A BIRDWATCHING
LESV

STEVE DUDLEY

in association with **MINOX**
VISIBLE INNOVATION

ARLEQUIN PRESS
A Division of CJ WildBird Foods Ltd

Cover artwork by David Nurney
Cinereous Bunting, Isabelline Wheatear and Alpine Swifts at Ipsilou

First published in 2009
Revised reprint in 2010

Copyright © Arlequin Press, 2009, 2010

Copyright © text, Steve Dudley, 2009, 2010

Copyright © site maps, Steven Hall, 2009, 2010

Copyright © photographs, Steve Dudley, 2009, 2010

Copyright © cover and illustrations, David Nurney, 2009, 2010

ISBN 978 1905268 061

All rights reserved. No part of this book may be reproduced, stored in a retrieval system, or transmitted in any form or by any means, electrical, mechanical, photocopying or otherwise, without the permission of the publisher.

A catalogue record of this book is available from the British Library.

Text set in Berlin Sans FB, Berlin Sans FB Demi & Trebuchet MS.

Design and typesetting by
Steve Dudley | WWW.LESVOSBIRDING.COM

Printed and bound in England by
Latimer Trend Co. Ltd | SALES@TRENDS.CO.UK

ARLEQUIN PRESS | WWW.ARLEQUINPRESS.COM
A Division of CJ WildBird Foods Ltd
The Rea, Upton Magna, Shrewsbury SY4 4UR

CONTENTS

ABOUT THE BOOK
  Birding sites covered   6
  How to use this guide   7
  Greek place names   8
  About the author   9
  Acknowledgements   10

INTRODUCING LESVOS
  The island   12
  Mythology   13
  Political history   13
  Economy   14
  Natural history   16
  When to go   16
  Weather   17
  Getting to Lesvos   18
  Health   18
  Money   18
  What to take   19
  Where to stay   20
  Eating & drinking   21
  Getting around the island   23
  Driving on the island   26

BIRDING ON LESVOS
  The birding year   28
  Birders' behaviour   36
  The environment   37
  Local people   38
  No go areas   38
  Military areas   39
  Other birders   40
  Photography & photographers   41
  Habitats   42
  Migration   46
  Resident species   53
  Vagrants   55
  Submitting your bird records   56
  Other wildlife   57
  Conservation   58
  Lesvos birding & conservation websites   59
  Other websites of interest to birders   59
  Hunting   60

BIRDING SITES ON LESVOS
  Lesvos place names   61
  Site maps   61
  Featured sites   61
  Island maps   64
  Photographs of sites and species   65

BIRDING SITES ON LESVOS (cont)

The Kalloni area	Skala Kallonis	97
	Skala Kallonis Pool	98
	Skala Kallonis Beach	99
	Christou River	100
	Potamia Valley & Reservoir	100
	Metochi Lake	102
	Tsiknias River	104
	Kalloni Saltpans	108
	Alykes Wetlands	112
	Madaros	115
	Kalloni Mini Soccer Pitch	115
	Kalloni Raptor Watch Point	117
The Napi Valley	Napi	120
	Koriani	120
	Platania	120
The North Coast	Kavaki	124
	Perasma	125
	Molivos	126
	Efthalou to Skala Sikaminias	128
	Korakas	131
	Mt Lepetimnos area	132
	Vafios to Klio	132
	Stipsi to Kapi	132
The Skalochori area	Aghias Taxiarchis	135
	Katapetros Valley	135
	Voulgaris River	136
	Lardia Valley	137
	Perivolis Monastery	137
The South West	Parakila Marsh	138
	Aghios Ioannis	139
	Makara	140
	Konditsia Valley	142
	Sideras	142
	Mesotopos	144
	Chrousos	145
The Far West	Ipsilou Monastery	147
	Petrified Forest	150
	Sigri Fields & Faneromeni	151
	Sigri Old Sanitorium	154
	Meladia Valley	156
	Pithariou Reservoir	160
	Vergias River, Skala Eresou	162

The Eastern Gulf of Kalloni	Mesa	164
	Vouvaris River Mouth	166
	Achladeri Forest	168
	Achladeri to Skala Vasilikon	169
	Skala Vasilikon to Skamnioudi	170
	Alikoudi Pool	170
	Mikri Limni	170
	Polichnitos Saltpans	171
The Vatera area	Almiropotamos River	174
	Agios Fokas	176
	Palia Vigla Chapel	176
	Vourkos River	176
	Ambeliko Valley	178
The Agiasos area	Agiasos	180
	Agiasos Sanatorium	180
	Megalochori Valley	182
	Dimitrios	182
	Panaghia Chapel	183
	Dipi Larisos Reedbed	184
The Far East	Mytilini	186
	Mytilini airport	186
	Cape Lena	186
	Haramida Marsh	187

AN ANNOTATED CHECKLIST TO THE BIRDS OF LESVOS — **188**

WILDLIFE CHECKLISTS
- Birds — 228
- Butterflies — 236
- Dragonflies — 238
- Other insects (selected) — 239
- Orchids — 240
- Mammals (selected) — 242
- Amphibians, Reptiles & Allies (selected) — 242

BIRD NAMES IN DUTCH AND GREEK — **243**

LESVOS PLACE NAMES — **251**

REFERENCES & BIBLIOGRAPHY — **254**

SCIENTIFIC NAME INDEX — **255**

ENGLISH INDEX — **261**

SITE INDEX — **272**

ESSENTIAL GREEK — **272**

ABOUT THE BOOK

This guide details some of the best birding sites on the Greek Aegean Island of Lesvos. Having led bird and wildlife holidays to the island for many years, and from my own personal holidays on the island (annually in spring and autumn), I have amassed an in depth knowledge of the island, its birds and the spring birding scene there.

Lesvos is unique in having such a concentration of birders, from all over Europe, birding the island each spring. It is this that marks Lesvos out as one of Europe's premier birding destinations.

Richard Brooks' *Birding on the Greek Island of Lesvos* published in 1998 was the first book to be dedicated to birding on the island. This privately published title, whilst crudely presented, at least brought together some detailed site and bird knowledge of the island for the first time. It has served visiting birders for the last decade, but I know from personal experience, and from the many hundreds of birders I have led around or met on the island, how frustrating accessing key information in that book can be.

In 2007 I set up Lesvos Birding — WWW.LESVOSBIRDING.COM — a website dedicated to birding on Lesvos. My aim was to provide improved information for birders visiting the island. I hope that together with this book I have now achieved this. The website will be used to keep information up to date between editions of this book.

BIRDING SITES COVERED

Lesvos became a popular birding destination in the early 1990s. Since then birders have followed the same routes around the island and visited the same sites year on year. Many of these remain ever popular and rewarding, whilst others have lost their appeal.

For an island with so many birders visiting each spring, the establishment of new sites has been very slow until recently. Some of us who have been visiting the island for many years have built up knowledge of the island wider than the traditional birding areas. Some (especially tour companies) have guarded sites from others in order to keep them to themselves. This is a somewhat selfish approach as most visitors, including groups, tend only to ever visit a single area once or twice during a week-long stay, so depriving others of a site for the remainder of the year. This guide brings together much of the collective knowledge of some of us who have come to know the island intimately.

Most sites used by birders remain in the central, northern and western areas. This largely reflects the continued practice of birders basing themselves in the Skala Kallonis areas. Anaxos, Petra and Molivos are becoming increasingly popular, but these bases still serve those same general, well known areas. The southeast, and in particular, the far west of the island, both seem to be 'too far' to venture for most spring birders.

Autumn is very different. The considerably fewer birders present on the island do not have the same focused areas as spring visitors do, and with the Polichnitos Saltpans in the southeast easily overshadowing the larger Kalloni pans in autumn, more time is spent here and the surrounding areas.

There are no nature reserves on Lesvos. All the sites are either publicly owned (by the local municipal authority) or private. Private, however, simply means the land around and between the tracks and accessible areas (such as beaches) which overlook such areas. All the sites included in this guide have been deemed to be able to cope with any pressure that visiting birders put on them. This is only true however as long as birders adhere to the birding code and do not abuse or disrupt sites. It is up to those using this guide and visiting the sites to help police and protect sites and their wildlife if such abuse is witnessed (see p. 36).

The sites have been condensed down to 10 main areas covering over 60 sites right across the island — from Haramida Marsh in the extreme southeast to Faneromeni in the far west, and Makara in the south to Korakas in the north. Each individual site is covered in detail within its own section with accompanying map of the area. Some sites are small single sites, whilst others are larger areas with details of many places within the area to look for birds. Between them they provide enough information for the visiting birder to sample all habitats and stand a good chance of seeing all the regular species during a week-long stay.

Any major changes to sites, or species status at sites or on the island, will in the first instance be covered on the Lesvos Birding website and then be covered in any future editions of this guide.

HOW TO USE THIS GUIDE

I very much hope that this book is simple to use. The book is broken down into separate, easy to use sections.

There are two **introductory chapters**. The first of these, **Introducing Lesvos** provides the visitor with useful background information about the island including when the best time is to visit, what the weather will be like, how to get there, what to take, where to stay and much more. The second introductory chapter, **Birding on Lesvos**, provides the visiting birder with detailed information on bird and wildlife aspects of the island including sections on the birding year, the many habitats on the island, migration through the island and species information. I encourage all visitors to read these introductory chapters, they should greatly improve your enjoyment of the island.

The bulk of the book is dedicated to birding sites across the island, presented in regional sections. Each region has an introduction with a small scale map of the region showing the sites covered. The sites included on these maps are then treated separately with their own annotated large scale map. The specially commissioned maps are detailed but should still be used in conjunction with one of the commercial maps available. I have purposely kept the maps 'clutter-free' and have introduced a unique annotation style for the maps. Most site guides try to cram information on to small maps. I've purposely left the maps as simple as possible, detailing the minimum information required regarding roads, tracks and paths needed to access the site, basic relief features showing some contour structure of each site, woodland plus rivers and wetlands. Key places (towns and rivers) are labeled. All bird, wildlife or visitor information is included around each map with arrows pointing to specific locations on the map. This has allowed me to include much more key information about the birds to be looked for at each site.

After the sites section is a **comprehensive annotated checklist** of the birds of Lesvos. The checklist provides the status for each species, the time of year they occur and details the individual records for rare species. Some resident or sought after migrant species have longer accounts to provide additional information to assist in finding these species during your stay.

This is the most accurate status ever published for birds occurring on the island to date. I have worked with the Hellenic Rarities Committee, resident birdwatchers and others to separate accepted records from the countless reports detailed in other publications and online. Officially accepted records are contained within the main systematic list of species. Non-accepted reports are included within two appendices to the main list (as many of these will simply be good records that have not been formally submitted). The checklist covers the 310 species recognised at 31 May 2009 as making up the official Lesvos List.

Following the main bird checklist are separate 'tick' checklists to the major wildlife groups on the island including birds, butterflies, dragonflies and orchids — all of interest to many visiting birders.

Lastly there are separate sections detailing the scientific, English, Dutch and Greek **names of birds** found on the island, and a section covering **place names** referred to in the book, along with the Greek form and English pronunciation (many rural signs are in Greek only so this section may prove helpful).

GREEK PLACE NAMES

Greek is a complicated language. It comes in two basic forms, Ancient Greek and Modern Greek. But the complication doesn't end there. Suffice to say then that there is often more than one version for individual place names. Throughout the book I have chosen to use the modern spelling of place names as used on the Road Editions map of Lesvos (no. 212, 1:70,000). This was last updated in 2007. The names on this map differ very slightly at times to road signs on the island, but since this is the most popular map used by visiting birders, I've chosen to stick with these.

ABOUT THE AUTHOR — STEVE DUDLEY

I'm one of Lesvos' most experienced bird and wildlife guides having led nearly 30 trips to the island. I'm also one of the few birders to visit the island in spring and autumn as well as leading groups, I annually holiday on the island with my wife Liz. Like many others, I fell in love with the island on my first visit and then fell deeper in love once I started exploring the island more with Liz in our weeks on the island without the responsibilities of tour leading. It is during these weeks I unearthed many new birding sites and discovered the real Lesvos, its friendly people and its fabulous food.

As well as leading bird and wildlife holidays to Lesvos, I also run Lesvos Birding (WWW.LESVOSBIRDING.COM), a free online resource for birders visiting the island. The website includes travel information, trip reports and, of course, bird news. The latter includes daily sightings summaries during the main spring weeks which allow those coming out to the island to see what is going on, and those on the island to plan their daily itinerary.

Since 1997 my full time occupation has been running the British Ornithologists' Union and I've previously worked for both the British Trust for Ornithology and the RSPB. My many freelance activities include marketing and design consultant for a host of bird and wildlife related companies including as a member of Leica's Optical Innovation Team (1991–2009), Minox GmbH and Vine House Farm Bird Foods, as acting publisher for both Subbuteo Natural History Books and Arlequin Press, and I contributed to *Bird Watching* magazine for over 20 years. As a wildlife tour leader, I also leads trips to many other destinations including Botswana, The Gambia, Spitsbergen and Shetland & Orkney (inc. Neolithic archaeology).

I've written two other books, *Watching British Dragonflies* (Dudley, Dudley & Mackay, Subbuteo Natural History Books, 2007) and *Rare Birds Day by Day* (Dudley, Benton, Fraser & Ryan, Poyser, 1996).

ACKNOWLEDGEMENTS

Needless to say a book of this nature cannot be produced without the help of many others. During my time visiting the island I have met countless birders with whom I have exchanged news, and at times shared views, of birds. If I have omitted anyone please do not be offended. There is simply not enough room for me to list all of those who I have shared Lesvos experiences with.

On Lesvos I would like to thank all the staff at the Hotel Pasiphae for their care and attention during my many, many stays, many of whom I am very proud to call friends. A friendlier group of people, typical of the Lesviot people, you could not expect to meet — Vasilis El. Vogiatzis, Evridiki (Erika) Stamatelli, Lefteris Vogiatzis, Stratos Vogiatzis, Erene Makaratzi Vogiatzi, Erene Petritzikli Vogiatzi, Vasilis Efst. Vogiatzis, Violeta Michaelidoy, Panagiota Mperteni, Anastasia Nazlidoy, Ntountoulaki Aliki, Maria

Mpaloma, Eleni Petrelli, Katerina Kalpaki, Panagiotis Afratoglou, Natascha Soumas, Erene Vogiatzi, Erene Zoumpourli, Acheleas Karakonstantis, Soula Artakianou, Nikos Mandamadiotis, Nikos Kalpakis and Stratos Baris. To all at Hotel Pasiphae, past and present, Σταυρό says a very warm ευχαριστώ.

Even from the hotel however, I must thank two people in particular. It is Erika Stamatelli's beaming smile which greets guests each morning of their stay. Erika, you are both wonderful and special, and many of your guests see this. And what can I say about my friend Vasilis El. Vogiatzis — the Lesvos equivalent of Basil Fawlty! Vasilis, you have given and done more for me than I ever dared ask for and always with your joyous and infectious smile and enthusiasm. Thank you.

Others from the island I would like to thank are George Tragellis and Stamatis Marathogiannis at the taverna Dionysos (Skala Kallonis) for looking after many of my groups, Nikos Mandamadiotis at taverna Ambrosia (Skala Kallonis), Kostas Tsiknas at taverna Australia (Sigri) and Sarandis Tzinieris at taverna Soulatso (Skala Eresou). I've enjoyed my time very much at each of these fabulous tavernas.

Lefteris Kakalis freely shared information on Krüper's Nuthatch from his research on the species on Lesvos as part of his PhD studies. Marius Bolck kindly checked the Dutch birds names used on pp. 243–50. Paul Manning kindly provided me with the information needed for the orchid section of the book and Brian Small provided additional butterfly information. Several people, notably Jim Robson, provided a list of corrections which have been incorporated in this revised reprint.

Of the many birders I have met and exchanged news, shared a drink, enjoyed a meal, and even watched a few birds with, I would like to thank in particular Dave Allen, Steve Bird, Steve Chalmers, Alan Currey, Bernie Forbes, Neil Glenn, Mike Hodgson, Adam Kennedy, Marcus Kohler, Ian Lewington, Paul Manning, Shena & John Maskell, Killian Mullarney, Dave & Jackie Nurney, Brian Small, Viv Stratton, Dave Suddaby, Reg Thorpe, Ralph & Brenda Todd and Duncan Walbridge, not to mention the countless paying guests I have shown the island and shared many magical moments with — thank you everyone

I would however like to pay special thanks to one Lesvos regular in particular. Bob (the birder) Buckler (Wingspan Bird Tours), we're two of a kind mate, thanks for being a friend and all your support and encouragement not to mention the occasional drink whilst watching the footie.

I've been extraordinarily lucky in having been paid (at times) to show people the wonderful birds of this fabulous island. Part of this luck has also been with whom I have had the privilege to lead my groups with over the years — Ian Rowlands, Mark Denman, Duncan Macdonald and Mark Newell — guys, simply thanks. I had a blast with you all. The others will forgive me for paying special thanks to Mark, with whom I first led on the island, following his every move and learning so much from him and with whom I've enjoyed birding the island with since he left the unreal world of wildlife tour leading!

Several key people contributed much in recent years to both www.lesvosbirding.com and to this book. Terry & Sue Robinson now live on the island and have provided much bird and visitor information on their area around Skala Polichnitou, photos for the website and Terry helped with several sections in the book and in particular the bird checklist. Mark Newell (again!) not only tour-led with me, holidayed on the island with me, but he read every section of the book in earlier drafts. Mark, I owe you more than you know. Eleni Galinou, although a native Lesviot studying tits on the island, since I've known her she has spent most of her time living on other Greek islands! Eleni provided help with information for both the website and this book — 'geia sou' Eleni.

Nikos Probonas (Hellenic Rarities Committee secretary) soon became a close web-friend and with whom I shared much about Lesvos, Greek birding and football during late night email exchanges! Nikos has provided immense help both for the website and this book from the Greek birding and national HRC end of recording, and spent much time helping with the preparation of the systematic bird list and checking all my Greek throughout the book, for which I thank him enormously.

Donald & Jennifer Rhodes have been visiting Lesvos for many years, so when Donald confessed to being a retired proof-reader I jumped at the chance to let him see the whole book! Donald has done a fabulous job in tightening up the text and making sure that I have been consistent throughout the book. Donald also help to 'road test' the guide on the island during his spring 2009 trip to the island.

Pete & Jan Deans and Fiona & Geoff Smith also road tested a complete draft of the book during spring 2009 and provided invaluable feedback and encouragement.

Dave & Jackie Nurney have spent a couple of weeks on the island with me and I'm pleased that Dave has been able to provide a set of fabulous line drawings, and a stunning cover for the book.

Steven Hall worked with me on my last book (*Watching British Dragonflies*) producing the excellent site maps required for that title. The requirements for this work were very different, but Steven has again come up with the goods and provided a set of simple, yet detailed maps to help guide the reader around the island and individual sites.

I'd like to thank Pete Deans and Joy Enston at Arlequin Press for their massive help and support in preparing this book.

Lastly, I would like to thank my wife Liz. She has accompanied me on many of my trips to Lesvos in recent years and shares my love of the island, its people and food. I'd like to thank her for compiling the Greek and Dutch bird lists and she has been an immense source of encouragement and at times much needed criticism.

Despite all this additional help with the book, I do of course take full responsibility for any errors or omissions! If you do spot an error, please don't keep it to yourself, but let me know via www.lesvosbirding.com. Likewise, if you find a new site you wish to share, please let me know. There are still many areas to explore and many gems to find.

INTRODUCING LESVOS

THE ISLAND

Lesvos is a small island and ideal for the visiting birdwatcher. If one stays centrally on the island, most main birding areas can be reached within an hour and a half — a bit longer if you enjoy your birding!

The Greek Aegean island of Lesvos lies within spitting distance of the Turkish mainland which wraps itself around the east and north of the island. At 1630 square km, Lesvos is the third largest Greek island (after Crete and Evia) with a population of around 87,000. Thankfully, the mass tourism which has blighted much of the Mediterranean basin has so far bypassed Lesvos. It is only in the last ten or so years that tourism has taken off, but it remains at a low level even at the main resorts, which are miniscule compared to the major Mediterranean resorts, and all the signs are it will stay that way.

Lesvos is a rural island with scattered towns and villages. The two main towns of Mytilini (capital) and Kalloni look largely 'modernised', but by and large other areas of human habitation look and feel very traditional. The undulating land is covered in a patchwork of olive groves, small-scale arable farmland, grassland, woodland and barren open country. Shepherds graze their sheep and goats just about everywhere on the island and the tinkling of their bells is one of the sounds of Lesvos.

The island is famed for the finest olive oil in the world, produced from over 11 million olive trees; great Greek food based on fresh fish and seafood caught daily in the warm, shallow offshore waters; the female poet Sappho (c.630-570 BC); it's fabulous Petrified Forest, one of the finest in the world; hot springs; and, yes, Lesbians. Yes, it is true, Lesvos is a favourite resort for gay women during the hotter summer months (mainly around Skala Eresou in the west). Lesvos is now however also known as one of the premier birdwatching locations in the Mediterranean.

In spring, Lesvos is a beautiful, lush green island with an amazing variety of scenery — green fields; olive grove covered hillsides; barren, volcanic mountainous areas; rich pine and sweet chestnut woods; beautiful beaches; and is dotted with traditional villages clinging to hillsides. From mid-May onwards, as temperatures begin to exceed 30°C, the island begins to dry and only the underground water resources maintain the plant life at the surface. The whole island abounds with birds, flowers and other wildlife to rival anywhere in Europe. The people are warm and welcoming and amongst the friendliest in Greece.

MYTHOLOGY

Lesvos has had many other names including Aithiope (sun-drenched island), Aiyeria (place of sun-browned people), Lassia (densely-forested) and Makaria (son of the Sun — Makaras, who reigned over the island and built the ancient settlements of Antissa, Avrisi, Issa, Mithymna (Molivos) and Mytilini – named after his five daughters).

The island's name may have two possible origins. Mythology says it comes from the brother of Makaras, Lesvos, whilst others say it derives from an ancient settlement called Lesvos which was sited near Lisvorios near where many ancient ruins have been found.

The island is mentioned by Homer when Odysseus defeated King Philomileidis and when Achilles attacked the island. Both Apollo and Artemis were said to be worshipped by the people of Lesvos and the historian Myrsilos said there was once an important sanctuary to Apollo at Mt. Lepetimnos. Local lore also says that the tomb of the inventor of letters and numbers, Palamides, lies on the slopes of the mountain.

One of the best known myths is that of the Greek musician Orpheus, whose music 'moved even the animals and rocks', and the men of Thrace were said to have left their wives in order to stay by Orpheus' side day and night in order to listen to his music. Orpheus was killed by the Maenades who discarded his dismembered body into the Evros river where it was taken out to sea. Orpheus' head and lyre were then carried across the Aegean Sea to the island of Lesvos where they were washed ashore near Antissa. The islanders buried his head, and his lyre was dedicated to the temple of Apollo. It is said that Orpheus' music still lives on in the song of the Nightingale.

POLITICAL HISTORY

Lesvos has been inhabited since the Neolithic period (c.7000 BC) and by the Early Bronze Age (c.3000 BC) an advanced civilization similar to the Mycenean had developed. By the Late Bronze Age (c.1000 BC) agriculture and shipping were the two main economies, and the island began to extend its commercial interests into Asia Minor. During an age when most civilizations were spreading their wings and flexing their muscles, it wasn't long before the people of Lesvos met with opposition and conflict from neighbouring peoples. In 427 BC the Athenians conquered the island, beginning what would be a regular feature of the island's history, including invasions by the Egyptians (323 BC) and the Romans (88 BC). Along with much of the Roman Empire, Lesvos flourished, but on the break up of the empire in 300 AD, Lesvos became part of the eastern Byzantine state. It is this period more than any other which formed the island's ideology. The island continued to be 'sacked' by invading armies including the Saracens, Venetians and Crusaders. Some stability was afforded under the rule of Francesco Gattelusi which benefited the island's commerce and culture until the great earthquake of 1401 which destroyed the capital town of Mytilini, and killed Gattelusi.

The Bulgarians were next to invade (1445) destroying the other main island town of Kalloni, and in 1462 the Turkish Sultan Mohamet II invaded and was the cause of much destruction across the island, which was the beginning of the 'dark period' of Lesvos' history. The 'dark period' lasted over 400 years, during which time the island's population suffered mass extermination and deportation and was reduced by 70%. The remaining populous of c.30,000 saw the cessation of both economy and culture, with non-Muslims subjected to huge taxes. Some resistance remained in order for the native islanders to hang on to their Greek Orthodox religion within the intellectual centres of the monasteries and churches, where secret schools were run in order to prepare for the fight for liberation. The Turks used the island as a major naval port and began repairing (Mytilini) and building (Sigri) major fortresses largely funded by huge taxes on the island's inhabitants.

Even during the 400-year Turkish occupation, attacks on the island continued. The Russian naval bombardment of Mytilini harbour in 1771 resulted in the Turks slaughtering the island's Christians. The Christians suffered another slaughter, known as 'the great assault', in 1821 following the attack on a Turkish frigate harboured off Eresos.

1850 saw a major exodus of islanders to Asia Minor following the destruction of huge numbers of the island's olive trees and in 1867 the island was devastated by another earthquake.

As part of the great Greek uprising against the Turks, triggered by the execution of the leader of the Greek Orthodox Church in Constantinople (now Istanbul), islanders rallied against the Turks. The island was eventually liberated in 1912 by the Greek navy. It was ceded to Greece in 1923 by the Treaty of Lausanne. The last 'invasion' occurred during the Second World War when the island was occupied by the Germans between 1941 and 1944.

ECONOMY

The island's economy is still largely focused on rural agriculture (inc. olive growing and sheep and goat herding), fishing and ouzo production. Fish, sheep and goats are for island consumption supporting both the local populous year-round and the swollen summer tourist season. Olives and ouzo are in part for local consumption, but the bulk of production leaves the island. Tourism contributes less than 10% to the islands economy.

Olives

Nowhere else in the Mediterranean basin is as dominated by olive production than Lesvos. The bulk of the 11 million olive trees date from after the devastating frost of 1851 which killed all but the hardiest of trees in some of the more sheltered spots. Some of these survivors are thought to be around 500 years old.

Olives are harvested between November and late December (as elsewhere in Greece). The best fruits come from the steeper hillside plantations such as those in the Agiasos area. The steeper slopes allow more of the trees to get maximum sunshine with minimum shade from their neighbours. Whole families take part in the harvest which is taken to the local mill (trvío) within 24 hours of picking. Good first-pressed oil produces extra virgin oil, whilst the remaining oil and waste is used to produce lower quality blended oils and soap. A lot of oil is exported, particularly to Italy. Lesvos alone accounts for around 25% of Greece's total annual olive production.

Oúzo

Oúzo is the Greek version of the grape-based spirit which is found throughout the Mediterranean basin. After pressing the grapes for wine production, the fermented waste (made up from grape skins, pips and stalks) are boiled in a copper still. Aromatic spices such as fennel or star anise are added to the distilled spirit (most distilleries have their own secret recipes) and the resultant spirit contains between 38% and 48% alcohol. The harmless reaction of turning milky when water is added is caused by the binding of anethole which occurs in the added spices.

Oúzo distilleries are dotted around the island but the best varieties are said to come from Plomari. No matter, many of the 'local' tavernas will have racks of it for you to try. If tempted, drink it whilst snacking (preferably on local mezedes) — as it is meant to be taken.

Lesvos oúzo, like its olive oil, is rated as some of the best (the locals tell you the best — but they would wouldn't they!).

Tourism

Whilst the majority of inhabitants will not have direct contact or a direct benefit from tourism, it is none-the-less still very important for several areas and industries on the island. The airport was extended because of the increase in tourism, and several local resorts would decline significantly without it.

NATURAL HISTORY

Once connected to the Turkish mainland, Lesvos remains more closely rooted geologically to Asia Minor than it does to the somewhat distant Greek mainland to the west.

Situated only 8km (5 miles) off the Turkish coast, the island is approximately 70km wide by 45km deep, and approximately 1630 square km.

The island can be divided into four main physiographical provinces –

i. the south-east – a mountainous area including Mt. Olympus (967 m),
ii. the centre – the coastal areas and gentle hills around the Gulf of Kalloni
iii. The north – a mountainous area north of the Gulf of Kalloni which includes Mt. Lepetimnos (968 m).
iv. The west – a barren, hilly area which is made up of volcanic pyroclastic rocks, and characterised by irregular peaks of up to 600 m.

It is the western side of the island which has proved to be the most important in both archaeological and natural history terms. Here the natural history of the island can be traced back over two million years through prehistoric fossils of many creatures including fish, mastodons, rhinos, camels and horses. These finds include a giant tortoise the size of a car, and amazingly, giant apes. The jewel in the island's crown is the Lesvos Petrified Forest, which is one of the finest in the world and larger than the much better known forest in Arizona, and has been given the status of Protected Natural Monument. The 'forest' was formed by millions of tonnes of pyroclastic material from numerous volcanic eruptions being deposited on the landscape and totally covering the western part of the island. Within the protective layer of the volcanic debris, plants and trees were preserved as fossils. Subsequent erosion of the volcanic rock over millions of years revealed many fossils, and further large scale excavations in recent times have revealed much of the extent of the island's value as a globally important geological landscape. The Petrified Forest can be visited via its centre, situated between Ipsilou and Sigri. There is also a fabulous new (2005) museum at Sigri which is definitely worth visiting.

WHEN TO GO

Like many coastal Mediterranean birding areas, Lesvos is primarily a spring migration location so most birdwatchers visit in spring, mainly between mid-April and mid-May, with a few birders also visiting in September. The 'peak' spring migration period depends on both weather and individual species, but the last week of April and first week of May tend to see the largest number of most migrant species passing through, and the best time to record the maximum number of species.

Although charter flights are now available from mid-April, the island as a tourist resort doesn't really wake up until mid-to-late May, and those visiting in April will find most places still closed and being prepared for the summer season. Hotels however will be open, but away from the main town centres, taverna lunches and dinners need to be hunted down.

Few birdwatchers visit outside spring which is a real shame. For those with a family, Lesvos can be a great destination, with early morning and evening birding enjoyed in the cool of the day either side of family activities.

Autumn birding on Lesvos can be very rewarding and I would urge anyone looking for a relaxing autumn break to consider visiting. Come September the tourist resorts are already very sleepy with dwindling visitor numbers and you can combine warm-weather birding with long relaxing lunches at fine tavernas.

See also — the birding year (p. 28)

WEATHER

The island has a typical Mediterranean climate. Winter is mild and short with a lot of rain and summer is hot with little rain. Strong north and north-west winds predominate.

Spring weather is typically variable. The main birding season is mid-April to mid-May during which time the weather typically moves from cool and damp (mid-April) to hot and dry (mid-May). Rain (even hail at high altitudes) can be encountered into June, but from early May such showers tend to be short-lived and followed by full sun and a return to warmth which soon dries both the land and any wet clothes!

Autumn (late August to end of September) is warm and dry and daytime temperatures are usually below 30°C.

Note that in all seasons, the predominating northerly winds are cool to cold, and can turn a perfectly warm day into a chilly one.

See also — the birding year (p. 28)

Typical monthly weather data

	JAN	FEB	MAR	APR	MAY	JUN	JUL	AUG	SEP	OCT	NOV	DEC
Air Temp (°C)	10	11	13	17	21	25	28	28	24	19	15	13
Sea Temp (°C)	15	15	15	17	22	25	26	26	24	20	17	15
No. of days 21°C +	0	0	0	8	24	30	31	31	30	23	4	0
Rainfall (mm)	130	95	73	50	25	8	2	3	10	50	100	140
No. rain days	30	26	21	13	9	3	0	0	4	16	27	29
Daily Sun (hrs)	4	6	7	8	10	11	12	12	11	9	7	5
Relative humidity (%)	71	70	68	64	63	57	56	57	60	66	71	72

GETTING TO LESVOS

For those visiting from Britain and western Europe, flying to Lesvos is the only viable option. For those visiting from Greece or neighbouring countries, you can reach the island by ferry (from the Greek mainland and Turkey).

Direct charter flights

Britain: flights are run weekly from Gatwick and Manchester by various operators who offer flights and package holidays which include hotels or self-catering accommodation. Flights usually start from mid-April and run to early October.

Germany: LTU airline (www.ltu.de) operates out of Munich and Dusseldorf.

The Netherlands: flights operate from Schiphol airport and can be booked via a number of Dutch travel agents.

Denmark, Sweden and Norway: flights are run by Apollo airline (www.apollo.no).

Scheduled flights

Both Aegean (www.aegeanair.com) and Olympic (www.olympicairlines.com) airlines run regular flights from Athens to Mytilini, Lesvos. Athens can be reached from most major European airports and from the UK with Aegean, British Airways (www.ba.com), Olympic and EasyJet (www.easyjet.com) offer flights to Athens.

Ferries

A daily ferry operated by Hellenic Seaways (www.ferries.gr) runs from Pireaus, south of Athens, to Mytilini (via Chios).

From Turkey, a ferry operates between Ayvalik and Mytilini. It runs daily during the high tourist season, but less regular outside this (www.danae.gr).

HEALTH

As Greece is part of the European Union, EU visitors are recommended to take a European Health Insurance Card (this replaced the old E111), but this is not mandatory. In the UK, these can be obtained from the Post Office (www.dh.gov.uk/travellers).

There are medical centres in the larger towns and most also have pharmacies for non-prescription items.

MONEY

Greece uses the Euro. It is recommended that you take these with you (you will get a better rate of exchange in the UK). There are banks in many of the towns, and cash machines are also available in Mytilini, Molivos, Kalloni, Plomari, Eressos and Mandamados.

WHAT TO TAKE

You are the best judge of what you need on a holiday, but as a wildlife tour guide, time and time again I see birders underestimate the terrain and climate of their destination. Here are some suggestions you may find helpful.

Clothing and personal items

The main spring weeks of mid-April to mid-May have variable weather conditions. Rainfall varies from a 50% chance (mid-April) to a 10% chance (mid-May) but can occur throughout both months. Temperature ranges from cool (10ºC) to hot (30ºC). Even the hottest days can turn cold when a north wind suddenly picks up.

Pack:

- layers — thin t-shirts, long-sleeved shirts, thin jumper
- a fleece
- a waterproof jacket
- one of your layers should be windproof
- gloves (advisable certainly in mid-April)
- zip-off trousers are versatile
- waterproof walking boots/trainers (non-waterproof shoes are OK for most places but beware the need to cross some fords on foot)
- sandals
- baseball cap or wide-brimmed hat
- sunglasses if you use them (not polarized if you use roof prism binoculars)
- swimsuit for the hotter periods (mid-May-late September) for hotel pool and/or sea swimming
- water bottle (tap water is fine to drink and saves you having to buy bottled water)
- high factor sun cream
- lip balm
- any medicines you require — there are pharmacies in the main towns for non-prescription items
- day rucksack
- bird guide (Collins Bird Guide!)
- Birding Lesvos checklist
- this book!

Also note that evenings can be cool and you may need a nightshirt/dress or pyjamas, especially in April and early May.

Optics

Obviously binoculars are a must. If you have a telescope take it. You will be viewing over medium to long distance constantly when searching areas like the saltpans and looking for raptors. Conditions, especially from mid-May and in autumn, can be very dusty, so take whatever cleaning items you use. Ensure your equipment is insured.

Camera

Again a must. There will be plenty of stunning scenery to photograph as well as excellent digiscoping and DSLR opportunities. Ensure your equipment is insured.

WHERE TO STAY (see also location map on p. 64)

Skala Kallonis

Skala Kallonis lies in the centre of the island at the northern end of the Gulf of Kalloni. It is ideally placed for exploring the whole of the island with ease and is the first choice for many visiting birders. Many main birding sites are on the doorstep including Skala Kallonis Pool (when wet), Tsiknias (East) and Christou (West) rivers, Kalloni Saltpans area, etc., as well as very good road links to the rest of the island.

There are several hotels, but Hotel Pasiphae has established itself as the hotel of choice for many birders. Lesvos Birding operates from here and runs a bird sightings log at the reception which non-residents are welcome to read and enter their own sightings.

Molivos / Mithymna

The Medieval name of Molivos is still preferred by many to the contemporary name of Mythimna. Molivos is situated in the very north of the island and is just over an hours drive from Mytilini (and most of the island).

Molivos is Lesvos' tourism capital and shows other places how to do it. It is truly spectacular and even at the busiest time of the year it can still be a relaxed place to stay or spend a day.

The town is set on a hill which rises up from its picturesque harbour to its medieval castle, sitting atop the town like a crown. From the castle you get spectacular views over the island as far as Ipsilou in the west and across the sea to neighbouring Turkey.

Molivos is a great place to base your stay. The north coast track along to Skala Sikaminias is great for migrants and breeding birds, and most of the main birding areas are within an hour's drive.

Vatera

Situated on the south coast, Vatera has the longest beach on the island. This is a real package holiday hotspot and during peak season can be absolutely bustling.

During the spring birding season the place is deserted and makes for a good base with its own local areas to explore. It is however a good drive to the main birding areas and a long way from the far west. But don't let this put you off staying here. Exploring a much neglected area and shunning the birding crowds around the main Kalloni area can be very rewarding. Very few birders based elsewhere on the island will bother you! Also be prepared for much of the resort being closed until late May.

Sigri

Sigri lies at the extreme western end of the island. Few birders stay at Sigri because it is simply too far from anywhere, including over a two hour drive to and from the airport at Mytilini.

The Sigri part of the island is however one of the best birding areas on the island and boasts some of the best migrant areas which can easily take up most, if not all, of your holiday. You will see other birders, as most will go to the Sigri area at least once during their stay. If you're thinking of a two-week stay, then consider spending your second week over here. You will have the place to yourself mornings and evenings!

Other places

Other towns where birders are increasingly staying include Skala Eresou (in the south-west), Anaxos (north) and Petra (north). Plomari in the south-east is a bit out on a limb and a long way from the main sites, and Mytilini is simply not suitable for most wildlife-interested visitors, and again away from the main birding sites.

EATING AND DRINKING (see also location map on p. 64)

Lesvos is famed for its fish tavernas, and eating at many of the fabulous tavernas should be one of the highlights of your holiday. For early spring visitors the choice may be limited as many do not open until the main season starts from mid-May, but many of those that are open are those open all year and patronised by the local populous.

Here are just a handful for you to try — but don't restrict yourself to these as you will be losing out! I keep finding new favourites each time I visit.

Skala Kallonis

The harbour area of the town boasts a plethora of tavernas, but here are some recommendations. The Dionysos, right on the harbour front, is run by the very personable duo of George Tragellis and Stamatis Marathogiannis, and offers a large and varied menu to suit all and has excellent service and value. It is a large taverna and great for group dining. Nikos Mandamadiotis will always offer you a warm welcome to Ambrosia which is a simple family run taverna by the church with a delightful terrace — try their fantastic zucchini flowers! The family-run Madousa on the main harbour front between the car park and the square is excellent, and Seahorse, along the beachfront heading out of town towards the Christou River, is also very good.

Molivos / Mithymna

The harbour area is crammed with tavernas, some good, some bad, some outstanding! 'To ouzadiko' is the best and Octopus is also excellent. For good real coffee, ice creams and snacks, try either Indigo or Cafe Habana. In the town centre there are several tavernas with spectacular balcony views, but you're largely paying for the view, so stick with the harbour! Avoid the Panorama taverna by the castle for all but drinks. Its classic tourist-located positioning unfortunately delivers mediocre food and lousy service.

Vatera

As with many real tourist traps good tavernas can be hard to come by in places like Vatera, but the Akrotiri fish taverna, situated on the headland of Agios Fokas to the west of the town, is better than most. Also, the Hotel Vatera Beach on the road west out of Vatera towards Agios Fokas is excellent.

Andissa

This hill town has a fabulous square shaded by three large plane trees under which there are several bars/tavernas.

Sigri

Australia (open all year) by the main harbour is an excellent taverna and is run by the very friendly Kostas Tsiknas. The Golden Key (May-September), situated along the narrow lane running into the town from the harbour, has views overlooking the fort and the offshore islands from its fantastic little balcony dining area. Also try Rezmessos (June-August) overlooking the castle.

Eresos

The main square has several good tavernas including 'Sam's' (The Tradition) in the top right corner as you come into the square along the main road.

Skala Eresou

This resort is the main Lesbian resort in Europe. The beach front is brimming with tavernas and bars. The leases of some do seem to change quite regularly, but as a rule, choose to eat where you find the locals eating! In particular, Soulatso (Σουλatso), midway along the seafront rates among the best tavernas on the island. This family-owned taverna is the pride of Sarandis Tzinieris who loves talking to birders about the wildlife around the local area. If you're staying June-August then a booking is essential. Adonis (at the far western end) is also worth trying and bar Agua (second establishment from the western end — next to Adonis) is excellent for drinks (good coffee!), non-Greek food (inc. excellent Italian dishes) and snacks; it also offers free Wi-Fi internet access.

Vafios

The hill-town of Vafios lies to the east of Molivos. The Taverna Vafios is situated by the side of the main road on the western edge of the town and has fantastic balcony views, an excellent menu and good service. This is a more formal taverna and slightly more pricey than resort areas, but it definitely rates as one of the finest tavernas on the island.

Skala Sikaminias

This tiny harbour village on the north coast is famed as being one of the most picturesque places on the island. It is also hugely popular with locals and holiday-makers alike. Choose from any of the tavernas. The Καβος café by the harbour (with the Scarlet Macaw) serves excellent coffee and ice creams. Note, it gets very busy on Sundays (so get there early if you want to lunch) and is best avoided altogether on public holidays (inc. Easter and May Day).

Near Mytilini airport

There are several tavernas a few km towards Mytilini from the airport. At Neapoli (just after the road signed for Pilgoni) look for taverna Νοσταλαγία set back from the road on your left. If this is closed, then walk along past Hotel Vigla and try the next taverna you come to. Also, Taverna Liminaki, a short way back towards the airport on the sea-edge is worth trying.

GETTING AROUND THE ISLAND

Visiting birdwatchers have little option other than to hire a car if they are to see more than the area around where they are staying. Taxis, buses, motorcycles and bicycles are also available. Throughout the guide it is assumed that the reader is travelling by car.

Car hire

If you are on a package deal (flight and accommodation) then your transport to and from the airport should already be included in the package. You can arrange car hire from your hotel (either direct with some hire companies or via many of the hotels themselves) or you can hire direct from the hire companies in many of the resort areas on a daily or weekly basis. If you are on a 'flight only' option you can do this from the airport, collecting your vehicle on arrival and dropping it back off on departure.

Search the internet (including Lesvos Birding) for car hire companies, or contact your travel agent or hotel. The local car rental companies can often offer the best deals, including competitive day rates.

Car hire is not unreasonable. Most visitors choose small 1 litre models, but it is worth considering a slightly larger, small family, 1.4 litre model for a more comfortable drive on the rough non-metalled roads (of which there are many). Four-wheel drive vehicles are available but are expensive and aren't needed other than for a few tracks or during wet periods. Most 4x4s are soft-top models, so check that your optics (and other items) are adequately insured if left in such vehicles.

For groups, small minibus-type vehicles such as the 9-seater (including the driver) Renault Skudo are available. Note that cramming nine people in one of these is not a great experience. I would recommend limiting these vehicles to a maximum of seven (including driver) to ensure some comfort. Also you are unlikely to get more than seven passengers and their luggage in one of these if you are collecting from the airport.

Ensure you choose unlimited mileage and air conditioning (although not very green) is a good option if you're visiting during the hotter months.

Hire companies are getting increasingly hot on damage to the underneath of the vehicle. Birdwatchers, unlike most general visitors, are more likely to go along the rougher dirt roads. You might be asked to sign a disclaimer with regards to the underside (see driving on the island on page 26). Collision Damage Waiver (CWD) is essential.

Taxis

Taxis are available from the airport, Mytilini and from the major towns and resorts, but are a relatively expensive way of seeing the island.

Buses

The island is served by public buses operated by KTEL Lesvos. They run from the terminal in KTEL Square (Πλατεία ΚΤΕΛ) in Mytilini (a ten minute walk south from the town centre bus terminus). Walk along the harbour southwards past the theatre, then right, then take the immediate left. The bus terminus is on the left at the end of this street.

Buses operate to serve the local communities and are not for tourists. Most places are served with one or two morning services into Mytilini with one or two return buses in the afternoon. If you intend to use buses then you should visit the terminus for up to date times of buses serving the area where you are staying.

Buses are slow (Mytilini to Petra takes around two hours) and in hotter months can be uncomfortable when temperatures exceed 40°C. Make sure you take lots of bottled water.

Ensure you ask about your destination when boarding. What it says on the front isn't always where it is going!

KTEL buses serve the main towns around the island only. A secondary service, connecting the KTEL through routes and smaller villages, operates (mainly from the central island town of Kalloni) but these are not publicised and operate mainly for local school children and shoppers and are of limited value for those wanting to explore the island.

Ask at your hotel or at local shops for information on services for your area.

Bicycles

Bikes for hire are available in most of the resorts from as little as €5 a day. This is a very good way of seeing the area around where you stay, but unless you are used to cycling in a hot climate you should think twice about cycling any distance on the island. Take the usual precautions of covering up, using high sun factor cream and drinking lots of fluid. Keep an eye on time and how long it is going to take you to get back to your base before it gets dark.

Scooters

These too are widely available in all resort areas but should be hired with caution. Scooters are popular in peak season and they can be a nuisance bordering on a danger around many resorts. Most scooters are unsuitable for many of the dirt tracks needed to navigate many birding areas.

Walking

The island is best enjoyed on foot. By whatever means you arrive at your desired destination, don't forget to get the most from your visit by walking. You will see more of the real Lesvos at walking pace, see more of its birds and wildlife and have a much greater opportunity to engage with the friendly locals. All of the sites included in this guide include the opportunity to walk to get the most from them. If you want good cross country walks, taking in different landscapes, villages, monasteries and other areas of interest, then I recommend you buy a copy of *Lesvos Landscapes* by Brian & Eileen Anderson (second edition, 2007, Sunflower Books) which is an excellent walking and car touring guide. Another excellent walking guide is Mike Maunder's *On Foot in North Lesvos* is available in both English and Dutch editions (www.lesvoswalks.net).

DRIVING ON THE ISLAND

Metalled roads

The island's roads are going through a major transformation due to European Union funding and all the main routes between major towns are now metalled. The most recent upgrades include the north/south Kalloni to Mandamados route through the well-known birding area of the Napi valley.

A metalled road lulls the visiting driver into a false sense of security. Just because you're driving on smooth tarmac doesn't mean you should forget you are still driving on a small, rural island and all the hazards that come with it. Be prepared for potholes, fallen or falling rocks (especially after rain), flash floods after heavy rain, slow moving local traffic (particularly the farmers), vehicles parked in unexpected and dangerous places (farmers again), and wildlife — tortoises are a favourite car-stopper!

Also, moderate your speed. There is no need to tear around the island as if you are back home. Apart from being a danger to yourself and others on unfamiliar roads, you stand more chance of seeing things of interest along the roadside or flying overhead if you are driving slowly and carefully.

In towns and villages, many roads are one lane only, so be prepared to give way and don't speed. Pay attention to road signs as one-way systems are common (inc. in Kalloni and Mytilini). Also, in built up areas it is an offence to turn across the lane of oncoming traffic into car parks. You can only turn across oncoming traffic at road junctions. Police will fine tourists for such misdemeanours.

On most roads you'll be able to stop and park safely if you do see something of interest. Park carefully away from bends and road junctions. You don't always have to get your vehicle off the road if others can pass safely. Do not block track entrances unless you are staying with the vehicle and can move it instantly if needed. Locals should not be inconvenienced by your desire to see something.

When pulling off a metalled road, then take care with the verge-side drop from the tarmac, and only pull off if you can see that it is safe to do so. Beware hidden holes and rocks within roadside vegetation.

Non-metalled roads

Away from the main routes, the roads vary from narrow metalled roads and dirt tracks of various widths and state of repair. When driving on any non-metalled surface you should take appropriate care for both your own and the other road users safety. Stones and small rocks can be flicked up even at slow speeds which can cause damage to your own vehicle, and even more damage to passing vehicles and pedestrians.

If you are visiting in any of the wetter months (including April) or during periods of unexpected, heavy showers, be extremely careful on these routes, particularly the lesser-used tracks in the remoter areas.

Potholes do of course mean puddles, and in drier months, birds will use any puddles they can find for drinking and bathing. The upgrading of many of the larger tracks to metalled roads has seen many traditional puddles lost.

Petrol

Petrol stations can be found at (list not exhaustive) Mytilini, Molivos, Kalloni, Parakila, Vatousa, Andissa, Eresos, Mandamados, Polichnitos, Plomari, Vrisa and Skala Loutron.

Petrol is readily available across the island during normal shop hours. Some stations in larger towns will be open through the day and evening, but in remoter areas most close early afternoon and open again late afternoon/early evening. Many stations (especially rural ones) close on public holidays (e.g. Easter Sunday and May Day) and some rural stations close on Sundays. Also be aware that petrol stations frequently run out of unleaded petrol, so do not run your tank dangerously low.

If you're returning your car to the airport, there are no petrol stations on the airport side of Mytilini. Ensure to fill up at one of the many stations on your way into Mytilini including at Keramia (8km out of Mytilini) when returning from the Kalloni area.

Touring

The island is a dream for those looking for a peaceful driving holiday, with every twist and turn bringing new and fascinating vistas. You can find your own way around the island with the help of a map, or you can buy the highly recommended *Lesvos Landscapes* by Brian & Eileen Anderson (second edition,

Middle Spotted Woodpecker
occurs in all woodland habitats, including olive groves, across the whole island

BIRDING ON LESVOS

LESVOS — A GREAT BIRDING DESTINATION

Since the early 1990s, Lesvos has quite rightly established itself as one of the premier birding destinations within the Mediterranean basin. It combines the excitement of migration with several key species which can be otherwise difficult to see elsewhere in Europe. It might not have the large numbers of raptors some other places enjoy, but even raptor passage can be exhilarating.

THE BIRDING YEAR

Spring, particularly late April and early May, remains the favoured time for birders to visit the island. Increasing numbers, however, do visit at other times, some (like me) return in autumn and others take family holidays during the summer months. These non-spring visitors are illustrating that Lesvos is more than a spring destination and they are providing valuable bird and wildlife records, particularly of breeding species in the summer, and autumn migration information.

The notes below should be used as a guide only. Most species migrate over many weeks and migration dates (departure, passage and arrival) are all dictated by the weather where a species is coming from, en-route, as well as on the island itself. Likewise the prevailing island weather will determine breeding activity for resident species.

Late winter

These are the coldest months but generally bright with regular rainfall and occasional frosts. Temperatures begin to increase from mid-February.

January

Ave. Air Temp (°C)	Ave. Sea Temp (°C)	No. of days 21°C+	Rainfall (mm)	No. rain days	Daily Sun (hrs)	Relative humidity (%)
10	15	0	130	30	4	71

February

Ave. Air Temp (°C)	Ave. Sea Temp (°C)	No. of days 21°C+	Rainfall (mm)	No. rain days	Daily Sun (hrs)	Relative humidity (%)
11	15	0	95	26	6	70

With wetland areas holding water, wildfowl numbers are at their highest, but no species ever occurs in very large numbers. These sites also hold increased Coot and Water Rail. The two saltpan areas hold over-wintering Greater Flamingos, herons, egrets and waders. Kingfisher is widespread both at inland freshwater sites and around the coast. The shallow basin of the Gulf of Kalloni holds significant numbers of wintering wildfowl and seabirds including Great Crested and Black-necked Grebes, Black-throated Diver, Great Cormorant and Shag. White Wagtail and Water Pipits are also widespread with smaller numbers of Grey Wagtail. Wintering gulls include Mediterranean and Lesser Black-backed (*intermedius* and *fuscus*). Lowland areas hold mixed flocks of seedeaters, mainly Corn Bunting, Skylark and commoner finches, but also including Serin and Woodlark. Raptors include Marsh Harrier and Goshawk. Merlin remain scarce. The reedbed at Dipi Larisos holds a large, winter Common Starling roost which attracts Eurasian Sparrowhawk and this coastal strip is one of the best places to search for wintering Pygmy Cormorant. Wintering warblers can be much in evidence with Blackcap, Chiffchaff and Cetti's and Sardinian Warblers. The latter are much more widespread throughout lowland areas than at any other time of year. The island can hold large numbers of Blackbird and Song Thrush, and Robin and Black Redstart are widespread and numerous. Hawfinch, Siskin and Crossbill are all usually present, and can be found in flocks in some winters. Numbers of many species vary from year to year depending on the severity of the winter, especially on the neighbouring Turkish mainland, where a hard winter can also lead to increased numbers of thrushes (including Fieldfare and Redwing), Lapwing and wildfowl (including geese).

Spring

March and April are unpredictable months weather-wise. As days begin to brighten the temperatures also pick up but it can be showery and windy. By the end of April and into May, air temperature becomes noticeably warmer and rainfall becomes less likely. May daytime temperatures can be tempered by northerly winds making it feel decidedly cool on some days.

March

Ave. Air Temp (°C)	Ave. Sea Temp (°C)	No. of days 21°C+	Rainfall (mm)	No. rain days	Daily Sun (hrs)	Relative humidity (%)
13	15	0	73	21	7	68

Migration is already underway in early March with early migrant species such as Chiffchaff, Garganey and Northern Wheatear in evidence. By mid-month hirundines and swifts (inc. Pallid) are moving through and by the end of the month the wetland areas in particular see an increase in both species and numbers – herons, egrets, storks, waders, raptors and the first crakes. The first Quail can be heard calling from lowland fields. Even highland areas will see increased activity as breeding birds begin setting up territories in earnest and the first Black-eared Wheatears arrive. Stone-curlews appear around the saltpans and river mouth areas, with some staying on to breed.

April

Ave. Air Temp (°C)	Ave. Sea Temp (°C)	No. of days 21°C+	Rainfall (mm)	No. rain days	Daily Sun (hrs)	Relative humidity (%)
17	17	8	50	13	8	64

Early April sees another push of migrants. Raptors include Lesser Kestrel and Short-toed Eagle from the start, both increasing in numbers during the month. Red-rumped Swallows and Crag Martins arrive back around breeding sites and even larger numbers pass through.

Mid-month is the best time for Pallid Harrier and the passage and arrival of many species seems relentless; it is the period with both greatest variety of species and total number of birds. Cretzschmar's Buntings are suddenly all over the mid-to-higher areas, Orphean and Rüppell's Warblers are on territory, and 'yellow' wagtails begin to pass through in considerable numbers. Flycatchers also pass through in large numbers, including many Collared and the occasional Semi-collared. Warblers include increasing numbers of Wood, Icterine and Eastern Bonelli's (on passage as well as returning breeding birds), good numbers of Golden Oriole, Hoopoe, Common Redstart, Whinchat (often in hundreds), and small numbers of Roller.

Lucky birders will chance upon Ortolan Bunting or a singing Thrush Nightingale. You won't fail to miss Great Reed Warblers around any of the scrub- or reed-lined rivers and wetlands. Raptors include good numbers of Marsh and Montagu's Harriers, the last of the spring's Hen Harriers, increasing numbers of Osprey, Hobby, Red-footed Falcon and Lesser Kestrel, and by the month's end, Eleanora's Falcon and Levant Sparrowhawk — the latter occasionally seen in small flocks, sometimes into double figures. Long-legged and Common Buzzards will be displaying over the open valleys, Goshawks are still much in evidence and the odd Black Kite and eagle species can be seen passing over to the north. In the west, Isabelline Wheatears are back on their breeding areas and offshore both Yelkouan (Mediterranean) and Scopoli's (Cory's) Shearwaters can be seen. Waders peak at wetland sites including the saltpan areas and wetter rivers and include good numbers of Wood, Common, Marsh and Curlew Sandpipers, Little and Temminck's Stints, Greenshank, Spotted Redshank and the occasional goody such as Spur-winged Plover or a downright rarity such as Caspian Plover. Rivers, especially river mouths, are the best place to look out for Citrine Wagtail, and the coastal areas are the places to look for Audouin's Gull. Any wetland area can see passage flocks of Mediterranean Gulls, the odd Slender-billed Gull, Gull-billed Terns or Collared Pratincoles. The latter can often be seen in good numbers in fields around the Kalloni Saltpans. Mid-month usually sees the last of the lingering wintering species such as Great Crested and Black-necked Grebes, wildfowl and a decline in Greater Flamingo numbers.

Mid-to-late April is probably the best time to catch up with two of the main target breeding species. Cinereous Buntings are now back on territory in the west of the island, with Ipsilou the best site to look for them, but they can also be encountered in many western areas including the Meladia Valley between Sigri and Eressos and at Aghia Ioannis just west of Parakila. Look for males singing from prominent rocks or small trees. They can be incredibly difficult to see!

Krüpers Nuthatch is also very obvious. Most pairs excavate their nest holes around the middle of the month. Once the nests are complete the females will be sat on eggs and males then make only irregular nest visits and turn all too quiet. From the last week of the month the first broods will have hatched and both parents will be busy collecting food and regularly seen at the nest.

The back third of the month sees the main arrival of Olivaceous Warbler, who soon set up territories along the river valleys and wetlands. Shrike numbers peak, with Woodchat, Red-backed, Lesser Grey and Masked Shrikes all in evidence, and occasionally all seen together around a single field! Hoopoes will also be much more evident and as the month progresses the wooded valleys will be filled with their far-carrying song and courting birds which often chase one another around suitable nesting areas. Check coastal areas for Red-throated Pipit and Short-toed Lark, while Barred and River Warblers, Wryneck, Red-breasted Flycatcher and other scarce passage passerines can pop up anywhere. The first flocks of Bee-eaters can be heard passing over, with some tempted down into the wooded valleys or fruit groves to feed or roost.

As water levels begin to reduce at places such as Metochi Lake, searching for Little and Spotted Crakes is made a whole lot easier! Little Bitterns too are more obvious now and Purple Herons are moving through and will often roost in tall trees at wetland sites or along river valleys. Night-herons are also best looked for at their day time roost sites, including the tamarisks around Metochi Lake. Both of these herons can occur in large flocks. These same areas often hold roosting hirundines, often in huge numbers. Common and Alpine Swifts pass over in much broader movements, but river valleys often funnel them northwards when clouds can appear overhead. During cooler, damper weather, birds are driven lower and will concentrate over water areas or along valley ridges to feed. The odd Pallid Swift might still be in amongst these flocks, but this species is best looked for earlier in the month.

White, and occasionally Dalmatian Pelicans can be seen this month, with both species occasionally occurring in small flocks with the odd bird lingering for a few days.

By the end of the month Masked Shrikes will be nesting, Rock Nuthatches will be feeding young in their funnel-shaped mud nesting chambers and Common Nightingales singing from any damp scrubby areas, including the hotel grounds at Skala Kallonis. The first broods of Sombre Tits will be hatching and the parents much more obvious as nest visits increase. The first Black-headed Bunting, Olive-tree Warbler and Rufous Bush Robin all arrive in the last few days of the month, and breeding Bee-eaters can be seen excavating their nest holes in the low river banks.

Spring raptor migration occurs broadly across the island, but several 'hot spots' stand out. In the west, mixed falcon flocks can be found hunting over hillsides between Ipsilou and Sigri. Ipsilou mount itself is excellent for many species, and watching from the top can often give views down on to birds moving along the valleys either side. In the centre of the island, the route north following almost exactly the road north to Petra is excellent. The Raptor Watch Point just north of Kalloni at the 'bandstand' (see p. 117) is excellent. Just to the east, Napi Valley is also excellent with several good viewpoints along its length. The north coast track between Efthalou and Skala Sikaminias provides several areas to view birds leaving to the north, and the main road inland of here running between Molivos and Mandamados (running below Mount Lepetimnos) offers vantage points looking south and north. In the south of the island, the Almiropotomas valley between Vatera and Agios Fokas can also be very good. The headland of Aghias Fokas is a natural arrival point for birds coming across the sea to the south (on a clear day the Turkish mainland and Chios can be seen to the south of here), and the valley to the north provides a natural corridor for migrants to follow northwards towards Polichnitos and over the Gulf of Kalloni (and then either north along the Napi Valley or the Kalloni-Petra route). The sheer size of Mount Olympus cannot be ignored as such a prominent area will attract migrating birds, particularly larger birds such as raptors, storks and pelicans in need of updrafts and thermals to lift them high over the island. Few birders however spend much time down this southern end of the island, and virtually no one visits the far south-eastern peninsula and the Haramida Marsh area where Sardinian Warbler is present throughout the year.

May

Ave. Air Temp (°C)	Ave. Sea Temp (°C)	No. of days 21°C+	Rainfall (mm)	No. rain days	Daily Sun (hrs)	Relative humidity (%)
21	21	24	25	9	10	63

With migration still in full swing, and temperatures decidedly on the warm side, the first week of May sees more birders on Lesvos than any other week.

Early May sees an increased chance of species such as Thrush Nightingale and White-throated Robin. The latter, although a vagrant, amazingly occasionally breeds with the odd pair popping up every few years, but rarely in the same location.

Marsh terns are much in evidence with good numbers of White-winged Black and Whiskered Terns gracing the saltpan areas, the wetter rivers and any remaining flooded fields (e.g. near the Kalloni saltworks entrance). These same wetland sites continue to attract waders including the occasional Great Snipe.

Red-footed Falcons peak in early May, but like most species, numbers are heavily dictated by the weather. Search through any flocks of falcons for Eleanora's, and make sure to check all small raptors for Levant Sparrowhawk. Honey-buzzard too should be much more evident.

Rufous Bush Robins arrive with a vengeance during the first week of May and territorial males are easy to pick out as they sing their thrush-like tune from a prominent bush-top. A territory can comprise a ridiculously small area of only a small group of bushes, and despite the limited cover, birds can go missing for long periods when disturbed.

As water levels recede in the heat, look for small pockets of water containing large numbers of tadpoles. Any such pools near cover will attract herons and egrets, including Little Bittern and Night-heron. Muddy margins along rivers and wetland areas are good for secretive crakes and early May offers the best chance to find a Baillon's.

By mid-month some of the breeding birds are easier to see. Krüpers Nuthatch young will be fledging and small family parties should be looked for in the usual woodland areas. Middle Spotted Woodpeckers are remarkably common and will be feeding young in the nest throughout the month. During nestling-feeding the parents are much more obvious and noisier than earlier in the season and nest holes are often easy to stake out from a respectable distance.

From mid-month numbers of many species begin to reduce, leaving one of the spring spectacles to take over — the passage of Rose-coloured Starling. Large flocks occur across the island, but particularly around water areas where they come down to drink in noisy groups before hiding in nearby trees. They have a distinct preference for Mulberry trees which concentrate the flocks to regular sites. This passage continues into June.

Other breeding birds to look for at the month's end include Nightjar which occurs across the island in open scrubby areas including Potamia Valley, Mesa area and throughout the west. Listen for their remarkable 'churring' song at dusk and watch for their delightful display flights, including 'wing-clapping' against the dusk sky.

Summer

June

Ave. Air Temp ($°C$)	Ave. Sea Temp ($°C$)	No. of days 21$°C$+	Rainfall (mm)	No. rain days	Daily Sun (hrs)	Relative humidity (%)
25	25	30	8	3	11	57

July

Ave. Air Temp ($°C$)	Ave. Sea Temp ($°C$)	No. of days 21$°C$+	Rainfall (mm)	No. rain days	Daily Sun (hrs)	Relative humidity (%)
28	26	31	2	0	12	56

August

Ave. Air Temp ($°C$)	Ave. Sea Temp ($°C$)	No. of days 21$°C$+	Rainfall (mm)	No. rain days	Daily Sun (hrs)	Relative humidity (%)
28	26	31	3	0	12	57

Summers are hot and dry. With virtually no rainfall most areas turn decidedly brown with green areas restricted to a few spots where natural underground water courses flow close to the surface and irrigated farmland. Unless its been a very wet spring, all the rivers will now be dry and standing water restricted to the irrigation reservoirs, such as at Perasma and Potamia, and the reservoir at Pithariou (near Eresos).

Migration tails off with the sudden surge in temperature. There remains a chance of lingering migrants during early June, but this hot summer period is largely left to breeding species. June can be a good month to see family parties of many species including Sombre Tit, Rock Nuthatch, shrikes, buntings and larks. Graniverous species begin to flock and finches, buntings and larks are soon flying around together in search of seedy areas. In upland areas wheatears are also easier to see now the young have fledged.

The late arriving Eleanora's Falcon are breeding by the end of June and small feeding parties can be seen hawking insects over hillsides and ridges, and chasing hirundines up and down the valleys. The west is by far the best area to look out for these magnificent falcons. They are thought to breed on the offshore islands around Lesvos and can be seen scything through flocks of Alpine Swifts. These large swifts are present throughout the summer. Some may be breeding on offshore islands or around the larger mountains, but most are probably feeding parties from the Turkish mainland. Swifts are well-known for their long-range foraging flights which can take them over 100km from their breeding sites.

Into July and the first returning waders begin to appear. Non-breeding birds are often the first to appear (some having never gone much further than Lesvos), and by the end of the month, the first young birds will be moving through. With standing water pretty scarce, concentrate your efforts on the saltpan areas, with the Polichnitos Saltpans now coming into their own. The Pithariou Reservoir is also worth covering as it holds water throughout the summer.

From mid-July and throughout August the breeding summer migrants begin to leave the island, many of them forming small flocks before departure. Black-headed, Cretzschmar's and Cinereous Buntings can form large flocks and are particularly obvious, along with large flocks of Corn Buntings.

As August progresses, raptors become more evident. Honey-buzzards and Goshawk begin to move south, and both species can be seen in good numbers from the middle of the month. Egrets, herons and storks are also on the move south, and the saltpan areas are a magnet for any wetland species.

During July and August birding is best confined to the cooler early morning and late evening when passerines are much more evident and raptors are often on the look out for the weak or unwary. Small birds will often be attracted to the smallest of water areas, including dripping or leaking irrigation pipes in the olive groves and arable fields.

Autumn

September

Ave. Air Temp (°C)	Ave. Sea Temp (°C)	No. of days 21°C+	Rainfall (mm)	No. rain days	Daily Sun (hrs)	Relative humidity (%)
24	24	30	10	4	11	60

October

Ave. Air Temp (°C)	Ave. Sea Temp (°C)	No. of days 21°C+	Rainfall (mm)	No. rain days	Daily Sun (hrs)	Relative humidity (%)
19	20	23	50	16	9	66

September sees only a marginal drop in temperature but northerly winds can still make it feel cool. October remains moderately warm, cooling towards the month's end with the chance of some rain. Standing water remains at a premium throughout.

September is an increasingly popular month for the visiting birder and offers great, relaxed warm weather birding. Raptors and storks are much in evidence. Goshawk and Honey-buzzard numbers peak and double figure day counts can be expected, and the chances of picking up species such as Golden, Bonelli's and Booted Eagles are greatly increased. Some of the best raptor watching can be either along the north coast (e.g. Molivos castle or near Sikaminia) with birds coming across the sea from Turkey, or in the south of the island (Polichnitos/Vatera area) as birds depart southwards.

White Pelicans begin to pass through and large flocks have been recorded. Birds arriving on the island late in the day might even roost on one of the saltpan areas or offshore in one of the shallow bays, moving on mid-morning the following day when the air temperature is warm enough to provide the thermals needed to help them on their southward journey.

The two saltpan areas and Pithariou Reservoir should be visited regularly. Not only do these areas attract and hold the wetland birds, but also the surrounding areas are the best areas to look for migrant passerines which are similarly drawn into these three major wetland sites.

Don't be afraid to wander though. Even the most barren areas in the west and the monoculture pine forests may appear devoid of birds at first look, but good searching of such areas will often produce rewards. The forest areas in particular, offering shade from the hot sun, hold shrikes, wheatears and warblers throughout the month.

Hirundines are on the move throughout, as are Bee-eaters, many of which go straight overhead, but others are attracted into woodland glades and sheltered valleys late in the day where they roost overnight. Common species such as Whinchat, Turtle Dove, Willow Warbler and Spotted Flycatcher pass through in large numbers and Kingfishers arrive at wetland sites and around the shallower coastal areas. The wetland areas and dry river valleys are often the best places to search. Even though dry, the river valleys are lined with trees and scrub which provide shelter and feeding sites along their length and a linear route for birds to follow southwards across the island. Rarer autumn passerines can be found including Collared Flycatcher, Eastern Bonelli's Warbler and real rarities such as Bluethroat.

Into October and winter visitors begin to arrive with increasing numbers of Chiffchaff, Song Thrush, White Wagtail and other passerines. The wetland areas hold increasing numbers of Greater Flamingo, egrets, herons, waders and wildfowl whilst Great Crested and Black-necked Grebe numbers build up offshore.

Early winter

November

Ave. Air Temp (°C)	Ave. Sea Temp (°C)	No. of days 21°C+	Rainfall (mm)	No. rain days	Daily Sun (hrs)	Relative humidity (%)
15	17	4	100	27	7	71

December

Ave. Air Temp (°C)	Ave. Sea Temp (°C)	No. of days 21°C+	Rainfall (mm)	No. rain days	Daily Sun (hrs)	Relative humidity (%)
13	15	0	140	29	5	72

Lower temperatures also bring increased rainfall (especially from mid-November) and the rivers begin flowing again. Metochi Lake and Pithariou Reservoir fill up and the irrigation reservoirs begin to fill. December sees a further temperature drop and even a chance of snow.

Pygmy Cormorant is one of the more unusual winter visitors with odd birds seen around coastal areas. Numbers of Great Cormorant increase too. Red-breasted Merganser join increasing numbers of wintering wildfowl, including scarcer species such as Pochard. Marsh and Hen Harriers hunt the open areas, particularly around the coast. Numbers of Black Redstart, Blackbird and Song Thrush continue to increase, and will increase further if mainland Turkey sees a cold snap.

BIRDERS' BEHAVIOUR

Birdwatcher's Code of Conduct

- The welfare of the birds must always come first
- Do not cause damage to habitats
- Keep disturbance to a minimum – do not intentionally disturb breeding, feeding or roosting birds
- Think about who you should tell about rare breeding birds

- Migrants will be tired and hungry and should not be harassed
- Birds are protected by law under the European Birds Directive
- Respect the rights of landowners — do not trespass
- Keep records and submit your records to the relevant recorder(s)

In addition, visitors to Lesvos should abide by the following:

- Consider the welfare of all wildlife
- Respect other birdwatchers and wildlife photographers
- Respect local people
- Do not litter
- Leave gates as you found them — close gates which were shut, leave open those which were not.

Unfortunately, each year bad behaviour from birdwatchers and photographers occurs — unneccessary trampling of sensative habitats; disturbance of nesting birds; harassment of breeding birds and hungry migrants; tramping of nests on the ground — conduct which would not occur in our home countries and conduct which is completely avoidable if the above code is adhered to and some general common sense is applied. Just because we are 'on holiday' shouldn't mean people can behave badly or those of us witnessing such behaviour should have to tolerate it.

THE ENVIRONMENT

Respect the environment you are birding in. Your actions and behaviour can and will impact on wildlife. Just because you are in a foreign country does not mean the high standards we apply at home should not be expected on Lesvos. Obey both the birders code of conduct (see page opposite) and the country code; keep to roads, tracks and paths, close gates, do not trample vegetation, do not pick flowers, do not litter. Do not foul water courses. Keep noise to a minimum!

We disturb birds by our very presence of walking through the countryside on paths and tracks. Unfortunately some choose to act without due care for both the birds and other wildlife. Breeding birds are chased from bush to bush, birders leave paths and tracks to enter 'closed' habitats containing breeding birds (sometimes rare breeding species). For some reason some birders think that conduct that would not be tolerated at home should be tolerated in Lesvos. They are wrong. If you witness anyone harassing any migrant or breeding bird, or walking through scrub in order to flush birds, please challenge them.

LOCAL PEOPLE

Please remember that you are a guest in someone else's country. Whilst some local economies depend heavily on tourism, birders are only a small percentage of the wider tourism the island enjoys. Birders also tend to be low-spend tourists on average, and because we visit before the majority of the island has opened for business, the number of hotels, tavernas, shops, etc. that benefit from our combined spend remains low. So, the majority of locals do not depend upon us. Yes, we are important and extend the holiday season for some local businesses, but please do not over estimate our importance to the island as a whole.

The nature of birding also means that the majority of us visit the same places time and time again. These also tend to be in the less populated central, north and west parts of the island. This puts pressure on small areas both on an environmental level as well as a local human level for those locals who on the whole graciously put up with us. Lesviots are a warm and friendly people. You can see the most stern, weather-worn face approaching only for it to suddenly break into a face-filling smile on eye contact or on the utterance of a simple greeting ('yassas' is the formal form of hello to be used with strangers). Lesviots never fail to surprise me with their generosity. I can recall numerous occasions of such friendliness, such as the time when a farmer watched a friend and myself birding his groves and small cultivated fields for a couple of hours, to appear suddenly with a water melon which he thrust upon us. He spoke no English, we little Greek, but he understood what we were doing, and seemed to like looking through our telescopes, and we later enjoyed his water melon very much!

To warm and friendly you can add inquisitive. Inquisitive to the extent of overcoming fear of the unknown and language. If a local stops to look at you, greet them ('yassas' is simply hello, 'kalimera' is good morning, 'kalispera' is good evening. If you want to go further, then 'ornithologos' is the Greek term for 'person studying birds' (similar to the near English word of ornithology). If you have something obvious to show them, let them look through your binoculars/telescope. Engage with the locals and you will be rewarded with some unexpected exchanges and help further our good relations with this local community.

NO GO AREAS

By and large you are free to wander around the island along any road or track. Even if the track is gated (a proper gate or a string of wire!), this is often simply to prevent livestock from wandering or to mark the boundary of the property. Unless you think there is a sign telling you not to progress any further, or the gate is actually padlocked, then if the gate is easily held open, proceed. But always leave gates as you found them – open or closed. Please do not park in such a way to block any road or track.

Fields are different. You should not routinely enter any field, grove or orchard unless a track or path takes you through it. Such land is private and any paths crossing it are not rights of ways but are for the benefit of the landowner. Most will not mind you using these paths and tracks as long as you stick to them and you do nothing to harm any livestock, trees, land, gates, fences, etc. Rule of thumb is to keep to tracks and paths. Do not climb fences or attempt to enter via a locked gate. Stay out of cropped fields. Be polite if challenged. Say sorry (sigh-no-mi) and retreat the way you came.

MILITARY AREAS

Lesvos is a military island. It lies only a few miles across the sea from the Greeks' long-time protagonists, Turkey. There are several permanent military bases that birders are likely to come across (see map) but the army also wanders around the island on manoeuvres when it will close off sections of road, tracks, forest, etc. It's pretty basic, but some simple rules to follow when around any army presence apply:

- never view a military area with binoculars or telescopes
- never take photographs around a military area
- never attempt to cross a checkpoint unless it is on a main road and other traffic are going through or you have been instructed to do so
- always stop if your vehicle is flagged down
- always move on if told to do so and never argue!

There have been instances of birders disobeying one or more of the above and the army taking offence and holding them for a short while (only hours) simply to make a point. But we know from other instances elsewhere in Greece that the military will go further as in the infamous case of the plane spotters on the mainland. Such unnecessary conflict should be avoided at all costs.

Some popular birding areas in particular have military bases/presence during the year.

Ipsilou

This has a permanent base next to the monastery. The personnel here are used to both general tourists inc. birders visiting one of the most popular tourist destinations on the island. Unlike normal tourists, many birders do walk up and down the access road to the top of the mountain where the monastery sits. This takes you right past the entrance to the base. You can still use your optics here, but just be aware of scanning and taking photographs in the direction of the base. I've never heard of any incidents here.

Agios Fokas

The southern headland west of Vatera also has a base just north of the tip. Most people drive past the guarded base entrance but birders often walk past kitted with optics, etc. A pleasant 'yassas' and smile will be greeted similarly by the guards. Just don't use your optics or camera until clear of the camp.

Achladeri forest

The popular forest area of Achladeri attacts both locals (for picnics, especially over the Greek Orthodox Easter weekend) and birders (searching for Krüper's Nuthatch). Birders are likely to come across two different military operations in this area:

- **the Krüper's Nuthatch site** (see p. 168) – this is used by the army for manoeuvres and camps. When in residence the entrance to the Krüper's Nuthatch area is out of bounds and guards are posted at the entrance to the site. Do not attempt to enter. Do not attempt to view the area from the road with optics. Either go elsewhere to look for Krüper's Nuthatch (see p. 214) or come back another day (but they may be present for many days, sometimes weeks!).

- **permanent bases** – of which there are two. The first is along the main road south (towards Vasilika) of the Krüper's Nuthatch site by the coastal area (just beyond the taverna on the beach-side). Unless you're visiting the taverna, most birders see this base from a moving vehicle and it should not present any concerns. The second base is in the forest itself just north of the Krüper's Nuthatch site between it and Mesa (on the blue Road Editions (212) 1:70,000 map it is marked with a 'no entry' sign). About 1km south of the Vouvaris River bridge towards the Krüper's Nuthatch site, there is a left turn into the forest marked by a small military guard box. Continue along this track, turn left across the river ford and eventually you will reach a large military base where the track takes you sharp left past it (and eventually back out on the main road at the southern end of Mesa). Do not stop in this area, and if anywhere along this track (before or beyond the base) you are stopped or moved on by the army, then co-operate. I have found that between the camp and the river ford is sensitive, but between the river ford and the main road is OK. Between the camp and Mesa is potentially more sensitive as there are several installations along the track, but I have never known anyone experiencing any difficulties other than being asked to move on.

OTHER BIRDERS

In the main spring weeks there might be several hundred birders on the island. Many are based in just one or two resort areas (mainly Skala Kallonis, with Anaxos and Molivos being the other popular places). The majority of all birding is concentrated in what amounts to just a few main areas. Avoiding other birdwatchers at the top sites around Kalloni (saltpans, Tsiknias River, Napi Valley, Achladeri, etc.) is nigh on impossible. Also expect to bump into other birders at the main sites in the west (Lardia Valley, Ipsilou, Meladia Valley, Faneromeni) and north (Kavaki, the north coast track between Efthalou and Skala Sikaminias). This doesn't mean you won't strike lucky and have any of these sites to yourself, and if you strike off the beaten track then you can spend a whole day on your own.

Lesvos attracts birders from all over Europe and is especially popular with the Dutch and Scandinavians. Birders, just like Lesviots, are on the whole a friendly tribe, but like wider society, our community does have its number of less friendly individuals (some even seem to take pleasure in winding other birders up). Keep it friendly. Keep noise down in the presence of others (you should want to keep the noise down anyway). Exchange news freely. Never suppress anything from another birder unless you know the bird is on private land (then how did you see it?), or if in the case of a breeding bird you feel that there is no way of observing it without disturbance to it. News of good birds should not be withheld. Share your sightings with other by entering your records in the Lesvos Birding log at the Hotel Pasiphae in Skala Kallonis. Don't block tracks, fords and access points.

PHOTOGRAPHY AND PHOTOGRAPHERS

Lesvos provides excellent opportunity for both the birder-cum-photographer and dedicated photographers. With the proliferation of digital cameras every man and his dog seems to be photographing birds, and unfortunately some users have the same impact on their subject as a dog would!

The rather unobtrusive practice of digiscoping is declining and giving way to DSLR photography. The experienced birder is still able to use his field craft to good effect, but as field craft skills wane, and more obviously, more and more non-birders pick up cameras and aim for the bird-filled regions of the globe, problems are bound to, and do, arise.

Every year the number of birder-photographer conflicts increase on the island. Those I have witnessed (and unfortunately they have been many) have largely been caused by the non-birder photographer (or put it this way, a photographer with so little grasp of his subject that I daren't ever describe them as birders!).

The Krüper's Nuthatch site at Achladeri has annual problems with photographers choosing to camp right below nest sites. I have no problem with this as long as the photographer stays put and makes no noise. Sat chatting on a mobile phone or getting up for frequent walkabouts does not constitute good, unobtrusive photographic skills. Think about finding your own nest site of this common pinewood species.

There are countless tales of thoughtless camera-toting birders and photographers foolishly climbing fences, wandering through crops, stopping on blind bends, and even trampling the nests of ground nesting birds, to know that there is an increasing problem on Lesvos. Some birders are equally culpable, and such actions should not be tolerated from anyone.

My advice to anyone witnessing such action is to be polite to the offender and explain that their actions are not welcome to the local wildlife, local people (if they are trespassing) and you and other visiting birders. If they are in a car consider taking their details and reporting them via your hotelier or holiday rep to the police. If the police choose to act, then the least it might do is inconvenience the perpetrator!

Birders should always be respectful of photographers when clearly in 'action'. Don't approach them. If you're in your car, stay in your car so as not to disturb their subject. If you're on foot, then wait until the photographer has finished or the bird has moved away. Likewise, photographers need to be equally understandable of birders.

HABITATS

Lesvos is a large island with a mosaic of habitats which makes it a fabulous holiday destination for the visiting birder.

Rivers and wetlands

Lesvos is basically a large, porous lump of rock. Much of the rain which falls on it goes straight down into the ground forming underground rivers and reservoirs (which the locals tap into right across the island for irrigation).

From November through to April the rivers fill up and some even hold water into May, but most by then are dry at the surface. Those with a watercourse following its length close to the surface are easily recognised by the increased vegetation along their banks and in the river beds themselves.

In such a dry landscape, those areas which do hold water in late April and May act as magnets for migrants which use them for refuge and refuelling. Chief among these is the Tsiknias River (p. 104) east of Kalloni, which is unrivalled. Situated at the northern end of the Gulf of Kalloni, and pointing due north inland, it is both an obvious staging post and route for birds to follow north across the island and beyond Lesvos' shores. In comparison, the other Kalloni rivers, Christou (to the west — p. 100) and Milopotamos (further still to the east) both attract birds but aren't a patch on the Tsiknias.

These rivers lie either side of the largest wetland on the island — the Kalloni Saltpans and adjacent seasonal Alykes Wetlands (p. 112). Combined with these three various rivers, this area alone covers some 20 square kilometres of the island which concentrates both birds and birders and the main reason why the Kalloni area remains the premier place for birders to base their stay on the island.

Situated within the Kalloni area is another important wetland, Metochi Lake (p. 102). This site clearly benefits from the pulling power of the Tsiknias River and Kalloni Saltpans, and provides a dense area of cover for herons, including Night-heron and Little Bittern, crakes (the islands premier site) and wetland warblers.

To the east of Kalloni, the Kalami River at Mesa (p. 164) forms a small marshland just in from the river mouth which sometimes holds decent water levels into May and can be good for egrets, herons, storks and wildfowl. Nearby Mesa Pool (p. 164) holds water year round and is one of the best sites on the island for Ruddy Shelduck.

Heading south along the eastern side of the Gulf of Kalloni (p. 163) the coastline down to Skala Polichnitou is peppered with little rivers reaching the sea, all of which are worth exploring for birds (and dragonflies). Just north of the coastal village of Skamnioudi is the coastal pool of Alikoudi (p. 170). This can be excellent in spring as, other than the saltpans, it is the only real pool of standing water in this area.

Continuing just a couple of kilometres you come to the second most important wetland on the island, Polichnitos Saltpans (p. 171). Whilst it's worth visiting these pans at any time of year, it's in the autumn that this site really comes into its own, for autumn waders in particular.

Vatera, on the south coast, has two important river mouths sitting either side of the town. The mouth of the River Almiropotamos (p. 174) lies to the west and is an important migration route north through this part of the island for herons, raptors and passerines. To the east of the town lies the mouth of the River Vourkou (p. 176) which provides an entry point to another deep valley system heading north through the island on the western flank of the Mt Olympus area.

To the northeast of Mt Olympus lies the largest reeded area on Lesvos, Dipi Larisos (p. 184). This is a much neglected site because it's not on the main circuit of main sites

Pygmy Cormorant
in autumn and winter can be found at coastal sites including river mouths or the coastal reedbed at Dipi Larisos

and can be difficult to work thoroughly, but it is certainly still worth paying a visit if you are covering any of the Agiasos area (p. 180).

North of Mt Olympus, the maps show a wetland area off the main Mytilini-Polichnitos road. Don't bother looking for this site in spring as what used to be an extensive damp wetland with reeds is now largely dry with more and more being taken up by farming.

The Mytilini peninsula has relatively little other than a trickle of a river by the north end of the airport (p. 186) and Haramida Marsh (p. 187). This latter site really warrants more attention but I fear it is simply too far out of the way for most birders. Why not make time for it before heading back to the airport?

The eastern coast has a few river mouths between Mytilini and Mandamados (p. 130) that are always worth checking including at Palios which is a regular Ruddy Shelduck breeding site. Nearby, the small roadside pool near Klio will take only a few minutes to check when passing. The only other permanent water body is Perasma Reservoir between Molivos and Petra, and other than this, the northern part of the island is pretty desolate when it comes to wetlands.

West of Anaxos you find a few more little river mouths worth spending time around, including the River Voulgaris which is another Ruddy Shelduck breeding site.

In the far west of the island, there are several wetland sites to visit – the River Faneromeni (p. 151), River Vergias (Skala Eresou – p. 162) and Pithariou Reservoir (p. 160). The Faneromeni valley is a major migration site and is a must visit at least once during your stay. The mouth of the Vergias River (Skala Eresou) holds water all year and is an excellent spring site, but can also be very good in autumn. Pithariou is the largest freshwater body on the island and in autumn is the only area of standing freshwater in this part of the island, and so is definitely worth checking.

The Meladia River valley (between Sigri and Eresos – p. 156) is one of the best migration sites on the island, and in spring the river ford, and nearby river mouth, can be a real pull for arriving migrants.

Running up the eastern side of the Gulf of Kalloni, the mouth of the River Makara (p. 140) can be good in spring, and Parakila Marsh (p. 138) is worth visiting at any time of year, but is at its best in winter and early spring.

Grassland and scrub

The winter rains usually mean that come spring the grassland and scrub areas are lush green. Much of the coastal areas are covered by grass and scrub, as are much of the non-olive producing upland areas (the lowland areas are reserved for what little passes for arable farming here) before the ground gives way to rock. Some coastal areas become damp grassland during winter, some remaining wet in spring, but by May, most of these sites are dry and become tinder dry during the baking summer months. These grassland areas are at their best in winter for wintering larks, pipits and buntings. In spring they attract migrating pipits, wagtails, chats and shrikes. In spring many grassland areas can be fabulous for wild flowers.

Another type of 'grassland' are the arable fields growing grass/hay and lucerne. These two crops are grown for cattle feed and are cropped twice a year — once in spring the other in autumn (irrigated sites). Recently cut fields are fabulous for feeding birds, which are attracted to the abundance of insects in the cut crop. Wagtails, chats, shrikes, warblers and the smaller falcons all hunt these fields.

Arable farmland

There is relatively little land available for arable farming on this rock of an island. What available land there is lies in the river plains and valleys near the coastal areas. These areas are still pretty much traditionally farmed. The fields are small, have weedy edges (and often weedy middles too), and often have fruit trees around their edges or nearby. This all adds up to excellent habitat for migrants and some of the commoner breeding species. An excellent example are the fields running between the Kalloni-Parakila road and Metochi Lake (p. 102). In spring and autumn these fields hold many migrants and a walk along the rough road here can be very rewarding.

Olive groves

The 11 million olive trees that cover a significant amount of the island create an important habitat. The groves on Lesvos are far from the intensively farmed olive groves of other Mediterranean areas which are a monoculture with limited birdlife. Lesvos olive groves are usually peppered with other trees and shrubs and a decent ground layer. They are an important breeding habitat for Middle Spotted Woodpecker and tits (inc. Sombre), but also attract many migrant breeding species including Turtle Dove and Olive-tree Warbler.

Deciduous woodland

Deciduous woodland is dotted all over the island. Throughout the centre, west and north, hillsides are often scattered with oaks and some areas have decent-sized oak woods. Ipsilou (p. 147) is an excellent example of scattered deciduous woodland which is excellent for both breeding species and attracting passage migrants.

The areas around Mt Olympus (p. 180) and Mt Lepetimnos (p. 132) are both swathed in sweet chestnut forests which provide a very different habitat for the island, and one in which a vast variety of scarcer birds and flowers predominate. These areas are rarely explored at length by visiting birders but are probably the habitat holding rare breeding species such as Hawfinch and Levant Sparrowhawk.

Pine Forest

Like much of the Mediterranean basin, coniferous woodland dominates large areas of the island. Woodlands such as Achladeri (p. 168) are fantastic for breeding species such as Krüper's Nuthatch, Long-eared Owl and Masked Shrike, as well as commoner species and passage migrants. If you have the time, or simply want to get away from the main birding areas, you could do a lot worse than checking some of these rarely covered woodland areas.

Barren uplands

Throughout the centre and west of the island, the rock forces through to the surface and grass and scrub are greatly reduced or driven out altogether. Barren and hostile these areas may look, but barren of wildlife they are not. Sought-after species such as Isabelline Wheatear, Rock Nuthatch, Cretzschmar's and Cinereous Buntings and Chukar occur throughout these areas, plus commoner species such as Woodlark and Black-eared Wheatear. Raptors too are present here and you can often get fabulous views of Short-toed Eagle and falcons in these areas. Ipsilou (p. 147) and the cross country route across the Meladia Valley (p. 156) between Sigri and Eresos are two excellent examples of bird-rich upland areas.

The coast and sea

Being an island, Lesvos has plenty of coastline and plenty of sea around it. Yellow-legged Gull is abundant around most coastal areas, while Audouin's Gull, whilst rare, can be found, particularly along the north coast. Yelkouan and Scopoli's Shearwaters can be seen along all coasts, but Scopoli's are best looked for along the south coast and can often give excellent views.

Two large gulfs penetrate the south of the island, and these shallow, nutrient- and fish-rich basins form major wintering grounds for several species. Great Cormorant and Great Crested Grebe occur in large numbers, along with smaller numbers of Black-necked Grebe and the occasional Black-throated Diver. Pygmy Cormorant occurs most winters around river mouths or the Dipi Larisos reedbed (p. 184).

MIGRATION

One of Lesvos' main attractions is the fantastic spring migration which is pretty much unrivalled in a European context (only places like Eilat in Israel surpass). The migration may not be vast in terms of numbers, but in terms of concentrated passerine movement and the 'anything can happen' feeling, spring birding here can be amongst the most exciting you'll ever experience.

Waterbirds

As detailed in the habitat section above, wetland birds occur at coastal sites, a handful of permanent wetlands and at seasonal wetlands, many of which are dry by late May.

Both Yelkouan and Scopoli's Shearwaters can be seen offshore in spring and autumn whilst White and Dalmatian Pelican occur occasionally. White Pelican is annual and has been seen in large flocks including a single flock of 144 in September 2007. Dalmatian isn't quite annual but can also occur in small flocks but singletons are the norm.

Greater Flamingo occurs year round with attempting breeding, and both White and Black Storks breed and can usually be seen at either of the saltpans and larger rivers.

Marsh Sandpiper is an annual passage migrant seen at the saltpan areas and larger rivers

Herons and egrets occur on most wetland areas. Little and Great White Egrets are common at both saltpans and along the larger river sections. Spoonbills are relatively scarce with singletons or small flocks occurring at both saltpans (but rarely elsewhere). Squacco and Purple Herons, Night-heron and Little Bittern occur on spring passage along reed- or bush-lined rivers and in particular at Metochi Lake. Purple Heron and Night-heron are occasionally recorded in large flocks such as in 2008 when a mixed flock of 53 Purple Herons and 32 Night-herons were seen together at Kalloni Saltpans. Glossy Ibis occurs in varying numbers, occasionally in sizable flocks. Cattle Egret is an increasingly regular species with three records alone between December 2007 and December 2008.

Seven species of rails and crakes occur regularly on the island. Of the migrants, Little Crake passes through in good numbers with Metochi Lake being the top site (double figure counts even being recorded!). Both Spotted and Baillon's Crakes are also occasionally seen here. The Meladia River Ford is another excellent crake site. Corncrake is a species rarely seen by birders, but we know from reports from islanders, as well as a case of illegal poaching in autumn 2007 (when 32 birds were found killed), that the species clearly passes through the island in reasonable numbers.

Waders are scarce around the coast preferring instead the southern rivers (particularly the Tsiknias) and the two saltpan areas. In spring the Kalloni Saltpans take centre stage but in autumn the Polichnitos pans are the better of the two. Regular species include

Black-winged Stilt (also breeds), Avocet (also breeds), Little Ringed, Ringed and Kentish Plovers, Grey Plover, Sanderling, Little and Temminck's Stint (the latter more common on the rivers), Dunlin, Ruff, Common Snipe, Black-tailed Godwit, Whimbrel, Curlew, Spotted Redshank, Common Redshank, Greenshank, Marsh, Green (also winter), Wood and Common Sandpipers and Turnstone. Spur-winged Plover are near annual in spring and one of the spring highlights is the passage of Collared Pratincole through the Alykes Wetlands and Kalloni Saltpans area, with the occasional Great Snipe also seen. Stone-curlew is one of the few waders that breeds and can be found around the Kalloni pans and the Christou river mouth. Both areas are also very good for passage birds.

Mediterranean Gulls are common spring migrants (as well as a wintering species) and both Little and Slender-billed Gulls pass through in small numbers. Both *intermedius* and *fuscus* Lesser Black-backed Gulls occur on passage (and in winter). Gull-billed Tern is a scarce spring migrant, but White-winged Black and Whiskered Terns are plentiful in spring, with a handful of Black Terns also seen annually.

Kingfisher can be found in sheltered bays and river mouths from September to April.

Raptors

Birds of prey are high interest for most birders lists. Migration through Lesvos, in spring and autumn, isn't about fantastic numbers but the range of species, and often close views.

Honey-buzzard is a scarce species but can be seen in numbers in autumn, yet Black Kite is surprisingly scarce with only a handful of records each year. Vultures are rare with only around ten records of both Egyptian and Griffon. There is a sole unsupported record of a Black Vulture in spring 2008 (one of the best raptor springs ever for the island).

Of the harriers, Montagu's is by far the commonest species in spring and is a scarce migrant in autumn. Marsh is regularly seen in spring and autumn with occasional winter records when Hen Harrier occurs with passage birds noted in spring. Pallid Harrier remains a sought after species with 1-3 records most springs.

Three accipiters occur on the island. Both Eurasian Sparrowhawk and Goshawk are thinly distributed breeders with passage birds of both species often seen. Goshawk can occur in numbers in autumn. Levant Sparrowhawk is thought to breed but has never been confirmed, but small numbers, including occasional flocks, have been seen in spring with the odd singleton seen in autumn.

Common and Long-legged Buzzard are resident breeders and both occur on passage.

Short-toed Eagle is a scarce breeder and passage migrant, but none of the other eagle species are anything but scarce. Bonelli's, Booted and Lesser Spotted Eagles are all recorded annually. There are a few records each of Golden, Imperial and Steppe Eagles. Osprey is a common passage migrant in spring and autumn.

Falcons can be one of the spectacles of spring on the island, with mixed flocks of up to four species seen in some years. Breeding species include Lesser and Common Kestrels and Peregrine (Eleanora's Falcon are thought to breed) — all of which also occur on passage. Lesser Kestrel and Eleanora's Falcon are species of the open areas of the west and north and both can occur in small flocks in these as well as central areas. Most springs witness good numbers of Red-footed Falcons with parties into double figures not uncommon. Small numbers of Hobby are seen passing through in spring and autumn. There are several reports of Lanner each year but there remains no evidence of breeding on the island. All falcons are scarce to rare in autumn.

Other migrants

Common Cuckoo is a fairly common passage species with the rufous female form frequent and a handful of Great Spotted Cuckoos are seen each spring.

Of all the species that pass through the island, swifts are one of the most obvious, on occasion filling the skies like an aerial soup. As elsewhere in Europe, Pallid Swift is the earlier passage species and occurs in good numbers through March to early April with a second small passage in late April/early May. Common Swifts pass through in huge numbers from late March with skies of many thousands not uncommon in late April and early May. The largest of the swifts, Alpine, passes through in good numbers in spring with fewer seen in autumn.

European Bee-eater occurs commonly in spring, with small numbers breeding along some rivers, and is a scarce migrant in autumn. Roller is a spectacular species and occurs annually in spring in varying numbers. It can occur in sizeable groups, e.g. a flock of 17 in off the sea at Vatera in May 2003. Hoopoes are another spectacular species and are common in spring and autumn. Wryneck is a scarce passage species in spring and autumn, and with their cryptic plumage and secretive nature, very few are reported.

Short-toed Lark can be seen in suitable grassland areas during spring passage, with small numbers remaining to breed, and in autumn large numbers of Skylark can pass over with some remaining for the winter. All other larks are rare, but there are over ten records of Calandra.

Hirundines add to the spring aerial soups with large numbers of Barn Swallow, House and Sand Martins passing through the island. Smaller numbers of Red-rumped Swallow and Crag Martins pass through, both species breed on the island and Crag Martin also occasionally winters in small numbers.

Red-throated Pipit is one of those breeding plumage species most birders want to connect with. Rosy-fronted birds are regularly seen on passage across the island, with the Alykes Wetlands and adjacent grasslands around the Kalloni Saltpans a real magnet for this species.

Wagtails are a real feature of spring. Racial identification of 'yellow' wagtails is not always straight forward, but at least seven subspecies/forms of 'yellow' wagtail occur on the island along with countless hybrids. Citrine Wagtail is an annual scarce spring passage migrant, unlike the rest of Greece where it is still extremely rare. In some years double-figure numbers can be seen (e.g. 15+ in 2004).

Small numbers of Thrush Nightingale are heard singing each spring — a few are even seen. Whinchat can occur in huge numbers whilst Common Redstart is a relatively scarce species. Black-eared, Isabelline and Northern Wheatears are all breeding and passage species and there are occasional records of Rock-thrush.

Large numbers of warblers move through the island with relatively few species staying to breed (see migrant breeders below). Commoner passage species include Chiffchaff, Willow, Wood, Icterine, Reed, Sedge and Barred Warblers, Common and Lesser Whitethroat and Blackcap. Scarcer species include Garden and Marsh Warblers. River Warbler, whilst extremely rare elsewhere in Greece, is an annual spring passage migrant in varying numbers.

All the breeding European flycatchers pass through the island. Spotted is very common in spring and autumn, whilst Pied occurs in reasonable numbers. Collared and Red-breasted Flycatchers occur in small numbers each spring and Semi-collared are near annual in recent years.

Penduline Tit is recorded most springs, including a pair breeding in 2002. Golden Orioles are common passage migrants across the whole island in spring.

Shrikes are another obvious family across the island. Red-backed Shrike is a very common spring and autumn passage species which also breeds in the west of the island. Woodchat is a common breeder and passage bird (the eastern race *niloticus* reportedly passes through in late May but there are no official Greek records). Masked Shrike is a breeding species with a few obvious migrants seen in autumn (separating migrants and breeders is difficult) whilst Lesser Grey Shrike is a relatively common migrant.

One of the annual spectacles is the passage of the amazingly coloured Rose-coloured Starling. These pink and black birds arrive en-masse in mid-May and for a brief time brighten up the late spring. Unfortunately their passage occurs after most birders have left the island. They have a real preference for Mulberry trees which concentrate numbers to just a few areas on the island.

In spring and autumn, flocks of sparrows can be seen dashing through the island at knee height. In spring most are Spanish, but in autumn both Spanish and House are noted, indicating that both species move through the island.

Migrant breeding species

Both White and Black Storks breed with nesting White Storks being very conspicuous with their roof- or chimney-top nests at Skala Kallonis, Mandamados, Polichnitos and other places. Greater Flamingo has attempted to breed without success.

Migrant breeding raptors include Honey-buzzard, Levant Sparrowhawk (suspected), Lesser Kestrel and Eleanora's Falcon (suspected).

Quail occur around coastal grasslands, the males calling their distinctive 'whit-whit-whit' song. Birds are frequently flushed from beach areas, presumably birds that have recently made landfall and are resting up before moving on.

Stone-curlew, Avocet, Black-winged Stilt and Little Ringed Plover all breed, as do both Common and Little Terns.

Turtle Dove breeds across the island along with Hoopoe and a few pairs of Great Spotted Cuckoo. Scops Owl is more often heard than seen, but most springs roosting birds are usually found in the Kalloni area. Nightjar is a common and widespread breeder occurring in a variety of habitats including olive groves. Common Swift breeds across the island, as do Barn and Red-rumped Swallows and a handful of Crag Martins breed around some of the higher and steeper crags. European Bee-eater breeds in small numbers along several dry rivers.

Scops Owl
often heard but seldom seen other than at one or two well-known sites

Both Short-toed Lark and Tree Pipit breed in small numbers whilst the Black-headed form of 'yellow' wagtail is the only one of the seven subspecies recorded on the island that breeds.

Small numbers of Rufous Bush Robin breed and there is a remarkable set of spring overshooting White-throated Robin breeding records on the island. Common Nightingale is common and widespread across the island in all suitable dense scrub areas.

Isabelline, Northern and Black-eared Wheatears all breed, the two former species are restricted to the west, but Black-eared is common and widespread.

Fewer warblers breed on the island than occur on passage. Small numbers of the wetland warblers breed including Reed and Great Reed. Olivacous is both widespread and common, whilst Olive-tree Warbler is thinly but widely distributed (under recorded due to birders tending to visit the same sites each year). Subalpine Warbler is common and widespread, Sardinian is thinly distrubted across the north, east and southeast (mainly within 1-2km of the coast) and Icterine and Barred Warblers may also breed.

Rüppell's Warbler is a very localised breeder and remains one of the most sought-after species for visiting birders, and thankfully the main breeding site in the north of the island near Petra remains active (despite declining numbers). Singing males do have a habit of popping up in other areas from time to time. Eastern Bonelli's Warbler whilst high on birders wish list often eludes. Few birders bother to search the breeding valleys near Agiasos and those picking one out during a spring fall remain the lucky ones. The odd territorial bird is occasionally found in the centre or west of the island.

Red-backed Shrike breeds across the west of the island, whilst Woodchat is thinly but widely distributed. Masked Shrike breeds across the island (most common in the central and eastern areas), and several pairs of Lesser Grey Shrike occur. Masked occurs in all types of scattered woodland including olive groves and pinewoods whilst the latter prefers open country with scattered trees.

Three distinctive migrant buntings come to breed on the island. Cretzschmar's Bunting is widespread occurring through much of the central, northern and western areas. Its Yellowhammer-like song is distinctive and easily picked out. Black-headed Bunting is common and widespread. They arrive en-masse at the very end of April and in next to no time singing males are everywhere and nest building is in full swing! Far less conspicuous is Cinereous Bunting which is restricted to the dry, rocky areas of the west of the island.

Its worth noting that nearly all the breeding passerines depart the island by late July, with later birds almost certainly passage migrants from further north.

Winter migrants

The island is little known for its winter species, but just because there are very few birders present to witness them, doesn't stop them occurring!

Huge numbers of Great Crested Grebes and Great Cormorants occur in the Gulf of Kalloni (with smaller numbers around other coastal areas) along with smaller numbers of Black-necked Grebe, Red-breasted Merganser and Black-throated Diver. Pygmy Cormorant are occasionally seen at coastal river mouths or at the coastal Dipi Larisos reedbed.

Wildfowl occur in relatively small numbers and are hunted during the winter months. Mallard is the most common species with small numbers of Teal, Wigeon and Pintail. Small numbers of Common Shelduck also occur.

Some raptor species increase over the winter months due to birds arriving from the north and east including Common Buzzard, Eurasian Sparrowhawk and Peregrine.

Green Sandpiper winters in small numbers, and both Common and Jack Snipe move in from the north, as do Woodcock. The latter two species are rarely seen by birders but are regularly reported as being shot by hunters.

Lesser Black-backed Gull (inc. *fuscus*) occurs mainly in winter as does Sandwich Tern.

Short-eared Owl occurs from November to March.

Skylark is a common and widespread winter visitor across the island, as is Meadow Pipit. Black Redstart is surprisingly common from November through to March and migrant Grey Wagtail, Wren, Robin, Dunnock and Song Thrush swell the island's small resident populations. Over this period Blackbirds pour in and are often hunted in the olive groves, but judging by the increasing number of birds in spring and remaining to breed, hunting of thrushes is dropping. Small numbers of both Redwing and Fieldfare occur and Goldcrests can be found in the pinewoods from November to March. Common Starling occurs between October and April.

Black Redstart
large numbers occur across the island during winter

RESIDENT SPECIES

Whilst Lesvos is clearly known for its migration, a number of species, including a few interesting ones, are resident on the island.

Chukar prefer the more open, rocky areas, and to this extent the west of the island is by far the best area for them, but they will occur in less rockier areas including along woodland edges. The species occurs at several sites close to Kalloni (e.g. Madaros).

Ruddy Shelduck is the only species of wildfowl that regularly occurs throughout the year. Whilst birds do pass through the islands, a small population is present year round. In winter they can occur on all the major wetland areas and along the larger rivers. A few pairs breed (e.g. Palios and the Voulgaris River).

Little Grebe is now resident with a number of pairs breeding at Metochi Lake and Pithariou Reservoir. Numbers increase in winter with arrivals presumably from nearby Turkey.

Shag is present in good numbers around the entire coast and can occur in large offshore 'rafts' in the winter months.

Resident raptors include Goshawk and Eurasian Sparrowhawk, Common and Long-legged Buzzards, Common Kestrel and Peregrine. Long-legged Buzzard tends to winter along southern coastal areas, in particular the Kalloni area.

Coot and Moorhen are resident with a handful of pairs of each breeding. No wader species is truly resident, although Stone-curlew can be encountered in all months.

Yellow-legged Gull is a common resident and can be seen around the entire coast and in many inland areas. Audouin's Gull is a rare resident, with breeding on offshore islands only recently discovered. Its main haunt is the north coast between Molivos and Skala Sikaminias, but odd birds can turn up along other coastal areas.

'Real' Rock Doves occur in several areas in the north and west where they breed on rocky cliffs or offshore islands (Feral Pigeons occur in most towns).

Owls are well represented on the island. Little Owl is very common and widespread and breeds in most towns and villages as well as throughout the countryside. Barn Owl is present in several areas including Skala Kallonis, Petra and Mytilini. Tawny Owl is known from the odd calling bird and the occasional road victim, whilst Long-eared Owl is thinly distributed throughout wooded areas in the centre and east, including the Kalloni area. Eagle Owl is reported to breed on the island but is never recorded by birders. Records come from local residents reporting calling birds in late winter and the more than reliable records of birds unfortunately shot by hunters (several of which end up in the wildlife hospital) in winter (which could simply be dispersing young birds from nearby Turkey).

Long-legged Buzzard
breeds in the uplands in the north and west with small numbers wintering along the coastal plains

Middle Spotted Woodpecker is a common resident across the island breeding in most woodland types including olive groves and pinewoods. There are small resident populations of Wren, Robin, Dunnock and Song and Mistle Thrushes. Most of these are restricted to the higher wooded mountain areas of Olympus and Lepetimnos. Blackbird is now common and widespread across the island due to reduced hunting in the winter. Blue Rock-thrush is relatively common throughout the centre and west of the island with occasional records from the eastern side inc. breeding at Mytilini castle.

Cetti's Warbler occurs along most river areas and around all scrubby wetland areas including Skala Kallonis Pool. Fan-tailed Warbler sadly appears to be extinct with former breeding areas around Christou River and Polichnitos Saltpans.

Great and Blue Tits are common and widespread and small, localised populations of both Long-tailed and Coal Tits occur around the pinewoods in the southeast of the island. Sombre Tit is fairly common in central and western areas occurring in most scattered woodland areas and olive groves.

Three species of nuthatch are resident on the island. Wood Nuthatch is relatively common in the woodland areas of the centre and north of the island (inc. olive groves) whilst Krüper's Nuthatch is restricted to the central and southeast pinewoods (see p. 214). Rock Nuthatch occurs in all rocky areas of the centre, north and west and the odd pocket in the east. This is an interesting species as the Lesvos birds show somewhat intermediate characteristics of the western and eastern species (see p. 215). Short-toed Treecreeper is common throughout the pinewoods of the southeast.

Hooded Crow is common across the island and Raven occurs in good numbers in the more mountainous areas but can be encountered almost anywhere on their wanderings. There are several populations of Jackdaw, all in coastal areas, with birds wandering to inland areas to feed in winter. The black-crowned *atricapillus* race of Jay is common and widespread.

House Sparrow is common and widespread and there are small pockets of Rock Sparrow dotted throughout the west of the island including Ipsilou. Goldfinch, Greenfinch and Chaffinch are all common, Linnets occur thinly across the island and Serin breeds throughout the pinewoods across the whole island. Hawfinch remains a bit of an oddity. Evidence suggests it breeds in the northern and eastern woodland areas. It certainly occurs in winter with flocks up to 200 reported, and presumed migrants are encountered in odd areas in spring. Cirl and Corn Buntings are both very common, breeding across the island, and the latter form large flocks in winter around coastal areas.

VAGRANTS

An island famed for migration will clearly be good for vagrants. Lesvos is ideally situated for overshooting spring migrants which should have put the brakes on somewhere to the south. Sat just a few miles off mainland Turkey means that some migrants which may normally follow the main land route east of the island, will drift west, cut the corner of the coast line (see map on p. 12) and drift over Lesvos. Some species, particularly raptors, are prone to wandering, and individuals of species which occur to the north and east will occasionally simply wander over to the island. This may apply to even some relatively sedentary species. As are the vagaries of vagrancy, some species simply turn up completely off course.

With so many birders visiting such a small island, many species are reported. Some reports are for totally unexpected and somewhat unlikely species which are often misidentified commoner species (e.g. Middle Spotted Woodpecker reported as Great Spotted). Unfortunately few records are submitted to the Greek recording authorities so many records remain unconfirmed and some species undoubtedly have occurred, yet are not officially on the Lesvos list due to lack of documentation.

Confirmed records of vagrants include Bewick's Swan (1), Whooper (3), Greater White-fronted Goose (5), Gadwall (3), Pochard (5), Ferruginous Duck (9), Tufted Duck (3), Goldeneye (1), White-headed Duck (1), Smew (1), Red Kite (2 — many reports refer to poorly seen Long-legged Buzzards), White-tailed Eagle (5), Egyptian Vulture (10+), Griffon (9 — the scarcity of Griffon Vulture seems surprising), Steppe Eagle (1), Imperial Eagle (10), Merlin (7), Saker Falcon (1), Dotterel (2), Knot (2), Pectoral Sandpiper (1 — only the fourth record for Greece), Bar-tailed Godwit (8), Red-necked Phalarope (10), Arctic Skua (3), Common Gull (3), Stock Dove (4), Laughing Dove (1), Little Swift (1), Blue-cheeked Bee-eater (2 — a further 13 unsubmitted records inc. seven (totalling 15 birds) from 2008 alone), Lesser Short-toed Lark (1), Black-bellied Dipper (1), Bluethroat (1) White-throated Robin (2 — a further seven remain unsubmitted), Pied Wheatear (10), Finsch's Wheatear (1 — despite annual claims which always turn out to be 'black and white' black-throated *melanolucea* Black-eared Wheatear), Penduline Tit (inc. a single breeding attempt), Bearded Tit (2), Great Grey Shrike (3+), Steppe Grey Shrike (1), Nutcracker (1), Red-fronted Serin (1), Common Crossbill (5+), Scarlet Rosefinch (2), Yellowhammer (3), Little Bunting (1).

The following species have been reported but no records have been submitted so they do not appear on the official Lesvos List: Lesser White-fronted Goose, Barnacle Goose, Red-throated Diver, Storm-petrel, Black Vulture, Lesser Sand Plover, Greater Sand Plover, Sociable Plover, White-tailed Plover, Pomarine Skua, Long-tailed Skua, Great Black-backed Gull, Lesser Crested Tern, Arctic Terns, Pied Kingfisher, White-fronted Kingfisher, Green Woodpecker, Great Spotted Woodpecker, Syrian Woodpecker, White-backed Woodpecker, Black Lark, Richard's Pipits, Ring Ouzel, Booted Warbler, Spectacled Warbler, Twite (not even on the Greek List) and Rustic Bunting.

There remains a need for records to be formally submitted in order for us to understand the true status of many species occurring on Lesvos.

SUBMITTING YOUR BIRD RECORDS

I encourage all visitors to submit their records via the Lesvos Bird Records Committee (http://lesvosbirdrecords.blogspot.com). The LBRC collect records of all species, in particular national rarities, which are forwarded to the Hellenic Rarities Committee (http://rarities.ornithologiki.gr/en/index.php), scarce Lesvos migrants (e.g. rare eagles) and scarcer breeding species (see pp. 188–227).

OTHER WIDLIFE

Lesvos offers much more than just birds to the interested birder and naturalist.

Around 50 species of butterfly can be found across the island (see p. 236) with more species sure to be added with more people paying more attention. I recently added two species to the Lesvos list (Lattice Brown and Marbled Fritillary) with photos found on the internet whilst researching this book! Dragonflies are also well represented on the island (see p. 228) including some species difficult to see elsewhere in Europe such as Odalisque and Small Skimmer. You will encounter countless other fascinating insects whilst birding including Europe's largest moth, Giant Peacock Moth, the day-flying Hummingbird Hawkmoth, grasshoppers, mantids and the amazing-looking Thread Lacewing. The equally fascinating Mole Cricket is usually only ever seen in the bill of a heron or Hoopoe!

Whenever you are near water you will never fail to miss the Marsh Frog chorus. Less conspicuous is the Common Tree Frog which can be found along most river courses and Metochi Lake (but take some finding!) and other species found on the island is the scarce Eastern Spadefoot and Green Toad. Lizards are plentiful and include Turkish Gecko (around buildings), the fantastic Balkan Green Lizard, the widespread Snake-eyed Lizard (Lacertid) and the rare Snake-eyed Skink. Snakes themselves are common and widespread once the ground temperature warms up from early to mid-May, but these are more usually seen dead on the road than alive in the field. The most common snake is actually a legless lizard — Glass Snakes are long, golden-brown with a yellowish head and completely harmless. Venomous species inc. the very rarely seen Ottoman Viper. Snakes will often scarper as soon as they hear your clomping feet, but care should be taken when leaving footpaths and tracks, particularly in rocky areas, when making your own call of nature!

Two species of 'turtles' occur on the island – the very common Stripe-necked Terrapin found on many rivers and Metochi Lake, and the much rarer European Pond Turtle known only from Metochi Lake. Spur-thighed Tortoise is relatively common and widespread throughout the centre and west of the island.

Mammals are rarely seen. Red Fox is thinly distributed across the island. Beech Marten is quite common judging by the number of road casualties you see, and much more so than Eastern Hedgehog which likewise is much more likely to be found dead on the road than seen alive. In the summer and autumn visitors might see Lesser Mole rats darting from holes in the ground to feed. In the sea, Common and Striped Dolphins occur, but a very lucky few might just chance upon the distinctive dark form of the very rare Mediterranean Monk Seal (total population c.300 animals).

Lastly, the flowers of Lesvos are spectacular. Across the island in spring the visitor will see countless flower meadows, poppy fields or flower-filled verges and river banks. Of note are the 80 species of orchid found on the island (see p. 240) including the endemic

Lesbos Orchid. Most species flower from March to May, so are accessible to birders.

Butterflies, dragonflies and orchids are all covered by excellent field guides (see respective species lists as detailed above) but the other groups are poorly covered by available guides.

CONSERVATION

Wildlife conservation on western European lines is pretty much non-existent. Some small scale efforts can be seen and initiatives such as the Lesvos Wildlife Hospital (WWW.WILDLIFEONLESVOS.ORG) contribute to an increase in awareness of wild animal welfare. But the destruction, much of it seemingly needless, of some areas (the straightening of water courses, bulldozing of scrub, draining of wetlands, etc.) continues pretty much unchecked.

An example of woeful conservation is the Skala Kallonis Pool. This was once one of the main spring sites. A fabulous little wetland in a resort area right by several of the main hotels favoured by birders, and one of the main reasons the hotels were favoured by birders. In recent springs the site has been at best a shadow of its former self or completely dried out thanks to so called 'improvements' which stopped the occasional flooding from the nearby sea (the salt water helping to control some of the less salt tolerant vegetation). Some local hoteliers have lobbied local politicians about the benefit the pool brings to them, extending their tourist season, but to date nothing has been done to save this wetland. Surrounding land has been developed and the wetland itself seems destined to be improved again so that it too can be built upon.

Another case of mismanagement (from a conservation perspective) is the occasional bulldozing of the rivers, straightening and clearing whole sections of river and making them almost sterile in a wildlife context. Such canalisation does away with much needed scrub and riverside vegetation which helps bind the otherwise loose soil and takes out the natural meander of a river and all the small pools, spits and margins a natural river course would otherwise create.

It is however very easy to treat any proposed development on an island such as Lesvos with deep scepticism and instant disapproval. Schemes to hold water, be these in irrigation reservoirs or the damming of rivers, can have less impact than first thought and can provide new habitat, especially those areas holding water during the otherwise dry summer months.

Rather than criticise what is done, we should try and encourage improved ways of doing things or new initiatives. This is best done via the local hotel, taverna and business owners. Those businesses dependent on tourism are beginning to understand the additional income the spring birding season in particular brings to them and the local economy. By talking to hotel and taverna owners about wildlife and conservation only helps them understand better why we visit the island, and why it is in their long term interests to encourage wildlife conservation in order to secure the future of birding tourism on the island.

This doesn't mean that none of the locals care. They do. Several groups including Friends of Green Lesbos, the Lesvos Wildlife Hospital and Naftilos en dras, national bodies such as WWF and the Hellenic Ornithological Society, and individual Lesviots such as Eleni Galinou and others contribute what they can within the confines of the unsympathetic authorities on the island. Some authorities are now beginning to understand, e.g. Agia Paraskevi council which have erected hides and viewing screens and undertaken some clearance of the illegally tipped rubbish, at some birdwatching sites.

LESVOS BIRDING AND CONSERVATION WEBSITES

WWW.GREENLESBOS.COM

This is the website of the Friends of Green Lesbos, an international internet-based society for all who want to see the rich and wonderful environment of Lesbos protected and enhanced.

WWW.LESVOSBIRDING.COM

This is the main birding website for the island providing a free online resource for visiting birders. In spring, Lesvos Birding runs a sightings log at the Hotel Pasiphae and posts summaries of each day's sightings on the website each evening during the main weeks. It also contains links to trip reports, photo galleries and details of Lesvos Birdingbird and wildlife holidays on the island

HTTP://LESVOSBIRDRECORDS.BLOGSPOT.COM

The Lesvos Bird Records Committee collects all bird records for the island.

WWW.WILDLIFEONLESVOS.COM

Website of the Lesvos Wildlife Hospital.

OTHER WEBSITES OF INTEREST TO BIRDERS

HTTP://RARITIES.ORNITHOLOGIKI.GR/EN/INDEX.PHP

The website of the Hellenic Rarities Committee inc. links to their annual reports and gallery of rare birds photographed in Greece.

WWW.ORNITHOLOGIKI.GR

The website of the Hellenic Ornithological Society.

WWW.WORLDBIRDS.ORG/V3/GREECE.PHP

Ornithotopos — submit your Greek bird records online.

WWW.PETRIFIEDFOREST.GR

The Lesvos Petrified Forest is one of the finest in the world.

HUNTING

Greece, like many other southern and eastern European countries, has a culture of hunting, much of it indiscriminate. Lesvos is no different. Hunting on the island is primarily with the gun. Liming and trapping, found elsewhere in the Mediterranean basin, doesn't appear to be practised. Being part of the EU, Greece is required to comply with the European Birds Directive and other EU legislation relating to hunting. This is not always the case and incidents of large scale poaching do still occur, as in the example of 32 Corncrakes illegally killed near Ambeliko in September 2007.

Although the legal hunting season in Greece is from mid-September to the end of February, Lesvos has a special dispensation to hunt outside this period, so expect to see hunting from August through to mid-March with the main quarry being Turtle Doves (in autumn), Quail (mainly autumn), Woodcock, thrushes (especially around olive groves), wildfowl (December to February) and Chukar. There are some attempts to captive breed Chukar for shooting, but nothing on the scale that we have seen in the UK with Red-legged Partridge and Pheasant.

Hunting periods for legal quarry species on Lesvos

Species	Period	Species	Period
Chukar	15/9 - 30/11	Woodcock	15/9 - 28/2
Quail	20/8 - 28/2	Snipe	15/9 - 10/2
Pheasant	15/9 - 29/12	Rock Dove	15/9 - 28/2
White-fronted Goose	15/9 - 10/2	Wood Pigeon	20/8 - 20/2
Gadwall	15/9 - 31/1	Turtle Dove	20/8 - 28/2
Wigeon	15/9 - 10/2	Magpie	15/9 - 28/2
Mallard	15/9 - 31/1	Jackdaw	15/9 - 28/2
Shoveler	15/9 - 10/2	Hooded Crow	15/9 - 28/2
Pintail	15/9 - 10/2	Skylark	20/8 - 10/2
Garganey	15/9 - 10/2	Starling	15/9 - 28/2
Teal	15/9 - 31/1	Blackbird	15/9 - 20/2
Pochard	15/9 - 10/2	Fieldfare	20/8 - 28/2
Tufted Duck	15/9 - 31/1	Redwing	20/8 - 28/2
Moorhen	15/9 - 10/2	Song Thrush	20/8 - 28/2
Coot	15/9 - 10/2	Mistle Thrush	20/8 - 20/2
Lapwing	15/9 - 31/1		

Source: Hunting Federation of Greece (www.ksellas.gr)

BIRDING SITES ON LESVOS

Lesvos is a birder's paradise. The whole island is pretty much open for us to enjoy with relatively little restriction. In this site section I have selected over 60 of the best birding sites I know of for birding. Some are already well known, others less so but soon will be! Please don't feel restricted by these sites. Explore the island far and wide. If you find any hidden gems and wish to share them, then please contact me and I will feature either on my website or in future editions of this book.

LESVOS PLACE NAMES

Greek is a complicated language and if you look at maps, road signs, etc. you will soon notice that many place names have several spellings. For this book I have used names found on the 1:70,000 Road Editions 212 Lesbos map. These names may differ slightly with some island road signs and may differ markedly with some of the names used on the 1:75,000 Freytag & Berndt Lesvos map. I have however used the latter map for several names where the Road Editions map does not give a name for a particular place and the Freytag & Berndt does (e.g. Kavaki headland where Rüppell's Warbler breeds between Petra and Molivos).

On p. 251 you will find a list of local place names in both lower and upper case (road signs on the island might be in either) and pronunciations.

I do not use the previously adopted birders' names for any site.

Short-toed Eagle
is the only eagle species which breeds on the island and also occurs on passage

SITE MAPS

For this book we commissioned a set of detailed maps from renowned magazine illustrator Steven Hall. These maps are not exhaustive but aim to provide the required information needed for each area or site and should be used in combination with the Road Editions 212 map.

I think the maps are so simple to understand, I have not provided a key!

FEATURED SITES

Each area is introduced with a large-scale map detailing the individual sites featured within an area. Within each section each individual site is then covered with most sites given a detailed and annotated map. This way the island is broken down into following sections —

Kalloni area

Skala Kallonis Pool	98	Tsiknias River (Upper)	107
Christou River	100	Kalloni Saltpans	108
Potamia Valley	100	Alykes Wetlands	112
Potamia Reservoir	100	Madaros	115
Metochi Lake	102	Kalloni Mini Soccer Pitch	115
Tsiknias River (Lower)	104	Kalloni Raptor Watch Point	117

Napi Valley

Napi	120	Platania	120
Koriani	120		

Petra to Mandamados

Kavaki	124	Korakas	131
Peresma	125	Vafios to Klio	132
Molivos	126	Stipsi to Kapi	132
Efthalou to Skala Sikaminias	128		

Skalochori area

Aghios Taxiarchis	135	Lardia Valley	137
Katapetros Valley	135	Perivolis Monastery	137
Voulgaris River	136		

Parakila to Mesotopos

Parakila Marsh	138	Sideras	142
Aghios Ioannis	139	Mesotopos	144
Makara	140	Chrousos	145
Konditsia Valley	142		

Sigri and Eresos

Ipsilou Monastery	147	Meladia Valley	156
Petrified Forest	150	Pithariou Reservoir	160
Sigri & Faneromeni	151	Vergias River, Skala Eresou	162
Sigri Old Sanatorium	154		

Mesa to Polichnitos
    Mesa 164
    Vouvaris River Mouth 166
    Achladeri Forest 168
    Achladeri to Skala Vasilikon 169
    Skala Vasilikon to Skamnioudi 170
    Alikoudi Pool 170
    Mikri Limni 170
    Polichnitos Saltpans 171

Vatera area
    Almiropotamos River 174
    Agios Fokas 176
    Palia Vigla Chapel 176
    Vourkos River Mouth 176
    Ambeliko Valley 178

Agiasos area
    Agiasos 180
    Agiasos Sanatorium 180
    Megalochori Valley 182
    Dimitrios 182
    Panaghia Chapel 183
    Dipi Larisos Reedbed 184

Mytilini area
    Mytilini 186
    Mytilini Airport 186
    Cape Lena 186
    Haramida Marsh 187

The text for each site includes the following sections —

Location and access
Areas to search
Species
Nearest amenities
Other information (where applicable).

Cetti's Warbler
occurs along rivers and wetland areas across the island

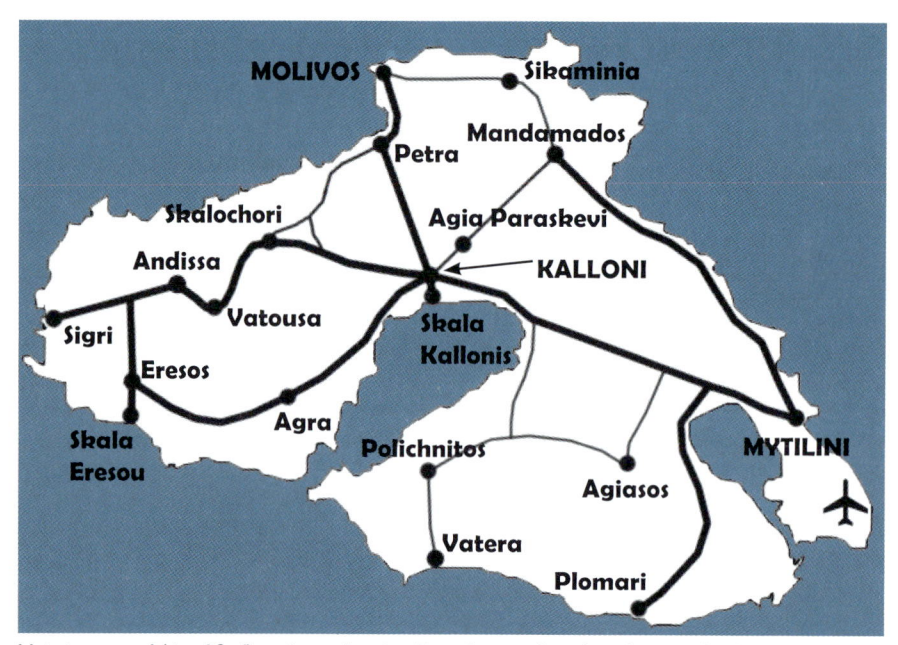

Main towns and (simplified) main road routes. For other roads and tracks see individual site maps.

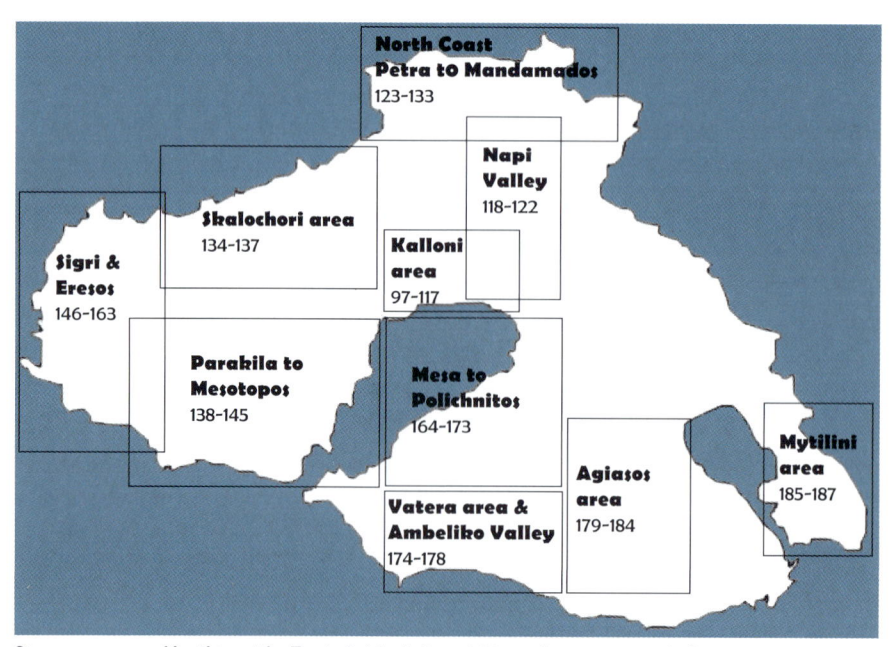

Site areas covered by this guide. For individual sites within each area see inside front cover or pp. 62-63 and first page of each area.

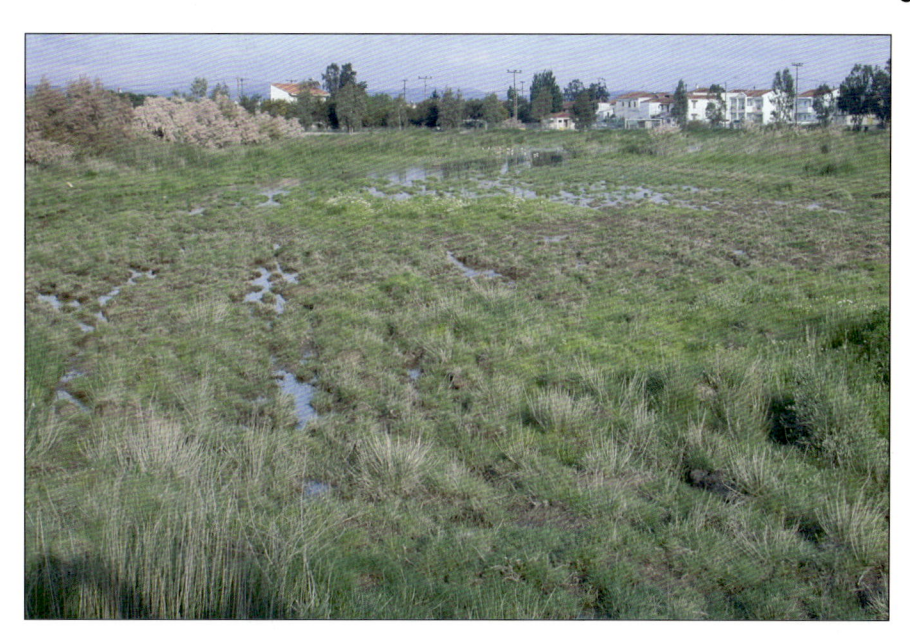

Skala Kallonis Pool taken in April 02 when the site was at its best. Unfortunately the site has now silted up heavily and is dominated by drier, tall, grass species with reduced water areas and reduced viewing. Will it ever be saved and reinstated to its former glory?

Christou River April 09. The wide river mouth and coastal plain is excellent for waders, egrets, herons and storks. Stone-curlew breed here and in autumn can occur in double figures. A viewing screen on the west side provides improved views of the river mouth.

Metochi Lake Apr 08. The best site on the island for crakes: Little Crake can occur in double figures. It is also excellent for Little Bittern, herons, marsh terns, warblers, and hirundines. The valley is excellent for raptors inc. Short-toed Eagle and Long-legged Buzzard.

Potamia Apr 08. This spur runs north above the irrigation reservoir at the Skala Kallonis end of the valley. It is an excellent area for commoner breeding species inc. Black-eared Wheatear, Subalpine Warbler and Cirl Bunting. Look for raptors over the ridges.

Potamia Left: lower river section Apr 07. The olive groves at the seaward end of the valley hold Masked Shrike and Olive-tree Warbler. Right: upper valley Apr 07. A good area for breeding and migrant raptors inc. Long-legged Buzzard, Short-toed Eagle and Peregrine.

Madaros April 09. Only a few kilometres north of Kalloni the terrain turns both hilly and rocky. This is an excellent site for breeding species and migrants alike. The former inc. Chukar and Rufous Bush Robin. River Warbler is sometimes heard singing from the valley bottom.

Tsiknias River Mouth May 09. This is one of the main rivers on the island and holds water most years into June. The wide river mouth has spits and muddy margins that attracts feeding and roosting waders, gulls and terns and is worth checking most evenings.

Tsiknias River Ford May 09. A superb area attracting migrants inc. Little Bittern, waders (inc. Temminck's Stint), Bee-eater, hirundines, wagtails (Citrine Wagtail seen here most years), warblers (inc. Great Reed and Olivaceous), shrikes and buntings.

Tsiknias River May 09. The river banks are heavily covered in some areas and hold breeding species such as Common Nightingale and Olivaceous Warbler, as well as cover for hungry migrants. View from the east bank in the morning and west bank in the evening.

Tsiknias River May 09. Shingle ridges and muddy margins are great for waders inc. breeding Little Ringed Plover and passage Temminck's Stint.

Fields alongside Tsiknias River May 09. A patchwork of small fields border the river and attract many migrants inc. falcons, shrikes and buntings.

Kalloni Saltpans May 09. A view from the northwest corner looking southeast towards Mount Olympus (peak distant right). The saltpans cover an area of around four square kilometres and are a magnet in spring for many wetland species.

Seasonal pool by the entrance of the Kalloni Saltworks Apr 07. The extent of seasonal pools depend on winter and early spring rains. When at their fullest, as above, they are excellent for Ruddy Shelduck, Garganey, waders, egrets, herons, Glossy Ibis and storks.

Kalloni Saltpans Apr 04. Looking east from the western side. This is one of the premier sites in spring and is excellent for egrets, herons, storks, waders, marsh terns. The number of Greater Flamingos increases annually and they have attempted to breed.

Kalloni Saltpans moat May 08. The moat running along the west (above) and south sides of the pans is excellent for waders. The ridge on the left is very good for attracting migrating falcons. The fields to the left should be watched for hunting harriers and buntings.

Kalloni Raptor Watch Point Apr 08. Looking south over Kalloni town. An ideal spot for spring raptors. Breeding species includes Cretzschmar's Bunting, Rock Nuthatch, Blue Rock-thrush, Subalpine Warbler and Black-eared Wheatear. Migrant passerines also occur.

Kalloni Mini Soccer Pitch Apr 09. Roosting Scops Owls are found in the eucalyptus trees here in the 'Scops Copse' each spring.

Arable fields nr Makara Pockets of arable land are excellent for migrant passerines. Irrigated areas concentrate birds.

Napi Valley May 08. North of Napi village. A typical view from this broad, long valley which is excellent for migrant raptors in spring. Breeding species inc. Short-toed Eagle, Long-legged Buzzard, Goshawk, Middle Spotted Woodpecker, Rock Nuthatch and Sombre Tit.

Platania May 08. The Platania track runs across the northern ridge at the top of Napi Valley. It is an excellent high point for migrants and for looking for raptors coming up the valley from the south. Olive-tree Warbler and Masked Shrike breed throughout the area.

Kavaki Apr 02. The headland looks north towards Turkey (in distance). This is the prime site for Rüppell's Warbler. Blue Rock-thrush, Black-eared Wheatear and Cretzschmar's Bunting also breed. It is also an excellent migration headland for passerines and raptors.

North Coast between Efthalou and Skala Sikaminias Apr 02. This 12km stretch of coastal track is fantastic for migrants passerines in spring and autumn. Hanging valleys, such as the one above, funnel birds into the trees and bushes. Keep a look out overhead for raptors.

North Coast between Sikaminia and Klio. Left: April 02. Looking north and over the sea towards Turkey. Right: May 08. Looking south into the interior. The heavily wooded hills across the far north hold many breeding species inc. Goshawk and Middle Spotted Woodpecker.

Lardia Valley Apr 02. This is an east-west river corridor through the middle of the island. Breeding species inc. Short-toed Eagle, Long-legged Buzzard, Middle Spotted Woodpecker, Crag Martin, Blue Rock-thrush and Rock Sparrow. Golden Oriole often occurs in spring.

Ipsilou Left: Apr 02. Looking west from Vigla. Right: May 09. Looking up from the bottom of the approach road. Both areas are excellent for open, rocky country species inc. Cinereous and Cretzschmar's Buntings, Rock Sparrow, Isabelline Wheatear and Rock Nuthatch.

Ipsilou Apr 05. Western slopes. Breeding birds inc. Chukar, Woodlark, Rock Nuthatch, Black-eared Wheatear and Rock Sparrow. Watch for migrating raptors and swifts. The flowers here are fabulous and this is a good area to look out for Spur-thighed Tortoise.

Ipsilou May 09. The old monastery path running up from the exit road. Left: looking up from the road. Right: looking back down towards the road. This path winds its way through the shelter of the trees providing outstanding views of migrants.

Ipsilou Apr 07. Eastern slope. This side of the mount is open to the valley leading south down through the Meladia Valley. The oak woodland provides shelter for migrant warblers, flycatchers, Golden Oriole and other species. Cinereous Bunting and Sombre Tit breed.

Sigri Apr 07. Appoaching from the east. The whole area is excellent for Lesser Kestrel, Eleanora's Falcon and migrant harriers.

Sigri Fields Apr 02. The fields north of Sigri are excellent for migrant passerines inc. chats, warblers, flycatchers and shrikes.

Faneromeni fords Left: Lower ford, May 09. Right: Upper ford, Apr 08. Both fords attract migrant passerines, inc. annual Collared Flycatcher, waders, and herons inc. Little Bittern and Night-heron. Migrating raptors follow the valley overhead.

Faneromeni May 09. The area northeast of the ford is excellent for migrants, inc. passage raptors, Roller and passerines.

Sigri Old Sanatorium May 09. A dry gully runs by the walled building and is excellent for migrants inc. Rufous Bush Robin.

Meladia Valley Left: between Sigri and the chapel, Apr 05. Right: between the chapel and river ford, Apr 08. This open country is excellent for raptors, Chukar, Black-eared Wheatear, Rock Nuthatch, Cretzschmar's and Black-headed Buntings.

Meladia Valley Chapel Sept 08. A small oasis of tall trees in an otherwise open landscape attracts migrants in spring and autumn. Breeding species in the area inc. Rufous Bush Robin, Woodchat, Red-backed and Lesser Grey Shrikes and Black-headed Bunting.

Meladia River Ford May 09. The sheltered shallow pools either side of the ford attract Little Bittern, crakes, warblers, flycatchers, shrikes and buntings inc. Ortolan on passage. An excellent site for Striped-necked Terrapin. The surrounding area is excellent for migrant shrikes.

Meladia Valley Apr 08. North of the river ford. Left: Looking north to Ipsilou. Right: Fig grove north of the ford attracts migrant passerines. One of the islands premier migrant spots. Look for raptors and storks overhead. Breeding Sombre Tit and Red-backed Shrike.

River Vergias, Skala Eresou May 09. View north from the road bridge. The river holds water year-round at the road bridge (the old ford). Look for Little Bittern, Squacco Heron, crakes, waders, wagtails, warblers, Spanish Sparrow. Follow the river north to Pithariou Reservoir.

Pithariou reservoir May 07. Looking north from the dam to the monastery. The reservoir holds water year-round so the area attracts migrants in spring and autumn. Search the tracks along either side of the reservoir and the track along the (dry) river approach from Eresos.

Voulgaris River Ford May 08. Looking north towards the river mouth. The area is very good for migrants inc. departing raptors coming up from the south and is a breeding site for Ruddy Shelduck and Bee-eater.

Gulf of Kalloni Apr 07. Looking east over Apothika (town middle right) across to the Polichnitos area (top left). The huge, shallow Gulf holds large numbers of winter seafowl. The open rocky country round Apothika holds breeding Chukar and Rock Nuthatch.

Makara Apr 07. Looking north from the coast. An excellent south coast migrant area for arriving raptors, wagtails, warblers, flycatchers and shrikes. Breeding species inc. Chukar, Black-eared Wheatear and Rock Nuthatch. Lesser Kestrel and Rock Dove breed offshore.

West of Agra Apr 07. Typical of the area, the scattered trees attract migrants. Rock Sparrow and Chukar breed.

Aghios Ioannis Apr 02. Breeding site for Cinereous Bunting, Rock Nuthatch, Sombre Tit and Black-eared Wheatear.

Mesa May 09. The wetland is partly seasonal and partly fed by the adjacent sea. It attracts herons, egrets (inc. Great White), storks, Ruddy Shelduck and waders. The rocky outcrop holds Little Owl, Black-eaered Wheatear, Rock Nuthatch and occasional Blue Rock-thrush. The area often attracts Red-footed Falcons which perch on roadside bushes and along fencelines.

Mirsinia Apr 02. In the south and east of the island, large areas of the interior are covered with scattered coniferous woodland which holds breeding European Nightjar, Woodlark and Black-eared Wheatear. Mature areas hold Krüper's Nuthatch and Short-toed Treecreeper.

Vouvaris river mouth May 09. A good site in spring and autumn. The fields to the south are good for migrant shrikes and occasionally Roller. Krüper's Nuthatch occurs in the pines here outside the breeding season. Ruddy Shelduck (spring) and Pygmy Cormorant (autumn/winter) occasionally seen around the mouth. Kingfisher occurs Sept-Apr.

Achladeri Forest Apr 02. Krüper's Nuthatch occurs throughout mature areas of the pinewoods but this remains the best site on the island with 1-3 pairs active most years. Long-eared Owl, Woodlark, Masked Shrike and Short-toed Treecreeper all breed.

Alikoudi Pool May 09. This small coastal seasonal pool attracts waders in spring and the surrounding area attracts migrant open country species inc. harriers. It is an often neglected site, but if you're venturing down to the Polichnitos Saltpans or Vatera area then this site should certainly be checked. The area is dry in autumn.

Olive grove near Skamnioudi Apr 07. Covering large tracts of the island, olive groves are an important habitat for resident species inc. Middle Spotted Woodpecker and Sombre Tit. Olive-tree Warbler occurs in areas with scattered oak or almond trees.

Almyropotamos River (Lisvorio) Apr 08. This small river lies just to the north-east of the Polichnitos Saltpans and is excellent in spring for herons, storks, wagtails and shrikes. Although dry in autumn, it is still worth checking for migrants.

Polichnitos Saltpans Apr 07. Overshadowed in spring by the Kalloni pans to the north, in autumn these pans are the premier wetland site and excellent for egrets, herons, storks, waders, gulls, terns and raptors.

Polichnitos Saltpans May 09. The fields to the north and east of these saltpans are excellent for migrant passerines such as pipits, chats, shrikes and buntings, and migrant harriers and falcons. The ridge to the east of the pans is used by migrating raptors and storks.

Ambeliko Valley May 09. A view over the plateau area above Kato Stavros. The area is good for breeding species inc. Sardinian Warbler as well as migrant raptors and passerines.

Mount Olympus Apr 02. The mixed deciduous woodland around Mount Olympus holds Eastern Bonelli's Warbler and commoner species such as Song Thrush and Robin (very rare elsewhere on the island). The area is also excellent for orchids.

Ruddy Shelduck Alykes Wetlands, Apr 08. Wetlands around Kalloni Saltpans remain the best sites to see this attractive species.

White Pelicans Polichnitos Saltpans, Sept 07. Flocks, some sizeable, are occasionally seen on autumn passage.

Little Bittern Almiropotamos River (Vatera), Apr 04. Encounters such as this are not uncommon for this usually skulking species.

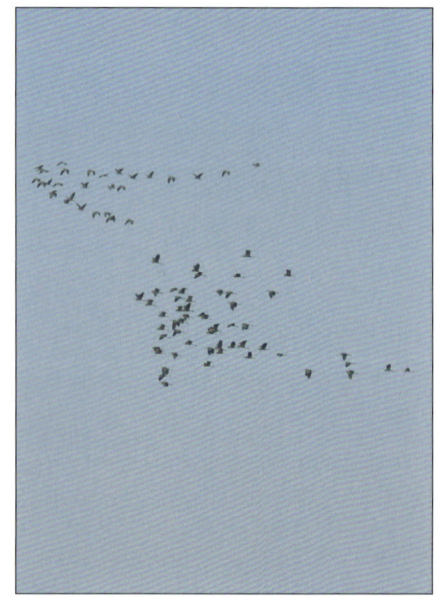

Night-herons (top group) and **Purple Herons** over Kalloni Saltpans, Apr 08. Migration in full swing!

Purple Heron Skala Kallonis Pool, Apr 02. A regular spring migrant found at most seasonal wetlands.

Squacco Heron Kalloni Saltpans seasonal floods, May 09. Found on most vegetated seasonal pools and rivers in spring.

White Stork Agia Paraskevi, Apr 07. This species breeds on chimneys and roof-tops across the island.

Glossy Ibis Alykes Wetlands, Apr 07. Flocks of migrating birds can drop into wetland areas at any time of day.

Red-footed Falcon female, Mesa, Apr 04. Usually encountered in small flocks, often in to double figures.

Long-legged Buzzard adult, Potamia Valley, May 07. A resident species with passage birds seen in spring and autumn.

Baillon's Crake Meladia River Ford, Apr 07. The rarest of the three crakes but now seen most springs.

Mixed waders Kalloni Saltpans south moat, May 08. The moat running around the entire saltpans is excellent for close views of many species.

Spur-winged Plover nr Kalloni Saltpans, Apr 07. Now an annual visitor most years to wetlands around the Kalloni Saltpans.

Scops Owls Kalloni Mini Soccer Pitch, Apr 04. Roosting birds are found in the eucalyptus trees at this breeding site each spring.

Common Nightingale Skala Kallonis, Apr 04. 'The' sound of Lesvos, and birds frequently sing from open perches.

Rüppell's Warbler Kavaki, Apr 05. A number of pairs breed on Lesvos with this site being the most accessible and reliable.

Rock Nuthatch Apothika, Apr 07. This resident breeding species occurs in most open rocky habitats on the island.

Krüper's Nuthatch singing male, nr Agiasos, Apr 05. Lesvos is the most accessible place in the Western Palearctic to see this species.

Collared Flycatcher female, Faneromeni, Apr 09. This is a regular spring passage migrant, particularly in the west of the island. It has also been recorded in autumn.

Rock Sparrow Ipsilou, Apr 04. A rare resident occurring throughout the rocky west with Ipsilou being one of the more regular sites to see the species.

Cinereous Bunting Ipsilou, May 09. This migrant breeder occurs throughout rockier areas of the west of the island.

Cretzschmar's Bunting Ipsilou, Apr 02. A common breeding migrant throughout the western half of the island.

Spur-thighed Tortoise Ipsilou Apr 05. Found throughout the centre and west of the island. Beware tortoises crossing roads!

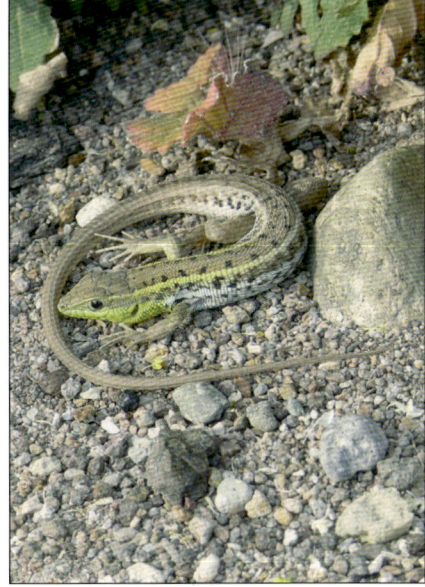

Snake-eyed Lizard Ipsilou, Apr 07. One of several lizards occurring on the island which also includes the stunning Balkan Green Lizard.

Small Pincertail Mylopotamos River, May 08. Over 40 species of dragonfly have been recorded on Lesvos.

Scarce Swallowtail Skala Polichnitou, May 09. One of many interesting butterflies found across the island.

Thread Lacewing Kavaki, May 07. Lesvos is fantastic for many other insects inc. crickets, mantids and this stunning lacewing.

Lesbos Orchid near Andissa, May 09. Around 75 species of orchid occur on Lesvos. This species is endemic to the island.

KALLONI AREA
Ευρύτερη περιοχή Καλλονής

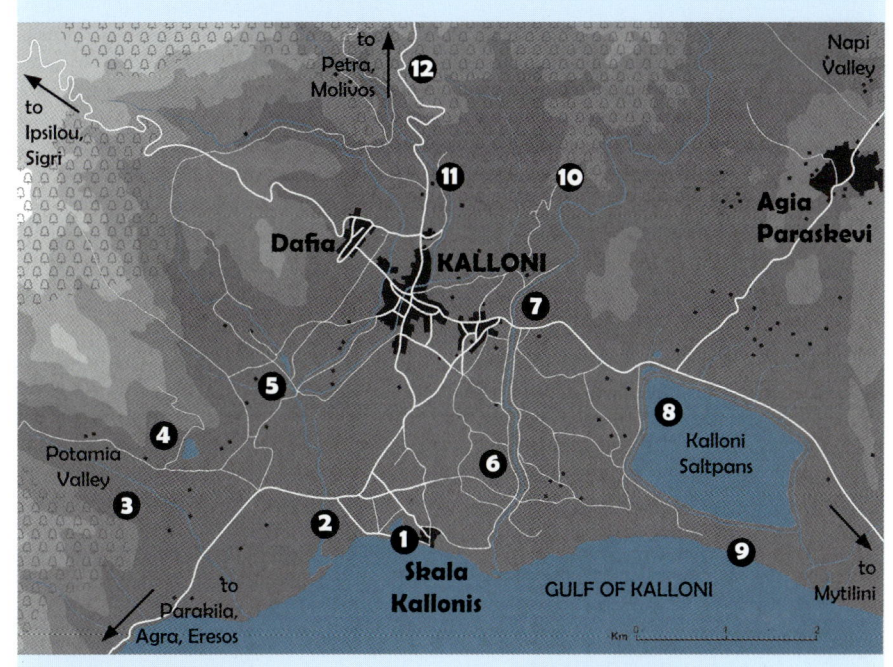

1. Skala Kallonis Pool
2. Christou River
3. Potamia Valley
4. Potamia Reservoir
5. Metochi Lake
6. Tsiknias River (Lower)
7. Tsiknias River (Upper)
8. Kalloni Saltpans
9. Alykes Wetlands
10. Madaros
11. Kalloni Mini Soccer Pitch
12. Kalloni Raptor Watch Point

Kalloni lies at the heart of the island on the northern edge of the dominating Gulf of Kalloni. The surrounding area provides the basis of most visiting birdwatchers' holidays on the island, with many excellent birding sites on the doorstep.

SKALA KALLONIS | Σκάλα Καλλονής

Once Lesvos gained its popularity, it wasn't long before the small harbour village resort of Skala Kallonis established itself as the focal point for visiting birders.

Skala Kallonis is situated in the middle of the island with good roads to all other parts of the island, and no place is much over an hours drive away. The resort itself has several good hotels situated just outside the village, two of which (the Pasiphae and Kalloni II) lie adjacent to the once outstanding Skala Kallonis Pool, and all are within a short walk of both the Christou River and Tsiknias River. The resort also boasts plenty of tavernas for lunchtime and evening dining.

1 SKALA KALLONIS POOL
Έλος Σκάλας Καλλονής

2 CHRISTOU RIVER
Ποταμός Χριστού

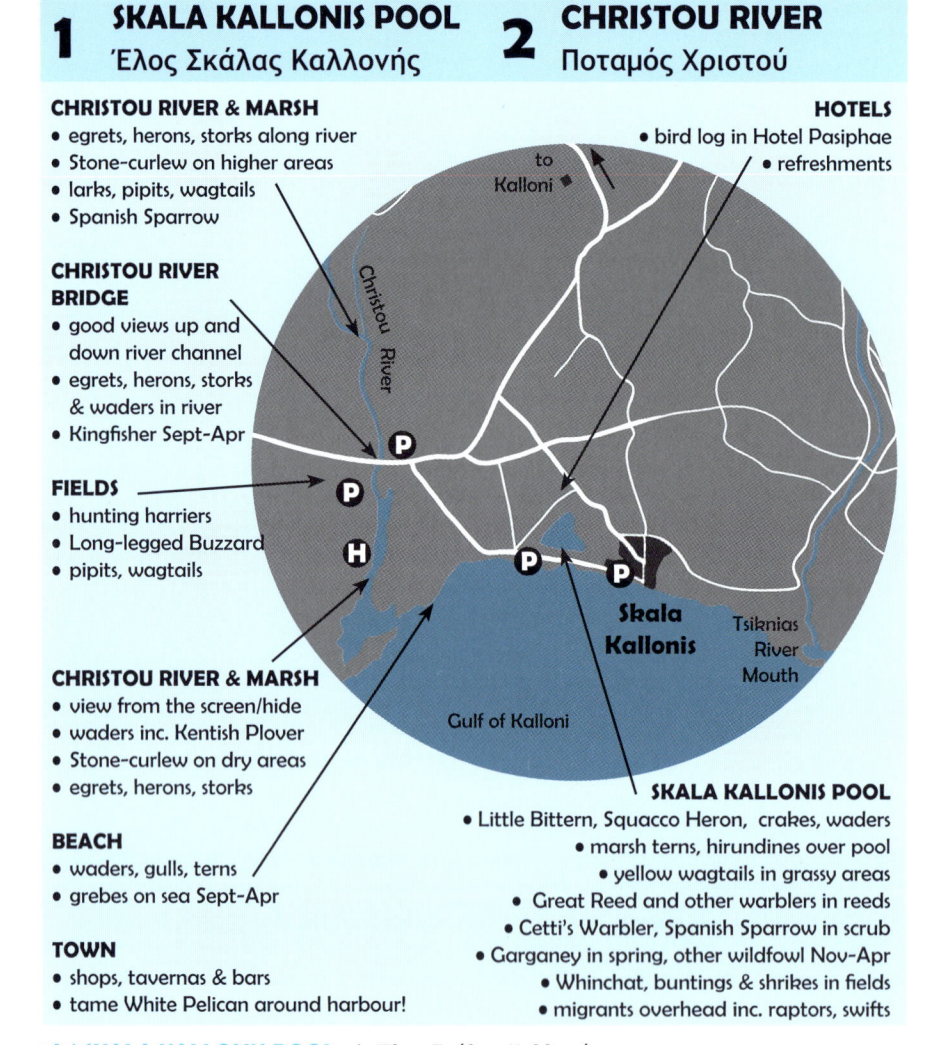

CHRISTOU RIVER & MARSH
- egrets, herons, storks along river
- Stone-curlew on higher areas
- larks, pipits, wagtails
- Spanish Sparrow

CHRISTOU RIVER BRIDGE
- good views up and down river channel
- egrets, herons, storks & waders in river
- Kingfisher Sept-Apr

FIELDS
- hunting harriers
- Long-legged Buzzard
- pipits, wagtails

CHRISTOU RIVER & MARSH
- view from the screen/hide
- waders inc. Kentish Plover
- Stone-curlew on dry areas
- egrets, herons, storks

BEACH
- waders, gulls, terns
- grebes on sea Sept-Apr

TOWN
- shops, tavernas & bars
- tame White Pelican around harbour!

HOTELS
- bird log in Hotel Pasiphae
- refreshments

SKALA KALLONIS POOL
- Little Bittern, Squacco Heron, crakes, waders
- marsh terns, hirundines over pool
- yellow wagtails in grassy areas
- Great Reed and other warblers in reeds
- Cetti's Warbler, Spanish Sparrow in scrub
- Garganey in spring, other wildfowl Nov-Apr
- Whinchat, buntings & shrikes in fields
- migrants overhead inc. raptors, swifts

1A | SKALA KALLONIS POOL | Έλος Σκάλας Καλλονής

This pool was undoubtedly one of the main reasons birders were attracted to staying in the area. Unfortunately, the pool's natural degradation has been accelerated by bad management of the site to the extent that by the time birders arrive in mid-April, unless it has been an exceptionally wet winter, the site can be bone dry. Even in a wet spring, the resulting inferior pool has grass and reed growth dominating with limited or no visible muddy margins and greatly reduced open water areas. Some of the surrounding land has also been built on.

At its best, mornings and evenings would find birders lining the road in their dozens to watch the rich birdlife of this tiny wetland. The place would be stuffed with crakes, herons large and small, marsh terns, Garganey, waders and numerous wetland passerines. Some local hoteliers are actively fighting for the pool to be restored as it remains an important feature of their local tourism economy. Visiting birders can help by speaking to hotel and taverna owners about writing to the local mayor.

LOCATION AND ACCESS The pool lies immediately to the north of the village in the triangle of land between the village, the coast road and the hotel road (along which the Pasiphae and Kalloni II hotels are located).

The pool is easily viewed from the hotel and coast roads.

AREAS TO SEARCH View the pool and the small fields opposite them along the road between the Pasiphae and Kalloni II hotels. Building has already begun on some of these fields and over time the others may be developed in this popular tourist area.

SPECIES Due to its location at the north of the Gulf of Kalloni, many birds migrate overhead without stopping. These can include flocks of Purple Heron, Night-heron, Collared Pratincole and Red-footed Falcon; raptors include also Hobby; Pallid Swift, Alpine Swift; European Bee-eater; Barn Owl breeds locally and can occasionally be seen hunting the pool edges (especially when water levels are lower) and the nearby fields; Scops Owl is occasionally heard, but rarely seen, around the hotels; Long-eared Owl also breeds locally and again is occasionally seen around the hotel area. **The pool in spring** When wet, the pool can still attract many wetland species inc. Little Grebe, Garganey, other scarcer wildfowl; Little Bittern, Night-heron, Squacco Heron, Purple Heron, Glossy Ibis; Marsh Harrier; Water Rail, Spotted Crake, Little Crake; Black-winged Stilt, Wood Sandpiper, Marsh Sandpiper; Whiskered and White-winged Black Terns; Common and Pallid Swifts; hirundines inc. Red-rumped Swallow; 'yellow' wagtails inc. Black-headed and Blue-headed; Cetti's, Great Reed and Olivaceous Warblers. **The pool in winter** The pool refills during winter when it becomes an important area on the island for wildfowl. **The fields in spring/early summer and autumn** Montagu's Harrier, Common Kestrel; swifts; hirundines; pipits, wagtails, Common Redstart, Whinchat; Spotted Flycatcher; Red-backed and Woodchat Shrikes; Rose-coloured Starling; Spanish Sparrow; other migrants. **The fields in winter** Hen Harrier; larks, pipits; Black Redstart. **Surrounding locality in spring** A pair of White Storks breed on the rooftops viewable from near the entrance of the Pasiphae hotel looking east.

1B | SKALA KALLONIS BEACH | Παραλία Σκάλας Καλλονής (map p.98)

LOCATION AND ACCESS The beach lies west of the village towards River Christou near and opposite the Skala Kallonis Pool and hotel road.

The beach is reached by walking along the hotel road, past the pool (on your left), to the T-junction with the coast road.

AREAS TO SEARCH View the sea from the beach. The roadside trees provide excellent shade when the sun is high. The spit to the west is at the mouth of the Christou River and is worth scoping for gulls and terns.

SPECIES The beach itself rarely holds anything interesting, but the sea can often hold grebes, wildfowl, gulls and terns. **Spring** small numbers of late winter species such as Great Crested and Black-necked Grebes; wildfowl; Avocet; Gull-billed and Sandwich Terns; Yellow-legged, Mediterranean and Slender-billed Gulls. **Winter** The Gulf holds large numbers of wintering Great Crested and Black-necked Grebes; Black-throated Diver; Great Cormorant; Red-breasted Merganser; wildfowl; Black Redstart; Chiffchaff along the coastal strip.

OTHER INFORMATION A tame White Pelican resides in the village around the harbour. In 2007 it was purposely knocked-down by one of the locals. The bird has had a foot amputated and she now hobbles around the harbour and nearby tavernas and still proves popular with both locals and visitors.

NEAREST AMENITIES Skala Kallonis itself for tavernas, shops. Kalloni | Καλλονή (3km) for banks, petrol, pharmacies, shops.

---

2 | CHRISTOU RIVER | Ποταμός Χριστού (map p.98)

Also known as Kamares River. Like other wetland sites, the wetness of the area depends largely on winter rainfall, but there is a saltwater creek which holds water year-round.

LOCATION AND ACCESS The river lies to the west of Skala Kallonis and is crossed by the Kalloni-Parakila road.

The river is within walking distance of the hotels and village. Cars can be parked either side of the Kalloni-Parakila road bridge.

AREAS TO SEARCH The area can be viewed from the two roads bordering it, the Kalloni-Parakila road and the road running from this road to Skala Kallonis, as well as from the beach. Recently the local council has erected a sunshade on the road bridge and a viewing screen on the west side of the river.

One of the main species to search for is Stone-curlew which occurs here Mar-Oct (occasionally over winter). In autumn this species can number up to 50 birds.

SPECIES (passage birds unless stated) Waders inc. Black-winged Stilt, stints, shanks and plovers inc. Kentish and Little Ringed (both breed), Stone-curlew (breeds); herons, storks, egrets; Long-legged Buzzard, Marsh, Hen Harrier (winter) and Montagu's Harriers; 'yellow' wagtails, pipits.

NEAREST AMENITIES Nearby Kalloni | Καλλονή for shops, banks, petrol, etc. Skala Kallonis (1.5km) for tavernas, shops.

---

3 & 4 | POTAMIA VALLEY & RESERVOIR | Κοιλάδα Ποταμιάς και Λιμνοδεξαμενή

LOCATION & ACCESS The Potamia River and valley lies west of Skala Kallonis. There are two different points of access.

Potamia Valley This is accessed off the Kalloni-Parakila road west of Skala Kallonis at the sharp left-hand bend from which the north (straight on) track takes you up the Potamia Valley and the right track turn takes you to Metochi Lake (and signed Metochi). The valley can also be reached from the lake (see map). The track up the Potamia is drivable (with care in places) all the way north to the town of Anemotia (Ανεμώτια – c.11 km).

Potamia River road bridge This lies further along the main road towards Parakila. Park either side of the road bridge.

AREAS TO SEARCH It is worth walking any section of this valley. The principal sites are (also see map):

Potamia Reservoir Park by the second track on your right by the little pumping house. Walk up the track on your right to view the reservoir. It is also worth walking along the track up the first hillside which provides a great view across the reservoir and wide valley mouth.

Potomia Valley bridge and weir Park either side of the bridge and walk either side of the river. The river (when wet) rarely holds any waders or herons, but does attract other species down to drink. The surrounding fields and olive groves are excellent. The weir lies just north of the bridge and is a good

3 POTAMIA VALLEY
Κοιλάδα Ποταμιάς

4 POTAMIA RESERVOIR
Κοιλάδα Λιμνοδεξαμενή

UPPER POTAMIA VALLEY (off map)
- raptors inc. Short-toed Eagle, Long-legged Buzzard, Peregrine
- Black Stork
- Red-rumped Swallow & Crag Martin
- Orphean & Subalpine Warblers
- Woodchat, Red-backed & Masked Shrikes
- track to Anemotia

ABOVE POTAMIA RESERVOIR
- Short-toed Eagle, Long-legged Buzzard
- Blue Rock-thrush, Black-eared Wheatear
- Orphean & Subalpine Warblers

POTAMIA RESERVOIR
- Little Grebe, gulls, waders
- Black-necked Grebe Nov-Mar
- dragonflies

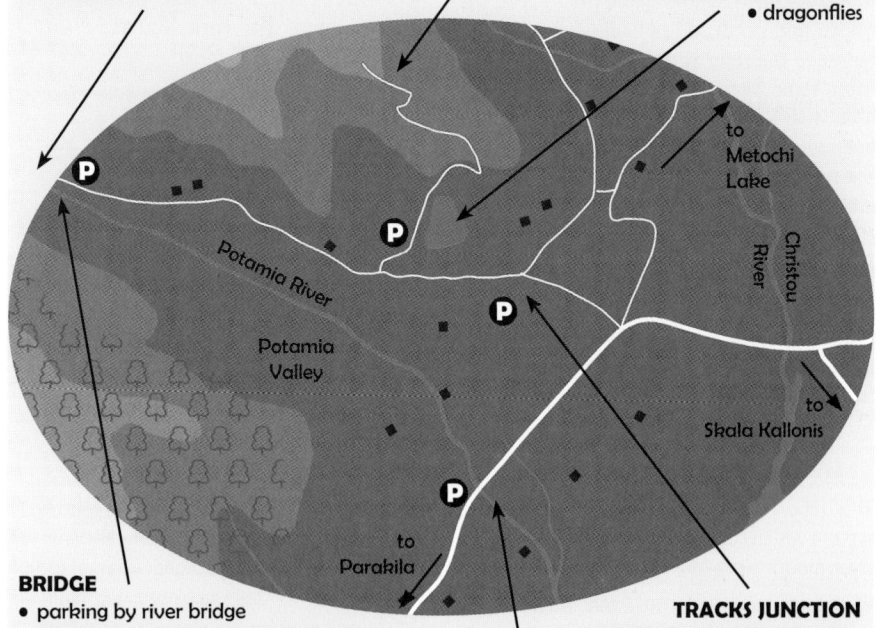

BRIDGE
- parking by river bridge
- Nightjar in open areas north of river
- chats & wheatears in fields (inc. autumn)
- Olive-tree Warbler can occur in olive groves on both sides of the river
- Woodchat & Masked Shrikes
- Black-headed Bunting
- dragonflies

TRACKS JUNCTION
- Middle Spotted Woodpecker
- Olive-tree Warbler in olive groves
- Woodchat & Red-backed Shrikes
- Sombre Tit
- Rock Nuthatch
- Black-headed Bunting

WEIR (above bridge)
- park by weir or walk from river bridge
- look for raptors inc. Short-toed Eagle, Long-legged Buzzard, Peregrine
- swifts, hirundines
- Nightingale, warblers
- Woodchat & Red-backed Shrikes
- dragonflies, Stripe-necked Terrapin

MAIN ROAD BRIDGE
- parking by bridge
- egrets & herons
- wagtails
- Olivaceous & Great Reed Warblers
- Black-headed Bunting
- dragonflies

place to access the open river and search for dragonflies.

This area lies at the head of the valley and is flanked on either side by steep ridges which are great for raptors. Common and Long-legged Buzzard and Short-toed Eagle breed with other species frequently seen over the ridges inc. Goshawk, migrating falcons, etc. The area is also a north-south route for other migrants inc. swifts and hirundines.

River rock pools Following the track across the bridge and north, do not take any left turn but keep the river within sight on your right. After some time you will come to an open area with a grassy slope leading down to an open section of the river which forms pools in the smooth worn sedimentary rocks. This is a great spot for a picnic lunch overlooking the river and craggy outcrops opposite.

Potamia River road bridge View from the tracks either side of the river.

SPECIES An excellent area for migrants and raptors.

Potamia reservoir Black-necked Grebe (winter); wildfowl; waders; gulls and terns on the reservoir (species and numbers depend on water levels); raptors; Black-eared Wheatear; Blue Rock-thrush; Subalpine Warbler; Sombre Tit; Rock Nuthatch; shrikes.

Potomia Valley bridge and weir Raptors; Nightjar; Middle Spotted Woodpecker; warblers inc. Olive-tree (can be heard singing from the olive groves to the southwest and northeast of the bridge and throughout the area); Sombre Tit; Rock Nuthatch; shrikes inc. Masked.

River rock pools Raptors; Middle Spotted Woodpecker; swifts; hirundines; Blue Rock-thrush; Wood and Rock Nuthatches; warblers; Sombre Tit; shrikes.

Potamia River road bridge Herons; waders; warblers; sparrows; buntings.

NEAREST AMENITIES Nearby Kalloni | Καλλονή (5km) for shops, banks, petrol, etc. Skala Kallonis | Σκάλα Καλλονής (3km) for tavernas, cafés, shops.

5 | METOCHI LAKE | Λίμνη Μετόχι

This lake forms part of the Christou River system which runs due south from here to the river mouth west of Skala Kallonis.

Like other wetland sites, the water levels depend largely on winter rainfall, but it is nearly always full throughout spring. Some mud-fringe is best for crakes which can occur in double figures here in a good year. Occasionally holds some water in summer and autumn.

This is a fantastic site and is best visited in the morning (dawn to 09.00h). Evening is not as productive and the setting sun can make viewing awkward, but the circular walk in particular can be enjoyable in the evening. Try and visit several times during each week of your stay.

LOCATION Metochi Lake lies to the southwest of Kalloni and northwest of Skala Kallonis (on the more popular blue Road Atlas 1:70,000 map look for the lake between Metochia and Limni).

ACCESS The lake is best reached off the Kalloni-Parakila road west of Skala Kallonis. Turn right at the sharp left hand road bend (the track straight at this point takes you up the Potamia Valley). Continue along this track and avoid all turns off it until you come to a low concrete bridge which is followed by a more obvious low concrete bridge with obvious water-filled channels running underneath and away from you on the left. Turn left immediately before this bridge, then next right, to the lake. There are signs for 'Metochi' (a chapel) but these occasionally fall down and take time to be replaced.

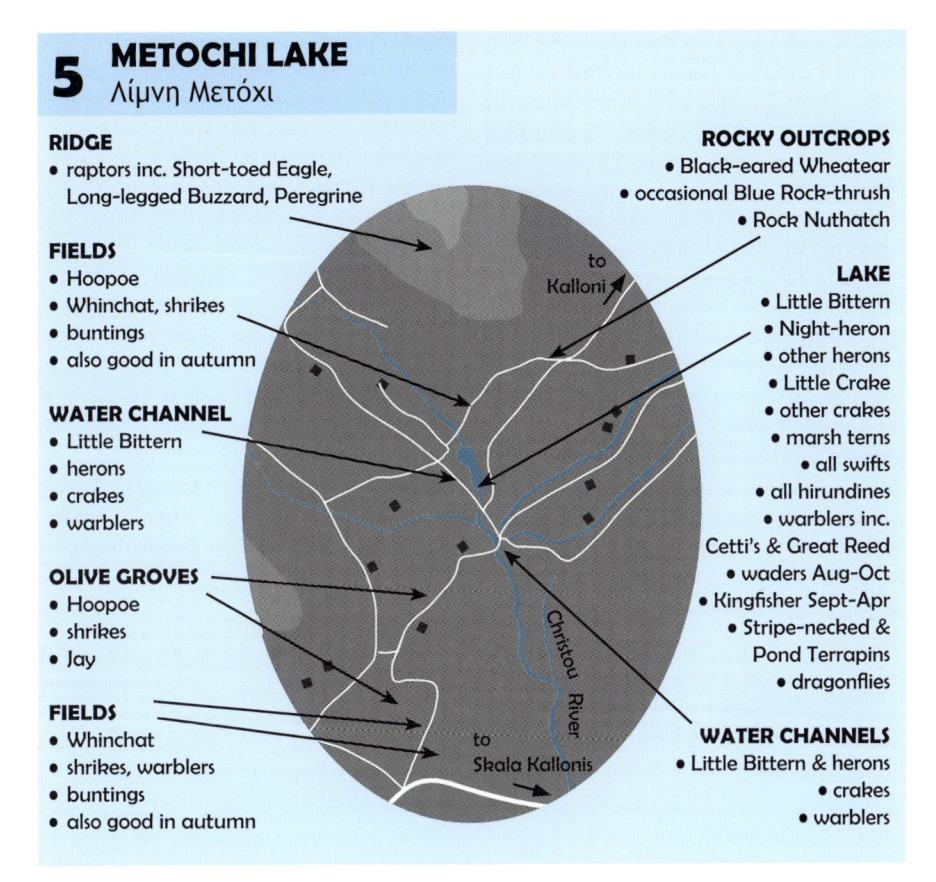

5 METOCHI LAKE
Λίμνη Μετόχι

RIDGE
- raptors inc. Short-toed Eagle, Long-legged Buzzard, Peregrine

FIELDS
- Hoopoe
- Whinchat, shrikes
- buntings
- also good in autumn

WATER CHANNEL
- Little Bittern
- herons
- crakes
- warblers

OLIVE GROVES
- Hoopoe
- shrikes
- Jay

FIELDS
- Whinchat
- shrikes, warblers
- buntings
- also good in autumn

ROCKY OUTCROPS
- Black-eared Wheatear
- occasional Blue Rock-thrush
- Rock Nuthatch

LAKE
- Little Bittern
- Night-heron
- other herons
- Little Crake
- other crakes
- marsh terns
- all swifts
- all hirundines
- warblers inc. Cetti's & Great Reed
- waders Aug-Oct
- Kingfisher Sept-Apr
- Stripe-necked & Pond Terrapins
- dragonflies

WATER CHANNELS
- Little Bittern & herons
- crakes
- warblers

to Kalloni
Christou River
to Skala Kallonis

Park on the east side of the lake taking care not to block the track (allow room for tractors and lorries). Try also not to block the 'spit' area at the north end of the lake with the pump. You can park here, but try and allow room for others to turn around here.

If you've got the time, and energy in an increasingly warming day, then it can be walked or cycled from Skala Kallonis in a morning.

AREAS TO SEARCH There are three main areas to search.

The Lake This is viewed from the track which runs up the east side of the lake. Bushes and reeds provide some cover to view between/over. Make sure you walk the entire length of this section carefully checking all available cover for skulking herons, crakes and warblers. Don't leave any area unchecked, no matter how small or useless you think it looks! Make sure to check the near side as much as you can as crakes and Little Bitterns can skulk right under your nose and will only take flight if it gets too noisy.

The Channel track (see map) Where the track meets the lake and forks right (along the east side of the lake), the left track goes north alongside a channel which runs the length of the lake. It is worth walking this channel from the main east side of the lake all the way up to the T-junction, or drive the track and park left of the T-junction. The channel by the T-junction can be particularly productive with crakes and herons seen here.

Circular walk (c.2 km) Park along the east side, you can then follow the track on foot north. The track turns away from the lake by the 'pumping' corner. Follow this and then take the next left. Follow the track past the rocky section, then a pump house with water trough (birds come to drink from the trough), then into an open field area. At the next junction turn left, and follow to the little bridge at the north of the channel track (see map). After searching this area, turn left along the channel (on your left) and then your next left at the southern tip of the lake back along the east side of the lake.

SPECIES An excellent area for wetland migrants, raptors. **Spring** The lake holds Little Grebe; crakes inc. Little, Spotted and even Baillon's; Little Bittern, Night-heron (roosting in lakeside bushes), Purple Heron, herons, egrets, storks (flyovers); raptors inc. Long-legged Buzzard, Short-toed Eagle, Peregrine; marsh terns; Middle Spotted Woodpecker; swifts (all species); Bee-eater, Hoopoe; hirundines (all species); Wren; Black-eared Wheatear; warblers inc. Great Reed; shrikes; Sombre Tit; Rock Nuthatch. **Autumn** If wet, then waders inc. Ringed, Little Ringed and Kentish Plover, Common, Wood and Green Sandpiper; Kingfisher; warblers; flycatchers; raptors. In autumn the cultivated fields on the approach from the main road can be very productive, especially any recently cut fields which can attract large numbers of pipits, wagtails, chats, wheatears, warblers, shrikes, etc.

NEAREST AMENITIES Nearby Kalloni Καλλονή for shops, banks, petrol, etc. Skala Kallonis | Σκάλα Καλλονής (3km) for tavernas, shops.

6 | TSIKNIAS RIVER | Ποταμός Τσικνιάς

The Tsiknias River begins life northeast of Kalloni, flows just east of the town and exits into the sea just east of Skalla Kallonis. Tsiknias is the Greek for heron (the heron river).

The shallow river follows a pebble and silt bed to a reasonably large silty river mouth with small spits and islands. Spring water levels will depend on previous winter rainfall, but even by late April there is little more than a shallow trickle with no more than a few inches covering the main concrete ford (see below). By July the freshwater flow has usually disappeared completely, with only the saltwater mouth section below the lower ford holding any water.

This is one of the premier birding locations on the island, with many Skala Kallonis-based birders starting and finishing their birding day here. Early morning in particular can be rewarding to the point of breathtaking if you hit it on a major spring arrival when waders, egrets, storks, etc. are dotted along the river, the bushes and fields drip with chats, shrikes and buntings and the air is full of swifts, hirundines and Bee-eaters.

6 | LOWER TSIKNIAS RIVER | Ποταμός Τσικνιάς

LOCATION AND ACCESS The river lies to the east of Kalloni with the river mouth to the east of Skala Kallonis. It is crossed by the main Kalloni-Mytilini road.

The main Kalloni-Mytilini road divides the river into the southern coastal 'lower' section and the northern, inland 'upper' section.

The river mouth and lower section can also be reached from Skala Kallonis.

The southern end and river mouth are in walking distance and driveable from the Skala Kallonis hotels and village. Raised dirt roads run alongside both the east and west banks between the main road and the

6 TSIKNIAS RIVER LOWER
Ποταμός Τσικνιάς

7 TSIKNIAS RIVER UPPER
Ποταμός Τσικνιάς

The whole area is fantastic for migrants, both grounded or flying over

SILOS AREA
- Middle Spotted Woodpecker
- warblers, shrikes, Jay in olive groves
- tracks to Kalloni (left) and Madaros (right: see p. 115)

BRIDGE
- egrets, herons, storks
- waders
- bathing gulls
- warblers
- Spanish Sparrow

FIELDS & OLIVE GROVES
- Middle Spotted Woodpecker
- Whinchat
- warblers
- shrikes

FORD
- Little Bittern
- crakes
- waders
- Bee-eater
- hirundines
- pipits
- wagtails
- warblers
- Spanish Sparrow
- Hoopoe

   Do not block ford — in constant use by locals and visitors

RIVER MOUTH
- view from track corner/ info board or canopy
- grebes, Cormorant
- egrets, herons, storks
- waders
- gulls, terns

WALK UP RIVER
- park just after left turn to silos and walk
- raptors inc. Peregrine, Short-toed Eagle, Long-legged Buzzard
- Ruddy Shelduck
- Black-eared Wheatear
- Rock Nuthatch

Walk or drive along tracks either side of the lower section

Only use the main road bridge and concrete ford to cross the river

View from east bank in morning, from west bank in evening

FIELDS
- Long-legged Buzzard
- harriers
- falcons
- Bee-eater
- Whinchat
- wheatears (aut)
- warblers
- shrikes
- Spanish Sparrow
- Black-headed Bunting
- Ortolan Bunting
- occasional Roller
- tracks to saltpans

SEASONAL POOLS
- herons
- Long-legged Buzzard (winter)
- harriers
- falcons
- Stone-curlew
- waders

main ford (just inland of the river mouth) offering direct viewing from the roads. The roads are wide enough to pull over and allow other vehicles to pass with ease. The main concrete ford is always driveable even when under water.

The northern part of the 'lower' section can be accessed off the Kalloni-Mytilini road bridge along the raised dirt roads either side of the river between the main road and the river mouth (c.3 km).

Cross the river only at the main road bridge and the main concrete ford just inland of the river mouth (see map). Do not attempt to cross using any other fords used by the local farmers.

AREAS TO SEARCH This is not only a very popular area, but is an incredibly easy area to work. The roads running from the road bridge down either side of the river to the mouth means that morning and evening viewing (best times to visit) can be enjoyed at all times with the rising or setting sun behind you.

Staying in the car has its benefits, including not flushing any storks, herons and egrets, but this limits your viewing of the river, but more so the adjacent fields which can be just as productive. For best results, walk sections which don't hold large wading species and try to drive past those areas which do hold such species.

River mouth Reached on foot or by car from Skala Kallonis or by car from the Kalloni-Mytilini road bridge. View from the recently (2008) erected canopy or road on the west side. You can walk down to the mouth behind the bushes to view the mouth spits and islands. Viewing from the east side is restricted and best avoided. The track down the east side turns inland before the mouth into a seasonally flooded area which can be worth exploring.

The ford This is an excellent area for riparian species. Despite this being a busy thoroughfare and heavily disturbed by birders' and locals' cars alike, as well as all manner of farm vehicles, the ford itself can be a very good area to concentrate on. Park on either side of the ford along the top banks away from the turning areas down to the ford itself. Do not park in the ford. In recent years the selfish behaviour, of photographers in particular, blocking the ford to take photos has led to flash points with birders and locals. If a birder or photographer is blocking the ford, do not hesitate to sound your horn and get them to move out of the way.

Even in a wet spring, the shallow river forms spits and edges here which waders and other species feed along. The stony reed-fringed edge on the inland side of the ford can even attract Little Bittern, crakes and Great Snipe, as well as roosting hirundines, and the overhanging bushes are worth searching for warblers, Spanish Sparrow and buntings.

Adjacent fields View the fields east and west of the river from the two dirt roads. Most fields are cultivated with the occasional livestock field.

SPECIES A superb area for migrants.

River mouth Waders; herons, storks, egrets; gulls and terns; Bee-eater; warblers; buntings; Kingfisher (Sept–Apr).

lower (crescent) river ford Waders; herons, storks, egrets; crakes; marsh terns; Kingfisher; Bee-eater; warblers; hirundines; sparrows; buntings. The ford is dry in summer and autumn.

Riverside fields Passage unless stated – larks, pipits, wagtails; chats, wheatears; shrikes; sparrows; buntings; Marsh, Montagu's, Pallid and Hen (inc. winter) Harriers, Long-legged Buzzard (inc. winter), falcons; Bee-eater; Middle-spotted Woodpecker (breeding).

NEAREST AMENITIES Nearby Skala Kallonis | Σκάλα Καλλονής (3km) for tavernas, shops. Kalloni | Καλλονή (3km) for shops, banks, petrol, etc.

7 | UPPER TSIKNIAS RIVER | Ποταμός Τσικνιάς (map p.105)

LOCATION AND ACCESS A track runs north from the Kalloni-Mytilini road bridge on the west side of the river. It is best to park near the bridge and walk this section as the track gets tricky after c.0.5km.

Cross the river only at the main road bridge. Do not attempt to cross using any other fords used by the local farmers.

AREAS TO SEARCH Park near the road bridge and walk north along the west side. The road bridge area should hold you for a time whilst you check the area for waders, warblers, sparrows and buntings. The river immediately north of the road bridge is used by resident Yellow-legged Gulls and other gulls for bathing. Further up from the bridge keep checking the river for waders, but numbers and variety reduces the further north of the bridge you venture. From the track view the valley slope above and the east slopes and hills across the river.

SPECIES Waders; herons, egrets; Ruddy Shelduck; warblers inc. occasional passage Ruppell's; Black-eared Wheatear; 'yellow' wagtails; buntings; Rock Nuthatch; raptors inc. Peregrine and Long-legged Buzzard; Raven.

NEAREST AMENITIES Nearby Kalloni | Καλλονή (1km) for shops, banks, petrol, etc. Skala Kallonis | Σκάλα Καλλονής (4km) for tavernas, shops.

Black-headed Bunting
the first spring arrivals are eagerly awaited, but once they arrive, they arrive en masse and suddenly they are everywhere!

8 | KALLONI SALTPANS | Αλυκές Καλλονής

The Kalloni Saltpans and surrounding area is without doubt the premier spring birding area on the island. The pans themselves are a large complex of rectangular pools surrounded by an isolation moat. They are surrounded by fields and scattered woodland to the north, west and east, and by the seasonal Alykes Wetlands to the south.

The saltpans cover over 260 hectares and can produce around 10,000 tons of salt a year. The area is made up of rectangular pans separated by raised banks or bunds, all interconnected by a series of sluices and channels. The whole area is surrounded by a large channel (the moat). The water levels on the pans vary considerably. The pans are a complex of moving saltwater with the central pans used for evaporation for salt production. The shallow outer pans are consistently good year on year, and the pans in the northwest and northeast corners are among the best for waders and marsh terns.

These are the larger of the two areas of saltpans on the islands, the other, at Polichnitos, are much smaller and lie to the south on the eastern shore of the Gulf of Kalloni. Some movement of birds occurs between these two sites.

Look at the saltpans on a map of the island and note their position (a) at the northern most point of the Gulf of Kalloni (b) at the mouth of the Napi Valley and just east of the northern road route between Kalloni and Petra which is also known as a raptor and stork corridor, (c) situated equidistant between the Rivers Tsiknias (to the west) and Milopotamos (to the east), and (d) as a major water feature in the landscape (the largest on the island) — and its not hard to see just why this whole area is a major migration point. Many birds will drop in to refuel at the pans or in the surrounding fields, or are simply funnelled by the Gulf to pass overhead on their way north up through the Napi Valley.

Birds crossing the Aegean Sea to the south will either come along the Turkish coast and over Chios, or from the open sea to the southwest. Thus birds arriving from the south and southeast will arrive over Lesvos near Mount Olympus. Many birds will be drawn by the large water body to the west of Olympus and follow the eastern side of the Gulf northwards. If they are crossing the island they bypass the smaller saltpans at Polichnitos (partly explaining why these attract fewer birds in spring) and move up the Gulf to the northern point – the Kalloni Saltpans.

Autumn wader passage is relatively poor here. The only available water areas are the pans themselves as the seasonal pools in the surrounding fields dry up by late May. The benefit of lying at the northern end of the Gulf works in spring, but goes against the area in autumn, when most waders use the Polichnitos Saltpans to the south.

Breeding species in this area (some not mentioned elsewhere) include Avocet, Black-winged Stilt, Stone-curlew, Little Tern, Quail (in adjacent fields). Greater Flamingo attempt to breed most years and often peak at over 1,000 birds.

LOCATION The Kalloni Saltpans lie at the very northern edge of the Gulf of Kalloni around 3km east of Kalloni.

ACCESS The area can be accessed from the north and west.

From the north From Kalloni, travel east towards Mytilini for around 3km and take the minor metalled road on your right (in the northwest corner of the pans) before the left turn signed for Agia Paraskevi, Napi and Mandamados (the Napi Valley).

A second access point lies at the northeast corner of the pans around 1.5km east of the Napi Valley junction along the Kalloni-Mytilini road. Turn off to the right at the northeast corner and park in the parking area by the raised hide.

8 KALLONI SALTPANS
Αλυκές Καλλονής

POOLS
- occ. herons, egrets & storks
- waders
- wagtails

MOAT
- occ. herons, egrets & storks
- waders

FIELDS
- Quail calling
- harriers
- chats
- warblers
- shrikes
- buntings

COASTAL SCRUB
- Rufous Bush Robin
- migrant warblers
- ! ground nesting birds inc. Stone-curlew

SEASONAL WETLANDS
- Ruddy Shelduck
- egrets & herons
- waders
- pipits & wagtails
- ! ground nesting birds inc. Stone-curlew

RIDGE
- Short-toed Eagle
- Red-footed Falcon & Lesser Kestrel

to Agias Paraskevi

to Kalloni

KALLONI SALTPANS

to Mytilini

MOAT
- waders
- terns
- egrets
- storks

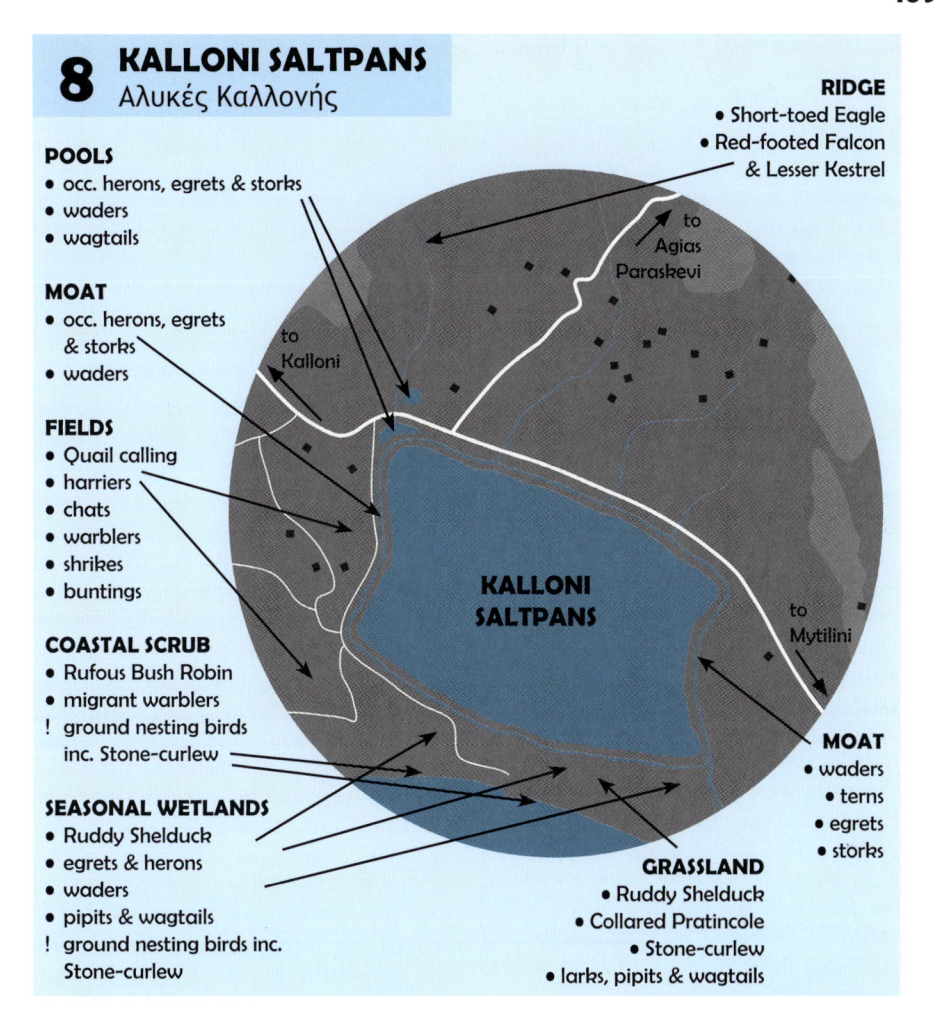

GRASSLAND
- Ruddy Shelduck
- Collared Pratincole
- Stone-curlew
- larks, pipits & wagtails

From Skala Kallonis Take the dirt road out of the village to the Tsiknias River mouth, north along the west bank and cross the river at the lower concrete ford. Turn northward (towards the Kalloni-Mytilini road) up the east river bank, then turn immediately right and follow the dirt road across the fields to the southwest corner of the pans.

AREAS TO SEARCH This is a large area but it can be easily broken down into individual areas.

The east pans track Whilst this is by no means the main access point for the area, it is now the most obvious being marked since 2006 by a raised hide right by the Kalloni-Mytilini road.

Park by the hide and view the area from the ground or from the hide (which holds about eight people). Do not drive down the track down the side of the pans. The hide obviously provides improved views over the pans, but as is all too often the case, the viewing slots are too high for shorter people and for most users of angled telescopes and using a tripod mounted scope on the wooden floor when the hide is full of shuffling birders isn't great.

You can walk along the track which follows the moat down the eastern side of the pans. The pans in this northeastern corner and along the track are often among the best for waders, marsh terns and Slender-billed Gull.

Several km to the east of this track is a track down to the beach (near some large greenhouses and signed for a beach taverna which is open from June-August only). Parking at the beach here and walking east along the coastal grassland you come to an area of damp grassland which can be very good for yellow wagtails and worth checking for the odd wader and heron.

The west pans road Start from the northwest corner by the Kalloni-Mytilini road, as soon as you turn south along the road, and park carefully on the right hand side of the road. You should search the northwest corner of the moat for waders and terrestrial passerines (pipits, wagtails, etc.). You can also view across the immediate pans for waders, egrets, storks, herons, gulls and terns. Once this area has been checked it is worth crossing the main road and checking the small pool on the north side of the road between the pans road and the main Napi Valley road junction (if driving past there is plenty of room to pull in by the pool). Also check the fields along the pans road and scan the hillside to the northwest for raptors, it can be very good for picking up flocks of migrant falcons such as Lesser Kestrel and Red-footed Falcon.

Continue south along the road stopping several times to view the moat, the different pans as they present themselves and to check the fields on your right. The fields here can be good for hunting harriers (all species) and calling Quail. Carefully check the bunds (banks) between the pans. These are used by breeding Stone-curlew as well as many species for roosting, inc. daytime roosting Night-herons. A scope is handy to check the more distant pans.

Always remember to check the sky. This is a major arrival point for species moving up from the south through the Gulf of Kalloni and a major feature for any bird flying high over the island. Raptors, storks, pelicans — anything — can be seen flying over or dropping in from high.

The south pans road When you reach the southwest corner of the pans the road turns sharp left. Ignore the tracks running west and south from this corner (for now) and continue along the main road along the south side of the pans. Again, you can a park up along the right hand side and view the moat and pans.

A new raised hide was erected in 2008 which offers improved views over the the pans and the fields/flood behind it.

The fields on the right behind the hide run the full length of the southern edge of the pans and down to the sea. There is no access to much of the area, but most of it can be viewed from the road. Opposite the saltworks entrance, the fields flood after a good wet winter and this seasonal pool area can be exceptional at attracting waders (inc. Collared Pratincole), egrets, storks, herons, Glossy Ibis, Ruddy Shelduck, Garganey, 'yellow' wagtails, Red-throated Pipit and Short-toed Lark. Raptors are usually much in evidence here with harriers hunting the taller grass areas in the middle of the fields and towards the sea, whilst Red-footed Falcons can often be found hunting from the overhead wires running over the fields. The best area is just beyond the saltworks entrance at the start of the dirt track where the tarmac road ends.

If you continue along the dirt track, at the sharp left before the tracks cross the moat (which runs towards the sea from here), you can go straight on to the beach café. Park here and walk along the coast to check the tamerisks for Rufous Bush Robin and migrant warblers — do not chase birds from bush to bush. Beware ground nesting birds in this area inc. Stone-curlew.

Back on the track, turn left at the café track the dirt track takes you past the salt mound and the horse racing track (on right). This is a drier area but the track often has puddles after heavy rain which attracts passerines, including migrant passerines, to drink. The horse track attracts expected dry grassland species such as Red-throated and Tawny Pipits, 'yellow' wagtails and Short-toed Lark.

If you continue further down, the track bends to the right at an obvious concrete bridge (which looks far from secure) with a renovated shepherds building with a red-tiled roof just to the left. Follow the track round to the right and where it widens and park on the right. You are now at the entrance of the Alykes Wetlands (see next section — p. 112).

Saltpans western fields In the southwest corner of the pans, there are two dirt tracks (one heading east and one south) either side of the large rectangular water treatment building set back just off the road. These two tracks cut through to the Tsiknias River.

The northern track turns east along a wet ditch running into the moat. This immediate area is worth checking and Temminck's Stint can often be seen along the wet ditch. It is worth walking down this track rather than driving. The track takes you into the interior of the fields and few birders tend to wander down here possibly due to the restricted viewing. It is none-the-less still worth checking for migrant shrikes, buntings and warblers and the area is often hunted over by Bee-eater, harriers (all species) and migrant falcons.

From this track there is a track on the right just beyond the wet ditch entrance section which joins up with the main Kalloni-Mytilini road (it comes out on what looks like a lay-by area by a farm truck outlet). Along this track is a wet grassy section with small seasonal pools. This is an excellent area for hunting harriers and the wet grassland used to hold breeding Fan-tailed Warbler, but like other sites for this species on the island, there are no records since about 2004.

Lotzaria (between the southwest pans corner and Tsiknias River) The southern of the two tracks turns south through the fields towards the sea. Most birders drive this track which eventually brings you out at the Tsiknias River ford (do not turn off this track in order to reach the ford). The more open fields near the pans are another excellent area for Collared Pratincole, harriers, falcons, 'yellow' wagtails, chats, pipits and larks. The whole area is worth spending some time in, either by walking or stopping frequently.

Saltpans northern fields The fields between the pans and the Kalloni-Mytilini road are difficult to view due to the dangerous main road. I do not advise stopping or birding from along this road which is used by large lorries and being a long and straight stretch of road is an area where locals speed and usually overtake other vehicles. Because of this little does get reported from this area, but it is an area which can hold good numbers of Stone-curlew in late summer and early autumn.

SPECIES For the whole area; passage birds unless stated; wintering birds can also be seen during passage periods; specific species mentioned for individual sites above.

Ruddy Shelduck, Garganey; Quail (breeds); Great Crested and Black-necked Grebes (winter offshore, some linger into spring); White and Dalmatian Pelicans (both rare); Night-heron, Squacco Heron, Little and Great White Egrets, Purple and Grey Herons, Glossy Ibis, Greater Flamingo, Black and White Storks; raptors inc. Marsh, Montagu's, Pallid (rare) and Hen (winter) Harriers, Common and Long-legged Buzzards, Short-toed Eagle, Osprey, migrant falcons inc. good numbers of Red-footed and occasional Eleonora's, Peregrine; waders inc. Oystercatcher, Black-winged Stilt (breeds), Avocet (breeds), Stone-curlew (breed), Collared Pratincole, Kentish Plover (breeds), Little Ringed Plover (breeds), Ringed Plover (winter), Golden Plover (inc. winter), Grey Plover (inc. winter), Spur-winged Plover (most records are from this area), Sanderling (scarce), Little and Temminck's Stints, Curlew Sandpiper, Dunlin (winter), Broad-billed Sandpiper (rare), Ruff, Great (rare) and Common Snipe, Whimbrel, Curlew, Black-tailed and Bar-tailed (rare) Godwits, Spotted Redshank, Redshank, Marsh Sandpiper, Greenshank, Green Sandpiper (winter), Common Sandpiper, Wood Sandpiper, Turnstone; gulls inc. Mediterranean, Little (scarce), Black-headed (winter), Slender-billed (scarce), Lesser Black-backed (inc. *fuscus*); terns inc. Gull-billed, Sandwich (offshore), Little (breeds), Whiskered, Black and White-winged Black; Little (breeds) and Short-eared (winter) Owls; swifts (all species over); Kingfisher (winter); Bee-eater (inc. local breeders); Calandra (rare) and Short-toed (breeds) Lark; hirundines (all species over); Tawny and Red-throated Pipits; Black-headed (breeds), Grey-headed, Blue-headed, Citrine (rare) and White (mainly winter) Wagtails; Rufous Bush Robin (rare breeder); Black Redstart (winter), Whinchat, Northern Wheatear; Fan-tailed Warbler (locally extinct?); Red-backed, Lesser Grey (breeds), Woodchat (breeds) and Masked Shrike (scarce); Rose-coloured Starling; Spanish Sparrow; Ortolan (scarce) and Black-headed Bunting (breeds);

NEAREST AMENITIES Nearby Kalloni | Καλλονή (3km) for shops, banks, petrol, etc. Skala Kallonis | Σκάλα Καλλονής (3km) for tavernas and shops.

9 | ALYKES WETLANDS | Υγρότοποι Αλυκών

This is a seasonal wetland which in a good year has many seasonal pools, damp grassland and high areas of dry grassland. It provides a great mix of open grassland habitats which attracts a wide selection of species.

LOCATION AND ACCESS Follow the south pans road past the saltworks entrance, onto the dirt track and round past the salt mound. After the mound the track bends to the right by a concrete bridge. Park here (do not block the bridge or track). Continue on foot over the concrete bridge over the drain. The rusty wire 'gate' is simply to keep the livestock in the sheep fields beyond. Carefully replace it as you found it and walk into the fields beyond.

AREAS TO SEARCH Ahead of you is a somewhat daunting large grassland area which can be difficult to work. The wetter areas are immediately to your left towards the saltpans boundary fence and further to the east in the distance. The ground is higher and drier as it runs up to the raised beach area on your right.

Before entering the wetlands proper, scan the immediate area just beyond the bridge. The small scrubby area on the right has held Rufous Bush Robin (from early May). Once you have scanned from the bridge/entrance, you can either turn left and follow and view from along the saltpans boundary or head straight on and keep to the obvious track. Try to avoid wandering around too aimlessly to avoid disturbing resting and feeding birds.

When wet, the **seasonal pools** will attract waders, egrets, storks, herons, Glossy Ibis and Garganey. The grassland areas here are among the best places on the island to look for Collared Pratincole, Red-throated and Tawny Pipits and Short-toed Lark. These species can occur across the whole area, but they are all often found within a few hundred meters of the entrance.

NOTE — you should consider not approaching the pools too closely, or attempting to reach the saltpans fence, in order to avoid flushing birds on the pools or putting incoming birds off from landing on the pools.

If you make it as far as the **eastern end** of the wetlands (few birders do), the pools here usually stay wetter later than the pools near the entrance, probably due to their proximity to the mouth of the River Milopotamos (which feeds the saltpans). These pools have taller vegetation and can be a good place to search for more secretive species such as Great Snipe,

9 ALYKES WETLANDS
Υγρότοποι Αλυκών

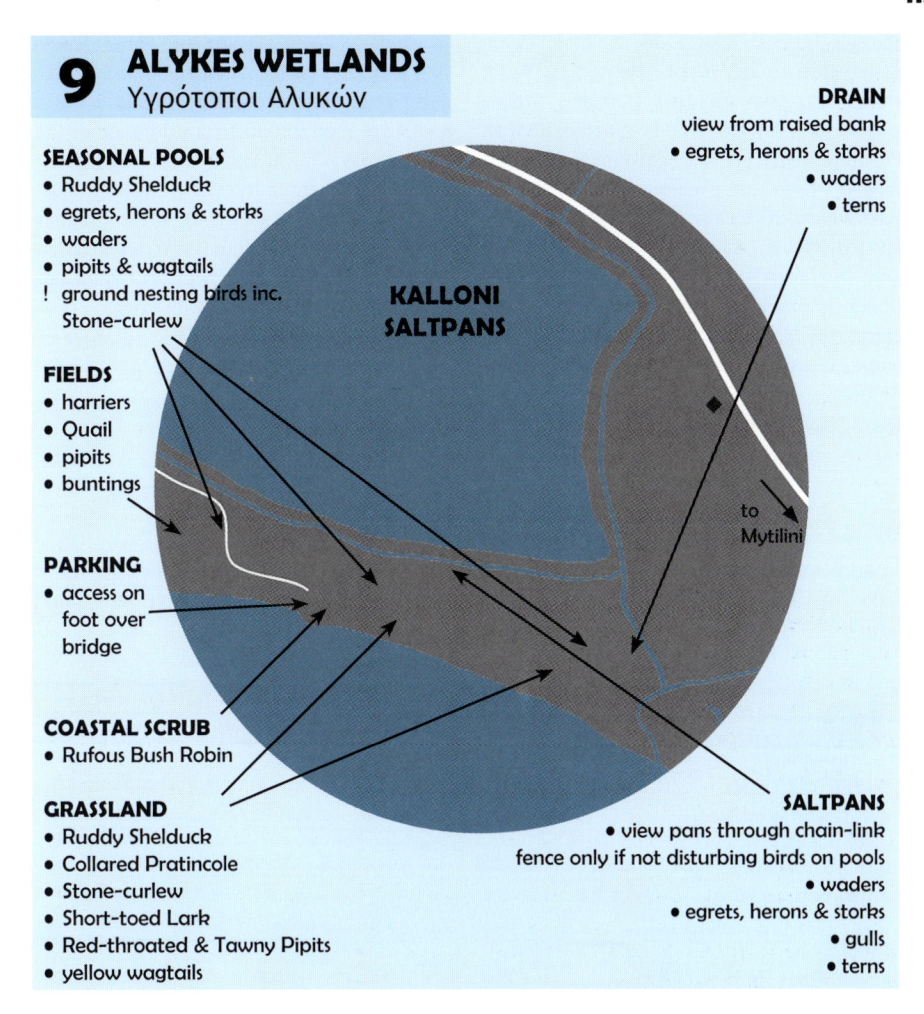

SEASONAL POOLS
- Ruddy Shelduck
- egrets, herons & storks
- waders
- pipits & wagtails
- ! ground nesting birds inc. Stone-curlew

FIELDS
- harriers
- Quail
- pipits
- buntings

PARKING
- access on foot over bridge

COASTAL SCRUB
- Rufous Bush Robin

GRASSLAND
- Ruddy Shelduck
- Collared Pratincole
- Stone-curlew
- Short-toed Lark
- Red-throated & Tawny Pipits
- yellow wagtails

KALLONI SALTPANS

to Mytilini

DRAIN
view from raised bank
- egrets, herons & storks
- waders
- terns

SALTPANS
- view pans through chain-link fence only if not disturbing birds on pools
- waders
- egrets, herons & storks
- gulls
- terns

(which could turn up on any pool in the area) and the area is usually good for taller wading species such as egrets, storks and herons and Glossy Ibis. The area is one of the best sites on the island for Ruddy Shelduck, but they are however very wary and are more likely to take flight long before you get anywhere near them. They will soon settle on another part of the wetland or fly over to the less disturbed pans.

The area is also good in mid-May to early June for passage Rose-coloured Starling.

BEWARE! Ground nesting species inc. Stone-curlew and Kentish Plover in this area.

Rarer and scarcer species found throughout the wetlands include Caspian Plover, Great Snipe, Citrine Wagtail and Calandra Lark.

Back at the car retrace your route back along the dirt track to the saltworks entrance and back along the tarmac road along the south side of the pans.

SPECIES (for wetlands only – for saltpans see p. 111) Passage birds unless stated; wintering birds can also be seen during passage periods. Ruddy Shelduck (especially at eastern end); Garganey; Great Crested and Black-necked Grebe (winter offshore, some linger into spring); herons, Glossy Ibis and storks on pools; raptors inc. Marsh, Montagu's, Pallid (rare) and Hen (winter) Harriers; Stone-curlew (breeds), Collared Pratincole, Kentish Plover (breeds), Little Ringed Plover (breeds), Ringed Plover (inc. winter), Golden Plover (inc. winter), Grey Plover (inc. winter), Spur-winged Plover, Sanderling (scarce), Little and Temminck's Stints, Curlew Sandpiper, Dunlin (inc. winter), Broad-billed Sandpiper (rare), Ruff, Great (rare) and Common Snipe, Whimbrel, Curlew, Spotted Redshank, Redshank, Marsh Sandpiper, Greenshank, Green Sandpiper (inc. winter), Common Sandpiper, Wood Sandpiper; Short-eared Owl (winter); swifts (all species over); Bee-eater (inc. local breeders); Calandra (rare) and Short-toed (breeds) Lark; hirundines (all species over); Tawny and Red-throated Pipits; Black-headed (breeds), Grey-headed, Blue-headed, Citrine (rare) and White (mainly winter) Wagtails; Rufous Bush Robin (rare breeder); Black Redstart (winter), Whinchat, Northern Wheatear; shrikes; buntings.

NEAREST AMENITIES Nearby Kalloni | Καλλονή (3km) for shops, banks, petrol, etc. Skala Kallonis | Σκάλα Καλλονής (3km) for tavernas and shops.

OTHER KALLONI SITES | Άλλες θέσεις στην Καλλονή

In addition to the main Kalloni area sites (Kalloni Saltpans, Tsiknias River, Metochi Lake, Skala Kallonis Pool, Christou River) the area boasts several other smaller sites which are of considerable interest to birders.

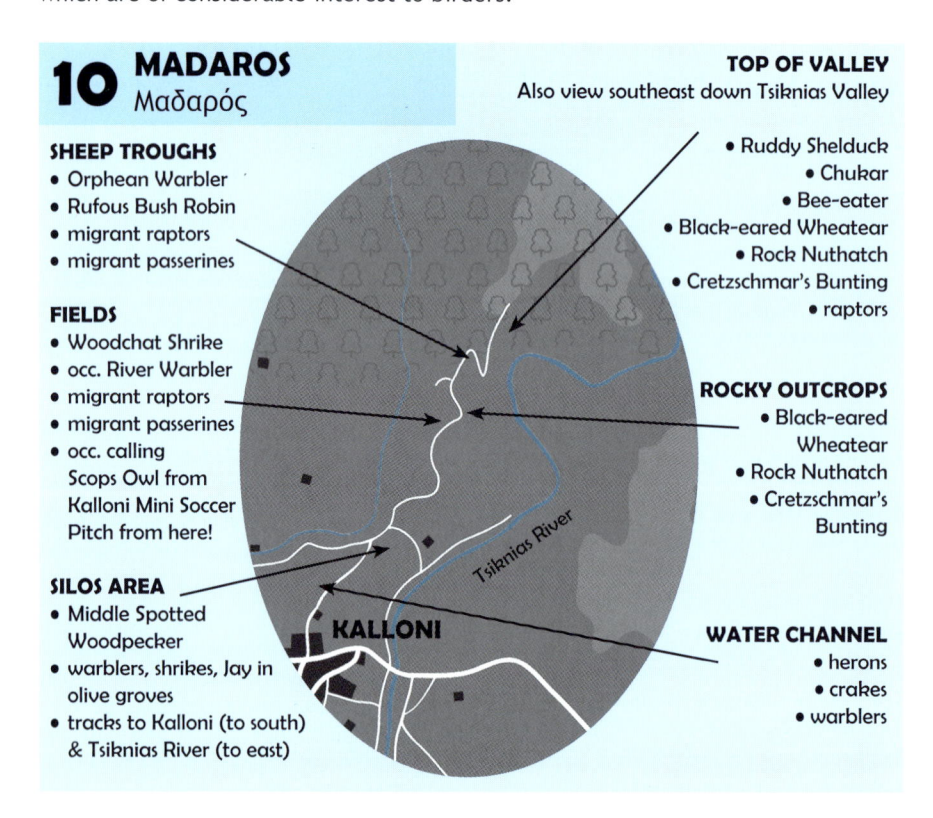

10 MADAROS
Μαδαρός

TOP OF VALLEY
Also view southeast down Tsiknias Valley
- Ruddy Shelduck
- Chukar
- Bee-eater
- Black-eared Wheatear
- Rock Nuthatch
- Cretzschmar's Bunting
- raptors

SHEEP TROUGHS
- Orphean Warbler
- Rufous Bush Robin
- migrant raptors
- migrant passerines

FIELDS
- Woodchat Shrike
- occ. River Warbler
- migrant raptors
- migrant passerines
- occ. calling Scops Owl from Kalloni Mini Soccer Pitch from here!

SILOS AREA
- Middle Spotted Woodpecker
- warblers, shrikes, Jay in olive groves
- tracks to Kalloni (to south) & Tsiknias River (to east)

ROCKY OUTCROPS
- Black-eared Wheatear
- Rock Nuthatch
- Cretzschmar's Bunting

WATER CHANNEL
- herons
- crakes
- warblers

10 | MADAROS | Μαδαρός

LOCATION AND ACCESS This is a rocky area to the north of Kalloni. The area is best accessed via the Upper Tsiknias River. Turn north off the Kalloni-Mytilini road as for the Upper Tsiknias River then take your next left which leads down to four large silos. At the silos turn right and follow this track past a goat farm. After the farm, the track bends to the right and the area opens up and the track drops away down to a second goat farm. You can either stop before this second farm or proceed past this second farm, then after the next right bend, park carefully along the track.

AREAS TO SEARCH Search the area from the track. It is worth walking back on yourself to check the area you've just driven down, but the main area to search is up the track beyond the second farm. Where the track begins to rise (there is a track dropping off to the left here) and then bends to the right and increases markedly in steepness, this is an excellent area to concentrate on. You can view the scrubby hillsides around you whilst you have a good view of the lowlands across to the Kalloni-Petra road. Before the right bend a track leads down to another goat farm. At the head of the track are a couple of concrete livestock troughs. This general area is a traditional breeding site for Rufous Bush Robin.

If you walk up the hillside further, where the track bends to the left you can view south down along the Upper Tsiknias River. Further up the track is an area of denser scrub and continuing onwards the track peters out in an area of taller trees. It is here where the 'dead goat pit' was located, but it is no longer in use.

SPECIES Spring Ruddy Shelduck (often seen looking down the Tsiknias River); raptors inc. Common and Long-legged Buzzards, Short-toed Eagle, migrants; swifts (all species); Bee-eater (over and often in trees down towards the Tsiknias River); Hoopoe; hirundines (all species); Rufous Bush Robin (breeds); Whinchat; Black-eared Wheatear; River (passage; heard), Olivaceous, Barred (passage), Orphean (breeds) and Subalpine Warblers; Rock Nuthatch; Red-backed and Woodchat Shrikes; Raven.

NEAREST AMENITIES Nearby Kalloni | Καλλονή for shops, banks, petrol, etc. Skala Kallonis (4km) for tavernas and shops.

11 | KALLONI MINI SOCCER PITCH | Γήπεδο Μίνι Ποδοσφαίρου Καλλονής (map p.116)

Also known as the 'Scops Copse'. This is usually a one species stop — Scops Owl.

LOCATION AND ACCESS Take the road north out of Kalloni towards Petra. Go past the left turn for Sigri (Σίγρι) and after c.100m turn right into a stand of eucalyptus trees by the mini soccer pitch. Park by the taverna building (June-Sept).

AREAS TO SEARCH Scops Owl breeds here and birds are found at daytime roosts. Birds always use eucalyptus trees, usuaully the ones along the roadside, but they have used trees behind the taverna building. If the birds are roosting on the road side of the trees, view from track opposite the mini soccer pitch — do not view from the road.

Scops Owls can be extremely difficult to find. They roost close to the tree trunks 4-10m up. They avoid direct sunlight and will often sit under pieces of peeling bark or dead twiggy areas, but never completely hidden as they like an open view to look over. There are several traditional roost sites which will be checked by regular visiting birders, but if they have moved, they can take some relocating.

Once an owl has been found please respect its wellbeing. View from 5+m from the roost tree.

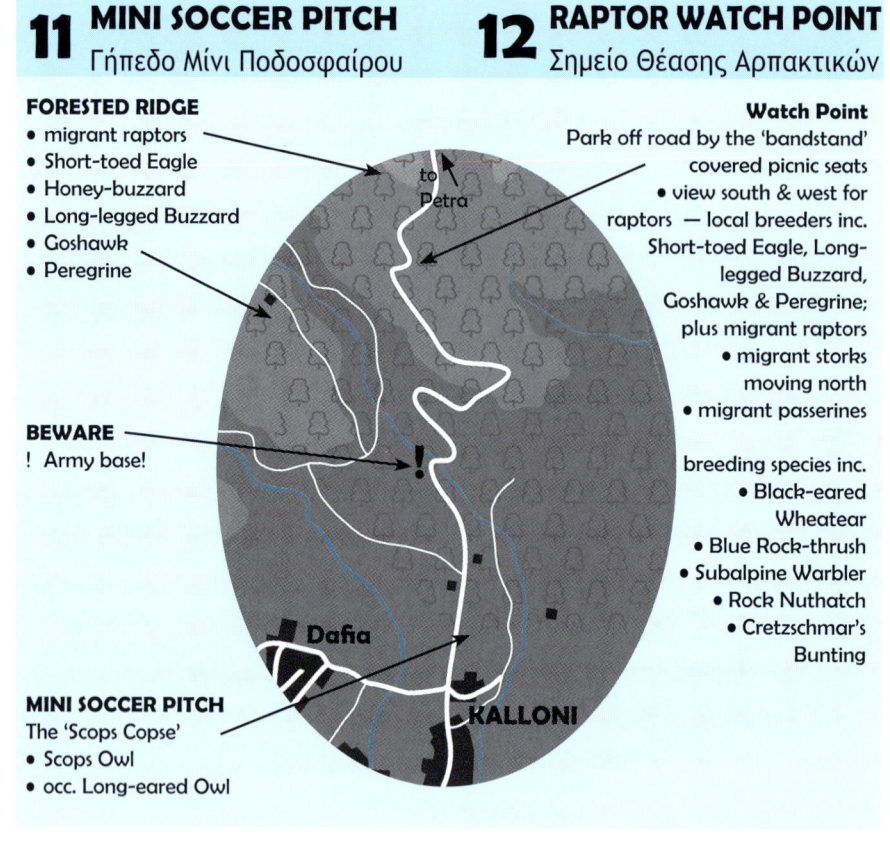

11 MINI SOCCER PITCH
Γήπεδο Μίνι Ποδοσφαίρου

12 RAPTOR WATCH POINT
Σημείο Θέασης Αρπακτικών

FORESTED RIDGE
- migrant raptors
- Short-toed Eagle
- Honey-buzzard
- Long-legged Buzzard
- Goshawk
- Peregrine

BEWARE
! Army base!

MINI SOCCER PITCH
The 'Scops Copse'
- Scops Owl
- occ. Long-eared Owl

to Petra

Dafia

KALLONI

Watch Point
Park off road by the 'bandstand' covered picnic seats
- view south & west for raptors — local breeders inc. Short-toed Eagle, Long-legged Buzzard, Goshawk & Peregrine; plus migrant raptors
- migrant storks moving north
- migrant passerines

breeding species inc.
- Black-eared Wheatear
- Blue Rock-thrush
- Subalpine Warbler
- Rock Nuthatch
- Cretzschmar's Bunting

They don't move so are ideal for scoping (and digiscoping). Do not stand closer, or worse, directly under the tree. Once disturbed they tend to move to more difficult to find roost sites. There is no need to approach within 5m once located. Those wishing to photograph birds without digiscoping equipment or telephoto lenses, please bear in mind if you approach the tree to take a photograph, you are unlikely to be alone in doing so. Others will have done the same and ask yourself do you want to be the person who flushes a bird, so spoiling the chance of others seeing these fabulous diminutive owls.

Some birders return at dusk and use lights to observe hunting birds. Lights on their own do not seem to bother the birds, but the playing of tapes is unnecessary at this site.

SPECIES Spring Scops Owl (breeds) and Long-eared Owl (occasionally breeds).

NEAREST AMENITIES Nearby Kalloni | Καλλονή for shops, banks, petrol, etc. Skala Kallonis | Σκάλα Καλλονής (4km) for tavernas and shops.

12 | KALLONI RAPTOR WATCH POINT | Άλλες θέσεις στην Καλλονή

LOCATION AND ACCESS This site lies on the Kalloni-Petra road about 2km from the northern outskirts of Kalloni. This is a spring season site.

Take the road north out of Kalloni towards Petra and Molivos. About 1km out of Kalloni the road makes a series of hairpin bends. After several bends you will see a covered seated picnic area (looks like a mini bandstand) on your right on the bend of a left hand hairpin. There is room for several cars to pull alongside the bend on the left, or proceed beyond the bend and there is room to pull off the road on the right. Park along the roadside, do not park nose facing towards the 'bandstand' as you may get blocked in by other cars and reversing back out on to the road on this bend can be dangerous.

AREAS TO SEARCH There is plenty of standing space around the 'bandstand'. The site looks south with views over Kalloni and beyond. It is one of only a few real north-south valley routes which migrating birds, particularly raptors and storks, follow on their way north across the island. It is probably unrivalled as the best single raptor spot on the island, but in order to reap the rewards you have to hit it at the right time on the right day and put in the hours! The surrounding area often holds plenty of smaller birds to keep you occupied if no raptor passage.

SPECIES Spring White and Black Storks; raptors – anything can occur and often does, with regular species including harriers (all species), Common and Long-legged Buzzard (inc. local breeders), Short-toed Eagle (inc. local breeders), Honey-buzzard (inc. local breeders from mid-May), Levant and Eurasian Sparrowhawks, Goshawk, Hobby, Common and Lesser Kestrel, Red-footed, Eleanora's and Peregrine Falcons; scarcer raptors in recent years have inc Lesser Spotted, Bonelli's, Booted and Imperial Eagles; Black-eared Wheatear; Blue Rock-thrush; Subalpine Warbler; Rock Nuthatch; Cretzschmar's (breeds) and Ortolan (passage) Buntings.

NEAREST AMENITIES Nearby Kalloni | Καλλονή for shops, banks, petrol, etc. Skala Kallonis | Σκάλα Καλλονής (4km) for tavernas and shops.

Red-throated Pipit
occurs at many sites in the Kalloni area including the Alykes Wetlands where you can encounter double-figure numbers during a good passage of the species

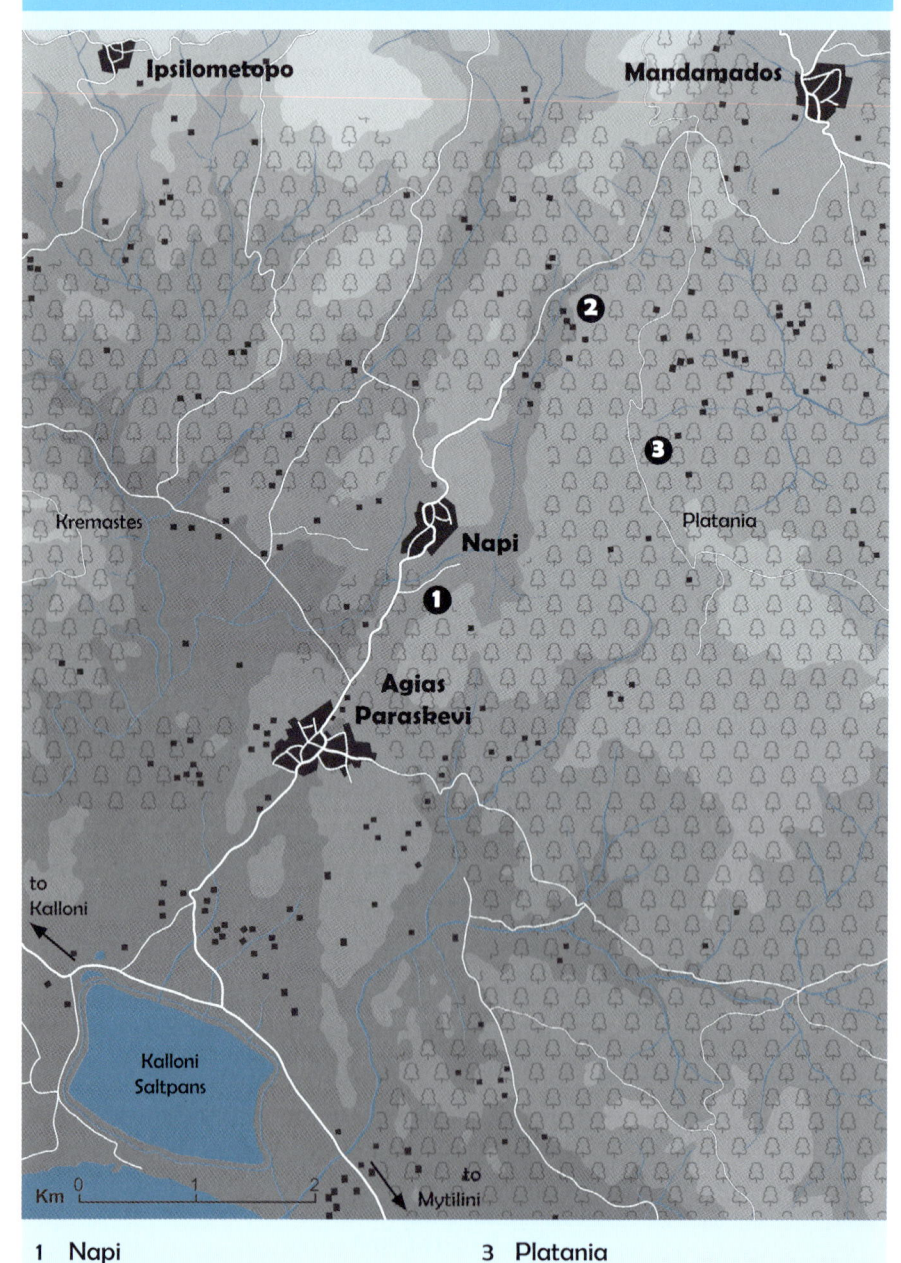

NAPI VALLEY
Κοιλάδα Νάπη

1 Napi
2 Koriani
3 Platania

NAPI VALLEY | Κοιλάδα Νάπη

The Napi Valley is a long (14km), broad valley running north through the middle of the island. It is an outstanding area for many breeding species as well as for observing migrants, in particular raptors and storks.

Like most areas this too is at its best in spring, but you can have some success looking for autumn moving raptors as they move south down the valley.

LOCATION The Napi Valley runs north from the Kalloni Saltpans north-northeast up towards Mandamados (Μανταμάδος) taking in the towns of Agias Paraskevi (Αγιάς Παρασκενή) and Napi (Νάπη) (half way along the valley).

ACCESS The whole area is accessed along the main road between the Kalloni Saltpans (off the Kalloni-Mytilini road east of Kalloni) and Mandamados (off the Mandamados-Mytilini road just east of Mandamados).

AREAS TO SEARCH The valley is c.14km in length and you can stop pretty much anywhere along its length and find birds. Here I describe some of the better sites on which to focus, but don't be afraid to stop and venture away from these.

NEAREST AMENITIES Kalloni | Καλλονή (up to 20km) for shops, banks, petrol, etc. Agias Paraskevi | Αγιάς Παρασκενή (up to 16km) for shops and simple tavernas. Mandamados | Μανταμάδος (up to 12km to north) for shops, simple tavernas and petrol.

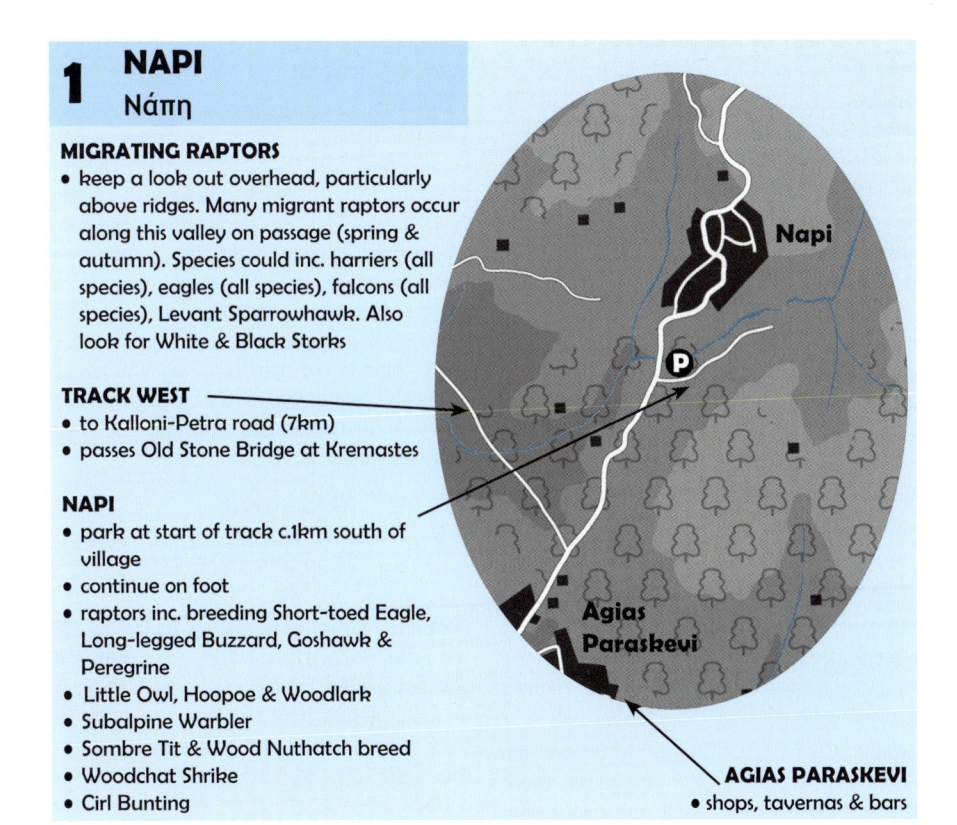

1 NAPI
Νάπη

MIGRATING RAPTORS
- keep a look out overhead, particularly above ridges. Many migrant raptors occur along this valley on passage (spring & autumn). Species could inc. harriers (all species), eagles (all species), falcons (all species), Levant Sparrowhawk. Also look for White & Black Storks

TRACK WEST
- to Kalloni-Petra road (7km)
- passes Old Stone Bridge at Kremastes

NAPI
- park at start of track c.1km south of village
- continue on foot
- raptors inc. breeding Short-toed Eagle, Long-legged Buzzard, Goshawk & Peregrine
- Little Owl, Hoopoe & Woodlark
- Subalpine Warbler
- Sombre Tit & Wood Nuthatch breed
- Woodchat Shrike
- Cirl Bunting

AGIAS PARASKEVI
- shops, tavernas & bars

1 | NAPI | Νάπη (map p. 119)

About 1km out of Agia Paraskevi pass the large track on your left (to Kremastes/Κρεμαστές and the old stone bridge/Παλιό Πέτρινο Γεφύρι). After a further 1.2km, where the road bends to the left, there is a track straight ahead on your right. Take this track and park almost immediately in the broad 'turning area' (often used by the local council to store road stone).

From here walk along the track. The area is excellent for breeding species as well as over-flying migrants.

SPECIES Breeding raptors inc. Common and Long-legged Buzzards, Short-toed Eagle, Eurasian Sparrowhawk, Goshawk, Peregrine; Little Owl; Hoopoe; Woodlark; Common Nightingale; Blue Rock-thrush; Subalpine Warbler; Sombre Tit; Wood and Rock Nuthatch; Woodchat Shrike; Cirl Bunting. **Passage** White and Black Stork; raptors inc. harriers, Honey-buzzard, buzzards, eagles, hawks, falcons; swifts (all species); Bee-eater; hirundines (all species); Golden Oriole.

2 | KORIANI | Κοριανή

About 2.5km north of Napi village the valley is broad. On the right (when travelling north) look out for a neat round wooded hill. Opposite here the banks on the west side of the road have been built up with concrete retaining walls with several obvious water channels and culverts. There is parking at several spots on the east side (right as you drive up the valley) and around the concreted areas on the west side.

The roadside verge is broad in places on the east side (do not attempt to park on here as it is unsafe) and is good to view the valley and hillside to the east of the road.

Further along the road, as the road bends gently to the right and two obvious masts are visible up to the left, note the crash barriers along the left (as you travel north) on the bends here before a sharper right hand bend. You can park just below these series of bends (or walk along the roadside from further south). On the crash barrier side of the road, 1-2 pairs of Olive-tree Warbler breed in the scattered olive and oak trees below the barriers. Care must be taken when standing along this roadside. Do not enter the trees and fields.

SPECIES Breeding raptors inc. Common and Long-legged Buzzards, Short-toed Eagle, Eurasian Sparrowhawk, Goshawk; Little Owl; Middle Spotted Woodpecker; Hoopoe; Woodlark; Common Nightingale; Subalpine Warbler; Sombre Tit; Wood and Rock Nuthatch; Masked and Woodchat Shrikes; Cirl Bunting. **Passage** White and Black Stork; raptors inc. harriers, Honey-buzzard, buzzards, eagles, hawks, falcons; swifts (all species); Bee-eater; hirundines (all species); Golden Oriole.

3 | PLATANIA | Πλατάνια

Not truly part of the Napi Valley, but this area is accessed from the northern end of the valley, and forms the northern spur running across the head of the Napi Valley.

Around 5.3km north of Napi, just beyond the Koriana Olive-tree Warbler site above, there is a left turn leading up to the two masts.

Continue beyond here and up to the top of the valley. When the road begins to drop and you can see the coastal area ahead, there is an area on your right to turn around. Travel back towards Napi and as you re-approach the masts track (now on your right) look for a track on your left at an acute angle (too

2 KORIANI
Κοριανή

MIGRATING RAPTORS
- keep a look out overhead, particularly above ridges. Any species of migrant raptor could occur along this valley on passage (spring and autumn). Species could inc. harriers (all species), eagles (all species), falcons (all species), Levant Sparrowhawk. Also look for White and Black Storks

TRACK TO MAVRIA (two masts)
- view for raptors • Woodlark

KORIANI
- park carefully on roadside
- view hillside to east
- raptors inc. Short-toed Eagle, Long-legged Buzzard & Goshawk
- Little Owl, Hoopoe & Woodlark
- Middle Spotted Woodpecker
- Sombre Tit
- Rock & Wood Nuthatches
- Woodchat & Masked Shrikes
- Cretzchmar's & Cirl Buntings

OLIVE-TREE WARBLER
- Occurs throughout the area but best areas are barriers on west side of main road and the Platania track (see text)

PLATANIA
- park carefully along track
- raptors inc. Short-toed Eagle, Long-legged Buzzard, Goshawk & migrants
- Little Owl, Hoopoe & Woodlark
- Olive-tree Warbler, Subalpine & Orphean Warblers
- Sombre Tit & Rock Nuthatch
- Woodchat & Masked Shrikes
- excellent for migrants inc. Roller, Bee-eater, Golden Oriole

3 PLATANIA
Πλατάνια

acute to turn in when approaching from the south hence having to go beyond and turn around). Take this track taking care where it meets the tarmac road as it can be rocky. You are now on the Platania track.

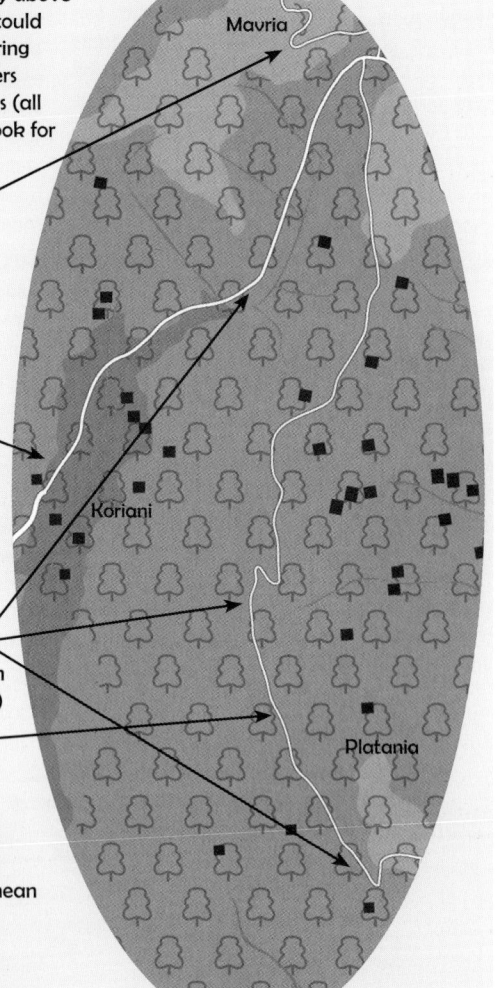

The most rewarding way of covering this area is to park as soon as you can on the trackside and walk east along the track. The area is a rich open habitat with fields, scattered trees and scrub and some denser wooded areas. It is excellent for many breeding species as it runs east along the northern spur at the head of the Napi Valley which is the high point before the land drops away to the coastal area to the north. This ridge is a magnet for migrants and a good place to watch for raptors. Among the many breeding species found along here, Olive-tree Warbler can occur in any of the oak and olive areas (beware singing Masked Shrikes) but can be very difficult to see from the track (do not enter fields).

After c.5km the track drops into a low section at the bottom of which is a cattle grid with room to park several cars just beyond the grid on the left. This area is probably the premier Olive-tree Warbler site on Lesvos. Most birds tend to be down to the left but they do occur either side of the track here. If it is necessary to leave the track, please try to keep in single file and form as few trails as possible through the long grass. This area is rich in flowers, grasses and other plants and there is no need to trample the whole area when this can clearly be avoided. Care should be taken if you cannot see your footing as the area is rocky and can also be muddy underfoot. At the bottom of the slope is a fence. Do not enter the fields beyond but you can walk along the length of the fence to view the trees beyond. The use of tapes should be avoided as with time most people enjoy excellent views of the warblers without them. Early mornings and evenings are best and the middle of the day is better avoided.

You can continue eastwards beyond the Olive-tree Warbler site and continue birding this excellent area. With care (and preferably using the blue Road Editions 1:70,000 map) you can find your way east and then south and out onto the main Kalloni-Mytilini road between Mesa and the village of Lambou Mill (Λάμπου Μύλοι).

SPECIES Breeding raptors inc. Common and Long-legged Buzzards, Short-toed Eagle, Eurasian Sparrowhawk, Goshawk; Little Owl; Middle Spotted Woodpecker; Hoopoe; Woodlark; Common Nightingale; Orphean, Subalpine and Olive-tree Warblers; Sombre Tit; Wood and Rock Nuthatch; Masked and Woodchat Shrikes; Cirl Bunting. **Passage** White and Black Storks; raptors inc. harriers, Honey-buzzard, buzzards, eagles, hawks, falcons; Great Spotted Cuckoo; swifts (all species); Bee-eater; hirundines (all species); Roller; Golden Oriole; shrikes; Ortolan Bunting.

Masked Shrike
occurs on passage and breeds in open woodland areas across the island

THE NORTH COAST — PETRA TO MANDAMADOS
Βόρεια Ακτή — Από Πέτρα προς Μανταμάδος

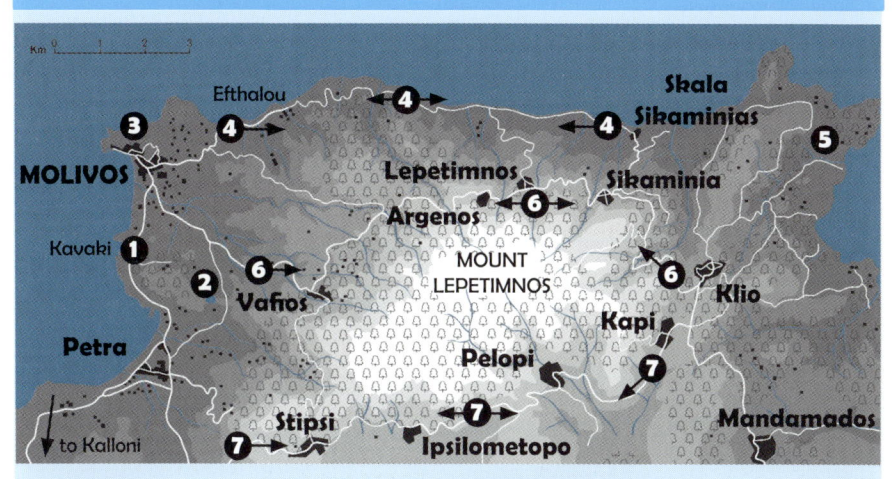

1 Kavaki
2 Perasma
3 Molivos
4 North Coast Track
5 Korakas
6 Vafios to Klio road
7 Stipsi to Kapi road

THE NORTH COAST

This is a large area dominated by the joint highest peak on the island — Mount Lepetimnos.

There are plenty of sites across this area holding key breeding species such as the highly-prized Rüppell's Warbler, as well as being a fantastic area for migrant passerines and raptors and the constant threat of passing shearwaters along this 25km stretch of coastline.

Between Petra and Molivos is Kavaki, the home for breeding Rüppell's Warbler, Blue Rock-thrush, Subalpine and Orphean Warblers, Cretzschmar's, Black-headed and Cirl Buntings plus migrants including regular Barred Warbler, pipits, shrikes and buntings.

Molivos nestles below its castle from which raptors can often be seen crossing the straight to or from Turkey. Autumn is usually more fruitful here, but its worth visiting in spring if nothing more than for the view!

The north coast between Efthalou in the west and Skala Sikaminias in the east is an excellent spring and autumn migrant area. Little valleys, stream beds and wood edges along the whole coastline attract plenty of hungry migrants. Breeding birds include Long-legged Buzzard, Sombre Tit and Rock Nuthatch.

The two roads which pass inland from west to east to the north and south of Mount Lepetimnos are worth checking mainly for migrant raptors. The Vafios to Sikaminia road is best in autumn looking for raptors crossing over from Turkey, whilst the Stipsi to Kapi road can be good for northward moving birds coming across the island.

In the east, the Korakas headland is good in spring and autumn for migrants and breeding birds inc. Middle Spotted Woodpecker, Sombre Tit and Wood Nuthatch. Ruddy Shelduck breeds at Palios and a pair of White Storks breed on top of the olive factory chimney at Mandamados.

PETRA AREA | Πέτρα

Petra is a resort town on the north coast 15km due north of Kalloni (Καλλονή) and 6km south of Molivos (Μόλυβος).

The scrubby, hilly area to north between the town and Molivos provides some excellent birding inc. the best site on the island for one of the Lesvos specialities, Rüppell's Warbler.

NEAREST AMENITIES Petra has shops, bars, tavernas, cafés and a petrol station. Molivos | Μόλυβος (6km) has shops inc. an excellent art gallery, banks, post office, bars and tavernas (by harbour). Vafios | Βαφειός has the excellent Taverna Vafios on the western side of the village by the main road. Kalloni | Καλλονή is 15km away.

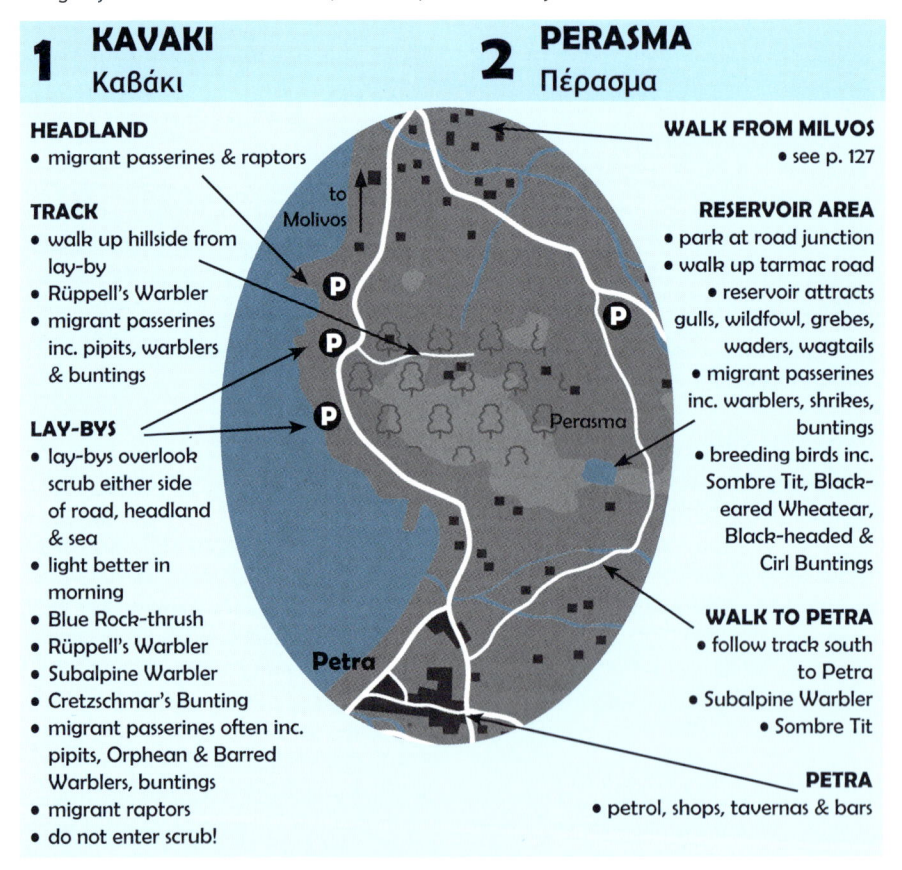

1 KAVAKI | Καβάκι

HEADLAND
- migrant passerines & raptors

TRACK
- walk up hillside from lay-by
- Rüppell's Warbler
- migrant passerines inc. pipits, warblers & buntings

LAY-BYS
- lay-bys overlook scrub either side of road, headland & sea
- light better in morning
- Blue Rock-thrush
- Rüppell's Warbler
- Subalpine Warbler
- Cretzschmar's Bunting
- migrant passerines often inc. pipits, Orphean & Barred Warblers, buntings
- migrant raptors
- do not enter scrub!

2 PERASMA | Πέρασμα

WALK FROM MILVOS
- see p. 127

RESERVOIR AREA
- park at road junction
- walk up tarmac road
- reservoir attracts gulls, wildfowl, grebes, waders, wagtails
- migrant passerines inc. warblers, shrikes, buntings
- breeding birds inc. Sombre Tit, Black-eared Wheatear, Black-headed & Cirl Buntings

WALK TO PETRA
- follow track south to Petra
- Subalpine Warbler
- Sombre Tit

PETRA
- petrol, shops, tavernas & bars

1 | KAVAKI | Καβάκι

ACCESS AND AREAS TO SEARCH This site lies c.2km north of Petra. Follow the main road around the beach front towards Molivos, round the harbour and up the hill. On your right look out for a metal building which looks like something out of Thunderbirds! (it's actually a disco/club). Opposite here is a small lay-by, and just beyond this, as the road starts to reach the brow of the hill, there is another parking area on the left (parking bays edged with a low stone wall with a taller stone wall behind). Take care turning across on-coming traffic.

This parking area affords views down over

Kavaki Bay and the Cape Kavaki headland (on your right as you face the sea) and up the hillside (Rachona | Ραχώνα) on the opposite side of the road. This area is the single most reliable site on the island for Rüppell's Warbler with several pairs breeding on either side of the road. The area is also excellent for other breeding species inc. Peregrine, Black-eared Wheatear, Blue Rock-thrush, Orphean Warbler, Woodchat Shrike and Cretzschmar's and Black-headed Buntings.

The parking area itself provides excellent views, but you can cross the road and walk up the track by the impressive stone house and on up the northern side of the hillside. The view of the hillside is more restricted than from the car park.

Rüppell's Warbler is best looked for in the morning when the sun is good for viewing the inland hillside in particular (the sun can be terrible here in the evening). The males are at their most active in late April and the first week of May, after which they sing much less and can be increasingly difficult to obtain good views of. During peak activity the males sing from bush tops or from the overhead wires and afford excellent views and photo opportunities.

Do not enter any of the scrub areas!

If you continue along the main road towards Molivos there are further parking areas on your left after a further 0.5km. This area is also good for migrants, and usually holds singing Orphean Warbler, but rarely holds Rüppell's Warbler which prefers the area around the main parking area.

SPECIES Breeding inc. Peregrine; Turtle Dove; Black-eared Wheater; Rüppell's, Subalpine and Orphean Warblers; Cretzschmar's and Black-headed Buntings. **Passage** inc. raptors, Common Cuckoo, Tree Pipit, warblers inc. Barred, Spanish Sparrow. **Butterflies** The whole area is also very good for butterflies.

---

2 | **PERASMA** | Πέρασμα

ACCESS AND AREAS TO SEARCH Continue towards Molivos, and just short of the town, take the right turn for Vafios (Βαφειός), Sikaminia (Συκαμινιά) and Mandamados (Μανταμάδος). Continue past the Eko petrol station (on right) and after a further 0.5km, turn right. You can park here by the main road and walk up the tarmac road to view over the old reservoir (formerly referred to by birders as Petra Dam, Petra Reservoir or Molivos Reservoir). The reservoir was drained in 2008 but was thankfully reinstated during the winter of 2009/10. It's worth continuing on foot beyond the reservoir, and this track eventually takes you back to Petra (3.5km) — see the Molivos to Petra walk p. 127.

The reservoir holds water throughout the is well worth exploring in spring and autumn and is a good area for migrants as well as breeding species inc. Ruddy Shelduck, Black-eared Wheatear, Orphean, Sardinian (rare) and Subalpine Warblers, Rock Nuthatch and Cirl and Black-headed Buntings. Great Spotted Cuckoo is seen in the area most years and may have bred. Rufus Bush Robin has been found here and River Warbler is occasionally heard. Sombre Tit can be found beyond the reservoir.

SPECIES Breeding Inc. Ruddy Shelduck; Turtle Dove; Black-eared Wheatear; Orphean, Sardinian and Subalpine Warblers; Sombre Tit; Rock Nuthatch; Cirl and Black-headed Bunting. **Passage** Raptors inc. Eleonora's Falcon quite regular in late summer and autumn; occasional marsh terns; Great Spotted Cuckoo; Common Cuckoo; Bee-eater; Tree Pipit; chats; warblers; shrikes; Spanish Sparrow. **Butterflies** The whole area is also very good for butterflies. **Drgonflies** The whole area is also very good for dragonflies.

3 MOLIVOS (MITHYMNA)
Μόλυβος (Μήθυμνα)

MOLIVOS CASTLE
- drive up to castle
- views across to Turkey
- migrant passerines
- can be very good for raptors
- use the tavernas in the harbour

MOLIVOS TO PETRA WALK
- see p. 127

WALK TO PETRA
- joins up at Perasma (see p. 125)
- good in spring & autumn for migrant passerines inc. warblers, shrikes, buntings
- breeding birds inc. Sombre Tit, Black-eared Wheatear, Black-headed & Cirl Buntings

MOLIVOS
- excellent tavernas, cafés & bars at harbour
- shops, post office & bank
- excellent art shop at harbour

3 | MOLIVOS | Μόλυβος

LOCATION Molivos lies at the far north of the island 22km from Kalloni (Καλλονή) and 60km from Mytilini (Μυτιληνη).

Molivos is arguably the most beautiful town on the island. Strict planning laws, inc. banning the building of dwellings over two-storeys high, has preserved the picture-postcard, red-tiled township clinging to the sides of the hill, between an equally picturesque harbour and castle. The town itself might be limited for bird and wildlife watching, but there is nowhere comparable on the island to spend an hour or so having lunch in one of the many excellent harbour-side tavernas. There is also a fabulous art gallery (inc. local and Greek art) on the harbour front (near taverna Octopus) and several souvenir shops.

3A | MOLIVOS CASTLE | Κάστρο Μόλυβος

ACCESS AND AREAS TO SEARCH As you enter Molivos, go past the turn on the right to Vafios (Βαφειός), Sikaminia (Συκαμνιά) and Mandamados (Μανταμάδος) and into the town proper. Take your next turn up a one way street which runs around a sunken car park (with lots of trees shading it). Continue up the hill, ignore the turn to the right near the top, but take your next left which is signed for the castle/kastro. Continue up to the castle itself and park there or back along the roadside approach.

The view from the castle is stunning, over the red rooftops of Molivos across to Petra and the distant mountains in one direction and across the narrow sea channel to the Turkish coastline in the other.

The trees and bushes along the approach road and around the castle attract migrants, but it is for raptors which most birders come to this vantage point. The view across to Turkey offers a great vantage point to look for raptors moving south in autumn.

The Taverna Panorama might look tempting, and whilst it is OK for a drink whilst watching for raptors, if you require lunch or dinner, head for the harbour!

SPECIES Passage species inc. raptors (literally anything); Black-eared Wheatear; warblers; flycatchers; shrikes.

3B | MOLIVOS TO PETRA WALK | Πεζοπορία από τον Μόλυβος στη Πέτρα (no map)

8km. 3-4 hours. Good trainers or walking boots/sandals. Take sunhat, sun cream and water. See also *Lesvos Landscapes* by Brian & Eileen Anderson (second edition, 2007, Sunflower Books) and Mike Maunder's *On Foot in North Lesvos* (WWW.LESVOSWALKS.NET).

This walk can be done from either Molivos or Petra by parking at one end, walking the route and getting a taxi back to your car.

As you enter Molivos, go past the turn on the right to Vafios (Βαφειός), Sikaminia (Συκαμνιά) and Mandamados (Μανταμάδος) and into the town proper. Take your next turn up a one way street with a sunken car park (with lots of trees shading it) immediately on your right. Park here. Walk up the hill towards the castle. At the road junction with the castle to your left, turn right and head away from the town with a sports area on the left. When the track bends to the left, turn right onto another track. A little further on, bear left onto another track over a concrete bridge. This track brings you out on the Molivos-Vafios road. Turn left along the road and then your next right on to a new tarmac road. This takes you up past the reservoir (see Perasma, Petra area, p. 125). Continue past the reservoir for about 0.75km and at the main fork bear right. Continue straight on this track which brings you out in Petra by the Panorama Taverna (on right). Turn right, then left down to the seafront.

Turn left again and you will find taxis around this area to take you back to Molivos. There are numerous tavernas and bars to have lunch or a drink (but Molivos is nicer if you can wait to get back there).

The whole area is great for birds, both breeding species and passage migrants (see below).

SPECIES Breeding (inc. wanderers from nearby areas) raptors inc. Long-legged Buzzard, Eleonora's Falcon (quite regular especially in late summer and autumn); Great Spotted Cuckoo; Turtle Dove; Black-eared Wheatear; Subalpine Warbler; Sombre Tit; Rock Nuthatch; Cirl and Black-headed Buntings. **Passage** species inc. raptors; Common Cuckoo; Bee-eater; Tree Pipit; chats; warblers; shrikes; Spanish Sparrow. **Butterflies** The whole area is also very good for butterflies.

NEAREST AMENITIES Molivos itself has shops inc. excellent art gallery and numerous souvenir shops, banks, post office, bars, tavernas (by harbour) and a petrol station. Petra | Πέτρα has shops, bars, tavernas and a petrol station. Vafios | Βαφειός (5km) has the excellent Taverna Vafios on the western side of the village by the main road. Kalloni | Καλλονή is 22km away and Mytilini | Μυτιληνη 60km.

4 EFTHALOU TO SKALA SIKAMINIAS
Ευθαλού στη Σκάλα Συκαμινιάς

OFFSHORE
- good views over sea north to Turkey
- Yelkouan (common) & Scopoli's (scarce) Shearwaters
- Audouin's Gull
- look for raptors crossing the straight between Lesvos & Turkey
- dolphins
- Mediterranean Monk Seal (very rare)

HOT SPRINGS
- pebble seabed along coast has 'hot spots' where thermal springs reach surface
- be careful on hot unstable rocks
- small shallow pool behind fence (rock with 'hot springs') good for dragonflies inc. Red-veined Darter

ALONG TRACK
- excellent for butterflies inc. Cleopatra

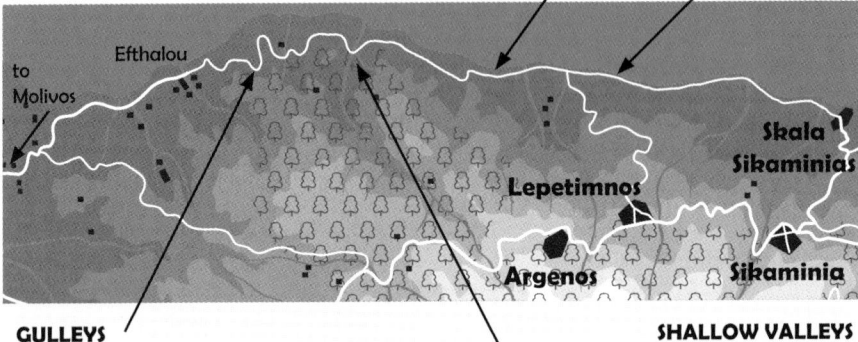

GULLEYS
- excellent for breeding birds & migrants
- look for raptors overhead in spring & autumn
- Hoopoe & Golden Oriole (passage)
- Bee-eater (passage)
- warblers inc. Subalpine, Orphean, Barred (passage), Wood (passage)
- Sombre Tit
- shrikes — all species
- buntings inc. Cirl, Cretzschmar's, Ortolan (passage)

OVERHEAD MIGRANTS
- keep an eye on the sky for storks, raptors, Bee-eaters, swifts & hirundines
- raptors — spring: departing birds will often appear low over coast before heading back inland to gain height to cross to the north; autumn: incoming birds from north often low and will either look for a sheltered roost tree or will gain height and continue south

SHALLOW VALLEYS
- excellent for breeding birds & migrants
- Chukar
- Bee-eater (passage)
- warblers inc. Subalpine, Orphean, Barred (passage)
- Sombre Tit
- Rock Nuthatch
- shrikes — all species
- buntings inc. Cirl, Cretzschmar's, Ortolan (passage)
- many scarce species seen along the length of this track inc. Thrush Nightingale, Red-breasted Flycatcher, Hawfinch

SKALA SIKAMINIAS
- occ. Audouin's Gull around harbour
- Kingfisher in harbour (autumn/winter)
- excellent tavernas, cafés & bars
- gift shops
- very popular on Sundays with locals & avoid on public holidays!
- boat to Molivos (need to book in advance — see text)

4 | EFTHALOU TO SKALA SIMAMINIAS | Ευθαλού στη Σκάλα Συκαμινιάς

LOCATION This track takes you along the most northerly coastline of the island between Molivos in the west and Skala Sikaminias to the east. A rough dirt track hugs the coastline for much of the 15km route and provides fabulous views of this beautiful coastal area with views across the sea to neighbouring Turkey.

ACCESS AND AREAS TO SEARCH From Petra, as you enter Molivos, go past the turn on the right to Vafios (Βαφειός), Sikaminia (Συκαμνιά) and Mandamados (Μανταμάδος) and into the town proper. Take your next turn up a one way street with runs around a sunken car park (with lots of trees shading it). Continue up the hill towards the castle/kastro (signed). Ignore the left turn to the castle and continue straight on along the road to Efthalou and along the seafront. It is worth stopping at the end of the tarmac section and check the sea from here which is excellent for Yelkouan Shearwater (and occasional Scopoli's), Shag and possibly Audouin's Gull, and occasional dolphins.

Continue up the rough track which runs straight ahead of the tarmac road. This first section is steep and very rough and you should take it in a low gear and beware of any traffic coming downhill. Do not stop until you round the couple of hairpins and the track gradient lessens as it turns inland along a straight section of a couple hundred metres. Park before the next hairpin and search the gully below you and the wooded slopes above. This area is excellent for migrants and breeding species here inc. Sombre Tit and Masked Shrike.

I recommend walking the track from here for as long as you can, or do a combination of short drives and walks along the entire length of the track. Take the usual sun precautions as you might end up finding anything along here and end up away from the car for longer than you think.

Whether you walk or drive, the main areas to search are the hairpin valleys which often follow along small streams or rivers. These water courses are usually dry but there is enough underground water to maintain good vegetation cover. Also check field edges, clumps of bushes/trees in open areas, buildings and the main wood edges.

There is simply too much to detail along this 15km track, safe to say that the whole coastline is great for migrants in spring and autumn inc. migrating raptors, and as such birds can be anywhere.

Some of the most productive migrant areas are the small valleys along the first 6km from Molivos, but make regular stops to check gulleys, shallow valleys, wood edges, open areas and remember to keep an eye on the sky. In spring larger raptors will occasionally wander low along the coastline before heading back inland in order to find a thermal to obtain the lift they require to cross the narrow sea straight. Birds crossing the straight do so at height and are difficult to pick up without seeing them at lower levels first. In autumn raptors will come in low from over the sea and may even seek to roost up in the wooded areas.

The area is usually full of Yellow-legged Gulls but this coastline is the best area of the island to look for Audouin's Gull. This rare gull is now known to breed on the islands off this north coast. Single birds are usually encountered, but occasionally you might see two together, with rare sightings of three or more birds. They can be encountered anywhere along this coast inc. around the small harbour of Skala Sikaminias. The sea is also worth keeping an eye on as quite large flocks of Yelkouan (common) and Scopoli's (scarce) Shearwaters can be seen along here.

Almost anything can occur along this coast and White-throated Robin has been reported along here during the breeding season, and Finsch's Wheatear has also occurred along this northern part of the island.

About halfway along the coastal track there is an area of hot springs. It lies where the track comes right down to the seashore below a steep earthy cliff-face on the right, at the end of which is a fenced off spring with rocks (look for steam around them) and a rusting vehicle (what else!). Although the pebble shore was heavily bulldozed in early 2008, it is still possible to paddle in this area seeking out the hot spring spots coming up under the shallow waters — very nice. Be warned — some of the rocks can be very hot — some sections even too hot to walk on bare-footed!

After 15km you come to the picturesque little harbour village of Skala Sikaminias and the instantly recognisable chapel of Our Lady of the Mermaid on the harbour front (which features on countless postcards and in virtually every book published on Lesvos — but not this one).

This route is probably more of a spring route and can provide an excellent day trip from the Kalloni area combining the Kavaki Rüppell's Warbler site on the way up and returning via the Napi valley and ending up around the saltpans or Tsiknias River in the evening. Alternatively ending up at this end of the island in the evening you could eat at the excellent Taverna Vafios in Vafios near Molivos.

There is a daily boat trip between Petra/Molivos and Skala Sikaminias (check with the tourist office (+30 22530 71347) in Molivos for sailings and cost). Some visitors arrange to walk the 15km track to Skala Sikaminias and return at leisure by boat (best to check that it isn't full before you do this). Others have also walked the track from Skala Sikaminias and returned from Molivos by taxi.

SPECIES Breeding (inc. breeders from nearby areas) inc. shearwaters; Chukar; Audouin's Gull; raptors inc. Short-toed Eagle, Common and Long-legged Buzzard, Goshawk, Peregrine; Little Owl; Middle Spotted Woodpecker; Turtle Dove; Hoopoe; Black-eared Wheatear; Orphean and Subalpine Warblers; Sombre Tit; Rock Nuthatch; Woodchat and Masked Shrikes; Cretzschmar's and Black-headed Buntings. White-throated Robin reported breeding in 1995 and 1996. **Passage** inc. raptors (all species); chats; warblers; flycatchers; shrikes; Golden Oriole; buntings. **Insects** The whole area is excellent for insects. Many butterflies occur along this coast inc. Scarce Swallowtail, Eastern Festoon, False Apollo, Cleopatra, Southern Comma and Orbed Red-underwing Skipper. The area is also good for dragonflies inc. Blue-eyed Hawker, Green-eyed Hawker, Broad-bodies Chaser, Southern Skimmer, Small Skimmer and Red-veined Darter.

NEAREST AMENITIES Molivos | Μόλυβος and Skala Sikaminias | Σκάλα Συκαμινιάς lie 15km apart. Molivos has shops inc. an excellent art gallery and numerous souvenir shops, banks, post office, bars, tavernas (by harbour) and a petrol station. Skala Sikaminias has several harbourside tavernas, cafés (try Καβος café) and bars and a couple of souvenir shops.

---

5 | MANDAMADOS AREA | Μανταμάδος

LOCATION Mandamados is the largest town in the northeast of the island.

NEAREST AMENITIES Mandamados has shops, basic tavernas and a petrol station. There is a petrol station just south of Klio (Κλειω).

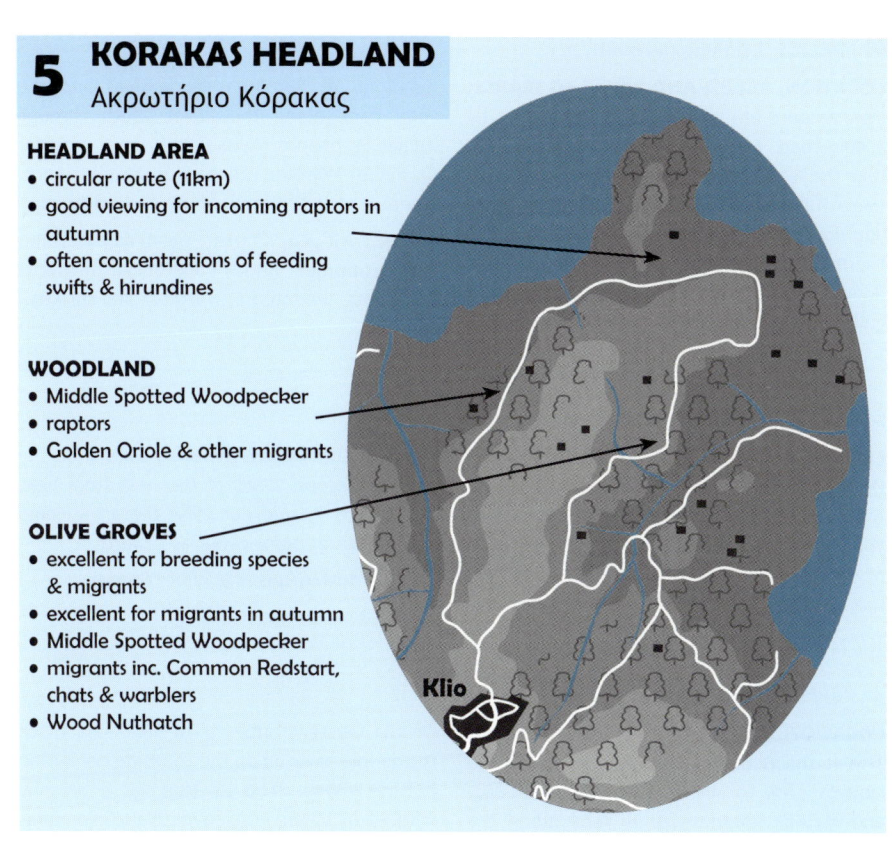

5 KORAKAS HEADLAND
Ακρωτήριο Κόρακας

HEADLAND AREA
- circular route (11km)
- good viewing for incoming raptors in autumn
- often concentrations of feeding swifts & hirundines

WOODLAND
- Middle Spotted Woodpecker
- raptors
- Golden Oriole & other migrants

OLIVE GROVES
- excellent for breeding species & migrants
- excellent for migrants in autumn
- Middle Spotted Woodpecker
- migrants inc. Common Redstart, chats & warblers
- Wood Nuthatch

5A | KORAKAS HEADLAND | Ακρωτήριο Κόρακας

LOCATION, ACCESS AND AREAS TO SEARCH
Heading north away from Mandamados, after c.4km there is a turn on your right signed for Klio. Just before this turn is a pool which is usually full of Yellow-legged Gulls but does occasionally hold Ruddy Shelduck and waders. Turn into Klio and through the village and follow the sign for Tsonia (Τσόνια). At a fork with Tsonia to your right, take the track to the left. This is a circular route of c.10km which if followed takes you back to Klio. It's worth stopping occasionally anywhere along the route to search, or park after a couple of kilometres and walk out to the northern part of the track with views over the headland.

Whilst this area is worth visiting at any time of year, it's probably at its best in autumn. This north-facing headland is an arrival point for migrants heading south. The sheltered woodland, olive groves and scrub provide plenty of shelter and feeding for hungry migrants, is an excellent area for feeding swifts (all species) and hirundines (all species) and a classic raptor crossing point. There are several good northerly viewpoints from which you can scan for raptors which pass low or even land in trees around the headland.

SPECIES All year Middle Spotted Woodpecker; Rock and Wood Nuthatches; Jay. **Spring/autumn** Migrant raptors, warblers; shrikes.

5B | PALIOS | Παλιός (no map)

LOCATION, ACCESS AND AREAS TO SEARCH
Mandamados has recently been by-passed by a new road. On the north side of the town take the road signed for Taxiarchon Monastery (Μονή Ταξιαρχών). The next right turn takes you down to Palios (8km). Just before Palios there are some pools which hold breeding Ruddy Shelduck and can attract waders and gulls (also excellent for dragonflies). The headland at Sarakina (Σαοαχήνα) and the road back along the coast south through Aghias Stephanos (Αγια Στέφανος) is good for Sardinian Warbler, Chukar, Short-toed Lark, wheatears and migrant chats and warblers.

SPECIES All year Chukar; Sardinian Warbler.
Spring/summer Ruddy Shelduck; migrants inc. chats, wheatears, warblers and shrikes.

5C | MANDAMADOS | Μανταμάδος (no map)

LOCATION, ACCESS AND AREAS TO SEARCH
On the eastern side of Mandamados itself, there is a White Storks nest on the chimney as you follow the main road around the east side of the town. It is best viewed by going past the chimney, up the hill and then turn into the right turn before the army camp. You can get good scope views of the nest from here but ensure you do not view the army camp with optics or point cameras towards it.

SPECIES Spring/summer White Stork.

6 | VAFIOS TO KLIO | Βαφειός – Κλειώ

LOCATION, ACCESS AND AREAS TO SEARCH
This is the main road route connecting the Molivos area to Mandamados (Μανταμάδος) and Mytilini (Μυτιληνη). It runs along the northern side of Mt Lepetimnos and passes through the villages of Vafios (Βαφειός), Agrenos (Αργενος) and Sikaminia (Συκαμνιά).

In autumn, if travelling along this route there are many viewpoints to search for raptors moving south. Several stops just east of Vafios and near Sikaminia are usually more rewarding as birds coming across the sea choose to skirt around Mt Lepetimnos rather than attempting to regain height in order to pass directly over it.

On the western outskirts of Sikaminia there is a simple taverna on the roadside below the hillside village. The taverna has a balcony with views to the north over Skala Sikaminias and across the sea channel to Turkey, views to the west and across a large ravine which runs up the side of the village. You can do worse than spend an hour or two here lunching whilst watching out for birds of prey.

The Taverna Vafios by the main road on the western side of Vafios is an excellent evening dining spot if you find yourself up this end of the island late in the day.

7 | STIPSI TO KAPI | Στύψη – Κάπη

LOCATION, ACCESS AND AREAS TO SEARCH This route follows a narrow metalled road from Petra in the west to Klio in the east via the villages of Stipsi (Στύψη), Ipsilometoro (Υψηλομέτωπο), Pelopi (Πελόπη) and Kapi (Κάπη).

This road is rarely travelled by birders but can be good in spring and autumn to watch for moving raptors. There is an excellent viewpoint immediately east of Ipsilometopo which looks south down the island. An ideal

6 VAFIOS TO KLIO
Βαφειός στη Κλειώ

- good views to north along much of the road
- look for raptors, swifts, Bee-eater, hirundines
- Taverna Vafios excellent
- roadside taverna at Sikaminia good for lunch/drinks whilst looking for raptors
- access up to Mt Lepetimnos between Sikaminia & Klio

7 STIPSI TO KAPI
Στύψη στη Κάπη

- good views to south along much of the road inc. large lay-by on east side of Ipsilometopo
- look for raptors, swifts, Bee-eater, hirundines
- access up to Mt Lepetimnos from Kapi

MT LEPETIMNOS
- breeding Chukar, Peregrine. Black-eared Wheatear, Blue Rock-thrush, Rock Nuthatch, Cretzschmar's Bunting

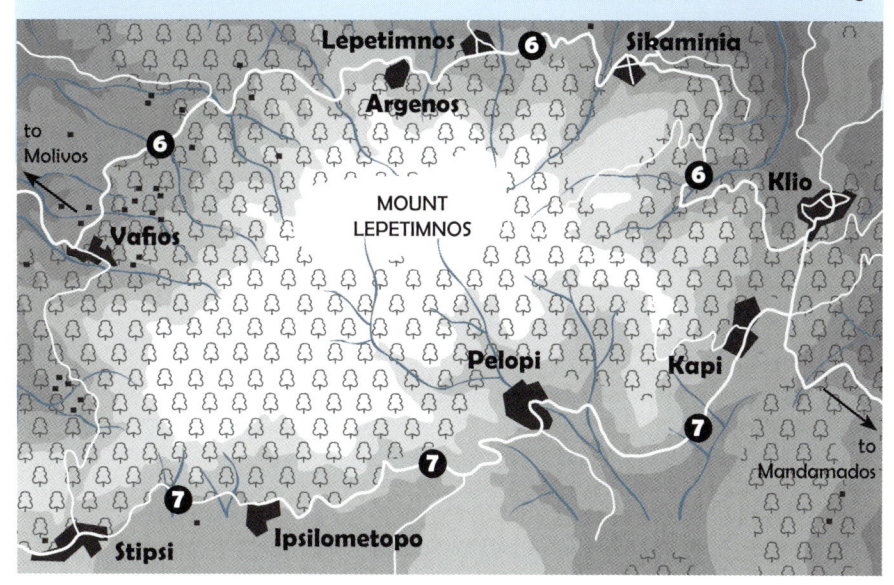

spring raptor spot which has produced flocks of Levant Sparrowhawk in spring and Honey-buzzard in autumn.

Mt Lepetimnos can be approached part way by car via the village of Kapi. Just as you enter the village from the west there is a left turn between the houses which is signed with a trekking sign (man with rucksack on yellow background). The track is rough but manageable and can provide excellent raptor watching as well as breeding Black-eared Wheatear, Blue Rock-thrush and Rock Nuthatch.

SPECIES Breeding species inc. Peregrine; Black-eared Wheater; Blue Rock-thrush; Rock Nuthatch; Cretzschmar's and Black-headed Buntings. **Passage** raptors; Bee-eater.

NEAREST AMENITIES Molivis | Μόλυβος and Klio | Κλειώ lie 21km apart; Petra | Πέτρα and Klio lie 17km apart.

Molivos has shops inc. excellent art gallery, banks, post office, bars, cafés and tavernas. Petra has shops, bars, tavernas (by harbour), cafés and a petrol station. Vafios | Βαφειός has the excellent Taverna Vafios on the western side of the village by the main road. Sikaminia | Συκαμινιά has a simple taverna. There is a petrol station just south of Klio.

SKALOCHORI AREA
Ευρύτερη περιοχή Σκαλοχωρίου

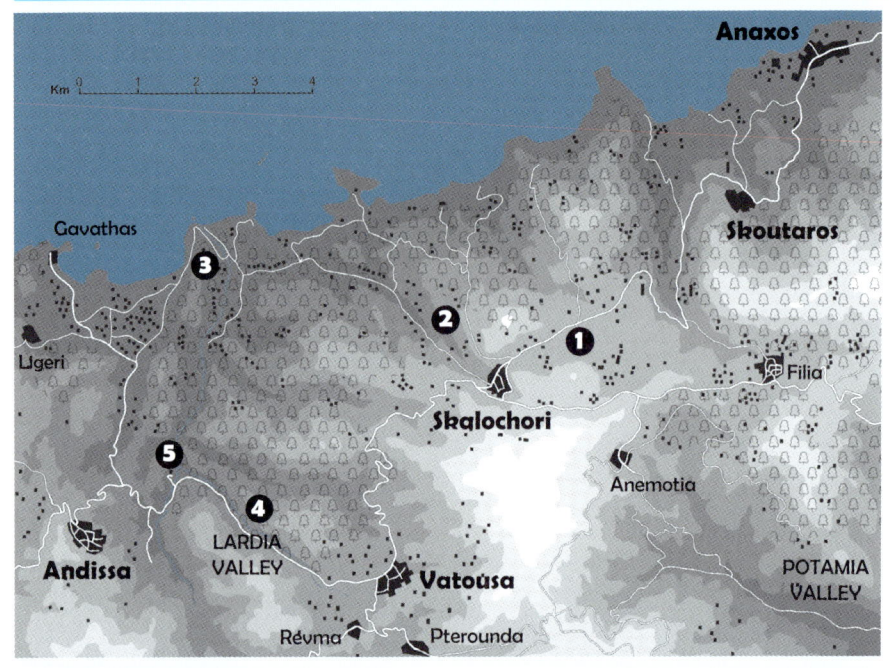

1. Aghios Taxiarchis
2. Katapetros Valley
3. Voulgaris River
4. Lardia Valley
5. Perivolis Monastery

Apart from the Lardia Valley, this area remains very underwatched by visiting birders.

Anaxos (Αναξος) is an increasingly popular resort with birders. It offers good links to Petra (Πέτρα) and Molivos (Μόλυβος) and the north coast, south to the Kalloni (Καλλονή) area, and west and south west to Andissa (Άντισσα), the Eresos (Ερεσος) area and Sigri (Σίγρι).

The whole coastal area west of Anaxos to Gavathas (Γαββαθάς), and the tracks inland up to the main Petra to Andissa road, offer fantastic scenery and are worthy of exploring with little chance of seeing any other birders – you'll have the area to yourself for as long as you like!

There is no coastal route along this section of coast and the area is best accessed off the main Petra to Andissa road and the road from Andissa to Gavathas. Here are a few suggestions, but this area is simply best enjoyed ad-hoc – just wander freely using a map, stopping where the scenery takes you and enjoy what you find.

SPECIES See individual site accounts.

NEAREST AMENITIES The coastal village of Gavathas is c.25km west of Anaxos and 8km from Andissa. Anaxos | Αναξος has shops and tavernas. Petra | Πέτρα (2km from Anaxos) has shops, bars, tavernas and a petrol station. Molivos | Μόλυβος (a further 6km) has shops (inc. excellent art gallery), banks, post office, bars and tavernas. Andissa | Άντισσα (15km from Skalochori) for petrol and town centre tavernas. In season there are beach bar/tavernas at Gavathas.

1 **AGHIOS TAXIARCHIS**
Άγιος Ταξιάρχης

2 **KATAPETROS VALLEY**
Κοιλάδα Κατάπετρος

3 **VOULGARIS RIVER**
Ποταμός Βούλγαρης

AGHIAS TAXIARCHIS
- Olive-tree Warbler
- Masked Shrike

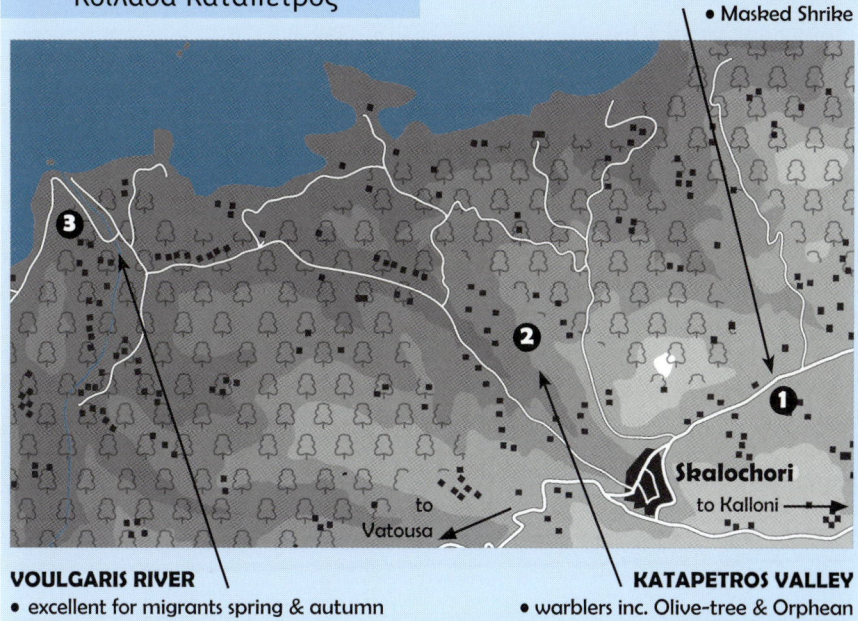

VOULGARIS RIVER
- excellent for migrants spring & autumn
- Bee-eaters, wagtails, chats, warblers, shrikes, flycatchers
- breeding Ruddy Shelduck

KATAPETROS VALLEY
- warblers inc. Olive-tree & Orphean
- shrikes — all species
- raptors inc. Short-toed Eagle, Long-legged Buzzard, Goshawk

1 | AGHIOS TAXIARCHIS | Άγιος Ταξιάρχης

From Skalochori (Σκαλοχωρι) head east towards Anaxos (c.12km). After c.2km east of Skalochori is the chapel of Aghia Taxiarchis. Just east of here is a track north to Koutamatsa Beach (Παρλία Κουταμάτσα). This track is worth exploring (particularly the pool by the track after c.300m). Also search the track running south just to the west of the chapel. This latter track gives great views along the shallow valley.

West of the chapel there is a roadside pool with covered picnic seating.

SPECIES The whole area is very good for Olive-tree Warbler, Masked Shrike, warblers, Golden Oriole, raptors.

2 | KATAPETROS VALLEY | Κοιλάδα Κατάπετρος

From Skalochori there are two tracks leading north out of the village down to the northern coast offering stunning scenery. The east track is in better condition than the west track, the latter at times not very suitable for non-4x4s. Both tracks can be very bumpy in places and I would advise not attempting them in the wet unless you're in a 4x4.

Both of these tracks link up with tracks west along the coast to Gavathas and provide an excellent circuit out to the coast, along to Gavathas and then back up to the main road at Andissa.

SPECIES The whole area is good for migrants inc. raptors and breeding species inc. Masked Shrike, the odd Oliver-tree Warbler and Orphean Warbler.

3 | VOULGARIS RIVER | Ποταμός Βούλγαρης (map p. 135)

The River Voulgaris (Βούλγαρης) runs out of the western end of the Lardia Valley north to the coast. The mouth of the river can be reached from the two Skalochori tracks above (2) or from Gavathas. Here the river inland can be viewed by tracks on either side of the river with a ford c.1.5km inland.

Another track c.0.5km inland from the ford leads back to the river c.2.5km further inland. Here is the confluence of the river and a secondary feeder river and the area is a natural migrant trap and worth checking.

SPECIES This is an excellent area for migrants, especially warblers and shrikes. Ruddy Shelduck breeds here. The river can still hold water even in autumn so should not be neglected later in the year.

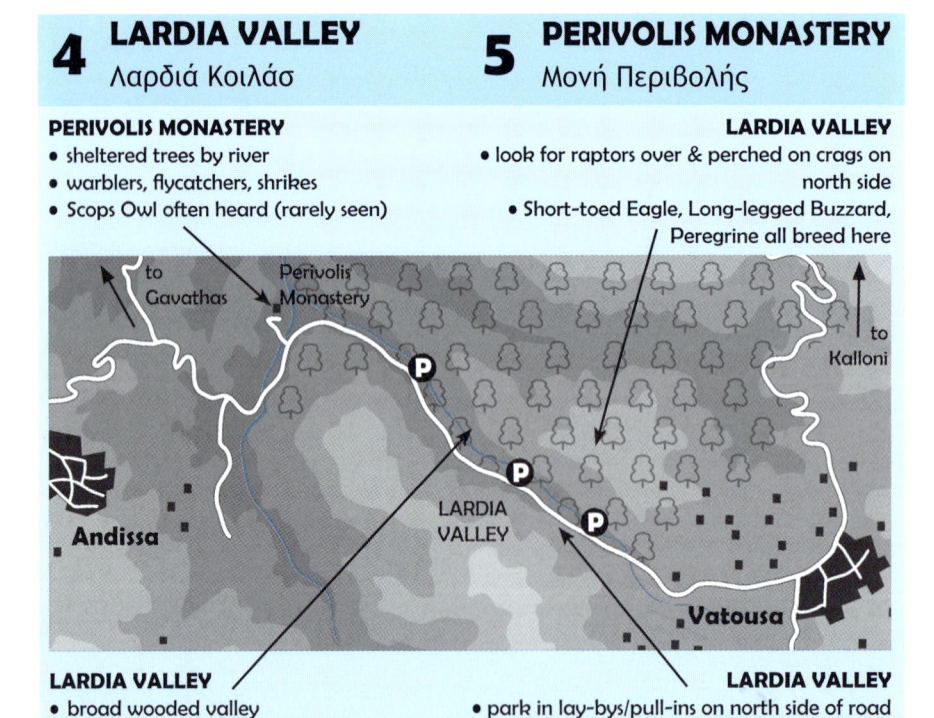

4 LARDIA VALLEY
Λαρδιά Κοιλάσ

5 PERIVOLIS MONASTERY
Μονή Περιβολής

PERIVOLIS MONASTERY
- sheltered trees by river
- warblers, flycatchers, shrikes
- Scops Owl often heard (rarely seen)

LARDIA VALLEY
- look for raptors over & perched on crags on north side
- Short-toed Eagle, Long-legged Buzzard, Peregrine all breed here

LARDIA VALLEY
- broad wooded valley
- Middle Spotted Woodpecker
- excellent for migrants inc. warblers, flycatchers, shrikes, Golden Oriole
- watch for migrant raptors & storks overhead

LARDIA VALLEY
- park in lay-bys/pull-ins on north side of road
- view across valley to north and crags above road to south
- breeding birds inc. Crag Martin, Black-eared Wheatear, Blue Rock-thrush, Subalpine Warbler, Rock Sparrow

4 | LARDIA VALLEY | Κοιλάδα Λαρδιά

This is a deep gorge running east-west along a 3km stretch of the Lardia River (which runs into the Voulgaris (Βούλγαρης) River which runs north into the sea). It is an excellent stop-off when travelling to and from the far west (better in the mornings).

LOCATION AND ACCESS The Lardia Valley lies midway between Vatousa and Andissa along the main Kalloni-Sigri road.

The drive from Kalloni, and beyond to Sigri, is scenic and there are plenty of opportunities to stop and explore (too many to mention). Drive slowly and keep alert. Like the rest of the island, birds can appear anywhere!

AREAS TO SEARCH Heading west out of Vatousa, after 2km the road enters the rocky gorge which runs for the next 3km. There are several lay-bys on the right in which you can park and view down into the gorge and up at the crags and slopes above you to the left.

The first lay-by is long and wide and has a small gate near its eastern end (Vatousa end) which opens onto a small path leading down into the valley. This lay-by is an excellent place to stop and has most of the regular resident and summer breeding species around it. Both Crag Martin and Rock Sparrow breed on the crags up to the left. In 2008 and 2009 a single Eastern Bonelli's Warbler took up residence about 100m west of this lay-by.

Continue along the valley stopping at the different lay-bys on your right. After several hundred metres there is a hairpin bend and a small parking area on the right by a large crag. This is an excellent area for Crag Martin and Red-rumped Swallow. Also Rock Sparrow frequently seen here.

SPECIES see below.

NEAREST AMENITIES see below.

---

5 | PERIVOLIS MONASTERY | Μονή Περιβολής

At the western end of the gorge is a turn (signed for the monastery) on your right down to this small monastery which lies next to the confluence of the Lardia/Voulgaris Rivers. There are tall trees offering shady parking on hot days and the valley can be good for warblers and flycatchers. Scops Owl is frequently heard calling here, although rarely seen at roost it is occasionally reported at dusk.

SPECIES (inc. Lardia Valley) **Breeding** Along the length of the gorge expect to see/hear: Black Stork; raptors inc. Short-toed Eagle, Common and Long-legged Buzzards, Peregrine (locally breeding Lesser Kestrel and Eleonora's Falcon also seen over occasionally); Scops Owl; Turtle Dove; Hoopoe; Middle Spotted Woodpecker; hirundines inc. Crag Martin and Red-rumped Swallow; Wren (scarce on the island); Nightingale; Black-eared Wheatear; Blue Rock-thrush; Subalpine Warbler; Rock Nuthatch; Woodchat and Masked Shrikes; Rock Sparrow; Cirl Bunting. **Passage** Regular species inc. raptors, swifts and hirundines over; Thrush Nightingale; warblers inc. Blackcap, Garden, Wood and Icterine; flycatchers; shrikes; Golden Oriole.

NEAREST AMENITIES Vatousa | Βατούσσα (2km) for simple tavernas and petrol, Andissa | Άντισσα (4km) for tavernas (in square), petrol, Sigri | Σίγρι (20km) for tavernas, Eresos | Ερεσος (16km) for bars, tavernas and petrol, Skala Eresou | Σκαλα Ερεσού (20km) for bars, tavernas and ATM and Kalloni | Καλονή (24km) for shops, ATMs and petrol.

PARAKILA TO MESOTOPOS
Παράκοιλα στη Μεσότοπος

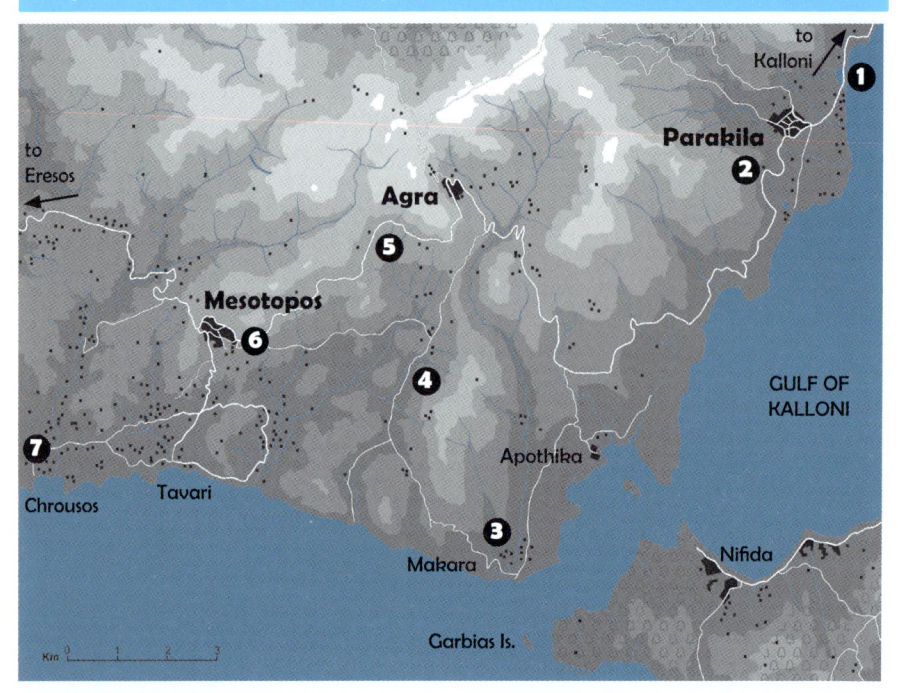

1. Parakila Marsh
2. Aghios Ioannis
3. Makara
4. Konditsia Valley
5. Sideras
6. Mesotopos
7. Chrousos

This is the southern of the two regular routes used by birders to and from the west from the Kalloni area. In addition to the detailed stops below (in order from Kallonis to Eresos), there are many other areas to explore along this southwest section of the island including roadside stops and along tracks north and south (some reaching the coast).

---

1 | PARAKILA MARSH | Βάλτος Παράκοιλων

LOCATION This small wetland lies along the main road 8km southwest of Kalloni (and 6.5km southwest of Skala Kallonis) just before you reach the town of Parakila. It is a difficult site to work without disturbing things and most people leave frustrated that a wetland can hold so little. It dries up from mid-May onwards. In winter it attracts good numbers of wildfowl, Water Rail and herons.

AREAS TO SEARCH There are tracks into the marsh off the main road which you can drive and walk along.

Most of the marsh is surrounded by tall bushes and is difficult to view. Small pools attract waders and herons and the bushes attract warblers.

1 PARAKILA MARSH
Βάλτος Παράκοιλων

2 AGHIOS IOANNIS
Άγιος Ιωάννης

PARAKILA MARSH
- park off road or along tracks
- view from car to avoid flushing birds
- spring — waders, herons, Marsh Harrier, wetland warblers
- winter — Water Rail, wildfowl

AGHIOS IOANNIS
- park in lay-by by bench
- view scrub gulley to north and open hillside to south
- walk up steps to chapel
- breeding birds inc. Nightingale, Black-eared Wheatear, Sombre Tit, Rock Nuthatch, Cinereous & Cretzschmar's Buntings
- passage — raptors, swifts, Bee-eater, hirundines, chats, warblers, shrikes, Golden Oriole

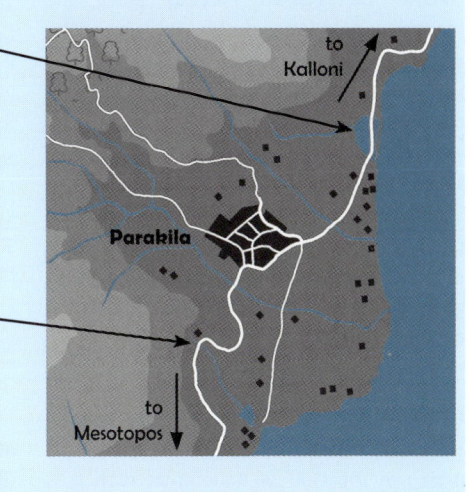

SPECIES Spring Herons; crakes (difficult); Marsh Harrier; waders inc. breeding Black-winged Stilt; chats; warblers inc. Great Reed and Olivaceous. **Winter** Wildfowl; Great Bittern; Water Rail.

NEAREST AMENITIES Parakila | Παράκοιλα (1km) has shops and petrol. Kalloni | Καλλονή (8km) for shops, ATMs and petrol (closed Sundays). Skala Kallonis | Σκάλα Καλλονής (6.5km) for tavernas and shops.

---

2 | AGHIOS IOANNIS | Άγιος Ιωάννης

This is the nearest site to Kalloni for breeding Cinereous Bunting.

LOCATION This is a small scrubby gulley c.1.5km southwest of Parakila. As you round a right hand bend 1km out of Parakila, pull into the lay-by on the right at the next bend on the left. Look for a bench under some trees, a drinking fountain and small gate leading through to steps up the gulley to a chapel. A culvert runs under the road. The lay-by itself affords excellent views up the scrubby gulley and down the hillside on the other side of the road with a fabulous view of Krakala (Κοαχάλα) and its harbour (which you can reach along the track from east of Parakila — see map). You can walk up the steps to the chapel for a great view of the gulley and the ridge running above the site.

AREAS TO SEARCH This is the nearest site to the Kalloni area to start experiencing the 'western' flavour of the island. You will notice the habitat is much rockier and more barren than other coastal areas to the east, and it is the nearest regular site to Kalloni to see Cinereous Bunting, which prefers the higher part of the gully by the chapel.

The ridge running above the site is good for raptors, in particular groups of falcons inc. Eleonora's and Red-footed and Lesser Kestrel.

The rocky area immediately above the lay-by is good for breeding Black-eared Wheatear, Rock Nuthatch and Cretzschmar's Bunting. Sombre Tit regularly breeds along the roadside inc. in fence posts.

The gulley itself can be viewed from the lay-by and along the steps running up its right hand side up to the chapel. It attracts warblers on passage (inc. records of Olive-tree, Great Reed and Eastern Bonelli's), flycatchers and Golden Oriole.

Looking south across the road, the hillside drops away down to Krakala. This slope is also good for chats, wheatears, Rock Nuthatch and buntings.

SPECIES Breeding species (inc. locally): raptors inc. Short-toed Eagle, Long-legged Buzzard; Black-eared Wheatear; Sombre Tit; Rock Nuthatch; Cirl, Cretzschmar's and Cinereous (scarce) Buntings. **Passage** species inc. raptors (especially falcons); swifts; hirundines; Bee-eater; chats; warblers; flycatchers; shrikes; Golden Oriole.

NEAREST AMENITIES Parakila | Παράκοιλα (1.5km) has shops and petrol. Kalloni | Καλλονή (12km) for shops, ATMs and petrol. Skala Kallonis | Σκάλα Καλλονής (10km) for tavernas and shops.

---

3 | MAKARÁ | Μάκαρα

Makara forms the western headland of the mouth of the Gulf of Kalloni. As such it is very good for migrants as well as many of the rockier habitat breeding species.

LOCATION From Aghia Ioannis, continue west towards Eresos and after c.8km the road runs through an open barren area and look for the left turn signed for Apothika (Αποθήκα). Take this turn and after 1.3km take the track on the right (continuing left along the tarmac road continues to Apothika). Follow this rough track down to the coast (4km) and park at the beach.

AREAS TO SEARCH The drive from the main road to the Makara track holds Chukar, Black-eared Wheatear and Rock Nuthatch.

The track from the Apothika road to the beach should be driven slowly with regular stops to look for Chukar, Black-eared and Northern Wheatear, Blue Rock-thrush, Rock Nuthatch and Cretzschmar's Bunting plus migrants inc. swifts, chats and shrikes. About 1km short of the beach the track straightens out and sits above a low flat valley bottom with scattered trees. This area can be viewed from the track and is excellent for migrant Hoopoe, Common Cuckoo, Turtle Dove, shrikes and Golden Orioles on passage.

At the beach you can view the island of Gabrias (Γαρμπιας) in the mouth of the Gulf. This island holds large numbers of breeding Yellow-legged Gulls and Shags, and appears to be a breeding site for Lesser Kestrels, which can be seen in numbers over the island going back and forth from the island to the nearby coast. Jackdaws and Rock Doves (real ones!) can also be seen flying back and forth from the island (the latter almost certainly breed there).

The beach is flanked by small fields and bushes which attract migrants. This whole area can be excellent for passage swifts (all species) with newly arriving birds often feeding low over the beach below knee level!

At the western end of the beach is a small pool flanked with tall bamboo-reed. This pool can attract the odd Little Bittern as well as smaller migrants such as warblers and flycatchers.

Continuing just around the corner there is a near-ruined footbridge and ford across the Makara River. The narrow inland stretch is good for herons, Little Bittern, warblers and flycatchers. The open river mouth is very good for waders and yellow wagtails.

3 MAKARA
Μάκαρα

4 KONDITSIA VALLEY
Κοιλάσ Κοντίτσια

KONDITSIA VALLEY TRACK
- drive slowly & stop often
- typical rocky country species inc. Chukar, Rock Nuthatch, Black-eared Wheatear, Cretzschmar's Bunting
- migrants inc. Golden Oriole, warblers, flycatchers, shrikes
- Spur-thighed Tortoise

MAKARA TRACK
- drive slowly & stop often
- typical open country species inc. Chukar, Rock Nuthatch, Black-eared & Northern Wheatears

- track joins the two areas
! 4x4s only

SHALLOW VALLEY
- migrants inc. chats, warblers, shrikes, flycatchers, Hoopoe, Bee-eater, falcons
- excellent for arriving swifts & hirundines in spring

BEACH, FORD & POND
- park at beach
- beach — early morning look for recently arrrived migrants inc. Quail & Stone-curlew
- pond — warblers, flycatchers
- ford — herons, wagtails, warblers, flycatchers
- to village — warblers, flycatchers
- offshore — look for shearwaters & Mediterranean Monk Seal (very rare)

Agra

to Kalloni

Apothika

GULF OF KALLONI

Makara

Garbias Is.

GARBIAS ISLAND
- view from Makara headland
- Lesser Kestrel, Rock Dove & Jackdaw all to and fro between headland and island

Just across the river, the field on the right is damp often holds Squacco Heron.

Walking up to the houses this area is excellent for migrants inc. chats, warblers, shrikes and buntings.

If your are in a 4x4 then you can take the track to the west beyond the ford which links with the southern end of the Konditsia Valley. Do not attempt in normal car!

SPECIES Breeding species (inc. locally) inc. raptors inc. Lesser Kestrel; Chukar; Black-eared Wheatear; Sombre Tit; Rock Nuthatch; Cirl, Cretzschmar's and Black-headed Buntings. **Passage** species inc. raptors (especially falcons); waders; swifts (especially Alpine); hirundines; Bee-eater; yellow wagtails; chats; wheatears; warblers; flycatchers; shrikes; Golden Oriole.

NEAREST AMENITIES Parakila | Παράκοιλα (13km) has shops and petrol. Mesotopos | Μεσότοπος (18km) for petrol. Kalloni | Καλλονή (25km) for shops, banks and petrol.

---

4 | KONDITSIA VALLEY | Κοιλάς Κοντίτσια (map p. 141)

LOCATION This valley area lies immediately south of Agra (Αγρα) and can be reached either off the main road east of Agra of via Makara (for 4x4 drivers).

ACCESS If you have a 4x4 you can access this area via Makara. Continue across the beach, across the ford and follow the track to the west along a narrow and rocky route.

It is however best accessed off the main road c.1.5 east of Agra, south along a very driveable track which takes you down to the coast. After 6km the track forks. The left fork takes you across to Makara and should only be attempted in a 4x4.

AREAS TO SEARCH From Agra, the top of the valley is broad with lots of tree cover. This area is excellent for Golden Oriole, raptors and shrikes, but many of the trees are too far away to scrutinize for anything smaller.

Continue south and make regular stops to check trees, bushes, ridges, banks, etc. The further south you venture the more chance you have of finding rock pools in what is otherwise a dry river bed. Such pools concentrate migrant passerines and can be good for other wildlife inc. dragonflies.

Along the length of the track look out for typical rocky area species such as Chukar, Rock Nuthatch and Black-eared Wheatear. Also a good area for Spur-thighed Tortoise.

This is a little visited area and is sure to prove fruitful the more time you spend here. Being a south-facing valley the chance of turning up anything in spring must be high!

SPECIES See above text.

---

5 | SIDERAS | Σιδεράς

LOCATION AND AREAS TO SEARCH This is an open stretch of road c.2.5km west of Agra.

Follow the main road west through the village of Agra towards Mesotopos (Μεσότοπος) and Eresos (Ερεσος).

The first place worth stopping is immediately outside the village by the 'two towers'. Park on your right at the top of the hill just before the towers. Search the surrounding area, before and beyond the towers, for Rock Sparrow, Cinereous and Cretzschmar's Buntings.

After c.1.5km the road runs downhill and begins to bear left forming a long sweeping bend. Look for a culvert running under the road and to the left the hillside slopes away

5 SIDERAS
Σιδεράς

AGRA TOWERS
- view either side of towers (species — see text)

OPEN HILLSIDE
- park carefully on roadside
- view down hillside into shallow valley
- check hillside above road
- Chukar
- raptors inc. breeding Short-toed Eagle & Long-legged Buzzard & frequent Lesser Kestrel & Eleonora's Falcon
- Cretzschmar's & Cinereous Buntings
- Rock Sparrow & occ. Rufous Bush Robin
- also a good area for migrants inc. raptors, swifts, Roller, Bee-eater & Golden Oriole

with scattered trees, boulders following dry streambeds and some old ruins. A line of telegraph wires cuts through the shallow valley heading east-west. Just beyond a culvert is a track on the right leading uphill with a small corrugated hut at the roadside. There is a small tree here by the road (where there is often a donkey sat in its shade).

The slope down below the main road holds Chukar, Black-eared Wheatear, Rock Sparrow and Cretzschmar's and Cinereous Buntings. Rufous Bush Robin has also been recorded here. The area also holds breeding Short-toed Eagle and Long-legged Buzzard and frequently attracts Lesser Kestrel and Eleonora's Falcon. It is also a good area for migrants inc. raptors, swifts, Roller, Bee-eater and Golden Oriole.

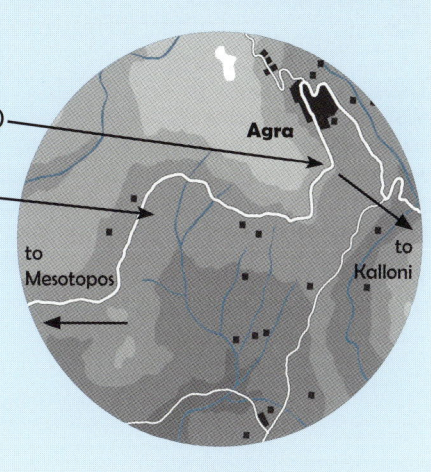

SPECIES See above text.

NEAREST AMENITIES Parakila | Παράκοιλα (20km) has shops and petrol. Mesotopos | Μεσότοπος (5km) for petrol. Eresos | Ερεσος (24km) for shops, bars, tavernas and petrol.

Cretzschmar's Bunting
breeds in rocky areas of the centre, north and west.

6 MESOTOPOS
Μεσότοπος

LANGADA VALLEY
- park carefully on roadside
- Middle Spotted Woodpecker
- Sombre Tit
- migrants inc. warblers, flycatchers, shrikes & Golden Oriole

DRINKING FOUNTAIN
- park in lay-by at fountain
- path up left hand side of fountain
- good for warblers & flycatchers

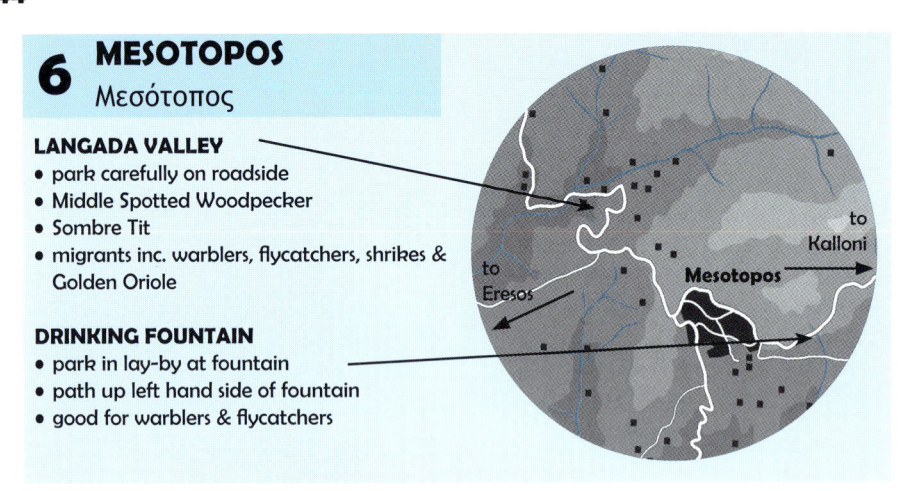

6 | MESOTOPOS | Μεσότοπος

LOCATION AND AREAS TO SEARCH There are two sites around Mesotopos worth checking.

Drinking fountain east of Mesotopos Just east of the town is a lay-by on the right as you approach the town (near an Eko garage) with a drinking fountain under some tall trees. This area is a little migrant trap for warblers (inc. Olive-tree), flycatchers, etc.

Langada (Λαγκάδα) Valley Around 2.5km west of Mesotopos the road gets very bendy. After a tight right bend, the road turns left over a culvert, straightens and then another sharp left bend. Here the road bisects a dry valley which is covered with scattered trees running downhill to your left. This little wooded valley is excellent for migrants inc. Golden Oriole and resident species inc. Middle Spotted Woodpecker and Sombre Tit. Look for raptors overhead inc. Short-toed Eagle and Long-legged Buzzard.

SPECIES See above text.

NEAREST AMENITIES Mesotopos | Μεσότοπος (2.5km) for petrol. Eresos | Ερεσος (16.5km) for shops, bars, tavernas and petrol.

7 | CHROUSOS | Χρούσος

This is a lush green valley by the sea southwest of Mesotopos. It is a real migrant trap in autumn when the valley remains irrigated keeping this area as a lush green oasis.

LOCATION AND AREAS TO SEARCH The main Kalloni-Eresos road by-passes the town of Mesotopos with the town below you on the left as you travel towards Eresos. At the west end of the town is a sharp turn on the left down into the town. The road drops steeply with a hard right turn at the bottom and continues through outskirts of the town. Follow the road south along the tarmac road towards Tavari (Ταβάρι). After c.2.3km from the town, there is a turn on the right along a rough track which fords a stream after only a few metres. Turn along here. Follow this track for 5km to Chrousos.

The ford off the Tavari road is worth checking for migrants and as conditions get drier into May, the water here becomes increasingly important for local breeding birds in the surrounding dry landscape. Species seen here inc. Rock Sparrow, Cretzschmar's Bunting and Rufous Bush Robin. Continue along the track down to a right turn where the track bisects a line of trees (following a dry stream bed). This little gulley of trees can be excellent for

7 CHROUSOS
Χρούσος

FORD
- migrants in scrub inc. warblers & flycatchers
- local breeding birds coming to drink inc. Rock Sparrow, Cretzschmar's Bunting & Rufous Bush Robin

CHROUSOS — IRRIGATED FIELDS
- can be exceptional in autumn
- migrants inc. hirundines, chats, yellow wagtails, warblers, shrikes, flycatchers

CHROUSOS — TRACK TO BEACH
- hillside on right excellent for hunting falcons inc. Eleonora's & Lesser Kestrel
- migrant wheatears, chats, shrikes
- taverna on edge of village very good for drinks — breeding Sombre Tit in garden!

RIDGE
- exiting raptors follow this ridge south in autumn
- excellent for hunting falcons inc. Eleonora's & Lesser Kestrel

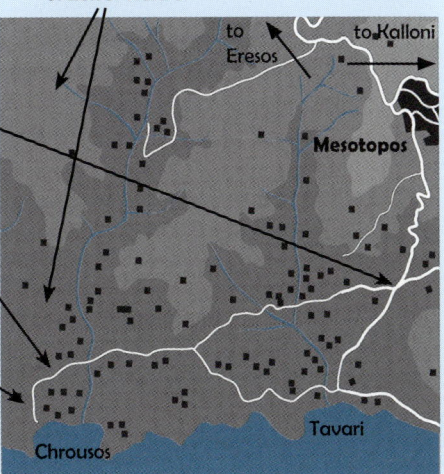

migrants. Follow the track looking out for Chukar and wheatears.

Continue along the track. You will see a left turn (to Tavari) just over 2km from the ford. Ignore and continue straight on to Chrousos.

At Chrousos go over the river bed (rarely holds water) and park just as you drop down into the village (you can drive down to the beach but you will miss a lot of the area if you do). You can walk from here along the main track through the village and fields and down to the beach (c.1km). This whole area is excellent for migrants, and comes into its own in autumn when much of this flat valley bottom remains irrigated and is a lush green oasis in an otherwise dry barren landscape. Wagtails, chats, wheatears, warblers, flycatchers and shrikes can all occur in good numbers (in autumn you might encounter hundreds of birds in the valley bottom). Hirundines and swifts feed overhead and being a south-facing valley it is an exit point for south-moving raptors in autumn. The ridge running down to the coast is excellent for both migrating and feeding raptors inc. Eleonora's Falcon and Lesser Kestrel.

The taverna along the beach access track is usually closed, but if you require only drinks, don't be afraid to knock or shout and ask. The owners are very friendly and always accommodating if around. The flower covered taverna veranda is a lovely place to rest with a cold drink watching butterflies on the flowers and Sombre Tits in the garden.

SPECIES Breeding (inc. local breeders) inc. raptors inc. Short-toed Eagle, Long-legged Buzzard, Lesser Kestrel, Eleonora's Falcon, Peregrine; Rufous Bush Robin; Black-eared Wheatear; Blue Rock-thrush; Sombre Tit; Rock Nuthatch; Rock Sparrow; Cirl, Cretzschmar's and Black-headed Buntings. **Passage** species inc. raptors (especially falcons); swifts; hirundines; Bee-eater; chats; warblers; flycatchers; shrikes; Golden Oriole.

NEAREST AMENITIES Mesotopos | Μεσότοπος (7km) for petrol. Eresos | Ερεσος (26km) for shops, bars, tavernas and petrol. If the taverna on the beach track appears closed, shout and if the owners are around they will sell drinks (ensure you have small change — no large notes).

SIGRI & ERESOS
Σίγρι και Ερεσος

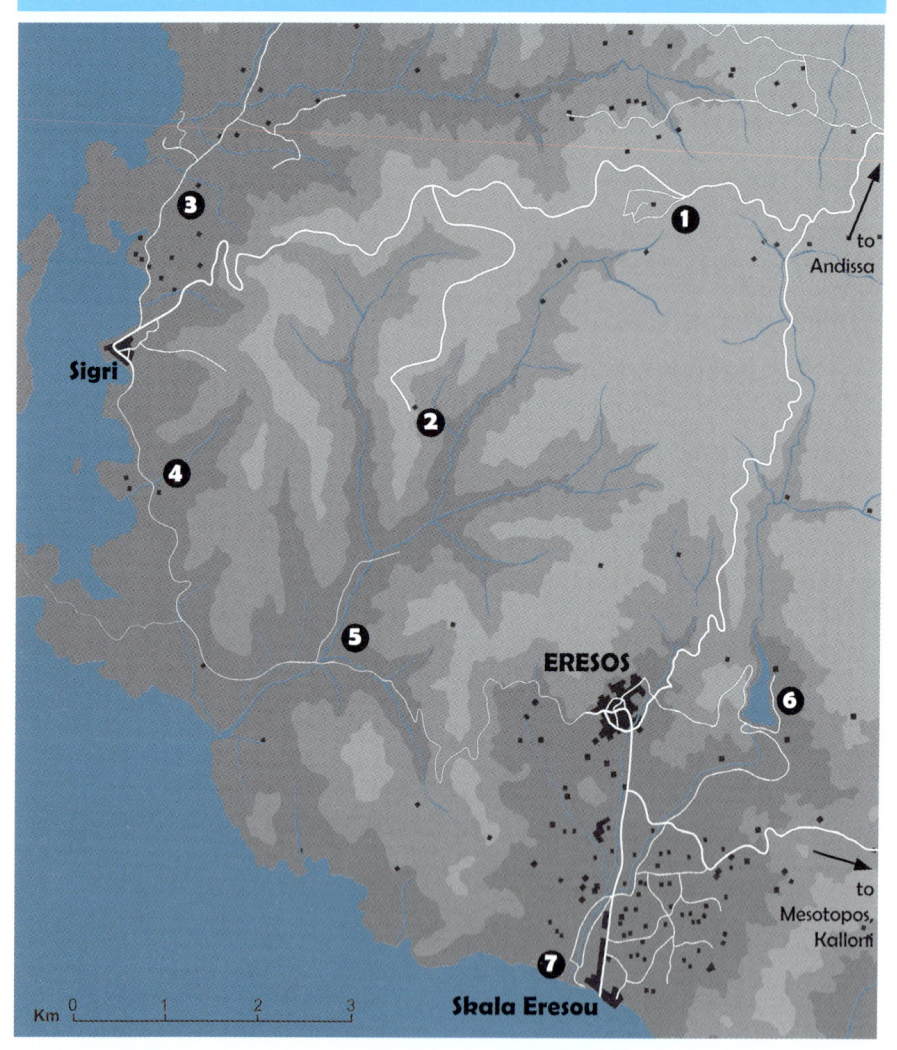

1. Ipsilou
2. Petrified Forest
3. Sigri Fields & Faneromeni
4. Sigri Old Sanatorium
5. Meladia Valley
6. Pithariou Reservoir
7. Vergias River

The far west of the island is dominated by open, barren, rocky country. It's a very contrasting landscape to the soft, more rolling wooded central and eastern areas with their olive groves and large areas of woodland. Migrants are concentrated along river valleys with good cover including scrub, arable fields, fig groves and some small wooded areas.

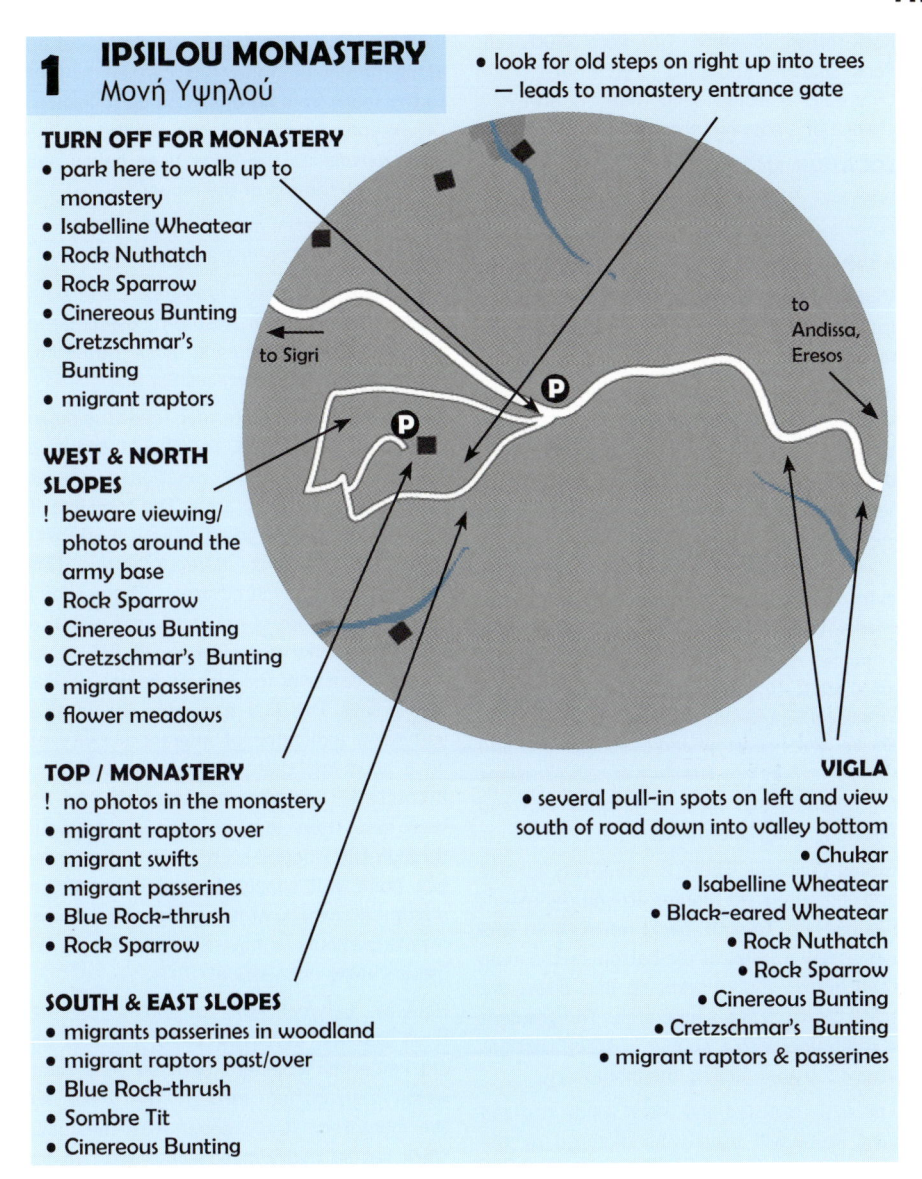

1 IPSILOU MONASTERY
Μονή Υψηλού

TURN OFF FOR MONASTERY
- park here to walk up to monastery
- Isabelline Wheatear
- Rock Nuthatch
- Rock Sparrow
- Cinereous Bunting
- Cretzschmar's Bunting
- migrant raptors

WEST & NORTH SLOPES
! beware viewing/ photos around the army base
- Rock Sparrow
- Cinereous Bunting
- Cretzschmar's Bunting
- migrant passerines
- flower meadows

TOP / MONASTERY
! no photos in the monastery
- migrant raptors over
- migrant swifts
- migrant passerines
- Blue Rock-thrush
- Rock Sparrow

SOUTH & EAST SLOPES
- migrants passerines in woodland
- migrant raptors past/over
- Blue Rock-thrush
- Sombre Tit
- Cinereous Bunting

- look for old steps on right up into trees — leads to monastery entrance gate

to Sigri

to Andissa, Eresos

VIGLA
- several pull-in spots on left and view south of road down into valley bottom
- Chukar
- Isabelline Wheatear
- Black-eared Wheatear
- Rock Nuthatch
- Rock Sparrow
- Cinereous Bunting
- Cretzschmar's Bunting
- migrant raptors & passerines

---

1 | IPSILOU MONASTERY | Μονή Υψηλού

Ipsilou is a spectacular conical mount with a small monastery sat on its peak. It is the highest part of the far western end of the island and its tree-covered slopes are a magnet for migrants in both spring and autumn. Falls of migrants here can be exceptional and during a major fall, the trees can be packed with birds and on its day is unrivalled on the island. Even during quieter migration periods there are always plenty of breeding species to look for inc. Chukar, Little Owl, Isabelline Wheatear, Blue

Rock-thrush, Sombre Tit, Rock Nuthatch, Rock Sparrow and Cirl, Cretzschmar's and Cinereous Buntings, and there is always a chance of a passing raptor.

LOCATION AND ACCESS Ipsilou lies midway between Andissa and Sigri along the main Kalloni-Sigri road.

AREAS TO SEARCH

Vigla (Βίγλα) This area lies 1.5km east of Ipsilou on the main road as you approach the monastery.

As you approach from Andissa and the Lardia Valley, at the Sigri-Eresos-Andissa junction turn right towards Sigri. The road bends left, then right, and along this next section are several rough pull-ins on your left to park and view the area. The second of these areas sits above a shallow dry valley with a narrow dry gully running down the slope to the left of the road with a culvert just beyond and obvious telegraph poles. This area in particular is very good for Isabelline and Black-eared Wheatears, Rock Nuthatch, Woodchat Shrike, Rock Sparrow and Cretzschmar's and Cinereous Bunting. The area is also excellent for migrants inc. raptors (inc. harriers and falcons), Roller and shrikes.

Ipsilou (Υψηλού) There is a one-way tarmac and concrete road running around the mount heading up to and back down from the monastery. Parking at the bottom by the main road allows you to walk up and down the track taking in the whole area. The gradient is moderate with a couple of steep sections at the top approaching the monastery.

This is an exposed and often windy site and your route will usually be dictated by the conditions in order to find the best areas out of the wind. On stiller days my preferred route is always to park at the main road and walk up the left hand (down for vehicles) road. The details which follow take this route. The main reason I prefer this route is that the view to the south is not only spectacular, but in spring allows you to keep an eye out for approaching raptors. Also, on good fall days, birds move up from the coast inland and up along the Meladia Valley (you can see the ford to the south from here) and on up to Ipsilou. On exceptional days you can experience the birds moving up the slope from below and past you to the top of the mount.

The walk up to the monastery should take 1+ hours depending on migrant activity.

Before leaving the main road area, check both sides of the road for Northern, Black-eared and Isabelline Wheatears, Rock Nuthatch, Rock Sparrow and Cinereous Bunting.

Walk up the left hand tarmac road (the down section when driving). You should continue checking for the above mentioned species along this open rocky area. The tree line is very obvious and as you approach it you will no doubt here singing Cinereous Bunting. This is one of their favoured areas. They usually sing from the tops of oak trees, but will also sing from rocks (inc. low down flat rocks — not necessarily the biggest or one with a high point). This first tree edge should give you some indication of migrant activity as on a good day there are usually warblers, flycatchers, Common Redstart, etc. to be seen here. How long it takes you to walk through the wooded section up to the army gun point will simply depend on how the migrant activity is. At its best it has taken me over three hours to move a couple of hundred meters along this section!

Halfway between the beginning of the trees and the first right bend, there is an old kalderimi (cobbled) path on your right which zig-zags up through the trees to the monastery. It is steeper than the main track but still very manageable and can be excellent to get in amongst the trees and see warblers and flycatchers at near-touching distance. It comes out by the gateway into the monastery itself (see below).

Beyond the path on the right up to the monastery, the road gradient reduces slightly and on your left is a hanging hillside leading round to a rocky outcrop ahead of you. This section can be exceptional for funnelling migrants up the slope to the top. It is also an excellent area to view to the south looking for passing raptors, swifts and hirundines.

Beyond the gun point is the approach up to the monastery. Be careful not to view the main army camp to your left with optics or point cameras towards it. The camp residents are more than used to binoculars and cameras at this very busy tourist site, but it is always better to be safe. This area can be very good for Woodlark.

All being well, you have spent most of the morning walking up to the monastery where you can lunch if you have brought a picnic lunch with you. Depending on wind direction, you can lunch at one of three great viewpoints: 1) just below the cobbled parking area there is a little flat plateau which acts as an overspill parking area and looks out due north across the island; 2) walk up to the monastery and at the main arched gateway take the cobbled path down to the right with a great view down over the wooded hillside and sky views to the east and south; or 3) walking through the archway, continue past the chapel (on your left), through the courtyard to a door in the far left corner. Go through the door and out on to the flat area with views to the east. All three spots are fabulous places to spend an hour relaxing and even when there are few migrants around there are always breeding bird activity around you and birds, inc. raptors, passing overhead.

Your descent route now takes you down the concrete road section which is the up route for vehicles. From the monastery follow the road below the army camp and past the meadow on your left. Woodlark is regular here and the flowers can be outstanding. Keep an eye out for Spur-thighed Tortoise in the meadow. Continue down through the trees searching for migrants. Keep an eye on the main rocky outcrop up on your right. This is another good area for Rock Sparrow. From under this outcrop, looking down and left to the road, look for the remnants of a track running off from the main road up onto the hillside to your left. This track area is also good for feeding Rock Sparrow. This wooded section, and the trees across on the other side of the main road is another excellent area for Cinereous Bunting. Continue on down to the bottom and the road junction to your parked vehicle.

SPECIES A brilliant area for migrants and several sought after breeding species. **Breeding** Expect to see the following locally breeding species around or from the mount: raptors inc. Short-toed Eagle, Common and Long-legged Buzzards, Peregrine, Lesser Kestrel and Eleonora's Falcon; Chukar; Little Owl; Turtle Dove; Hoopoe; Middle Spotted Woodpecker; hirundines inc. Crag Martin and Red-rumped Swallow; Northern, Isabelline and Black-eared Wheatears; Blue Rock-thrush; Subalpine Warbler; Rock Nuthatch; Woodchat Shrike; Sombre Tit; Jay; Raven; Rock Sparrow; Cirl, Cretzschmar's and Cinereous Buntings. **Passage** Regular species inc. Black Stork; raptors, all species, but can be very good for Honey-buzzard, falcons inc. Red-footed, Levant Sparrowhawk; Common and Great Spotted Cuckoos; swifts (all species); hirundines (all species); Thrush Nightingale; Common Redstart; wheatears; warblers inc. Orphean, Blackcap, Garden, Wood, Willow, Chiffchaff, Eastern Bonelli's and Icterine; flycatchers (all species); shrikes (all species); Golden Oriole.

OTHER WILDLIFE The area is good for butterflies inc. Eastern Rock Grayling and Large Wall Brown. Persian Squirrel occurs around the monastery. Look out for Spur-thighed Tortoise in the flower meadows. Snake-eyed Skink occurs around the overflow monastery car park area. The soil verges along the access roads are good for ant-lion 'pits'.

NEAREST AMENITIES Andissa | Άντισσα (5km) for tavernas and petrol. Sigri | Σίγρι (12km) for tavernas. Eresos | Ερεσός (12.5km) for bars, tavernas and petrol. Skala Eresou (16.5km) for bars, tavernas and ATM. Kalloni | Καλονή (39km) for shops, ATMs and petrol.

2 PETRIFIED FOREST
Απολιθωμένο Δάσος

ROADSIDE RIDGES
- if stopping for raptors, park carefully away from bends
- hunting flocks of Lesser Kestrels often joined by other falcons inc. Red-footed & Eleonora's

ROADSIDE POOLS
- birds drink & bathe
- Black-eared Wheatear
- Cretzschmar's Bunting
- migrant passerines

ROADSIDE
- Chukar
- raptors inc. harriers & Short-toed Eagle
- Black-eared Wheatear
- Rock Nuthatch
- Rock Sparrow
- Cretzschmar's Bunting

PETRIFIED FOREST PARK
- entrance charge
- Café & toilets for park visitors
- walks of different lengths (1-5km)
- few petrified trees standing — one 11m tall specimen
- no cover once in park
- museum in Sigri is possibly better for forest history & café & toilets (entrance charge for museum)

FROM ROADSIDE & CAR PARK
- Chukar
- Isabelline Wheatear
- Black-eared Wheatear
- Rock Nuthatch
- Rock Sparrow
- Cinereous Bunting
- Cretzschmar's Bunting
- migrant raptors & passerines

2 | PETRIFIED FOREST | Απολιθωμένο Δάσος

Travelling from Ipsilou towards Sigri, after 7km you will see a turn on your left signed for the Petrified Forest Park. The 5km drive down to the park centre is excellent for Chukar, Rock Nuthatch, Black-eared Wheatear and other open country birds. There are a couple of roadside pools which are worth checking for drinking and bathing birds.

For more information about the Petrified Forest Park and Museum see Sigri & Faneromeni (p. 154).

To Sigri As you near Sigri you get terrific views of the fertile coastal strip across to Faneromeni. This area is excellent for Lesser Kestrel and passage raptors. The Lesser Kestrel flocks are worth stopping for, as they frequently attract other falcons. I've regularly seen Red-footed Falcons hunting with them, and on one occasion a flock over 40 birds also inc. Hobby and Eleonora's Falcon. The approach to Sigri provides fabulous views of this stunning coastal area.

SPECIES Mainly an area for breeding species inc. Short-toed Eagle, Long-legged Buzzard, and Peregrine Falcon; Chukar; Little Owl; Isabelline and Black-eared Wheatears; Rock Nuthatch; Rock Sparrow; Cinereous and Cretzschmar's Buntings.

NEAREST AMENITIES Andissa | Άντισσα (15km) for tavernas and petrol. Sigri | Σίγρι (15km) for tavernas. Eresos | Ερεσος (23km) for bars, tavernas and petrol. Skala Eresou (27km) for bars, tavernas and ATM. Kalloni | Καλονή (50km) for shops, ATMs and petrol.

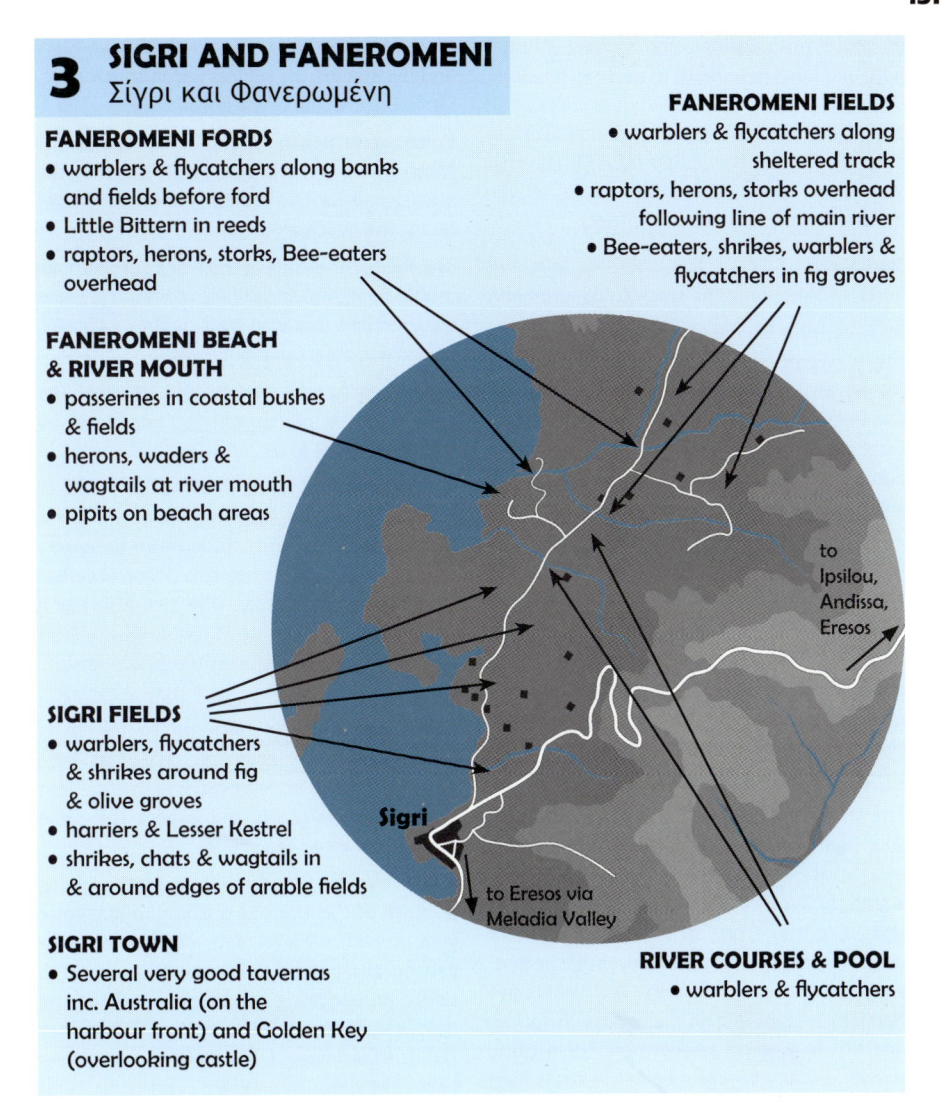

3 SIGRI AND FANEROMENI
Σίγρι και Φανερωμένη

FANEROMENI FORDS
- warblers & flycatchers along banks and fields before ford
- Little Bittern in reeds
- raptors, herons, storks, Bee-eaters overhead

FANEROMENI BEACH & RIVER MOUTH
- passerines in coastal bushes & fields
- herons, waders & wagtails at river mouth
- pipits on beach areas

FANEROMENI FIELDS
- warblers & flycatchers along sheltered track
- raptors, herons, storks overhead following line of main river
- Bee-eaters, shrikes, warblers & flycatchers in fig groves

to Ipsilou, Andissa, Eresos

Sigri

to Eresos via Meladia Valley

SIGRI FIELDS
- warblers, flycatchers & shrikes around fig & olive groves
- harriers & Lesser Kestrel
- shrikes, chats & wagtails in & around edges of arable fields

SIGRI TOWN
- Several very good tavernas inc. Australia (on the harbour front) and Golden Key (overlooking castle)

RIVER COURSES & POOL
- warblers & flycatchers

---

3 | SIGRI and FANEROMENI | Σίγρι και Φανερωμένη

Sigri lies at the very western tip of Lesvos. This fertile coastal strip immediately north of the town is excellent for migrants. Fed by rivers, and intensively irrigated, this shallow, sheltered valley is a lush green area surrounded by sea and barren rocky country, and forms an ideal staging post for tired and hungry migrants.

LOCATION AND ACCESS Sigri can be reached along the main Kalloni road via Andissa and Ipsilou, or from the south, via Eresos and approached either along the main roads via Ipsilou (p. 147) or across country via Meladia Valley (p. 156).

AREAS TO SEARCH Most birders arrive here from mid-morning onwards having stopped on route from Kalloni. Try dashing straight here and into these fields as early as possible. Despite there being relatively few workers in any of the fields in spring, birds do seem to start moving up the valley by mid-morning. Viewing is strictly from the tracks as the fields can't be disturbed by birders

Sigri Fields (Λιβάδια Σίγριου) This area lies north of Sigri along the track to Faneromeni.

Arriving from Ipsilou, as you drop down into the town, you pass a new road on the left (at an angle running uphill and signed for the Petrified Forest Museum – see p. 154). Continue straight on heading for the harbour, but as the sea comes into view, there is a sharp turn along the seafront on your right. This is the Faneromeni road-cum-track. The fields just past the houses on your right are good for Jackdaw and White Wagtail. In winter and spring you might chance a Kingfisher along the sea edge here.

Park carefully anywhere along this track taking care not to block field entrances. Beware also that farm machinery and lorries use this road, so leave plenty of passing space.

The sheltered fields, olive and fig groves on your right are excellent for songbird migrants inc. chats, wheatears, yellow wagtails, warblers, flycatchers, shrikes, Golden Oriole and buntings. The area is excellent for observing larger birds passing over inc. herons, storks and raptors. Marsh and Montagu's Harriers are present on many days in spring, and this is as good as anywhere for a Pallid Harrier. Locally breeding Lesser Kestrels hunt the area and you can get staggering views along this section. Check flocks of falcons for Red-footed, while Eleonora's Falcon also occurs throughout the area.

Faneromeni Lower Ford (Κάτω Πέρασμα Ποταμού Φανερωμένης) After 2.7km there is a left turn down to the sea (signed for the beach). Take the first right turn to the ford.

View the river from the ford and search the fields before and after the ford. The ford area in particular can be busy with passerine migrants inc. wagtails, warblers and flycatchers, as well as heron species inc. Little Bittern and Night-heron.

Faneromeni Beach (Παραλία Φανερωμένης) After 2.7km there is a left turn down to the sea (signed for the beach). Continue straight on for the beach area.

The fields either side of the track cuts through arable fields which can be excellent for close views of Red-throated Pipit, yellow wagtails, chats, wheatears and buntings.

At the beach, park on your left. Beware! The sand is soft in places and you would not be the first to sink in it!

Continue on foot along the track to the river mouth. This area is excellent for waders, herons, Little Bittern, storks, etc. Audouin's Gull has been seen along this beach area but is by no means regular. The site also has a good record for Citrine Wagtail. Tawny Pipit can often be found around the beach area.

Faneromeni Lower Fields (Νότια Λιβάδια Φανερωμένης) Head back up to the main Faneromeni track and turn left. This next section of fields and groves is also excellent for songbird migrants and expect the same sort of species as Sigri Fields.

If you have the time it really is worth walking as much of this track as possible to maximise your search. During fall conditions birds can be everywhere – on the tracks, in the fields, on hedgerows and fences, around the field edges, in the olive groves. I find that the further away from Sigri you go along here, the more birds there tend to be. This might be due to birds moving north through the shallow valley during the morning and settling in the better feeding areas further away from the town.

Along the track on your right is a little pool set into the bank. It's not worth standing by the pool as your presence will put off many birds coming down to the pool. Try pulling your car up on the left and sitting and seeing what comes down to drink and bath. Flycatchers often get in here, as do warblers, and species such as Penduline Tit and Rufous Bush Robin have been seen.

There are a couple of minor tracks to explore along here, but again, do not enter fields.

The olive and fig groves along here hold breeding Masked Shrike and occasionally attracts passage Olive-tree Warbler.

Faneromeni Western Fields (Δυτικά Λιβάδια Φανερωμένης) Beyond the pool, the main track forks with a turn to the right (straight on for the ford — see below). Follow this track through the fields in this area. The main track eventually fords the river after c.2km. The fields and groves along here are excellent for migrants inc. flycatchers and Roller. After c.300 from the Faneromeni track at the top of the hill is a right turn down to another small river ford. This too is excellent for migrants. The whole area is excellent for falcons inc. Red-footed, Eleonora's and Lesser Kestrel plus other raptors inc. harriers, Long-legged Buzzard and Short-toed Eagle.

Faneromeni Upper Ford (Πάνω Πέρασμα Ποταμού Φανερωμένης) The track leads down to the Faneromeni Upper Ford (known as the upper ford). Park here but take care not to block any route across the ford or along the river (which the locals use as a track once it starts to dry out), and take care that no one can block you in! Beware also getting grounded or stuck in the softer gravel spots here. I do not recommend you attempt to drive along the river course like the locals do! You can drive across the ford to park on the other side, but I don't recommend you drive up the narrow lane across the ford either.

The ford area itself can be bustling with birds. Warblers, particularly *acrocephalus* species, and flycatchers (this is one of the most regular sites for Collared) can be found in the tall 'bamboo' phragmites here which flank both banks of the river. Little Bittern is often found here taking refuge in the reeds or along the bank on the left downstream of the ford. Herons and egrets sometimes drop in. Great Snipe is among the waders to look for here, but they can disappear along and under the banks.

If you walk downstream you come to a second ford where a rough track crosses the river. Penduline Tit has bred in this area.

Faneromeni Northern Fields (Βόρεια Λιβάδια Φανερωμένης) If you cross the main river ford on foot, the track goes up a narrow lane. If you're in a group, then very often only those leading the party will get good views of any warblers and flycatchers feeding along here. After 50m the lane meets what is obviously a watercourse which flows down the track ahead of you and off to the left. This is usually wet into early May and birds come down to drink and bathe in the puddle area on your left where the watercourse diverts away from the track. It's also worth sitting and waiting looking down this section as all manner of things have been seen here coming to drink. Olive-tree Warbler occurs in the olive grove here. Continuing on up the lane you come to a track on your right which has low walls and fences and leads into an area of fig groves with a disused small building on your left by a large pine. This area is excellent for many passerines inc. warblers, flycatchers and shrikes, plus Bee-eater, Common Cuckoo, Turtle Dove and Golden Oriole. Having been enclosed by the ford and lane, you have a good skyscape to search, and raptors and storks can often be seen from here heading north along the river valley.

Head back to the lane and turn right and a little further up you come to a second track on your right which leads into fields behind a small farm. You can enter here and walk up to the field opening by the tall trees which looks over a large open field up to a rough hillside. This area can be very good for hunting harriers, Lesser Kestrel, Bee-eater, swifts and hirundines.

These two tracks can be used as picnic spots with good open views to watch out for raptors, etc.

Walk back to the ford along the lane.

SPECIES (for whole area — also see text) **Breeding** inc. Peregrine, Lesser Kestrel and Eleonora's Falcon; Little Owl; Turtle Dove; Hoopoe; Middle Spotted Woodpecker; Woodchat, Masked and Red-backed Shrikes; Spanish Sparrow. **Passage** Regular species inc. raptors, all species but can be very good for Red-footed Falcon, Levant Sparrowhawk; Common and Great Spotted Cuckoos; swifts (all species); hirundines (all species); Thrush Nightingale; Common Redstart; Whinchat; wheatears; warblers; flycatchers (all species); shrikes (all species); Golden Oriole.

OTHER INFORMATION Sigri is home to the **Petrified Forest Park and Museum.** The Park is a massive site (larger and reputed to be better than the more famous Arizona Petrified Forest) and holds the designation of Protected Natural Monument. It is accessed off the main road back towards Ipsilou (see p. 147). There is a small centre and café at the Park centre.

Park opening hours: open daily throughout the year; 1 July – 30 September 0830-1900; closing at 1630 at other times of year. Small charge. Café, toilets.

The new Museum (opened in 2005) is situated in the centre of Sigri and is signed.

The Museum is fantastic with lots of local petrified forest artefacts as well as artefacts from other petrified forests from all over the world. It has some fabulous petrified tree specimens both outside and inside and to some extent is far better than suffering the Park in the raging heat!

Museum opening hours: open daily throughout the year; 1 July – 30 September 0830-2000 (2200 on Fridays); 1 October – 30 June Tuesday-Friday 0830-1630, Saturday and Sunday 0900-1700 (closed Mondays). Small charge. Café, toilets, shop.

Further information on the forest available online at www.petrifiedforest.gr.

Recommended tavernas Sigri has some excellent tavernas inc. Australia (open all year) by the harbour, Remezzo's (June-August) near the castle, and Golden Key (May-September) up the narrow lane towards the beach.

NEAREST AMENITIES Sigri | Σίγρι has tavernas (see above), Andissa | Άντισσα (17km) for tavernas and petrol. Eresos | Ερεσος (via Meladia Valley 16km, via main road 23km) for bars, tavernas and petrol. Skala Eresou | Σκαλα Ερεσού (20/28km) for bars, tavernas. ATM and Kalloni | Καλονή (50km) for shops, ATMs and petrol.

---

4 | SIGRI OLD SANATORIUM | Παλιό Σανατόριο Σίγρι

LOCATION The old sanatorium lies c.2km south of Sigri along the Meladia Valley track.

ACCESS The track to the Meladia Valley is accessed via Sigri town.

From Sigri Take the harbour turn up into the village between the harbour-side tavernas (taverna Australia on your left). Continue through the narrow streets and out on to the beachfront road. Follow this beyond the beach and up onto the rough track at the southern end of the beach. Keep going!

AREAS TO SEARCH The 15km track through the Meladia Valley is excellent for open, rocky country species such as Chukar, Little Owl; Northern and Black-eared Wheatears (and occasional Isabelline on passage), Blue Rock-thrush, Rock Nuthatch, Cretzschmar's Bunting (and occasional Cinereous). I won't mention these species again as they are expected along the length of the route.

Above Sigri beach As soon as the track rises up off Sigri beach the track bears left and stopping here you can see some remains of the marvellous Petrified Forest (on left behind the fence – see page opposite for more information on the Petrified Forest) and

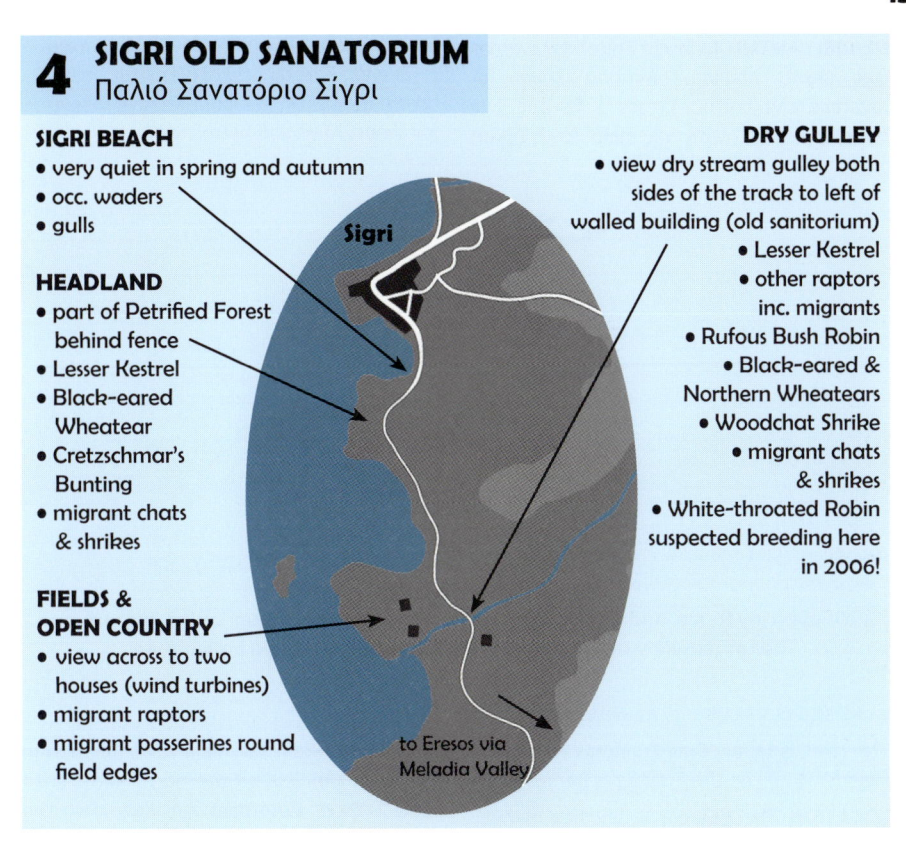

4 SIGRI OLD SANATORIUM
Παλιό Σανατόριο Σίγρι

SIGRI BEACH
- very quiet in spring and autumn
- occ. waders
- gulls

HEADLAND
- part of Petrified Forest behind fence
- Lesser Kestrel
- Black-eared Wheatear
- Cretzschmar's Bunting
- migrant chats & shrikes

FIELDS & OPEN COUNTRY
- view across to two houses (wind turbines)
- migrant raptors
- migrant passerines round field edges

DRY GULLEY
- view dry stream gulley both sides of the track to left of walled building (old sanitorium)
- Lesser Kestrel
- other raptors inc. migrants
- Rufous Bush Robin
- Black-eared & Northern Wheatears
- Woodchat Shrike
- migrant chats & shrikes
- White-throated Robin suspected breeding here in 2006!

Sigri

to Eresos via Meladia Valley

looking back towards Sigri a stunning coastal view. This area can be very good for Lesser Kestrel and occasional Eleonora's Falcon.

Old Sigri Sanatorium Continue past the Petrified Forest area and the track runs down into a shallow valley to a rough riverbed with a walled building beyond and two new houses (with little wind turbines) out towards the sea. Stop at the dry river. This dry gulley area is excellent for migrants and summer breeders inc. Rufous Bush Robin, Woodchat Shrike, Black-headed Bunting. The gulley often holds chats, warblers, flycatchers, shrikes and buntings on passage. White-throated Robin was seen here in 2006 and suspected to be breeding.

SPECIES Many passage and breeding species. **Resident** Peregrine Falcon; Chukar; Little Owl; Sombre Tit; Rock Nuthatch. **Spring Passage** Lesser Kestrel, Eleonora's and Red-footed Falcons; Bee-eater; Hoopoe; hirundines (all species); chats; Thrush Nightingale; shrikes (all species). **Summer breeders** (in and around the area) Raptors inc. Short-toed Eagle, Lesser Kestrel and Eleonora's Falcon; Northern and Black-eared Wheatear; Rufous Bush Robin; Woodchat and Red-backed Shrikes; Cretzschmar's and Black-headed Buntings. White-throated Robin suspected breeding in 2006.

OTHER INFORMATION See Sigri (p. 151–4). **Recommended tavernas** Australia (open all year) by the harbour, Remezzo's (June-August) near the castle, and Golden Key (May-September) up the narrow lane towards the beach.

NEAREST AMENITIES Sigri | Σίγρι has tavernas (see above). Andissa | Άντισσα (20km) for tavernas and petrol. Eresos | Ερεσος (via Meladia Valley 13km, via main road 26km) for bars, tavernas and petrol. Skala Eresou | Σκαλα Ερεσού (17/31km) for bars, tavernas and ATM. Kalloni | Καλονή (53km) for shops, ATMs and petrol.

Collared Flycatcher
is always a joy to see, and this dazzling flycatcher is a scarce annual spring migrant and occurs regularly at sites in the west including Ipsilou and Faneromeni

5 | MELADIA VALLEY | Κοιλάδα Μελαδιάς

The river is labelled as Tsihliotas River (not Meladia River) on the Freytag & Berndt map.

LOCATION The Meladia Valley lies midway between Eresos and Sigri along a rough dirt track between these two towns. The drive and stops along this 16km route can provide some of the most memorable scenery and birding experiences of your stay on Lesvos. It takes you through the truly barren rocky habitat and gets you up close to many species, and cuts across the Meladia River Valley at its coastal plain which is a major migrant hotspot, especially in spring.

ACCESS The track to the Meladia Valley is accessed from either Eresos or Sigri.

From Sigri From the harbour turn up into the village between the harbour-side tavernas (taverna Australia on your left). Continue through the narrow streets and out on to the beachfront road. Follow this beyond the beach and up onto the rough track at the southern end of the beach. Keep going!

From Eresos From the main road junction in the town (Andissa to the north and signed Skala Eresou, Mesotopos and Kalloni to the east), turn towards the town square (opposite direction to Skala Eresou, etc) and then take your next left into a wide, pale dusty track area between the buildings (the area is used for parking by the locals). Then take your next right between the houses up a narrow concrete road (signed for Sigri), follow this up past the church (on right) and at a mini crossroads, turn left, out past the last houses (on right) and out into the open countryside. Keep following this track!

AREAS TO SEARCH The whole drive is great for open, rocky country species such as Chukar, Little Owl, Northern and Black-eared Wheatears (and occasional Isabelline on passage), Blue Rock-thrush, Rock Nuthatch, Cretzschmar's and Cinerous Buntings. I won't mention these species again as they are expected along the length of the route.

5 MELADIA VALLEY
Κοιλάδα Μελαδιάς

CHAPEL
- migrant passerines in trees
- pipits, wagtails & shrikes in fields
- Black-headed Bunting

FIG ORCHARD
- can be outstanding in spring
- excellent for migrant passerines
- check small building on left beyond orchard
- Sombre Tit
- watch sky for raptors

RAVINE
- Little Owl on shepherds building
- Lesser Kestrel
- Black-eared Wheatear
- Cretzschmar's Bunting
- chats & shrikes

UPPER VALLEY
- good in spring & autumn
- can be very good for raptors inc. falcons
- migrant passerines
- Chukar

COASTAL MARSH & RIVER MOUTH
- walk down track east of chapel
- raptors inc. harriers
- migrant passerines in fields & scrub
- occ. waders in marsh
- herons & storks in river
- Bee-eater

TRACK TO ERESOS
- raptors
- Chukar
- Woodlark
- Cinereous Bunting
- Cretzschmar's Bunting

LOWLAND SCRUB
- outstanding for migrant chats, shrikes (all species) & buntings
- Rufous Bush Robin, Lesser Grey Shrike & Black-headed Bunting breed

FORD
- can be outstanding in spring
- excellent for migrant passerines
- crakes
- watch the sky for arriving raptors, egrets, herons, storks, swifts, hirundines, Bee-eaters, etc. from the sea

Above Sigri beach (από πάνω Σίγρι παραλία) See p. 154.

Old Sigri Sanatorium (Σίγρι σανατόριο) See p. 154.

Meladia River Plain (Μελάδια Ποτάμι Κάμποσ) Continue past the old sanatorium and follow the track for around 6km. This whole open country is good for raptors inc. Lesser Kestrel, Eleonora's Falcon, Long-legged Buzzard, Short-toed Eagle and migrant harriers (all species), so make regular stops to scan.

At the western end of the plain lies a **small chapel** surrounded by conifers. Park around here (do not block gateways). Search the chapel trees (from outside) and the fields and area around it, including walking back up the track for 200-300m to check the fields. This is a brilliant little site for migrant wagtails, warblers (inc. records of Olive-tree, Eastern Bonelli's, Sardinian, Rüppell's), flycatchers (all species), shrikes (all species) and buntings.

A few hundred metres beyond the chapel is a track on the right leading to the **Meladia River mouth**. You can either walk to here from the chapel or park by the track entrance. Do not drive down the track. The track leads down the western side of the River Meladia out to its mouth. To the west of the mouth is a small wetland area of shallow brackish pools. The river can attract anything – herons, egrets, storks, raptors, Bee-eaters (inc. a flock of seven Blue-cheeked in the influx of this species in spring 2008), warblers, flycatchers, shrikes, etc. The open grassland holds typical open country species and can attract harriers, pipits, wagtails, chats, wheatears. The brackish pools attract little other than the odd wader.

Back at the track junction, the area between here and the river ford (1km) is excellent for shrikes and breeding Rufous Bush Robin.

At the **ford**, park on the left around the track to the left (which leads up the Meladia Valley).

In spring the ford holds water which creates pools either side of the concrete ford pad. These are excellent for herons (especially Little Bittern), crakes (has recorded Baillon's) and migrant passerines such as warblers (inc. Great Reed) and flycatchers (Collared annual here). Swifts (all species) and hirundines can fill the sky as they arrive from the south and feed over the insect-rich aerial soup over the wet river valley. Larger migrants such as raptors, herons and storks can be seen arriving from the south, circling overhead looking for a safe area to land or searching for food.

As this route gets ever more popular, arriving here in spring and finding the place deserted is getting increasingly rare, but if you can get here as early in the day as possible the experience can be magical. During major falls it matters little what time you arrive, or how many people are here, as the place can be literally dripping with migrants.

Walking along the **track inland** up the valley you come to a **small fig grove** after 500m (do not enter the fig grove). This grove can be fabulous, holding warblers (Great Reed, Wood and Icterine regular and has occasional records of Olive-tree and Eastern Bonelli's), flycatchers (all species), shrikes and Sombre Tit (breeds). Migrant Sardinian, Rüppell's and Subalpine Warblers can also be occasionally found in the low surrounding scrub. Beyond the olive grove, set back on the left is an old shepherd's building covered in vegetation and vines. This can be a great little corner for migrants inc. species such as Thrush Nightingale.

You can proceed on foot up the valley, but it's probably best to drive if you want to cover much or all of the next 2km up the valley (you could walk up the valley as far as the Petrified Forest is you want). There are numerous sheep gates across the track. Ensure to leave them all as you found them (closed means closed, open means open – do not close open gates – they may be intentionally left open by the farmer). The track follows the river (crossing it at one point) and is usually lined with migrants and is very good for raptors moving up and down the valley inc. breeding Long-legged Buzzard and Short-toed Eagle, but virtually anything can occur on passage. Common and Lesser Kestrel, Eleonora's (suspected) and Peregrine Falcons all breed around the wider area, and Red-footed Falcon and harriers are regular in spring and autumn. Although you can chance upon Chukar anywhere in this area, this valley has delivered my only ever double-figure count of the species.

Although this valley can be fabulous in spring (a spring visit is rarely anything other than good), it can also be very good in autumn. The river is completely dry in September, but migrant herons, storks, raptors and passerines all follow the valley south from the middle of the island to the north. Looking from the ford north you can see Ipsilou Mount and you can see why this valley is part of a major north-south migration route through the west of the island.

Back at the river ford, you can cross the ford and search the area immediately beyond. A track takes you down into the scrubby area on your left. Again, expect anything on a good day inc. migrant chats, wheatears, warblers and shrikes. Rufous Bush Robin and Sombre Tit breed in the area.

Meladia River Ford to Eresos This 8km is probably the most neglected stretch of the 15km route. Those leaving the valley tend to find they've used up all their day before heading back east, or those arriving are itching to get to the plain! Expect to see more of the same regular species and stops will provide the chance of scarcer species such as Cinereous Bunting and Chukar. Many passerines dust-bathe on the track along this section, in particualr flocks of Crested Lark and Woodlark congregate near dusk.

Just short of Eresos is the **chapel of Agias Konstantinos and Eleni**. The valley area to the west of the chapel hs scattered trees and is good for migrants. The chapel itself is surrounded by lush bushes and is another little migrant trap attracting warblers, flycatchers and Golden Oriole. Sombre Tit breeds here.

Arriving in Eresos, as you come past the first houses on your left, you will come to a mini-crossroads where you turn right. After about 50m the road forks, bear left. On your left is a church with a prominent cross. Follow the concrete road down the narrow lane between the houses and when it reaches an open area, turn left up to the main road. Turn left for the town (tavernas, cafés and shops), or right to the main road juction — left to Ipsilou and Andissa, straight on for Skala Eresou, Mesotopos and Kalloni.

SPECIES The whole area is excellent for migrants and many breeding species. **Resident** Raptors inc. Long-legged Buzzard and Peregrine; Chukar; Little Owl; Blue Rock-thrush; Sombre Tit; Rock Nuthatch. **Spring Passage** inc. herons, egrets and storks; raptors — pretty much anything going through but regular harriers, Honey-buzzard, Lesser Kestrel, Eleonora's and Red-footed Falcons; crakes; waders; swifts (all species); Bee-eater; Hoopoe; hirundines (all species); chats inc. Rufous Bush Robin; Thrush Nightingale; warblers — pretty much anything but regular Wood and Icterine; flycatchers (all species); shrikes (all species); buntings (inc. annual Ortolan). **Summer breeders** (in and around the area) inc. raptors inc. Short-toed Eagle, Lesser Kestrel and Eleonora's Falcon; Bee-eater; Black-eared Wheatear; Woodchat, Lesser Grey and Red-backed Shrikes; Cretzschmar's, Cinereous (rare) and Black-headed Buntings.

NEAREST AMENITIES From the river ford, Eresos | Ερεσος (8km) has shops, tavernas, bars and petrol. Sigri | Σίγρι (8km) has several good tavernas. Skala Eresou | Σκαλα Ερεσού (12km) for bars, tavernas and ATM.

6 PITHARIOU RESERVOIR
Λιμνοδεξαμενή Πιθαρίου

RESERVOIR
- view from tracks either side or dam at southern end
- largest freshwater body on the island
- holds water year-round
- very good during summer & autumn
- wildfowl especially at northern arm
- waders when shallow edges exposed
- occasional herons, egrets, storks & flamingos
- Yellow-legged Gulls year-round
- hirundines over water
- Great Crested & Black-necked Grebes in winter

TRACKS
- excellent reservoir views — west side best in morning, east side in evening
- good in spring & autumn
- migrant passerines
- check ridges & crags for raptors, Crag Martin & Blue Rock-thrush

REEDS & FORD
- migrant warblers
- birds come to drink

OLD BUILDINGS
- open area
- migrant passerines inc. warblers, flycatchers, chats, wheatears
- buntings inc. roosting flock of Cirl in autumn & winter

BRIDGE & GULLEY
- migrants inc. warblers, flycatchers

RIDGE & CRAGS
- raptors inc. Long-legged Buzzard, Common Kestrel, Peregrine
- Crag Martin
- Blue Rock-thrush

RIVER VERGIAS
- warblers, flycatchers
- wagtails — White & 'yellow' on passage, Grey in winter
- waders in spring inc. Common Sandpiper & Temminck's Stint

---

6 | PITHARIOU RESERVOIR | Λιμνοδεξαμενή Πιθαρίου

This little known reservoir just happens to be the largest area of standing water on the island! It remains little known because it is still not marked on the more popular blue Road Editions 1:70,000 map (even the 2007 edition still doesn't have it marked). It is however marked on the red Freytag & Berndt 1:75,000 map (which few birders appear to use). All maps do however have the monastery marked.

The reservoir was formed by the damming of the River Vergias (Βεργιάς) just below the monastery and although the water level gets much reduced during the summer, it still holds water in the autumn with muddy margins to attract waders.

LOCATION AND ACCESS Pithariou Reservoir lies only 5km from Eresos. There are two access roads, one (the better for birders) lies 1km east of Eresos along the Mesotopos/Kalloni road. Just after an obvious bridge turn left on to a wide dirt track which is signed for the monastery (Μονη). Follow the track along the river (on left) up to the reservoir.

This track can also be reached direct from Skala Eresou by taking the track along the east side of the river from the road bridge at the old ford area. This track leads back up to the main Eresos road. At the main road go straight across and follow this track (with the river still on left) up to the next tarmac road (Eresos-Mesotopos/Kalloni road). Go straight ahead and follow this track to the monastery.

The second approach track is from Eresos itself and lies just north of the town centre road junction along the Andissa road. Take the right turn after 200m signed for the monastery.

AREAS TO SEARCH

The river All rivers, wet or dry, act as migrant traps and routes through the island. This river is no exception. In spring, if the river holds any water by late April it can attract the usual herons, egrets, waders, hirundines, wagtails, warblers, etc. In autumn, warblers, flycatchers and shrikes in particular follow the river south through the island to its mouth at Skala Eresou.

Below the dam As the southern approach track nears the dam, it swings away from the riverbed into a wide, open area with some old buildings on the right. The beginning of the area is marked by a bridge over a tributary to the river. This whole area is worth exploring, particularly the bushes and trees along the right hand side of the area, while the craggy cliffs ahead and to the left may yield raptors.

The open ground can be good for larks, pipits, wheatears and buntings. In autumn there is an impressive pre-roost of Cirl Buntings.

Directly below the dam on the far (left) end, there is a tiny reedbed with a stream fording the track. There is usually a puddle of water in the middle of the forded track which attracts birds down to drink and bath inc. the occasional rarity (Bluethroat was recorded here in autumn 2007).

The dam affords excellent views of nearly all of the open water and in autumn any muddy fringe on the reservoir side. It's also a good spot to scan for raptors.

Monastery track Crossing the dam you can follow (on foot or by car) the track up to the monastery itself (1.5km). This track is best walked in the morning so the sun is behind you when viewing the reservoir (terrible looking across the dam into the afternoon/evening sun). The bushes along this side of the dam can be excellent for migrants, particularly in autumn.

Eresos track Follow the track up the west side of the reservoir, the track itself hugs the reservoir for much of its length before swinging off to the left and back into Eresos (3.5km).

SPECIES A year-round site which can be good for migrants. **All year** Long-legged Buzzard; Little Grebe; Crag Martin; Sombre Tit, Rock Nuthatch; Cirl Bunting. **Spring** Raptors inc. Long-legged Buzzard, Short-toed Eagle, Eleonora's Falcon, Peregrine; swifts (all species); Bee-eater; Hoopoe; hirundines (all species); Black-eared Wheatear; warblers; shrikes. **Autumn** Wildfowl; grebes; herons, egrets, storks, Greater Flamingo occ. occurs here; waders; swifts (all species); Bee-eater; hirundines; pipits; wagtails; chats; wheatears; warblers; flycatchers; shrikes, etc.

NEAREST AMENITIES Eresos | Ερεσος (5km) for shops, tavernas, bars and petrol. Skala Eresou | Σκάλα Ερεσού (8km) for bars, tavernas and ATM.

7 VERGIAS RIVER
Ποταμός Βεργίας

RIVER
- view from road on west side or track on east side (track has less traffic and more riverside over which to search)
- waders inc. Common Sandpiper & Temminck's Stint
- wagtails
- Spanish Sparrow

BEACH
- scan for shearwaters
- migrants sometimes resting up in vegetation on beach occ. inc. Quail & Stone-curlew

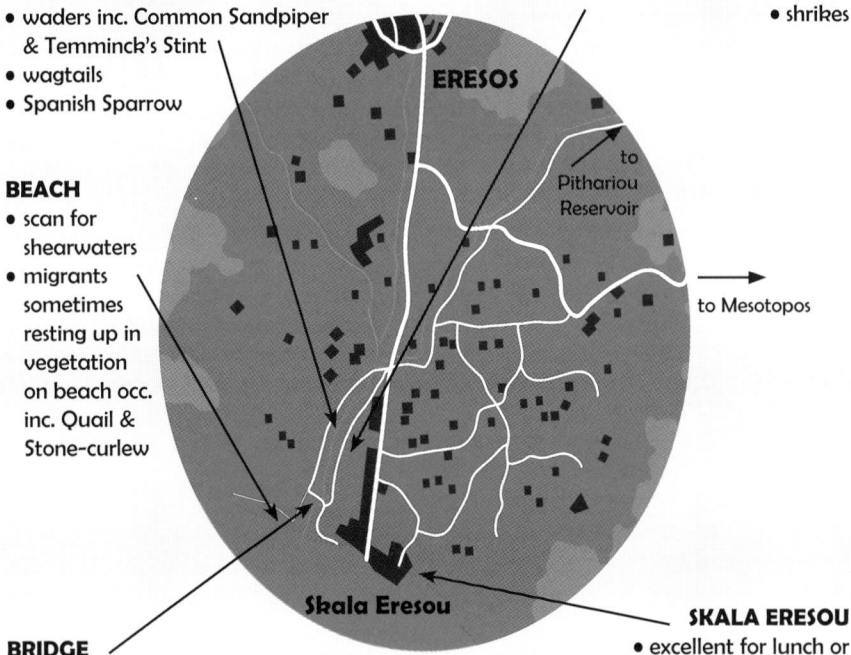

BRIDGE
- park on Skala Eresou side of bridge
- view from bridge
- Little Bittern & Squacco Heron regular
- occ. Little Crake
- waders inc. Common Sandpiper & Temminck's Stint
- wagtails
- warblers inc. Cetti's & Great Reed
- Spanish Sparrow

RIVERSIDE TRACK
- check fields, especially in autumn
- cut fields will hold wagtails & chats
- warblers in field boundaries
- shrikes

SKALA ERESOU
- excellent for lunch or afternoon drinks
- choose one of the seaside tavernas
- watch for Scopoli's (occ.) and Yalkouan (regular) Shearwaters

7 | VERGIAS RIVER | Ποταμός Βεργίας

Skala Eresou is the thriving little seaside resort of Eresos, whose inhabitants spend much of their time there during the peak tourist season. It is also probably the premier Lesbian (as in gay women) resort in Europe. This is due in main to Sappho (poet) originating from nearby Eresos and its reputation as a gay resort continues to be fuelled by TV programmes (many of them sensationalised of course!). Even in peak season it is however a mix of lesbian tourists and Greek nationals from the mainland mingling along the sandy beaches and in the beachfront tavernas and bars. The village itself might be nothing to shout about, but the beachfront tavernas and bars are excellent for relaxing during the hotter hours of a late spring or autumn day and can have a party atmosphere at night.

In spring the place is a ghost town until late May when the main tourist season begins to pick up. Most seasonal bars and tavernas close at the end of September.

The River Vergias (Βεργιάς) (also known as Chalandra River) reaches the sea to the west of the village and is on most birders' stops when out west.

LOCATION AND ACCESS Skala Eresou lies 4km due south of Eresos. Follow the road signs from Eresos. It can also be reached direct from Pithariou Reservoir by following the Vergias River south, across the Eresos-Mesotopos road, then along the river again, across the Eresos-Skala Eresou road, and continue following the river to the new road bridge by the old ford just inland from the river mouth.

AREAS TO SEARCH There are two main areas to search.

River Vergias Turning off the Eresos road you follow the lower reaches of the river down to the sea. The river can be good for waders, wagtails, herons, egrets, occasional crakes and rails and warblers.

If you are either approaching from, or heading up to, Pithariou Reservoir along the east bank track, don't neglect the fields along here which can be excellent for migrants especially wagtails, chats and shrikes.

River road bridge (old ford area) The west bank road and east bank track which follow the river south towards the sea both converge at the road bridge which crosses the river, at what used to be the old ford. Here the river dams slightly and a small pond is formed which also holds water in autumn and is excellent for herons (inc. Squacco), egrets, Little Bittern, wagtails, warblers (inc. Great Reed and Cetti's).

SPECIES A good area for migrants. **Spring** Raptors inc. Long-legged Buzzard, Short-toed Eagle, Eleonora's Falcon, Peregrine; swifts (all species); Bee-eater; Hoopoe; hirundines (all species); chats; warblers; flycatchers; shrikes. **Autumn** Herons, egrets; swifts; Bee-eater; hirundines; pipits; wagtails; chats; wheatears; warblers; flycatchers; shrikes.

NEAREST AMENITIES Skala Eresou has bars, tavernas and an ATM (by Sappho Travel). Eresos | Ερεσος (4km) for shops, tavernas, bars and petrol.

Recommended tavernas Soulatso (Σουλatso) in Skala Eresou is one of the best tavernas on the island. Adonis is also good. Agua is excellent for coffees and snacks and has free wi-fi. In Eresos, 'Sam's' (The Tradition) is the pick of the tavernas in the square.

Little Crake
occurs at several wetland sites in spring, but Metochi Lake remains the number one locality with regular double-figure counts

EASTERN GULF OF KALLONI — MESA TO POLICHNITOS
Ανατολικός Κόλπος Καλλονής, Από Μέσα προς Πολυχνίτος

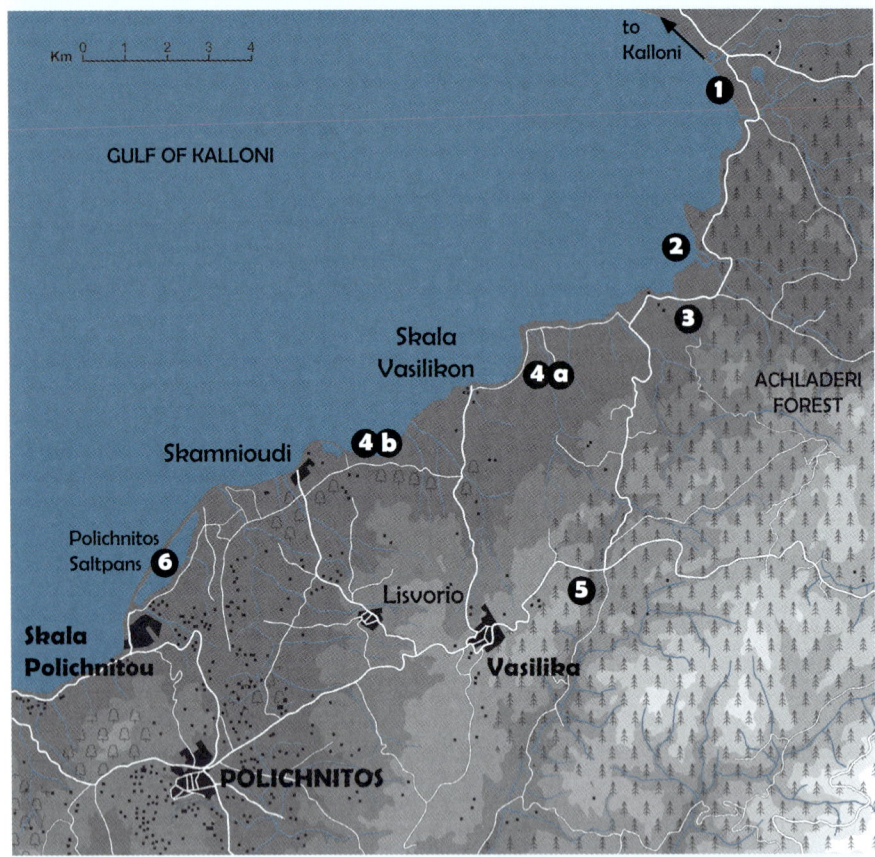

1. Mesa
2. Vouvaris River Mouth
3. Achladeri Forest
4a Achladeri to Skala Vasilikon
4b Skala Vasilikon to Skamnioudi
5. Mikri Limni
6. Polichnitos Saltpans

1 | MESA | Μεςα

This is quite a large area of seasonal coastal wetlands. It is at its best in spring but the main pool holds water throughout the summer as it is fed by the 'tidal' creek at the southern end.

LOCATION Mesa is the area between the Achladeri (Αχλδερή) road and the Kalloni-Mytilini road junction and the creek bridge c.1.3km to the south. On the inland side of the road is a large rocky outcrop with a large pool set behind it. To the southern end is a creek which feeds a marshy area. On the seaward side of the road is an area of low, undulating ground with short sward and pebble areas. The area can be damp and pools form at the northern end near the main road junction. It also includes the wetland area on the north side of the junction which is fed by

1 MESA
Μέσα

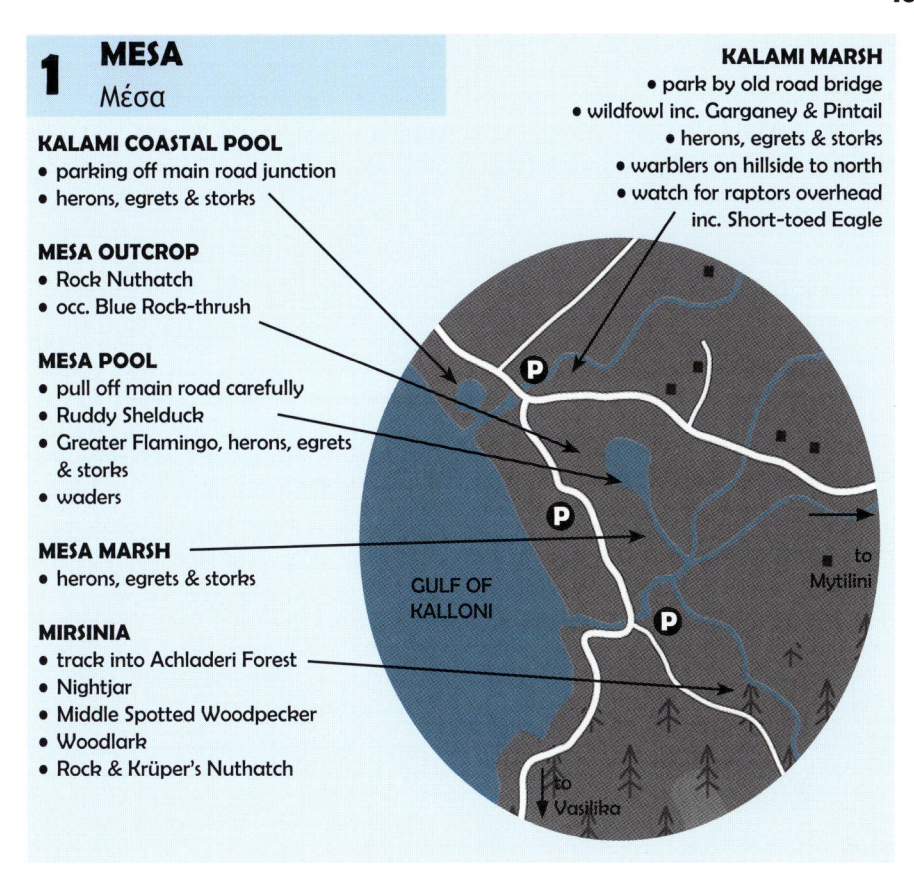

KALAMI COASTAL POOL
- parking off main road junction
- herons, egrets & storks

MESA OUTCROP
- Rock Nuthatch
- occ. Blue Rock-thrush

MESA POOL
- pull off main road carefully
- Ruddy Shelduck
- Greater Flamingo, herons, egrets & storks
- waders

MESA MARSH
- herons, egrets & storks

MIRSINIA
- track into Achladeri Forest
- Nightjar
- Middle Spotted Woodpecker
- Woodlark
- Rock & Krüper's Nuthatch

KALAMI MARSH
- park by old road bridge
- wildfowl inc. Garganey & Pintail
- herons, egrets & storks
- warblers on hillside to north
- watch for raptors overhead inc. Short-toed Eagle

GULF OF KALLONI

to Mytilini

to Vasilika

the Kalami (Καλάμι) River which itself forms a coastal pool by the road junction.

ACCESS The area is accessed from the main Kalloni-Mytilini road east of Kalloni, and the Achladeri road.

AREAS TO SEARCH

Kalami Marsh There is parking by the old road bridge immediately north of the main road junction and you can view the marsh from the old bridge as well as walking down the track on your left running away from the main road.

The marsh is excellent for the expected wildfowl (inc. Garganey in spring and Pintail in autumn and winter) and heron species. The scrubby hillside above the track is good for breeding species such as Subalpine Warbler and Cirl Bunting and has held Rüppell's Warbler.

Kalami coastal pool You can cross the road from the road bridge, or, as you turn onto the Achladeri road, then a right turn into a dirt parking area looks over this coastal pool.

The pool often attracts egrets, herons, storks and waders.

Mesa Rock and Pool There is ample room at several spots to pull off either side of the road in order to view the rocky outcrop and main pool behind.

The rocky outcrop is good for Little Owl, Black-eared Wheatear, occasional Blue Rock-thrush and Rock Nuthatch, and Rufous Bush Robin has bred here. The pool attracts the expected wildfowl inc. good numbers of

Ruddy Shelduck, egrets, herons and waders, but views of the latter aren't great due to the distance of the pool from the road. Do not enter the fields/fenced off areas.

Mesa beach Parking as for the rock and pool. The area holds ground-loving species such as larks, wheatears, Linnet, etc.

The whole area is good for migrant falcons with Hobby and Red-footed Falcon seen regularly, the occasional Lesser Kestrel and Eleonora's Falcon. Lanner has been recorded.

Mirsinia The track running inland from the creek bridge at the south end of the area can be worth exploring. If you follow the main track you pass through the pine forest (past the army camp marked with a 'no entry' symbol on maps), across the Vouvaris River in the forest and brings you out between the Vouvaris River mouth and Achladeri Krüper's Nuthatch site. Nightjar breeds in many of the more open areas along this track (especially at the Mesa end) and Krüper's Nuthatch occurs throughout the forest. The Mesa end of this area is also good for Woodlark, Orphean and Subalpine Warblers, Red-backed and Woodchat Shrikes, Rock Nuthatch. Rufous Bush Robin is occasionally reported from this area.

SPECIES Spring/summer Wildfowl inc. Ruddy Shelduck; Purple Heron, Little and Great White Egrets, Greater Flamingo; Stone-curlew; falcons inc. flocks of migrant Red-footed; waders; Little Owl; Nightjar (along forest tracks); Bee-eater; Tawny Pipit; Short-toed Lark; Rufous Bush Robin (has bred); Blue Rock-thrush; Krüper's Nuthatch (in forest), Rock Nuthatch (rocky outcrops); Linnet. **Autumn/winter** Wildfowl numbers increase as the site gets wetter from late autumn; herons; large numbers of Corn Bunting feed and roost in the area.

NEAREST AMENITIES There is an excellent little seaside taverna just north of the Achlederi army camp (7km) by the turn to Ancient Pyrra. Kalloni | Καλλονή (10km to north) for shops, banks, petrol, etc. Skala Polichnitou | Σκάλα Μολιχνίτου (19km to south) for simple tavernas, shops.

---

2 | VOUVARIS RIVER MOUTH | Εκβολή Ποταμού Βούβαρη

LOCATION The Vouvaris River mouth lies in the northeast corner of the Gulf of Kalloni along the Achladeri (Αχλδερή) road between Mesa (Μεςα) and the Achladeri Krüper's Nuthatch site.

ACCESS Turn off the Kalloni-Mytilini road south along the main road to Achladeri, through Mesa and continue along the Gulf coastal road for a further 3.5km beyond the Mesa creek bridge. After 3.5km you will arrive on a straight section of road sloping gently downhill. Ahead of you is the river mouth and the remains of the former fish ponds. Halfway down the downhill section is a track on your right which leads to the beach. Park here and follow the track down to the river mouth to view the coastal section and the marsh.

Continue further along the road and after a sharp left bend the road turns sharp right through the trees and over the river bridge. There is parking either on the right under the trees before the bridge, at the track on the left before the bridge or along the section of straight road beyond the bridge.

AREAS TO SEARCH

River mouth This coastal section is possibly at its best in autumn and winter. Kingfisher and Grey Wagtail are regular; look for Lesser Black-backed Gull offshore and Stonechat around the reed areas. Pygmy Cormorant has been recorded at the river mouth and feeding along the river up to road bridge. Offshore in winter look for grebes and wildfowl.

2 VOUVARIS RIVER MOUTH
Εκβολή Ποταμού Βούβαρη

3 ACHLADERI FOREST
Δάσος Αχλαδερής

RIVER MOUTH
- gulls offshore inc. 'fuscus' Lesser Black-backed in autumn/winter
- wildfowl inc. Ruddy Shelduck
- winter species inc. Kingfisher, Grey Wagtail & Stonechat
- Pygmy Cormorant has been recorded

ROAD BRIDGE
- Krüper's Nuthatch autumn/winter
- Long-eared Owl (has bred)
- Night-heron (occ. spring roost site)
- Blue Rock-thrush on crag to north

FIELDS
- chats
- warblers in hedges & field edges
- shrikes
- occ. Roller
- poppies — fabulous from late Apr

FOREST TRACK
- drive to/from Mesa ! Army Camp — move on if requested to do so
- fords Vouvaris River — look for waders, Bee-eater & dragonflies
- Krüper's Nuthatch

PICNIC SITE
- park near white building & search forest from track past building
- Krüper's Nuthatch
- Long-eared Owl
- Woodlark
- Masked Shrike
- Long-tailed Tit
- migrants inc. warblers & flycatchers
- raptors & storks over
- Short-toed Treecreeper
- woodland butterflies inc. Woodland Grayling
- dragonflies inc. Odalisque & Lesser Emperor

Road bridge The trees here have held roosting Night-heron in spring and Long-eared Owl has bred. Krüper's Nuthatch ventures out from the forest here (autumn and winter). The **rocky outcrop** overlooking the trees on the Kalloni side of the bridge can hold Black-eared Wheater, Blue Rock-thrush and Rock Nuthatch. The fields beyond the road bridge are good for shrikes inc. Lesser Grey, and Roller has been recorded in this area. Local raptors inc. Common and Long-legged Buzzards and Short-toed Eagle, plus the chance of many migrant raptor species.

SPECIES Spring/summer Egrets, herons inc. Night-heron (occ. roosts), storks; Common and Long-legged Buzzards, Short-toed Eagle; Long-eared Owl (rare); Black-eared Wheatear; Roller; Blue Rock-thrush; Rock Nuthatch; shrikes. **Autumn/winter** Great Crested and Black-necked Grebes; occ. Pygmy Cormorant; Lesser Black-backed Gull; Kingfisher; Grey Wagtail; Stonechat; Krüper's Nuthatch.

NEAREST AMENITIES There is an excellent little seaside taverna south of here and just before the Achlederi army camp by the turn to Ancient Pyrra. Kalloni | Καλλονή (15km to north) for shops, banks, petrol, etc. Skala Polichnitou | Σκάλα Μολιχνίτου (16km to south) for tavernas, shops.

3 | ACHLADERI FOREST | Δάσος Αχλαδερής (map p. 167)

This is undoubtedly the most popular Krüper's Nuthatch site on the island.

LOCATION Achladeri Forest lies between Mesa (to north) and Achladeri army camp (to south) on the road to Vasilika (Βασιλικά).

ACCESS Turn south off the Kalloni-Mytilini road at Mesa and continue for c.6km and the forest area is situated on the left (inland) side of the road south of the Vouvaris River bridge and north of Achladeri army camp.

Park in the large open picnic area with the white-washed building. There are plenty of trees to park underneath in the shade.

Important — do not attempt to enter the area if the army is using the site (the main entrance to the site will be blocked but the access track a little further south along the road might be open — do not be tempted to access here). It is also best to avoid the site on bank holidays (e.g. Easter Sunday, May Day) when the site is used as a picnic site by the local Lesviots.

AREAS TO SEARCH Search the following areas.

Car park area The area around the car park is worth scrutinising before moving off into the woodland proper. This open area usually holds breeding Woodlark, Black-eared Wheatear, Masked and Woodchat Shrikes and Cirl Bunting. Krüper's Nuthatch rarely breeds this close to the road, but birds can be found feeding in the trees around the parking area. Also check the area on the other side of the road (view from the road) which is often good for migrants such as warblers (inc. Orphean), shrikes, Roller, etc.

You should also watch the hilltops from here which can be very good for local breeding raptors (inc. Long-legged Buzzard and Short-toed Eagle), storks, raptors and swifts.

Pine wood Once you have exhausted the car park area, follow the main track away from the road up through the pine woodland. You can walk between the trees but be careful not to trample flowers. Krüper's Nuthatch can breed anywhere from just beyond the white building onwards either side of the track up to where the track forks, but can also occur beyond the fork along either track (inc. along the stream ravine between the two tracks). The same pair rarely uses the same nest hole in consecutive years, but the first birders arriving in spring usually locate the nest site(s) pretty quickly. They have a preference for tall, shattered trunks (snags — trees which have had their tops blown out). They usually nest c.2-4m off the ground.

The woodland area also holds breeding Long-eared Owl, Short-toed Treecreeper, Long-tailed Tit (*A.c. tephronotus* occurs on Lesvos) and migrants. Night-heron occasionally found roosting here.

The area is also excellent for butterflies (inc. Woodland Grayling) and dragonflies (inc. Odalisque along the stream right of the main track).

SPECIES All year Long-eared Owl; Middle Spotted Woodpecker; Long-tailed Tit; Krüper's Nuthatch; Short-toed Treecreeper. **Spring/summer** Long-legged Buzzard, Short-toed Eagle, migrant raptors; swifts (all species); Common Cuckoo; Black-eared Wheatear; Orphean Warbler; flycatchers; Woodlark; Masked and Woodchat Skrikes; Cirl Bunting. **Winter** Coal Tit.

NEAREST AMENITIES There is an excellent little seaside taverna just south of here and just before the Achlederi army camp by the turn to Ancient Pyrra. Kalloni | Καλλονή (17km to north) for shops, banks, petrol, etc. Skala Polichnitou | Σκάλα Μολιχνίτου (14km to south) for tavernas, shops.

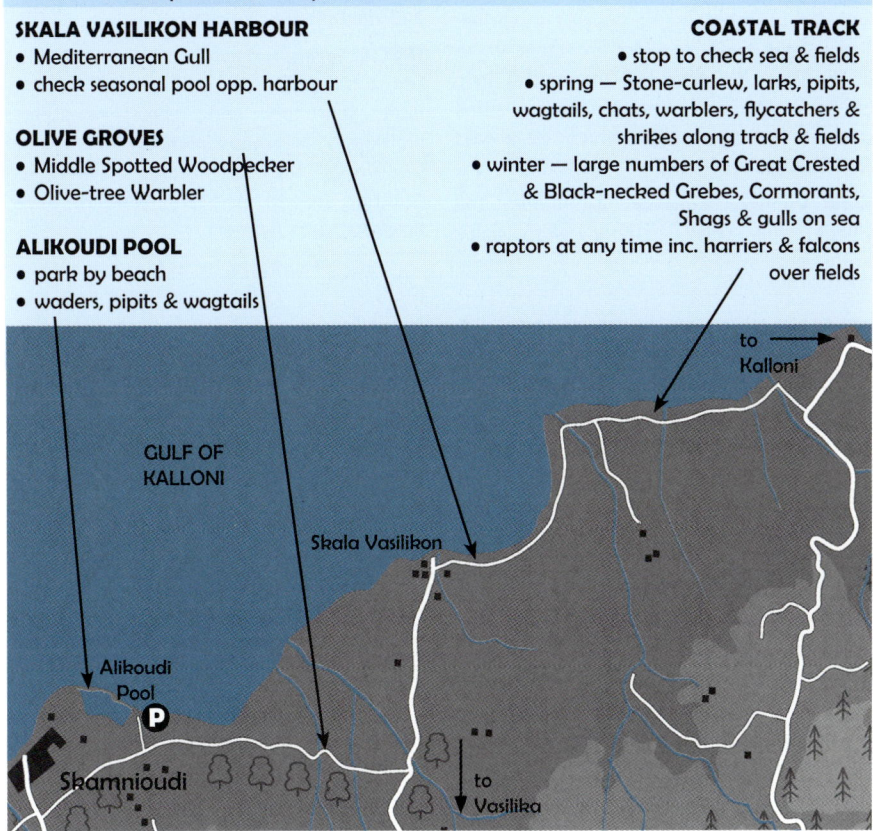

4 ACHLADERI TO SKAMNIOUDI
Αχλαδερή στη Σκαμνιούδι

SKALA VASILIKON HARBOUR
- Mediterranean Gull
- check seasonal pool opp. harbour

OLIVE GROVES
- Middle Spotted Woodpecker
- Olive-tree Warbler

ALIKOUDI POOL
- park by beach
- waders, pipits & wagtails

COASTAL TRACK
- stop to check sea & fields
- spring — Stone-curlew, larks, pipits, wagtails, chats, warblers, flycatchers & shrikes along track & fields
- winter — large numbers of Great Crested & Black-necked Grebes, Cormorants, Shags & gulls on sea
- raptors at any time inc. harriers & falcons over fields

4 | ACHLADERI TO SKAMNIOUDI | Αχλαδερή στη Σκαμνιούδι

Apart from the Polichnitos Saltpans (which are actually at Skala Polichnitou), this south-eastern area remains desperately neglected by birders.

NEAREST AMENITIES There is an excellent seaside taverna off the main road just north of the Achladeri army camp by the turn to Ancient Pyrra. Kalloni | Καλλονή (17km to north) for shops, banks, petrol, etc. Skala Polichnitou | Σκάλα Μολιχνίτου (14km to south) for tavernas and shops. Polichnitos | Μολιχνίτος (20km) for tavernas, shops and petrol.

4A | ACHLADERI TO SKALA VASILIKON | Αχλαδερή στη Σκάλα Βασιλικών

LOCATION AND ACCESS Turn south off the Kalloni-Mytilini road at Mesa and continue beyond Achladeri Forest area and past the Achladeri army camp. Just beyond the camp is a long, straight section of road lined with conifers either side. At the end of this road section, take the right turn on to the dirt track signed for Skala Vasilikon. The track runs out to the seafront and then south along the seashore to Skala Vasilikon.

AREAS TO SEARCH Check the **roadside fields** along the conifer lined straight section of road south of the army camp can hold shrikes and can be fabulous for poppies in spring. The **coastal track** provides excellent views of the Gulf of Kalloni and the coastal strip of fields. It crosses/passes several small streams and marsh areas which are always worth checking.

Skala Vasilikon harbour Just before the village, this small harbour often holds Mediterranean Gulls. In spring there is usually a small wetland (Farmakies) opposite the harbour which is good for herons, waders and wagtails (inc. Citrine).

SPECIES Spring/summer herons; waders; gulls; terns; falcons; Little Owl; wagtails; Tawny Pipit; Short-toed Lark; chats; wheatears; buntings. **Autumn/winter** Wildfowl and seafowl on the Gulf; Lesser Black-backed Gull (inc. *fuscus*); Mediterranean Gull; terns; Black Redstart (winter).

4B | SKALA VASILIKON TO SKAMNIOUDI | Σκάλα Βασιλικών — Σκαμνιούδι (map p. 169)

LOCATION AND ACCESS From Skala Vasilikon, turn inland along the tarmac road for 1.6km, then on a sharp zig-zag bend, take the right dirt track signed (in Greek) for Σκκαμνιουδι (Skamnioudi) and Σκάλα Μολιχνίτου (Skala Polichnitou). The track takes you through an olive grove area before opening out just short of Skamnioudi (after c.1.5km).

The Alikoudi Pool (Αλικούδι λίμνη) situated on the beach just north of the Skamnioudi village and accessed from the main track.

AREAS TO SEARCH Again, you can stop almost anywhere along this route.

Olive groves It is worth stopping and either viewing the trackside groves from the car or walking along the track. The area just before a turn to the right, with a sign on the junction pointing left for Σκκαμνιουδι (Skamnioudi), can be good for Middle Spotted Woodpecker and Olive-tree Warbler.

Alikoudi Pool Just short of the village is a seasonal pool right by the beach which is usually wet until June, but is dry through the summer and autumn until the rains. It is reached by taking a right turn down to the sea from the main track (look for 'Santa Maria' sign — also see map). The pool can be viewed from this track or from the beach track. It is not advisable to try and access the village along the beach track. Go back to the main track, turn right and continue along the main track.

SPECIES Spring/summer egrets, storks; waders; gulls; terns; falcons; Tawny Pipit; Short-toed Lark; chats; wheatears; buntings. **Autumn/winter** Wildfowl and seafowl on the Gulf; Lesser Black-backed Gull (inc. *fuscus*); Mediterranean Gull; terns; all the above when the pool is wet from October onwards.

---

5 | MIKRI LIMNI | Μικρή Λίμνη (map p. 164)

LOCATION AND ACCESS From Achladeri follow the main road south to the T-junction with the Vasilika road. Park along the woodland track opposite.

In winter this is a large expanse of water which attracts wildfowl and Water Rail. By mid-May the site is largely dry and is bone dry from June-October.

AREAS TO SEARCH View the lake from the woodland edge. Walk through the dry grassland in spring/summer. The wooded ridge above the site attracts raptors, particularly during passage periods.

SPECIES Spring/summer woodland edge, scrub and grassland species inc. Woodchat Shrike. Dragonflies. **Winter** Wildfowl; Water Rail.

6 | POLICHNITOS SALTPANS | Αλυκές Πολυχνίτου (map p. 172)

This is the smaller of the two areas of saltpans on the island. It is an under-watched area, and although better in autumn than in spring for waders, the area is worth searching for migrants in spring and autumn.

The reason that these pans are better in autumn is down to the two different sets of saltpans being worked at different times of years. The Kalloni pans are flooded in autumn which means that they are ideal for birds in spring. The Polichnitos pans however are flooded in spring, reducing their appeal for birds, but making them ideal for the return autumn migration period. The two saltpans are of course commercial sites and can be affected by the fluctuations of the international salt market. The Polichnitos pans, being smaller than the Kalloni pans, are more susceptible in this respect. They survived threatened closure in 2008 (which despite no spring flooding due to the threat of closure was a very good for autumn wader migration on the pans inc. the Lesvos' first Pectoral Sandpiper, and only the fourth for Greece). The threat remains real in 2010. It would be a major loss of habitat for migrating wetland birds if they did close.

LOCATION The saltpans lie on the coast north of Skala Polichnitou village which is to the northwest of the larger town of Polichnitos.

ACCESS The area is best approached from the north along the coastal route from Achladeri (Αχλδερή) via Skala Vasilikon (Σκάλα Βασιλικών) and Skamnioudi (Σκαμνιούδι).

Turn south off the Kalloni-Mytilini road at Mesa and continue through Achladeri and then after the conifer-lined road section turn right on to the coastal track to Skala Vasilikon. From the village turn inland and after c.1.6km on a sharp zig-zag bend, take the right dirt track signed (in Greek) for Σκκαμνιουδι (Skamnioudi) and Σκάλα Μολιχνίτου (Skala Polichnitou). When you come to the next tarmac road, continue straight across on a dirt track (turning right would take you to Skamnioudi) and follow track to the saltpans area.

You can also approach from Polichnitos. From Polichintos follow the main road to Skala Polichnitou, continue through the village to the saltpans.

AREAS TO SEARCH This is a large area and you can easily spend half, or even a full day covering the area well.

Skamnioudi road to the saltpans Most of this area is uninteresting unless you see something from the car. However, after c.1km the track crosses an obvious stream. Park here and search the small river, the Almyropotamos River (Lisvorio), which runs out to the sea. You can drive along the northern side of the river down to the beach and then along the beach. The next right turn brings you back out on the main track and turning right again will bring you back to the bridge (see map). Halfway between the bridge and the sea is a ford across the stream which is navigable in a 4x4 and is a short cut across to the pans. This river area can be excellent for migrants inc. herons, crakes, waders (inc. Temminck's Stint), wagtails, chats, shrikes.

Northern Fields Between the Almyropotamos River and the saltpans, the track weaves its way through fields to the pans. These are the 'northern fields'. This area is very good for migrants inc. raptors (especially harriers and falcons), pipits (inc. Tawny), shrikes and buntings. Stop along the track and scan the fields. Do not enter fields. These fields can also be accessed along the track which fords the Almyropotamos River (see above) and along the coastal track from the northwest corner of the pans.

Saltpans Unlike the Kalloni Saltpans, these pans are small and easily viewed with easy access around the entire site.

The main track takes you down past the eastern (inland) side of the pans and into Skala Polichnitou village. You can either drive this route, making regular stops to scan the pans and fields (on your left), or park as soon as you reach the pans and walk.

6 POLICHNITOS SALTPANS
Αλυκές Πολυχνίτου

FIELDS
- harriers & falcons
- Hoopoe, wagtails, chats, shrikes, buntings — cut fields in particular excellent in autumn

SALTPANS — FROM COAST
- walk along beach to view
- circular walk around entire pans
- species — see below

SALTPANS — FROM TRACK
- at best in autumn but should still be visited in spring
- park anywhere along track
- walk along entire length of track
- egrets, herons, storks & Spoonbill
- waders inc. Marsh, Broad-billed Sandpiper (rare) & Curlew Sandpipers, Little Stint, Spotted Redshank, Kentish Plover (breeds)
- wildfowl inc. Ruddy Shelduck (passage & winter), Garganey (passage), Pintail & Teal (both autumn/winter)
- egrets, herons, storks, Spoonbill

GULF OF KALLONI
- winter — large numbers of Great Crested & Black-necked Grebes, Cormorants, Shags & gulls on sea

ALMYROPOTAMOS RIVER
- track loops around fields & along river
- river — look for warblers, shrikes & buntings along its length
- herons, egrets, storks & waders at river mouth & bridge
- short cut to saltpans across ford — only in 4x4

Skamnioudi
GULF OF KALLONI
Almyropotamos River
Polichnitos Saltpans
Skala Polichnitou

FIELDS
- harriers & falcons
- wagtails, chats, shrikes & buntings
- in spring check the trackside pool and marsh area half way along track for waders & wagtails

WOODED RIDGE
- watch for migrant raptors following ridge in spring & autumn
- species can inc. Levant Sparrowhawk, Eleonora's Falcon, Goshawk, eagles

SKALA POLICHNITOU
- for simple tavernas & shop
- coastal road west to Nifida
- main road to Polichnitos, Vasilika & Vatera

The obvious disadvantage of the latter is that you risk flushing birds using the trackside pans, although they are quite used to traffic and people along this side. If birds are flushed they rarely fly far before settling on another pan.

There is a track along the north of the pans to the beach. In theory you can drive left and right at the beach, but it is advisable to walk from here unless you are in a 4x4 and experienced in driving in soft sand and mud. Birds are far more easily disturbed along the seaward side of the pans when birding on foot and you should be aware of the sun behind you in the afternoon and evenings. Try and keep as low as possible in order to keep the risk of disturbance to a minimum.

You can walk round the whole site (6km). Park at the northeast corner of the pans and walk down the main track into the edge of the village. Turn right here along the seafront and past the saltworks buildings. Continue along the beach track and back along the northern edge of the pans. This is a long walk and you should ensure you have plenty of water with you and the usual sun protection. You can break this up with a taverna stop in the village which will add another 1km to your walk.

The pans are obviously good for wetland species including Greater Flamingo, Little and Great White Egrets, Spoonbill, White and Black Storks, wildfowl, waders inc. Black-winged Stilt, Avocet, Little and Temminck's Stint, Marsh, Common, Green (winter) and Wood Sandpipers, gulls and terns. Other species include larks, pipits, wagtails and raptors. Rare species such as White Pelican and Broad-billed Sandpiper are recorded occasionally. Pectoral Sandpiper (first record for Lesvos) was recorded here in autumn 2008.

The pans rarely compete with the larger Kalloni Saltpans in spring, partly a geographic issue, but mainly a management issue as detailed above. Even with limited coverage rare birds such as Terek Sandpiper (May 09) are found in spring, and more will be found with increased coverage. In autumn however the pans are at their best and are great for waders and the chance of finding a good wader, such as Broad-billed Sandpiper is much higher than at the Kalloni pans.

Eastern Fields These are the fields which run alongside the main track down to the village. The area is very good for raptors, larks, pipits, wagtails, chats, wheatears, shrikes, buntings. In spring check the pool and marsh area by the track half way along the pans for waders and wagtails. Check the wooded ridge to the east which is used in spring and autumn by migrating raptors and storks.

SPECIES Spring/summer Little and Great White Egrets, Spoonbill, White and Black Storks, Greater Flamingo; Long-legged Buzzard, Short-toed Eagle, Marsh and Montagu's Harriers, Red-footed Falcon, other migrant raptors; Quail; Black-winged Stilt, Avocet, Kentish Plover (breed), Little and Temminck's Stint, Curlew, Marsh, Common and Wood Sandpipers; Mediterranean Gull; Common Cuckoo; Turtle Dove; swifts; Bee-eater; Roller; Short-toed Lark; Tawny Pipit; 'yellow' wagtails; Whinchat; wheatears; Red-backed, Woodchat and Lesser Grey Shrikes; Black-headed Bunting. **Autumn/winter** Common Shelduck, Teal, Pintail, Garganey; Black-throated Diver; Great Crested and Black-necked Grebes; Marsh and Hen Harriers; Black-winged Stilt, Avocet, Ringed Plover, Kentish Plover, Little and Temminck's Stint, Curlew, Marsh, Common, Green and Wood Sandpipers; Mediterranean Gull; Sandwich Tern; Kingfisher; Skylark; hirundines; Tawny Pipit; 'yellow', White and Grey Wagtails; Black Redstart (winter); Northern Wheatear; Red-backed, Woodchat and Lesser Grey Shrikes; Ortolan Bunting; Reed Bunting (winter). Black Stork and Black Kite have over-wintered in this area.

NEAREST AMENITIES Skala Polichnitou | Σκάλα Μολιχνίτου has several simple tavernas (those by the harbour are open year round), shops. Polichnitos | Μολιχνίτος (5km) for shops, banks, petrol, etc.

VATERA AREA & THE AMBELIKO VALLEY
Βατερά στη Κοιλάδα Αμπελικού

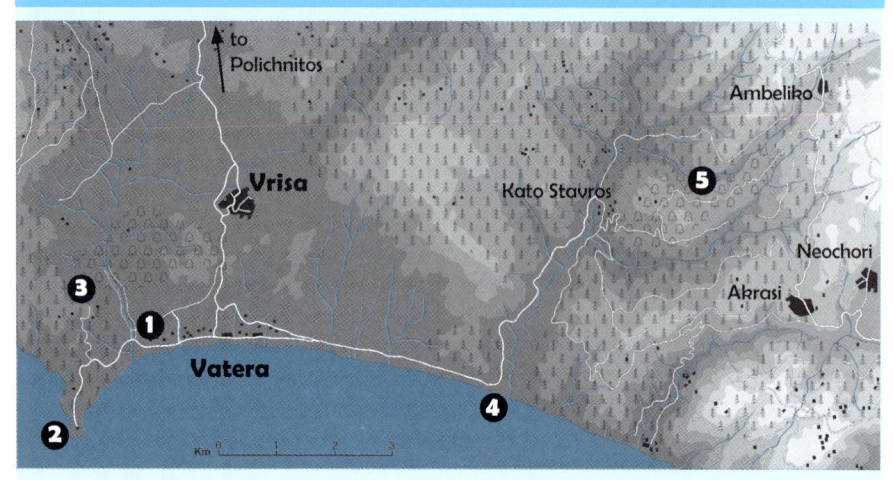

1. Almiropotamos River
2. Agios Fokas
3. Palia Vigla Chapel
4. Vourkos River Mouth
5. Ambeliko Valley

Vatera is located on the south coast to the east of the mouth of the Gulf of Kalloni and west of Plomari (Πλωμάρι). It is the island's largest resort area which in summer is full of package holiday makers, but in spring and autumn is largely deserted. Tavernas and shops don't usually open until mid- to late May or later. Some tavernas are still open throughout September. Hotel Vatera Beach is both an excellent hotel and taverna (open from mid-May to late September).

Birders who have based themselves here have found it a long way from the regular birding sites. For a quiet week exploring a relatively little known area, then a week based here may prove to be very rewarding.

Most birders combine the area with a drive down the east side of the Gulf of Kalloni and the Polichnitos Saltpans (Μολιχνίτος Αλυκές). The direct drive (and the quick return option to the Kalloni area) is along the main road south off the Kalloni-Mytilini road, through Achladeri (Αχλδερή), on to Vasilika (Βασιλικά) and Polichnitos (Μολιχνίτος) and then south past Vrisa (βρίσα) and on to Vatera. There is very little to be seen in Vatera itself.

1 | ALMIROPOTAMOS RIVER | Ποταμός Αλμυροπόταμος

LOCATION AND ACCESS Arriving in Vatera turn right (west) along the seafront. Beyond the edge of the resort the tarmac road turns to a dirt road and turns to the right. Park at the bend and walk out to the sea here to view the river mouth. Drive a little further round the bend and you will come to the main road bridge over the river.

AREAS TO SEARCH The river edges are lushly vegetated with tall phragmites reed, and north of the bridge, the river has in recent years been allowed to completely overgrow

1 ALMIROPOTAMOS RIVER
Ποταμός Αλμυροπόταμος

2 AGIOS FOKAS
Άγιος Φωκάς

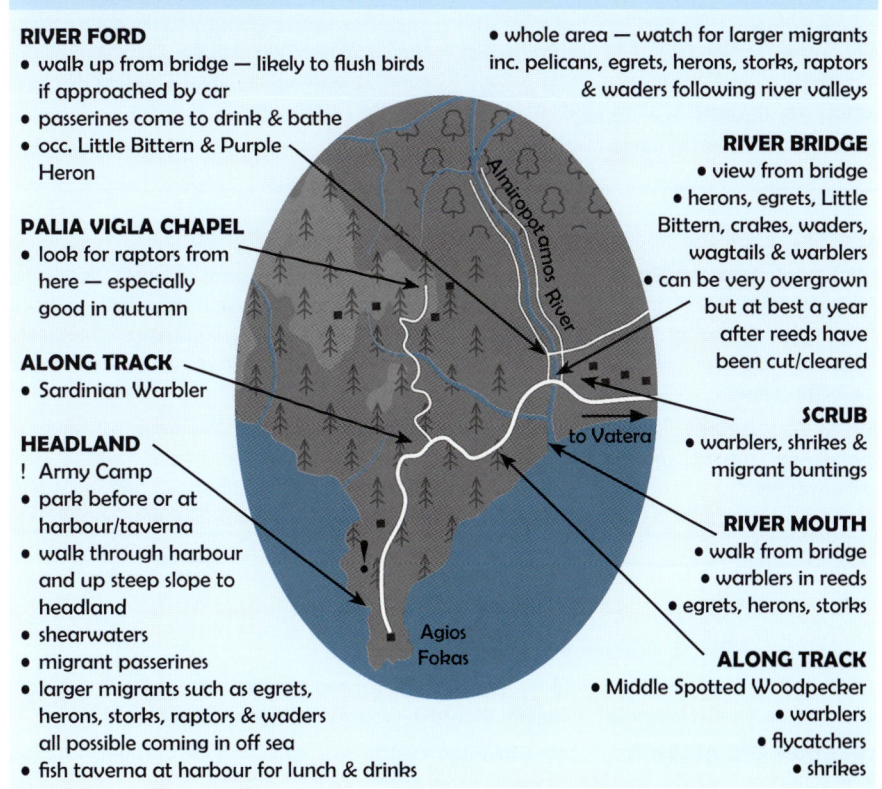

3 PALIA VIGLA CHAPEL
Παρεκκλήσι Παλιά Βίγλας

RIVER FORD
- walk up from bridge — likely to flush birds if approached by car
- passerines come to drink & bathe
- occ. Little Bittern & Purple Heron

PALIA VIGLA CHAPEL
- look for raptors from here — especially good in autumn

ALONG TRACK
- Sardinian Warbler

HEADLAND
! Army Camp
- park before or at harbour/taverna
- walk through harbour and up steep slope to headland
- shearwaters
- migrant passerines
- larger migrants such as egrets, herons, storks, raptors & waders all possible coming in off sea
- fish taverna at harbour for lunch & drinks

- whole area — watch for larger migrants inc. pelicans, egrets, herons, storks, raptors & waders following river valleys

RIVER BRIDGE
- view from bridge
- herons, egrets, Little Bittern, crakes, waders, wagtails & warblers
- can be very overgrown but at best a year after reeds have been cut/cleared

SCRUB
- warblers, shrikes & migrant buntings

RIVER MOUTH
- walk from bridge
- warblers in reeds
- egrets, herons, storks

ALONG TRACK
- Middle Spotted Woodpecker
- warblers
- flycatchers
- shrikes

with reed. This dense cover provides excellent shelter for heron species, but seeing them is a different matter! However, viewing from the river mouth and bridge can have its rewards.

North of the bridge is a ford (driveable in 4x4) which is excellent for small birds coming to drink and the occasional Little Bittern, Purple Heron and Little Crake feeding along the reed edge.

The scrub area around the bridge and along the nearby tracks are also worth walking and search the fields and scrub area for migrant warblers, chats and shrikes. Being at the mouth of a south facing river mouth with a due north river course, and just east of the headland of Agios Fokas, you should always keep an eye on the skies for flyover raptors, herons, storks and even pelicans!

Its worth walking along either side of the river. There remain some open sections.

The river often holds water in September.

SPECIES Spring Herons, egrets; crakes; migrant raptors; chats; warblers; shrikes. **Autumn** Herons; migrant raptors; warblers; shrikes; buntings.

2 | AGIOS FOKAS | Άγιος Φωκάς (map p. 175)

LOCATION AND ACCESS Drive over the Almiropotamos River bridge and turn left. Follow this track, up the hill and at the T-junction turn left and continue down to the small harbour. It is best to park just before the harbour and walk down, past the taverna and round to the right and up on to the headland.

AREAS TO SEARCH The T-junction area is worth searching for Sardinian Warbler.

Note — there is an army base between the T-junction and the harbour. Do not use optics and/or cameras around the base.

SPECIES Spring/autumn (unless stated) Scopoli's and Yelkouan Shearwaters; migrating egrets, herons, storks and raptors; Middle Spotted Woodpecker (all year); Black-eared Wheatear; Sardinian Warbler (all year); Sombre Tit (all year).

3 | PALIA VIGLA CHAPEL | Παρεκκλήσι Παλιά Βίγλας (map p. 175)

LOCATION AND ACCESS Drive over the Almiropotamos River bridge and turn left. Follow this track, up the hill and at the T-junction turn right. Follow the track up to the little chapel.

AREAS TO SEARCH This area is used by the birders for autumn raptor watching with some success.

The T-junction area is worth searching for Sardinian Warbler.

SPECIES Spring (unless stated) Migrating herons, storks and raptors; Middle Spotted Woodpecker (all year); Black-eared Wheatear; Sardinian Warbler (all year); Sombre Tit (all year).

NEAREST AMENITIES The little fish taverna by the harbour offers simple taverna food and drinks. Vatera (Βατερά) for shops and tavernas. Vrisa (βρίσα) (6km) for petrol.

4 | VOURKOS RIVER | Ποταμός Βούρκου

This is a little known area which forms part of a circular route when combined with the sites down the east side of the Gulf of Kalloni (Καλλονή Γέρας) down to Vatera (Βατερά).

LOCATION AND ACCESS From Vatera take the coastal road east for c.9km where the road then turns north at the Vourkos (Βούρού) River mouth. At Kato Stavros (Κάτω Σταυρός) the road forks, the track to the left following the Vourkos River north to Ambeliko (Αμπελικό), and following the road across the bridge to the right, through the village and up into the hills through to Ambeliko (follow the occasional signs for ΑΜΠΕΛΙΚΌ).

4a | VATERA TO VOURKOS RIVER MOUTH | Βατερά προς Εκβολή Ποταμού Βούρκου

AREAS TO SEARCH Once you have left Vatera its worth stopping along here to check clumps of trees and bushes, especially those around some of the larger buildings and hotels. As with any south-facing coastline it attracts arriving migrants in spring and departing migrants in autumn.

SPECIES Spring/autumn Shearwaters; chats; wheatears; warblers; flycatchers; shrikes.

4 VOURKOS RIVER
Ποταμός Βούρκος

5 AMBELIKO VALLEY
Κοιλάδα Αμπελικού

ROAD BRIDGE IN VILLAGE
- check river for herons, waders & wagtails

ROAD TO VILLAGE
- views over river valley — watch for larger migrants inc. raptors & storks following valley

ALONG TRACK
- straight section of track plateaux beyond hairpin section
- good views for raptors inc. Short-toed Eagle, Long-legged & Common Buzzards & migrants inc. Honey-buzzard, Levant Sparrowhawk & falcons
- Middle Spotted Woodpecker
- Sardinian, Subalpine & Orphean Warblers

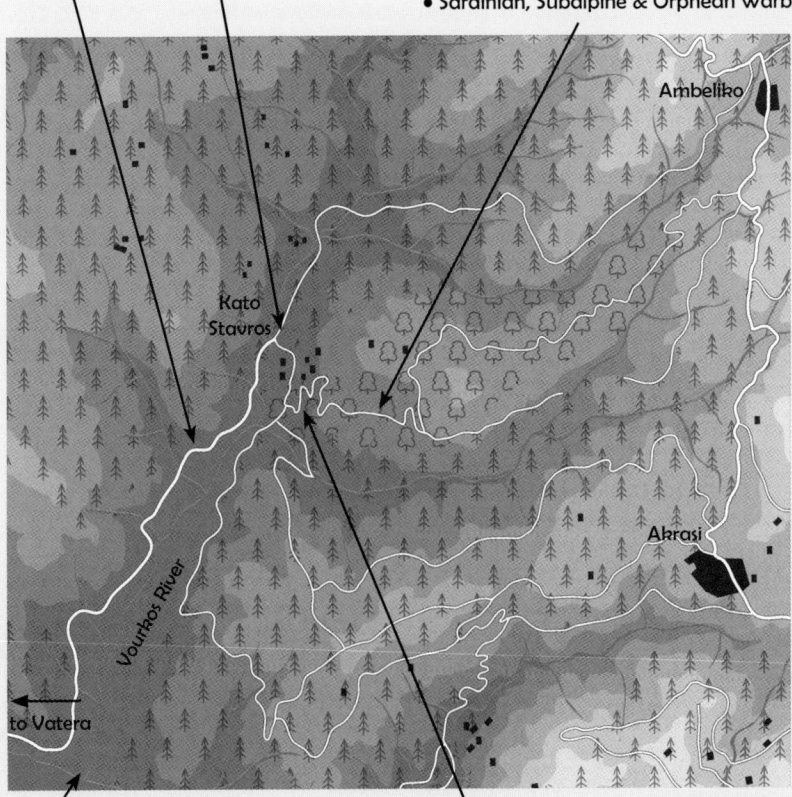

RIVER MOUTH
- take track down to mouth
- egrets, herons, waders, wagtails & warblers
- larger migrants such as egrets, herons, storks, raptors & waders all possible coming in off sea

HAIRPINS JUST OUTSIDE VILLAGE
- park along the 'hairpin' section & walk
- Middle Spotted Woodpecker
- Blue Rock-thrush
- Sardinian, Subalpine & Orphean Warblers

4b | VOURKOS RIVER MOUTH | Εκβολή Ποταμού Βούρκου (map p. 177)

This is a south-facing river mouth 9km east of Vatera. Before the road turns north, you can turn off to the right and down the track to the river mouth.

AREAS TO SEARCH Like many river areas on the island, this site has been cleared of vegetation in an attempt to canalise the river and is used regularly as a dumping site. In spring however it remains wet until mid-May and as such does attract arriving migrants. Also in autumn, it is at the bottom of the two valleys running south from Ambeliko and often holds departing migrants.

SPECIES Spring/autumn Little Bittern, Squacco Heron; crakes; migrant raptors; warblers; flycatchers; shrikes.

4c | VOURKOS RIVER MOUTH TO KATO STAVROS | Εκβολή Ποταμού Βούρκου προς Κάτω Σταυρός

(map p. 175) The tarmac road follows the river north up to Kato Stavros. It's difficult to view the river and the steep sided hillside on your left is difficult to view.

AREAS TO SEARCH The river can be viewed from the road bridge at Kato Stavros and there are tracks north running alongside the river which are worth investigating.

SPECIES Spring/autumn Little Bittern, Squacco Heron; crakes; migrant raptors; warblers; flycatchers; shrikes.

---

5 | AMBELIKO VALLEY | Κοιλάδα Αμπελικού (map p. 177)

There are two routes between Kata Stavros and Ambeliko. The southern track is by far the more interesting and rewarding with excellent views of the area to look for migrating raptors.

Crossing the river bridge at Kato Stavros, bear right through the village and onto the dirt road which runs up into the hills and through to Ambeliko (7km — with occasional signs for ΑΜΠΕΛΙΚΌ).

AREAS TO SEARCH There are numerous places to stop along this road and few places are the same from visit to visit. My advice is to park at the first main bend and walk up the track. You'll soon find out if it's busy or not, and if it is you'll get nowhere fast and get swept up the track with bird after bird. If it's quiet, then take the car further up the valley and repeat.

Once you go beyond the main hairpin bends rising up the valley, the road plateaus with a longish straight section of track. About c.200m along this straight section there is a small concrete building (looks like a bus stop!) on the left with a track to the left just beyond it before a stand of pine trees. This plateau area can be excellent in spring and autumn for migrant passerines and to watch for raptors. Sardinian Warbler breeds in this area.

Driving up to Ambeliko there remains many opportunities to stop and walk the track — just take pot luck! At several points the track reveals stunning views across the valley. These provide natural stops and photo opportunities and frequently turn up plenty of interest (Serin, Long-eared Owl, raptors).

SPECIES Spring/autumn Long-legged Buzzard, Short-toed Eagle, Goshawk, migrant raptors inc. Honey-buzzard, Levant Sparrowhawk, falcons; Long-eared Owl; Bee-eater; Middle Spotted Woodpecker; White Wagtail; chats; Blue Rock-thrush; Orphean (breed), Subalpine (breed) and Sardinian (all year) Warblers; flycatchers; Golden Oriole; shrikes; Serin.

NEAREST AMENITIES Vatera (Βατερά) and Ambeliko lie 16km apart. Vatera has shops and tavernas. Vrisa (Βρίσα) (3km north of Vatera) for petrol.

AGIASOS AREA
Ευρύτερη περιοχή Αγιάσου

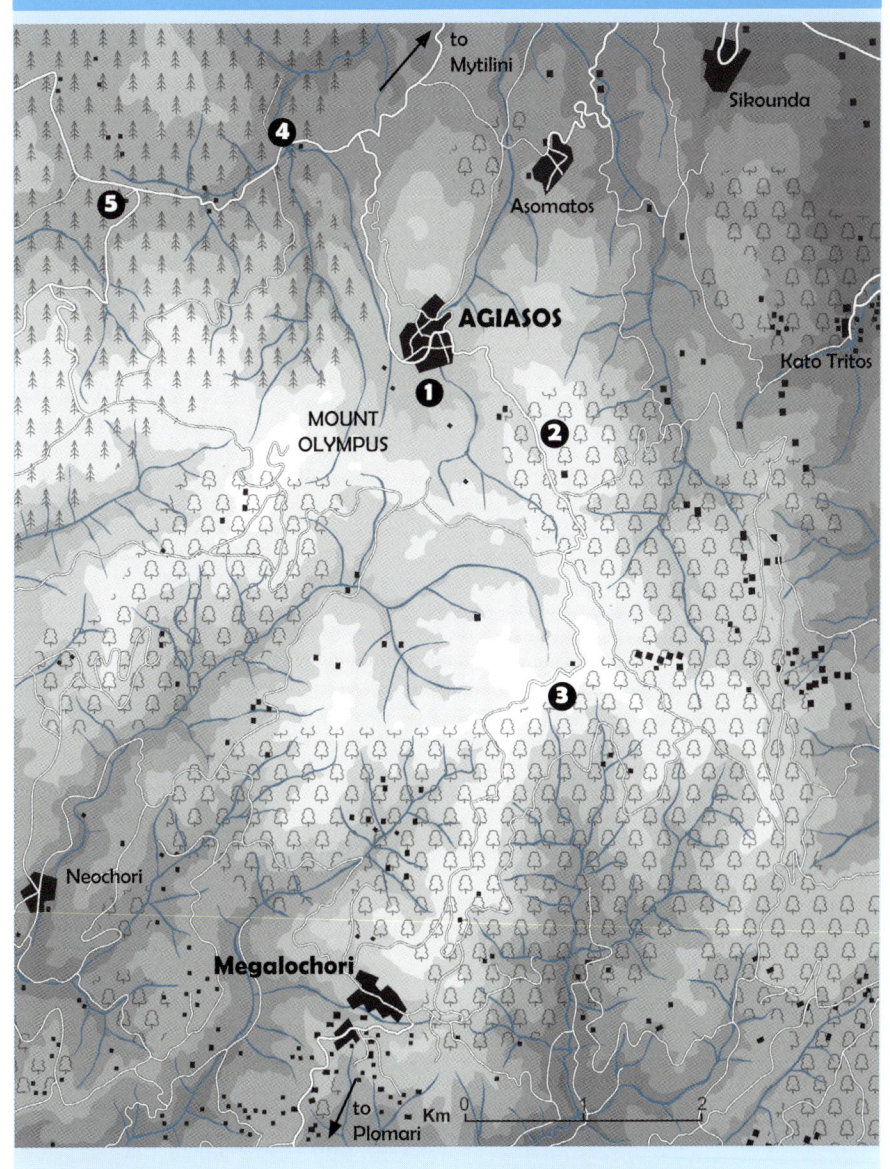

1 Agiasos
2 Agiasos Sanatorium
3 Megalochori Valley
4 Dimitrios
5 Panaghia Chapel
6 Dipi Larisos (off map — see text)

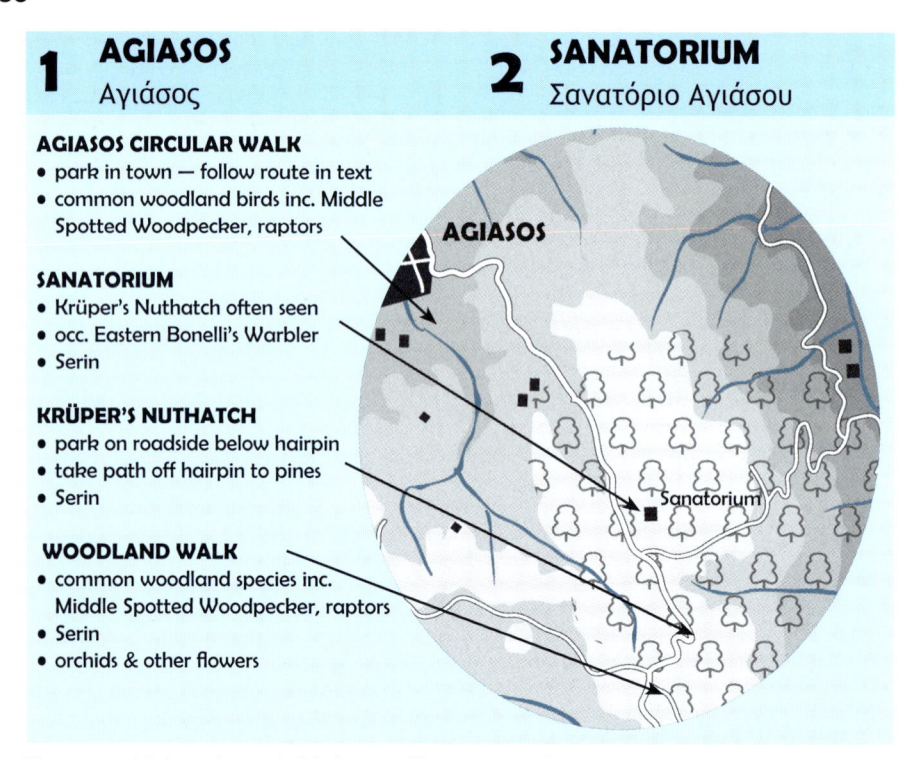

1 AGIASOS
Αγιάσος

2 SANATORIUM
Σανατόριο Αγιάσου

AGIASOS CIRCULAR WALK
- park in town — follow route in text
- common woodland birds inc. Middle Spotted Woodpecker, raptors

SANATORIUM
- Krüper's Nuthatch often seen
- occ. Eastern Bonelli's Warbler
- Serin

KRÜPER'S NUTHATCH
- park on roadside below hairpin
- take path off hairpin to pines
- Serin

WOODLAND WALK
- common woodland species inc. Middle Spotted Woodpecker, raptors
- Serin
- orchids & other flowers

The town of Agiasos is nestled below Mt Olympus (Ορ Ολνμπος). It is surrounded by fabulous forest areas which contain island rarities such as Robin and Mistle Thrush and is also an excellent area for plants, in particular orchids.

LOCATION AND ACCESS The area is usually, and best, approached from the north. It lies south of the road that runs between Polichnitos (ΜολιΧνίτος) and Keramia (Κεραμεία — on the Kalloni-Mytilini road). Birders staying in the Kalloni (Καλλονή) area would normally approach past Achladeri (Αχλδερή), turning left on to the Polichnitos-Keramia road and then follow signs for Agiasos (Αγιάσος).

---

1 | AGIASOS | Αγιάσος

Agiasos itself is a fascinating town. It oozes character and characters.

From Agiasos there is an excellent circular walk (c.5km) which is good for flowers (inc. orchids) and woodland birds.

Park in Agiasos. From the bus station, walk up into town and turn right by the library. Continue past the sunken courtyard with a church (Zoodchion Rigis) and the road begins to climb and bend to the right. At the fork by the memorial spring (dated 1995), turn right following the 'trekking sign' (man with backpack and stick on yellow background) and follow the cobbled path up the hill. At an obvious junction, follow the old cobbled donkey path (kalderimi) to the left, along the hillside below the Sweet Chestnut wood. The path drops into a shady stream. On the opposite bank is a walled enclosure. Cross the stream here. Follow the left side of the enclosure along the woodland path.

Stay on the obvious path as it winds around the hillside and through several wet areas. This area is particularly good for paeonies.

When you come to a second stream, look for four trees on the opposite bank, the centre two have red marks on their trunks. Cross the stream here. Follow the path to the left, away from the stream, to the cobbled track which crosses the path. Turn left down the track to a small pink chapel, bear to the right and past two further chapels. Cross the stream at the bridge and bear right down a concrete road which takes you up back to the cobbled street in town and you can then follow this back down to the car park.

For a fuller and more detailed account of this walk (and others in the area) see *Lesvos Car Tours and Walks* (Anderson, B & A. 2007).

SPECIES All year Raptors inc. Goshawk, Eurasian Sparrowhawk; Middle Spotted Woodpecker; Grey Wagtail; Wren; Robin; Blue Rock-thrush; Mistle and Song Thrushes; Long-tailed and Coal Tits; Krüper's Nuthatch; Short-toed Treecreeper; Raven; Serin; Cirl Bunting. **Spring** Raptors inc. Honey-buzzard, Short-toed Eagle; swifts; Turtle Dove; Common Cuckoo; Hoopoe; hirundines; Common Nightingale; Common Redstart; Black-eared Wheatear; warblers inc. Subalpine, Eastern Bonelli's and Wood; flycatchers; shrikes. Orchids and other flowers. **Autumn** A good chance of raptors over to the south.

2 | AGIASOS SANATORIUM AREA | Περιοχή Σανατόριου Αγιάσου

LOCATION AND ACCESS Drive through Agiasos and take the road south towards Megalochori (Μεγαλοχωρι) and Plomari (Πλωμάρι). After c.2km you will see a large building set back behind a set of large gates on your left. This is Agiasos Sanatorium. Park along the road before the gates. You can walk the road and follow tracks in this area which is good for woodland and meadow birds inc. Eastern Bonelli's Warbler.

Continue past the sanatorium and park by the next hairpin bend to the right (parking on right just before the bend). Off the bend on the left (going up hill) is a narrow path. Follow this into the trees and it continues into an open area. This area can be very good for Krüper's Nuthatch. Back down the road on the right is a deep-sided water tank which often has a leaking feeder pipe. This attracts birds to drink, particularly in summer and autumn, inc. Krüper's Nuthatch.

Continuing further still, go past one farm on the right and look for a goat farm on the right at a left hand bend (a track goes through the goat farm). Park on right just round the bend (look over the fence for some pig sties below the road). Continue to walk along the road to a concreted track entrance on your left. The track rises quite steeply and slightly back on the road you've just walked along. Follow this track for a fabulous woodland walk with lots of flowers incl. orchids, fritillaries and anemones. Please do not enter any fenced areas.

SPECIES All year Raptors inc. Goshawk, Eurasian Sparrowhawk; Middle Spotted Woodpecker; Wren; Robin; Mistle and Song Thrushes; Long-tailed and Coal Tits; Krüper's Nuthatch; Short-toed Treecreeper; Raven; Serin; Cirl Bunting. **Spring** Raptors inc. Honey-buzzard, Short-toed Eagle; swifts; Turtle Dove; Common Cuckoo; Hoopoe; hirundines; Common Nightingale; Common Redstart; warblers inc. Subalpine, Eastern Bonelli's and Wood; flycatchers; shrikes. **Autumn** A good chance of raptors over to the south.

3 | MEGALOCHORI VALLEY | Κοιλάδα Μεγαλοχωρίου (see area map on p. 179)

LOCATION AND ACCESS If you continue along the road away from Agiasos it turns into a track. Stick on the main track and you will wind down the valley towards Megalochori. Stop anywhere and search the woodland areas and open views. The couple of kms above Megalochori, inc. an open green valley, is very good for Eastern Bonelli's Warbler and Middle Spotted Woodpecker. See map for the circular route which takes you down to Megalochori and then back to the Sanatorium – this is a roughly indicated route and should be used in conjunction with your more detailed Lesvos road map.

SPECIES All year Raptors inc. Goshawk, Eurasian Sparrowhawk; Middle Spotted Woodpecker; Wren; Robin; Mistle and Song Thrushes; Long-tailed and Coal Tits; Krüper's Nuthatch; Short-toed Treecreeper; Raven; Serin; Cirl Bunting. **Spring** Raptors inc. Honey-buzzard, Short-toed Eagle; swifts; Turtle Dove; Common Cuckoo; Hoopoe; hirundines; Common Nightingale; Common Redstart; warblers inc. Subalpine, Eastern Bonelli's and Wood; flycatchers; shrikes. **Autumn** A good chance of raptors over to the south.

4 DIMITRIOS
Δημήτριος

- park on north of road to west (left) of river bridge
- Grey Wagtail breeds under bridge
- Serin
- Middle Spotted Woodpecker
- woodland walk along track north of road inc. Krüper's Nuthatch & Long-eared Owl
- raptors, swifts and hirundines overhead

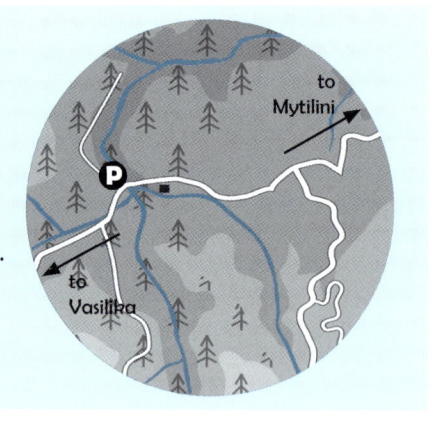

4 | DIMITRIOS | Δημήτριος

LOCATION AND ACCESS From Agiasos take the road north back to the main Mytilini-Polichnitos (Μυτιλήνη -Μολιχνίτος) road. Turn left towards Polichnitos and, after c.1km a new road section sweeps over a bridge and around a chapel (on left). Park at the far (west) end of the bridge on the right (north) side of the road where there is a large pull-in-cum-lay-by area at the start of a forest track.

AREAS TO SEARCH Bridge View the river gorge either side of the road for Grey Wagtail and birds coming to drink and bathe in the river.

Forest track Take the forest track north from the car park area, down the hill following the river. This forest track is good for Krüper's Nuthatch, warblers and butterflies.

SPECIES All year Common Buzzard, Long-eared Owl; Middle Spotted Woodpecker; Grey Wagtail; Krüper's Nuthatch. **Summer** Serin.

NEAREST AMENITIES Agiasos | Αγιάσος has shops and tavernas. Nearest petrol at Polichnitos | Μολιχνίτος or Keramia | Κεραμεία.

5 PANAGHIA CHAPEL
Παρεκκλήσι Παναγιάς

CHAPEL
- park on corner by covered picnic seats (bandstand)
- Fire tender usually present in summer/autumn
- walk up track to chapel
- open area surrounded by trees & bushes
- small chapel with trees
- Krüper's Nuthatch often comes to dripping tap by gate into chapel
- good for migrants inc. Redstart, warblers, flycatchers

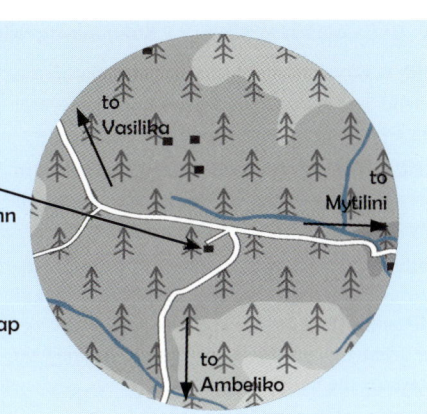

5 | PANAGHIA CHAPEL | Παρεκκλήσι Παναγιάς

LOCATION AND ACCESS From Agiasos take the road north back to the main Mytilini-Polichnitos (Μυτιληνη -ΜολιΧνίτος) road. Turn left towards Polichnitos and, after 3.5km take the left turn to Ambeliko (Αμπελικό). Park by the covered picnic table (bandstand) on the left by the junction (in autumn expect to see a fire engine parked here and the bandstand occupied by firemen).

AREAS TO SEARCH Walk up the track through the trees to an open area surrounded by trees with the chapel sat towards the back as you approach. This little site can attract migrants all year round, but the deep-sided water tank in the bottom right corner attracts birds to drink, as does the dripping water pipe by the gate into the chapel. Krüper's Nuthatch is a regular visitor to the leaky pipe at the chapel, especially in summer and autumn when ground water is scarce.

Also check the pinewood north of the main road from here and to the east of Megali Limni (flooded in winter but dry in spring/summer) for Krüper's Nuthatch, Middle Spotted Woodpecker, Long-tailed and Coal Tits.

SPECIES All year Krüper's Nuthatch. **Passage** Migrants inc. Common Redstart, warblers and flycatchers.

NEAREST AMENITIES Agiasos | Αγιάσος has shops and tavernas. Plomari | Πλωμάρι is 10km from Megalochori and has shops, banks, tavernas, petrol.

Kruper's Nuthatch
a sought after resident species which breeds throughout the pinewoods in the centre and southeast of the island

6 | DIPI LARISOS REEDBED | Καλαμιώνας Ντίπι Λαρσός (no map)

This is by far the largest reedbed area on the island and as such is important for several breeding and wintering species.

LOCATION The reedbed lies on the northern shores of the Gulf of Gera c.8km west of Mytilini.

Either turn off the Kalloni-Mytilini (Καλλονή-Μυτιληνη) road south towards Plomari (Πλωμάρι) by a garage opposite the large crag, or from the south, from Plomari heading up towards the Kalloni-Mytilini road.

ACCESS AND AREAS TO SEARCH The only real access is about 1km off the main Kalloni-Mytilini road by the road bridge which crosses the Evergetoulas (Ενερέτουλας) River. You can park here and follow the track just back towards the main road, down to the coast. This track is usually gated and secured with a bolt. The Greek sign asks you to 'close the gate' and not 'no entry' as some think. Follow the track on foot. Depending on the winter rains, the track takes you through a damp to wet area. Small pools form here in some years, but these have become smaller over the years due to silting of the site. The track eventually leads you down to the beach area.

The reedbed continues for c.1.5km beyond this bridge, and several tracks afford limited access and viewing to the coastal edge of the site.

Back at the bridge, tracks on the inland side of the road along the river channel run for c.3km through to Keramia (Κεραμεία) and access back on to the Kalloni-Mytilini road. The area attracts migrant chats, warblers and shrikes as well as expected breeding species such as Olivaceous Warbler and Woodchat Shrike.

OTHER AREAS Few birders venture far from here. The coastal road south along the edge of the Gulf can be worth exploring, but apart from the occasional pool or a few waders on the beaches, the main interest is looking for grebes etc. on the Gulf itself.

The Oros (Όρος) headland (the western headland overlooking the mouth of the Gulf of Gera) can be reached by following the gulf road down through Perama (Πέραμα) and Pirgi (Πύργοι) and then the track down past the mouth of the gulf to Katsinia Bay (Παραλία Κατσίνια). Park here and walk out to the headland for views over the mouth of the gulf over to Haramida and the open sea to the south.

SPECIES All year Little Grebe; raptors inc. Long-legged Buzzard, Marsh Harrier; Water Rail; warblers inc. Cetti's. **Spring/autumn** Egrets, herons, Great Bittern (winter), Little Bittern (breeds), Night-heron; Garganey; raptors inc. Short-toed Eagle, Osprey; crakes (very difficult to see here); waders; gulls inc. Mediterranean and Slender-billed; terns inc. occasional Caspian; wagtails (inc. large roost of yellow); warblers inc. Reed and Great Reed; flycatchers; shrikes. **Winter** Great Crested and Black-necked Grebes; Great White Egret; occ. Pygmy Cormorant; wildfowl; Sandwich Tern; waders inc. Green Sandpiper; Kingfisher; occ. Moustached Warbler (winter); Common Starling (large winter roost); Reed Bunting.

NEAREST AMENITIES Mytilini | Μυτιληνη (8km) has shops, banks, petrol and tavernas. Kalloni | Καλλονή (26km) has shops, banks and petrol. Plomari | Πλωμάρι (28km) has shops, banks, petrol and tavernas.

MYTILINI AREA
Ευρύτερη περιοχή Μυτιλήνης

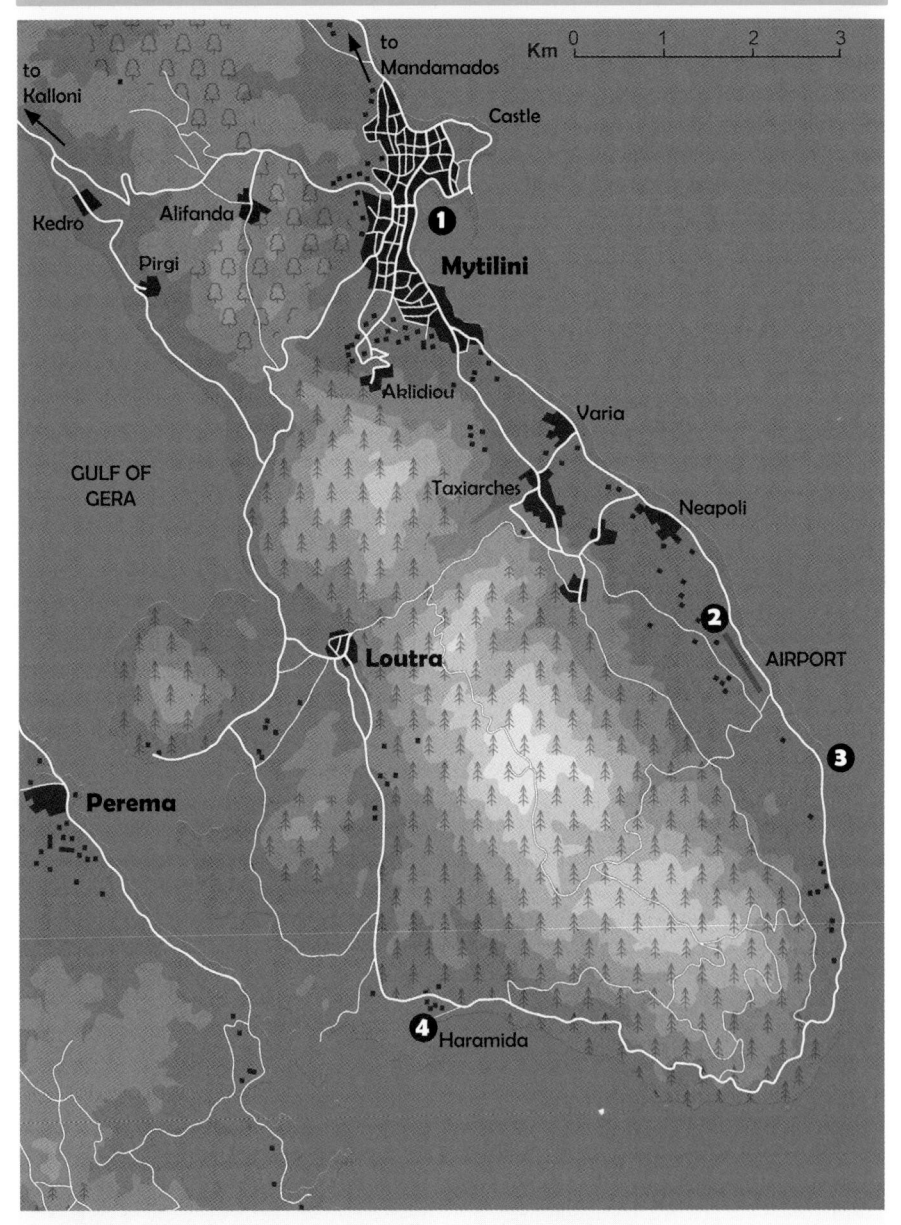

1 Mytilini (Castle & Harbour areas)
2 Airport
3 Cape Lena
4 Haramida Marsh

MYTILINI AREA | Ευρύτερη περιοχή Μυτιλήνης (map p. 185)

Mytilini is the capital town of Lesvos. It is quite a typical, bustling port town being a blend of old and new.

Most people's experience of Mytilini is restricted to navigating your way along the one way system to and from the airport (αεροδρόμιο). Accommodation and eating out is probably at its cheapest on the island here (if you search for it — avoid the harbour and sea fronts), but few birders choose to base themselves here as it's simply too far from the main birding sites in the centre (an hours drive) and west of the island (2+ hours drive).

LOCATION Mytilini lies in the south east of the island just (4km) north of the airport.

ACCESS AND AREAS TO SEARCH Mytilini holds little for the birder. The road between the airport and the town borders the sea and you can stop and scan for shearwaters and grebes. The tamarisk bushes along here can be dripping with birds after a fall (especially in autumn) and when in flower can attract hundreds of butterflies.

Mytilini harbour (1) tends to hold very little apart from the ubiquitous Yellow-legged Gull. Mediterranean Gull can occur and grebes, Sandwich Tern and Kingfisher in late autumn, winter and early spring. The beach areas can hold waders.

The Castle (1) at the north end of the town is the one site which does get some attention as birders turn tourist. Blue Rock-thrush and Black-eared Wheatear breed here. Migrants reported here inc. swifts, chats, wheatears, warblers, flycatchers and shrikes. Scops and Barn Owls are also occasionally reported from here and elsewhere in the area.

Airport (2) There is limited birding around the airport itself. To the north (towards Mytilini), immediately beyond the northern perimeter of the airport, a stream comes down from the left and is bordered by a track. The stream itself can hold waders such as Wood Sandpiper and the area of reeds and scrub holds migrants inc. warblers (inc. records of River), chats and shrikes.

Cape Lena (3) A walk or drive to the south of the airport takes you along the coast which holds Sardinian Warbler and views over the sea for shearwaters and grebes. Look for shearwaters, including close views of Scopoli's, following fishing boats back in to harbour (especially in the evenings).

SPECIES All year Sardinian Warbler. **Spring/autumn** Shearwaters; passage raptors inc. Short-toed Eagle, Osprey; waders; gulls inc. Mediterranean; terns; yellow wagtails; chats; warblers; flycatchers; shrikes. **Winter** Great Crested and Black-necked Grebes; Black-throated Diver; Sandwich Tern; Reed Bunting.

NEAREST AMENITIES Mytilini has shops, banks, petrol, bars and tavernas. There is a snack bar and toilets at the airport.

---

4 | HARAMIDA MARSH | Βάλτος Χαραμίδας

Haramida is situated at the southern end of the Mytilini peninsula. It is an area of scrub and reed just at the mouth of the Gulf of Gera.

LOCATION Haramida is c.10km due south of Mytilini and is reached either by following the coastal road south past the airport and around the Agreilia (Αγριελιά) headland, or from Mytilini follow the road south to Loutra (Λουτρά).

ACCESS AND AREAS TO SEARCH At the west end of Haramida take the track west off the bend down to the beach. There is a large beach bar building at the end and you will see the reeds on your right.

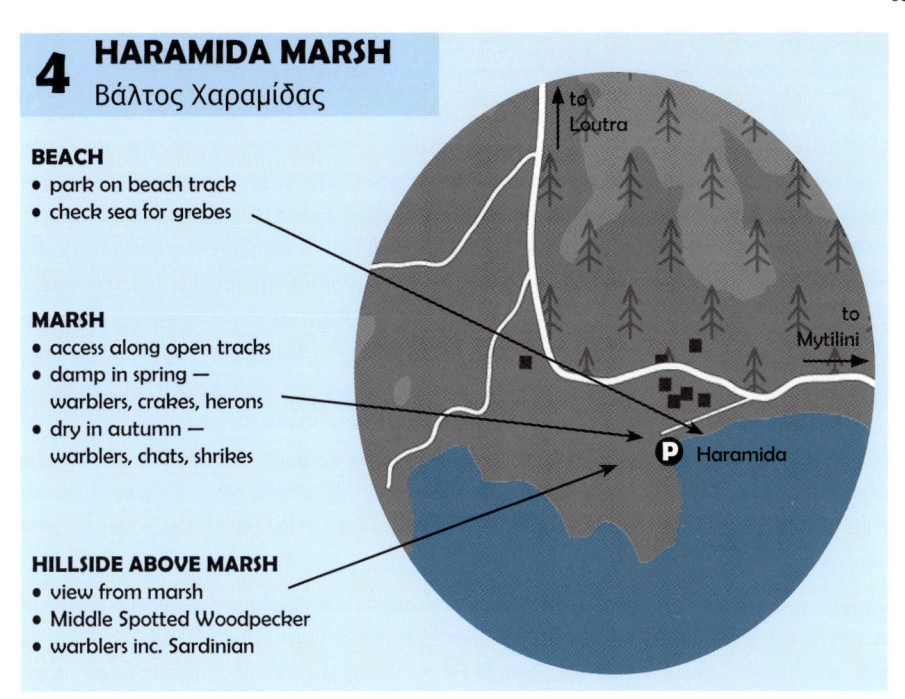

4 HARAMIDA MARSH
Βάλτος Χαραμίδας

BEACH
- park on beach track
- check sea for grebes

MARSH
- access along open tracks
- damp in spring — warblers, crakes, herons
- dry in autumn — warblers, chats, shrikes

HILLSIDE ABOVE MARSH
- view from marsh
- Middle Spotted Woodpecker
- warblers inc. Sardinian

Park here and explore the area on foot. A track runs in front of the bar, through the reeds and into an open area with a scrubby hillside on your left. You can follow the tracks throughout the area.

Please do not enter any gated or fenced off areas.

In spring the ground is damp to very wet depending on winter rains. There are usually no open pools, but the presence of water in the reeds is evident by the species present including wintering warblers and Water Rail.

The scrubby hillside holds Sardinian Warbler and is good for migrants inc. chats, warblers and shrikes.

Check the beach areas for waders, gulls and terns and offshore shearwaters.

OTHER AREAS Sardinian Warbler occurs across this headland south of the airport (including at the southern end of the airport itself). It is worth looking for shearwaters and grebes off the coast here between the airport and Haramida. Check the beach areas for waders, gulls and terns.

SPECIES All year Middle Spotted Woodpecker; Sardinian Warbler. **Spring/autumn** Passage raptors inc. Short-toed Eagle, Osprey; waders; gulls inc. Mediterranean and Slender-billed; terns inc. occasional Caspian; swifts; hirundines; yellow wagtails; chats; warblers; flycatchers; shrikes. **Winter** Great Crested and Black-necked Grebes; Water Rail; Sandwich Tern; Kingfisher; Reed Bunting.

NEAREST AMENITIES Mytilini (10km) has shops, banks, petrol, bars and tavernas. Loutra | Λουτρά (4km) has a petrol station.

AN ANNOTATED CHECKLIST OF THE BIRDS OF LESVOS

I have worked with both the Hellenic Rarities Committee (HRC) and Greek and Lesvos birdwatchers to produce as near a definitive list of accepted species recorded on the island. References are provided where previously published inc. for accepted records HRC annual reports and *The Birds of Greece* (Handrinos & Akriotis 1997) (BoG in text), and *Birding on the Greek Island of Lesvos* (Brooks 1998) and various updates by the same author (up to 2004) for many records of commoner species and from where many of the unconfirmed records (e.g. records not submitted to HRC) are taken. Most of the records of scarcer species (e.g. non-HRC species which are none-the-less scarce or rare on Lesvos) have never been formally submitted to the Greek recording authorities. In this respect we have decided to take many of these at face value. Some have been excluded (e.g. woodpeckers) on the basis that they are considered very unlikely and without formal documentation will not be admitted to the the Lesvos list. Most records from 2005 onwards are from HRC or collated by myself. Observers, where known (e.g. from HRC reports) are included for some of the rarer species (unfortunately not all publications provide details of observers). 'MO' in the text refers to Many Observers.

Lesvos is unique in respect of the concentration of western European birders present on the island in spring. It's inevitable that many of the reported sightings do not get formally submitted to HRC. Nevertheless, this coverage does help to record the truer status of some species on Lesvos which remain nationally rare at the national level, e.g. Citrine Wagtail is an annual scarce passage migrant on Lesvos yet remains rare elsewhere in Greece. The same is true for other species.

For completeness, records published in other publications but not formally submitted to HRC have been included within the species accounts to indicate these records are known and if observers are able to submit further details these will be considered by HRC. 2009 records marked † are pending acceptance.

At the end of the list are two appendices detailing 1) species submitted to HRC but rejected and species reported but never formally submitted by HRC (so these species are not on the Lesvos list) and 2) reported escapes.

RECOMMENDED BIRDING GUIDES

Collins Bird Guide (second edition) by Lars Svensson, Killian Mullarney & Dan Zetterstrom (HarperCollins, ISBN 978 0 00 726726 2 (hbk)/ 978 0 00 726814 6 (pbk) — quite simply the best bird guide in the world.

The Macmillan Birder's Guide to European and Middle Eastern Birds by Alan Harris, Hadoram Shirihai & Davis Christie (Macmillan, ISBN 0 333 58940 8) — out of print but definitely worth buying if you find a copy second-hand.

KEY TO STATUS CODES

c	= common	s	= scarce
r	= rare	f	= former
RB	= resident breeder		
MB	= migrant breeder		
CB	= casual/occasional breeder		
IB	= introduced breeder		
SP	= spring passage		

AP = autumn passage
PM = passage migrant (spring and autumn)
W = winter visitor
V = vagrant
? = status uncertain
* = species requiring supporting notes/evidence (LBRC and HRC — all records to be submitted via LBRC — see p. 56)

TAXONOMY AND NOMENCLATURE

This is based on the International Ornithological Congress (IOC) list of bird names as listed by Gill, F., Wright, M. & Donsker, D. (2009). *IOC World Bird Names* (version 2.0), and is available at www.worldbirdnames.org. I have deviated from this reference as follows:

1. where subspecies have a different name to the nominate name listed by Gill & Wright, e.g. Bewick's Swan *Cygnus columbianus bewickii*

2. in respect of hyphenated names, I do not use a capitalized letter for a name following a hyphen, e.g. the Lesvos list will use Stone-curlew and not Stone-Curlew.

3. Night-heron is used in preference to Night Heron to denote that Night-herons are their own family of 'herons' and not part of the *Ardea* group of herons.

4. Honey-buzzard is used in preference to Honey Buzzard to denote that this species is not a *Buteo* buzzard species

4. Rock-thrush is used in preference to Rock Thrush to denote that these species are not a *Turdus* thrush species

6. where identifiers such as 'Eurasian' are not the common vernacular name used in Europe, or rarely used, these have been left in regular type to denote their irregular usage among field birders.

7. where a Gill & Wright name differs markedly from the common vernacular name used in Europe this has been given on the line below the common name.

8. note that due to space issues, the English names listed on the bird list on pp. 228–35 are the common names and not the full Gill & Wright names.

SPECIES LIST

Chukar Partridge *Alectoris chukar* sRB
Occurs mainly in the rocky areas of the centre, north and west of the island. Its distinctive call will give the bird away — finding it is another matter! A couple of the better localities to search are Madaros, Ipsilou area, Petrified Forest area and the Meladia Valley.

Common Quail *Coturnix coturnix* rMB, sPM
Small numbers breed, their presence given away by calling males. Most usually encountered in spring Apr-May, when non-calling birds are also flushed from grassy areas bordering south-facing beaches. Also occ. recorded Aug-Sept.

Common Pheasant *Phasianus colchicus* rIB
A small naturalised population persists due to birds being released for hunting.

Greater White-fronted Goose *Anser albifrons* sW
Most recent records: 1 nr Kalloni Saltpans Mar 03 (Brooks 2003); 12 over Polichnitos Saltpans Dec 08 (T. Robinson).

Red-breasted Goose *Branta ruficollis* V *
Two records: 2 found shot Kalloni Jan 06 (E. Kakalis, A. Karamitros: HRC06); 1 Tsiknias River Jan 06 (E. Galinou, K. Zorbas: HRC06).
Records not submitted to HRC: 1 Kalloni Saltpans Feb 02 (Brooks 2002).

Mute Swan *Cygnus olor* sW
Small numbers usually Dec-Apr.

Bewick's Swan *Cygnus columbianus bewickii* V *
One record: 4 Kalloni area Jan 06 (E. Kakalis, E. Galinou, K. Zorbas, S. Laing: HRC06).

Whooper Swan *Cygnus cygnus* V *
Four records: one with Mute Swans at Skala Kallonis Pool Dec 93-Feb 94 (Brooks 1998); 9 Alikoudi Pool, Mesa and Kalloni Saltpans Jan 03 (Dirk Raes); 1 off Kalloni Saltpans (with the 4 Bewick's swans) Jan 06 (E. Galinou); 4 on sea off Mesa Jan 09 (T. Robinson).

Common Shelduck *Tadorna tadorna* sW, sPM, CB
Small numbers winter Nov-Apr, with passage noted Mar-May and less so Sept-Oct. Pr bred 2002 (Brooks 2003).

Ruddy Shelduck *Tadorna ferruginea* sRB, sPM
Birds present all months with small numbers breeding across the island, e.g. nr Palios, nr Gavathas,

Perasma Reservoir. Peak numbers in spring when passage birds also occur Mar-May, with flock of double-figures expected. Smaller numbers on passage Aug-Sept.

Gadwall *Anas strepera* V *
Three records: male nr Kalloni Saltpans May 03; fem Metochi Lake Aug 03 (Brooks 2003); 1 Metochi Lake May 06 (T. Robinson).

Eurasian Wigeon *Anas penelope* sW
Small numbers Oct-Apr.

Mallard *Anas platyrhynchos* sW
Small numbers Nov-May. Mating observed but no confirmed breeding.

Northern Shoveler *Anas clypeata* sW
Small numbers Sept-May.

Northern Pintail *Anas acuta* sW, sPM
Small numbers Sep-Apr.

Garganey *Anas querquedula* cSP, sAP
Common offshore and on reservoirs and Saltpans Mar-May, with smaller numbers Aug-Sept.

Eurasian Teal *Anas crecca* sW, sPM
Small numbers Aug-Apr.

Common Pochard *Aythya ferina* V *
Seven records, most recent: fem Skala Kallonis Pool Apr 2000; 1 Skala Kallonis Pool Apr 03 (Brooks 2000, 2003); 1 Kalloni Saltpans Jan 06 (E. Galinou), 1-2 Potamia Reservoir Mar, May & Sept 06 (E. Galinou, T. Robinson); 1 Polichnitos Saltpans Aug 07 (T. Robinson).

Ferruginous Duck *Aythya nyroca* V *
Nine records, most recent: male and fem Parakila Marsh Apr 2000 (Brooks 2000); male off Skala Kallonis Apr 2002 (MO); male Peresma Reservoir May 07; female Skala Kallonis Pool Apr 08 (MO).

Tufted Duck *Aythya fuligula* V *
Three records, most recent: 1 Tsiknias River Apr 01 (Brooks 2001).

Greater Scaup *Aythya marila* V *
One record: 1 on sea off Kalloni Saltpans Jan 06 (E. Galinou).

Common Goldeneye *Bucephala clangula* V *
One record: 3 off Achladeri Apr 86 (Brooks 1998).

Smew *Mergellus albellus* V *
One record: 4 Kalloni Saltpans Jan 06 (E. Galinou).

Red-breasted Merganser *Mergus serrator* sW
Small numbers offshore Oct-Apr.

White-headed Duck *Oxyura leucocephala* V *
One record: female shot Dec 91 (Brooks 1998).

Black-throated Diver *Gavia arctica* sW
Black-throated Loon
Small numbers offshore Nov-Apr, sometimes in small groups.

Scopoli's Shearwater *Calonectris (diomedea) diomedea* sPM, ?rSB?
Small numbers (but flocks of 100+ not unusual) offshore Mar-Oct. May breed on some of the offshore islands. Best looked for off the south (e.g. Agios Fokas) and west coasts (e.g. Skala Eresou).

Yelkouan Shearwater *Puffinus yelkouan* cRB
Present offshore all months with flocks of several hundred, even over a thousand, not unexpected.

Little Grebe *Tachybaptus ruficollis* sRB
Small numbers breed along the wetter rivers (e.g. Potamia) and the larger inland water bodies such as Metochi Lake.

Great Crested Grebe *Podiceps cristatus* sW
Gulf of Kalloni hold large numbers (1200+) Dec-Feb, otherwise small numbers offshore Oct-May.

Red-necked Grebe *Podiceps grisegena* V *
Relatively few records. Most recent: 20+ Gulf of Kalloni Mar 02 (Brooks 2002); off Skala Kallonis Mar 03 and presumed same bird off Skala Polichnitou Apr 03 (Brooks 2003).

Black-necked Grebe *Podiceps nigricollis* sW
Small numbers offshore, in river mouths and on inland reservoirs from Nov-May.

Greater Flamingo *Phoenicopterus roseus* sW
Present Sep-May with some non-breeding birds Jun-Aug. Has attempted to breed Kalloni Saltpans 2000 (8-9 nests — all abandoned) & 02 (33 nests — all abandoned) (Brooks 2000, 2003). Most birds

seen at Kalloni and Polichnitos Saltpans, with occasional birds at Mesa pool and at river mouths. Numbers can exceed 1000 birds.

Black Stork *Ciconia nigra* sMB, sPM, rW
Occurs Mar-Oct, mainly on passage, but with 10+ breeding pairs in pine forests. Birds have occasionally over-wintered, e.g. Kalloni Saltpans Jan 05 and Jan 06 (E. Galinou) and Polichnitos Saltpans winter 08/09 (T. Robinson).

White Stork *Ciconia ciconia* sMB, sPM, rW
Occurs Feb-Oct, mainly on passage, but a number of breeding pairs on rooftops, church steeples, poles and chimneys. Recent nests in Eresos (pole), Skala Kallonis (rooftop), Mandamados (chimney), Agias Paraskevi (chimney) and Polichnitos (chimney). Has over-wintered, e.g. 3 birds winter 08/09 (E. Galinou).

Glossy Ibis *Plegadis falcinellus* cSP, sAP
Can occur in sizable flocks Mar-May, with much smaller numbers Aug-Oct.

Eurasian Spoonbill *Platalea leucorodia* sPM
Small numbers Mar-May. Increasing numbers (especially Polichnitos Saltpans) Sept-Oct.

Great Bittern *Botaurus stellaris* sW, sPM
Eurasian Bittern
Single birds usually encountered Oct-May around obvious wetland and river areas.

Little Bittern *Ixobrychus minutus* cSM, sAP
Common in spring (Apr-Jun) around any wetland and river areas inc. even the smallest of culverts and drains with cover. Scarcer during autumn (Aug-Oct).

Black-crowned Night-heron *Nycticorax nycticorax* cSM, sAP
Occurs more commonly in spring (Mar-May) but small numbers Sept-Oct. Large flocks, e.g. 32 Apr 08 are exceptional.

Squacco Heron *Ardeola ralloides* cSM, sAP
Common around wetland and river areas Apr-May and smaller numbers Aug-Oct.

Western Cattle Egret *Bubulcus ibis* V *
Only three recently accepted records: 1 nr Sigri Dec 07 (E. Kakalis, E. Gribylakou: HRC07); 1 nr Tsiknias River Mouth Apr 08 (S.P. Dudley: HRC08); 1 Skala Eresou May 08 (R. Ulph: HRC08); 1 Polichnitos Saltpans Dec 08 (T. Robinson: HRC08).
Records not submitted to HRC: 1 Sigri May 95; 1 Vassilika May 96; pr Tsiknias River Apr 99; 1 Tsiknias River Apr 2000; 1 Kalloni Saltpans Apr 01; 1 nr Sigri Apr 02 (Brooks 1998, 1999, 2000, 2001, 2002).

Grey Heron *Ardea cinerea* sW, sPM
Small numbers Aug-May.

Purple Heron *Ardea purpurea* sPM
Small numbers, inc. flocks into double-figures, (mainly) Mar-May and (smaller numbers) Sept-Oct. Flocks of 60+ Chalandra River nr Skala Eresou Apr 02 and 53 Kalloni Saltpans Apr 08 are exceptional.

Great White Egret *Ardea alba* rW, sPM
Western Great Egret
Small numbers Oct-May.

Little Egret *Egretta garzetta* cSP, sAP, rW
Common around wetland sites and along the coast Mar-May and in smaller numbers Aug-Oct. Several birds over-winter.

Great White Pelican *Pelecanus onocrotalus* sPM
A near annual passage migrant Mar-May and Sept-Oct. Usually 1-2, but occasionally small flocks (e.g. 18 in Sept 07) and movements, e.g. large movement in Sept 07 inc. largest confirmed flock of 144 south nr Nifida (S.P & E.F. Dudley). Some individuals have been caught and tamed by fisherman (e.g. bird at Skala Kallonis harbour from 1998 to present). Single over-wintering record from winter 06/07 (T. Robinson).

Dalmatian Pelican *Pelecanus crispus* rPM
Much rarer than White Pelican but occurs in similar periods, Apr-May and Aug-Sept. Recent records: 27 over Kalloni/Potamia area Apr 2000; 15 (of flock of 17) over Kalloni Saltpans and Molivos Mar 02; Kalloni Saltpans Apr 2003 (Brooks 1998, 2000, 2002, 2003); 1 Polichnitos Saltpans Aug-Oct 06; 1 Kalloni Saltpans Sept 07; 1 Perasma Reservoir May 09. 2 Kalloni Saltpans Jan 09 the only winter record (E. Galinou).

Pygmy Cormorant *Phalacrocorax pygmeus* rW
Single birds recorded from coastal sites Nov-Apr. Earliest mid-Sept 08 Vouvaris River mouth.

Great Cormorant *Phalacrocorax carbo sinensis* sW
Gulf of Kalloni holds large winter population of c.3500 birds, otherwise small numbers around coast Sept-May.

European Shag *Leucocarbo aristotelis desmaresti* sRB
Present around the coast in all months.

Osprey *Pandion haliaetus* sPM
Recorded in reasonable numbers Mar-May and Sept-Oct.

European Honey-buzzard *Pernis apivorus* rMB, cPM
A relatively common passage migrant, occasionally in good numbers, Apr-May and Aug-Oct. Small numbers breed in both deciduous woodland and pine forests across the island.

Red Kite *Milvus milvus* V *
Two records: 1 Sigri Apr 84 (Brooks 1998); 1 nr Kalloni Apr 02 (Brooks 2002).
Note, confusion not only with Black Kite, but also with the much commoner Long-legged Buzzard which has very similar colouring to Red Kite.

Black Kite *Milvus migrans* sPM
Surprisingly only a handful of records noted most years Mar-May and Aug-Oct. One winter record, Feb 09 (T. Robinson).

White-tailed Eagle *Haliaeetus albicilla* V *
Five records: an imm and ad off Sigri May 94; 1 Vatousa May 95; 1 off Molivos Apr 98 (Brooks 1998); sub-ad Tsiknias River May 09 (I. & S. Bambrough, S.P. Dudley)†.

Egyptian Vulture *Neophron percnopterus* V *
Ten records: singles around Skala Eresou May 87 and May 91; one Ipsilou and Agiasos (believed to be the same bird) May 95; 1 Ipsilou Apr 98; 1 Napi Valley May 99; ad Skala Eresou May 00 and an imm nr Vatousa, both May 2000; 1 Makara Apr 04; 1 Molivos May 04 (Brooks 1998, 1999, 2000, 2004); 2 nr Ipsilou May 08 (per S.P. Dudley); 1 Vouvaris River mouth May 09 (T. Robinson)†.

Griffon Vulture *Gyps fulvus* V *
A surprisingly rare bird on the island, and with the rapidly declining European population, an increase in the level of records is unlikely. Only 10 recent records: 1 Eresos May 93; 3 over Filia May 96; 3 between Filia and Skoutaros May 97; 1 over Skala Sikaminias then at Vatera (taken in to care) Sept 97 (bearing a Croatian ring; released on Crete); 1 south over Efthalou Apr 02 (S.P. Dudley, M. Newell, V. Stratton); 2 over Molivos May 03; 3 over Potamia Valley May 03 (Brooks 1998, 2002, 2003); 1 over Ipsilou May 08; 3 over Skala Kallonis May 08; 1 Eresos, Agiasos & Kalloni areas May 09 (MO)†.

Short-toed Eagle *Circaetus gallicus* sMB, sPM
Short-toed Snake Eagle
Small numbers breed across the island. Seen on passage Apr-May and Aug-Oct. Occasional winter records. Often seen hovering over open hillsides.

Western Marsh Harrier *Circus aeruginosus* cPM
Regularly seen Mar-May with smaller numbers Aug-Oct. Occasional winter records.

Hen Harrier *Circus cyaneus* sW, sPM
Northern Harrier
Small numbers Nov-Apr, with passage birds Mar-May.

Pallid Harrier *Circus macrourus* sPM
Small numbers Mar-Apr. Very rare in autumn.

Montagu's Harrier *Circus pygargus* cPM
Common in spring Mar-May with small numbers Sept-Oct.

Levant Sparrowhawk *Accipiter brevipes* sPM, ?rMB?
Small numbers, occasionally double-figure flocks, recorded Apr-May, with smaller numbers Aug-Sept. Usually seen heading up/down obvious valleys (e.g. Napi) or from/near obvious hilltops (e.g. Ipsilou) or migration headlands/points (e.g. Sigri, Agias Fokas). Birds have been seen during the breeding season (BoG).

Eurasian Sparrowhawk *Accipiter nisus* rRB, cW, sPM
A handful of pairs almost certainly breed. Common Sept-Mar. Passage noted Mar-Apr and Aug-Oct.

Northern Goshawk *Accipiter gentilis* sRB, sPM
Small numbers breed across the island in both deciduous and coniferous woodland. Passage noted Mar-May and Aug-Oct.

Common Buzzard *Buteo buteo* sRB, cW, sPM
Small numbers breed across the island. Common Nov-Mar. Passage noted Mar-Apr and Aug-Oct.

Long-legged Buzzard *Buteo rufinus* sRB, sPM
Small numbers breed across the island. Common Nov-Mar. Passage noted Mar-Apr and Aug-Oct. Commoner in the western half of the island.

Lesser Spotted Eagle *Aquila pomarina* rPM
Recent records: singles nr Vatousa and between Agra and Eresos, both May 99; 5 over Agias Paraskevi Apr 2000; 4 over Molivos Reservoir May 2000 (Brooks 1998, 1999, 2000); birds seen daily late Aug/early Sept 02 during exceptional movement (P. Manning); 1 Metochi Apr 03 (S.P Dudley, M. Newell); 1 Vatera Bay Sept 07; 1 Ancient Antissa Apr 08; 1 Anaxos Apr 08; 1 Parakila Apr 08; 1 nr Ipsilu May 09; 1 Kalloni Raptor Watch Point May 09.

Greater Spotted Eagle *Aquila clanga* V *
Odd birds recorded Sept-Apr, most recent: 1 over Faneromeni Apr 99 (Brooks 1999).

Steppe Eagle *Aquila nipalensis* V *
Only one accepted record: 1 Petra Apr 08 (S.P. Dudley: HRC08).
Records not submitted to HRC: 1 over Liminos monastery and 2 over the Petrified Forest 11 May 97; 1 between Agiasos and Mytilini May 98; 1 nr Sigri May 01; 1 over Skoutaros Sept 02 (Brooks 1998, 2001, 2003).

Eastern Imperial Eagle *Aquila heliaca* V *
Eight records: 1, Sept 89 (BoG — no location); 2 over the 'south' of the island May 94; 1 Kalloni/Potamia Valley Sept 98; 1 north over Vatera Mar 99; 1 over Skala Sikaminias May 99; pr nr Vatousa May 99; 1 over Efthalou Apr 04; 1 over Vafios May 04 (Brooks 1998, 2004); 1 30 Apr-14 May 08 various sites (D. Walbridge, S.P. Dudley; photo); sub-ad Efthalou (presumed same Kalloni Raptor Watch Point) May 09 (I. & S. Bambrough, S.P. Dudley, I. Pitts, A. Bowley et al) [†]; 2CY & sub-ad Aghia Ioannis (nr Parakila) May 09 (P. & S. Solly, J. & F. Carden; photo)[†].

Golden Eagle *Aquila chrysaetos* rPM
Only c.14 recent records inc: 2 Kalloni Saltpans Apr 86; 2 nr Petra Aug 92; singles Petrified Forest Oct 94 and May 96; 1 nr Mandamados Aug 96; 2 Sigri Apr 97; one Potamia Valley May 2000 (Brooks 1998, 2000); 1 Napi Valley Apr 03 (P. Manning); 1 nr Sikaminia Sept 07 (S.P. & E.F. Dudley); 1 between Efthalou and Skala Sikaminias Apr 08 (S.P. Dudley; M. Denman); 1 Ancient Antissa Apr 08 (per S.P. Dudley); 1 nr Mandamados May 09 (S.P. Dudley).

Bonelli's Eagle *Hieraaetus fasciatus* rPM
Passage birds Apr-May. Brooks (1998, 2004) suggests breeding occurs around Mt Lepetimnos and Mt Olympus but there remains no evidence of this.

Booted Eagle *Hieraaetus pennatus* sPM
The odd single bird recorded most years Apr-May and Aug-Oct.

Lesser Kestrel *Falco naumanni* sMB, sPM
Small numbers breed on offshore islands at Sigri and possibly other offshore islands such as Is. Garbias (at the mouth of the Gulf of Kalloni) Apr-Aug. Most common in the west of the island. Also recorded on passage Apr-May and Sept when can be encountered anywhere.

Common Kestrel *Falco tinnunculus* sRB
A surprisingly scarce species with small numbers breed across the island.

Red-footed Falcon *Falco vespertinus* cPM
Common in spring Apr-May with smaller numbers recorded Aug-Oct. Occurs commonly in small parties of up to 30+ birds.

Eleonora's Falcon *Falco eleonorae* sPM, ?rMB?
On passage Apr-May and Sept-Oct. Even on passage, most often encountered in the west and north of the island. Can occur in numbers, e.g. 73 in one hour over Kalloni Raptor Watchpoint May 03. Thought to breed on offshore islands off Sigri.

Merlin *Falco columbarius* V *
Around seven records inc: 1 Mesa Mar 2000 (Brooks 2000); singles Kalloni Saltpans Apr 03 (S.P. Dudley, M. Newell) and Christou River Apr 03 (Brooks 2003); Kalloni Saltpans Apr 04 (S.P. Dudley, M. Newell); Mesa and Kalloni Saltpans area Mar 06 (E. Galinou); Ipsilou Apr 08 (S.P. Dudley, D. Nurney).

Eurasian Hobby *Falco subbuteo* sPM, ?rMB?
Small numbers seen on passage Apr-May and Sept-Oct. May breed (BoG).

Lanner Falcon *Falco biarmicus* ?rRB?
If this species is resident on the island, it is only a couple of pairs at most, as this remains a rarely sighted species. The higher western side of the island could provide breeding cliffs, but I suspect a lack of prey is the limiting factor for this and other predatory species. Odd records annually from anywhere on the island. Greek birds belong to the race *F. b. feldeggii* (BoG).

Saker Falcon *Falco cherrug* V *
One accepted record: Oct 92 (location unknown) (BoG)
Records not submitted to HRC: Apr 98 at Kalloni Saltpans; 2 Ipsilou Apr 02, 1 Upper Tsiknias River Apr 02; 2 Ipsilou Jun 03 (Brooks 1998, 2002, 2003).

Peregrine Falcon *Falco peregrinus* sRB, sW
Small numbers breed across the island with increased numbers in winter Nov-Mar. Greek breeding birds belong to the race *F. p. brookei* with nominate *P. p. peregrinus* occurring on passage (BoG).

Water Rail *Rallus aquaticus* rRB, rW, rPM
Small numbers breed at suitable wetlands (e.g. Dipi Larisos) but most usually encountered late winter and spring Mar-May.

Corncrake *Crex crex* V *
Around 15 records: 1 Loutropoli Thermis Apr 98 (LWH: HRC07); 1 ringed Haramida Sept 98 (HBRC: HRC06); 1 ringed Haramida Oct 02 (HBRC: HRC06); 1 Mytilini Sept 06 (LWH: HRC07); 1 Plomari Aug 07 (LWH: HRC06): 32 Ambeliko (illegally hunted) Sept 07 (per E. Kakalis, E. Gribylakou: HRC07)

Records not submitted to HRC: 1 Faneromeni River mouth spr 2000 (Brooks 2000); 1 Meladia Valley Apr 08.

Little Crake *Porzana parva* sSP, rAP, ?rW?
Recorded at most wetlands with cover Mar-May. Occasionally recorded Aug-Oct. Some may winter.

Baillon's Crake *Porzana pusilla* rSP
The rarest of the crakes with around 14 records, most recent inc: 1 Apr 84; 1 dead 98; 2 Makara Apr 2000; River Tsiknias May 03 (Brooks 1998, 2000, 2003); 1 Metochi Lake May 06 (T. Robinson *et al*); 1 Meladia River Ford Apr-May 07 (I. Lewington); 2 Metochi Lake Apr-May 08 (P. Manning *et al*); 1 Skala Kallonis Pool May 09 (D. Allen); 1 Metochi Lake May 09 (MO).

Spotted Crake *Porzana porzana* sPM
A handful of birds seen Apr-May. One autumn record: Skala Kallonis Pool Sept 98 (Brooks 1998).

Moorhen *Gallinula chloropus* sRB, sW
Small numbers breed with increased numbers in winter.

Coot *Fulica atra* rMB, sW
Small numbers occur in winter with occasional pairs staying on to breed.

Common Crane *Grus grus* rPM
The only recent records are: heard calling over Gulf of Kalloni in Apr 95; over Kalloni Saltpans May 96; 1 on flooded fields near Kalloni Saltpans Apr 97; one over Kalloni Saltpans Apr 99; 1 Sigri Apr 03; c.15 over Molivos May 03 (Brooks 1998, 1999, 2003).

Eurasian Stone-curlew *Burhinus oedicnemus* sMB, sPM
Small numbers breed inc. the Kalloni area (inc. Saltpans). Passage Feb-Apr and Aug-Oct. Large flocks (50+) can be encountered in autumn (e.g. 60+ near Kalloni Saltpans in Sept 03).

Oystercatcher *Haematopus ostralegus* sW, sSP
Small numbers occur in winter and spring Sept-May.

Black-winged Stilt *Himantopus himantopus* sMB, cPM
Small numbers breed (e.g. Saltpans) and also on passage Mar-May and Aug-Oct.

Avocet *Recurvirostra avosetta* sMB, sPM
Small numbers breed (e.g. Saltpans) and also on passage Mar-May and Aug-Oct. Occasionally over-winters on saltpan areas.

Northern Lapwing *Vanellus vanellus* sW
Small numbers Oct-Mar.

Spur-winged Plover *Vanellus spinosus* sPM
Spur-winged Lapwing
Usually single birds seen Mar-Mar, and rarely Aug-Sept. 2 together May 08 (MO) unusual.

Sociable Plover *Vanellus gregaria* V *
Sociable Lapwing
One record: 1 River Christou May 94 (BoG).

Caspian Plover *Charadrius asiaticus* V *
One accepted record: 1 nr Kalloni Saltpans May 02 (P. Marshall, T. Golding, D. Cleary, D. Mossman, D. Barker, I. Goshawk: HRC05).
Records not submitted to HRC: 1 dead Molivos Apr 84; 1 Skala Polichnitou Apr 87; nr Kalloni Saltpans May 02 and Mar-Apr 03 (Brooks 1998, 2002, 2003).

Eurasian Dotterel *Charadrius morinellus* V *
One accepted record: 1 Sept 06 Skala Polichnitou (T. Robinson: HRC08).
Records not submitted to HRC: 1 Mesa Sept 97; 1 nr Sigri Apr 99; nr Kalloni Saltpans Apr 01; 2 nr Kalloni Saltpans Apr 03; 3 River Christou Apr 03 (Brooks 1999, 2001, 2002, 2003).

European Golden Plover *Pluvialis apricaria* sW, rPM
Small numbers Oct-Mar. On passage Mar-Apr and Sept-Oct.

Grey Plover *Pluvialis squatarola* sW, sPM
Small numbers Mar-Apr and Sept-Oct.

Common Ringed Plover *Charadrius hiaticula* sPM
Occurs Mar-May and Aug-Oct.

Little Ringed Plover *Charadrius dubius* sMB, sPM
Small numbers breed along rivers and also on passage Mar-May and Aug-Sept.

Kentish Plover *Charadrius alexandrinus* sRB, sPM
Breeds in suitable habitats such as saltpans, drier areas of marshes, etc. Also on passage Apr-May and Sept-Oct.

Woodcock *Scolopax rusticola* cW
Another species known from hunting reports, Oct-Mar, but rarely seen by birders.

Jack Snipe *Lymnocryptes minimus* cW
Reported to be a common winter visitor, Oct-Mar, by hunters, but rarely seen! Only several records from birders: 1 Dipi Larisos Apr 2000; 6 Skala Kallonis Pool Mar 02; 1 flushed near Faneromeni River mouth Apr 04 (Brooks 2000, 2002, 2004); 1 Dipi Larisos Jan 06 (E. Galinou).

Great Snipe *Gallinago media* rPM *
A near-annual migrant with most recent records inc: 1 Tsiknias Valley May 99 (Brooks 1999); 1 Faneromeni River Ford Apr 2000 (Brooks 2000); singles nr Kalloni Saltpans Apr 04, Apr 06 & May 06; 1 Alikoudi Pool Apr 08; 2-4 reported at the Meladia River Mouth Apr 08; 1 Faneromeni River Apr 08. 1 Tsiknias River May 09 (MO)†; 1 Haramida Marsh May 09 (S.P. Dudley)†.

Common Snipe *Gallinago gallinago* cW, sPM
Present Aug-May.

Black-tailed Godwit *Limosa limosa* sSP
Occurs on larger wetlands and rivers Apr-May.

Bar-tailed Godwit *Limosa lapponica* V
Around eight records inc: 1 Polichnitos Saltpans Apr-May 2000; 18 Christou River May 01; Kalloni Saltpans Apr 04 (1) & May 04 (1); Kalloni area Apr 02 (Brooks 1998, 2000, 2002); 1 Polichnitos Saltpans Sept 07; Kalloni Saltpans and Tsiknias River mouth Apr-May 08.

Whimbrel *Numenius phaeopus* sSP
Small numbers occur Mar-May and Jul-Sept.

Eurasian Curlew *Numenius arquata* sW, rPM
Small numbers Aug-Mar.

Spotted Redshank *Tringa erythropus* sPM, rW
Small numbers Mar-May and Aug-Oct. 1-2 over-winter.

Common Redshank *Tringa totanus* cW, sPM
Occurs mainly Aug-Mar, with smaller numbers Apr-May

Marsh Sandpiper *Tringa stagnatilis* sPM
Small numbers move through the island Mar-May and Aug-Sept.

Common Greenshank *Tringa nebularia* sPM, sW
Small numbers move through the island Mar-May and Aug-Sept. Small numbers over-winter.

Green Sandpiper *Tringa ochropus* sW, sPM
Occurs mainly Oct-Mar, with passage Apr-May and Jul-Sept.

Wood Sandpiper *Tringa glareola* cPM
Very common on all water areas Mar-May with smaller numbers Jul-Sept.

Terek Sandpiper *Xenus cinereus* V *
Four accepted records: 1 Kalloni Saltpans May 93 (BoG); 1 Mesa May 95 (BoG); 1 Kalloni Saltpans Aug 2000 (A. Nicoli, M. Sighele: HRC05); 1 Polichnitos Saltpans May 09 (W. Lopau, T. Robinson, S.P. & E.F. Dudley: accepted, due in HRC 09).
Record not submitted to HRC: River Christou mouth May 03 (Brooks 2003).

Common Sandpiper *Actitis hypoleucos* sPM, rW
Small numbers Mar-May and Aug-Oct. Over-wintering birds recorded 97/98, 06/07 and 08/09 winters.

Turnstone *Arenaria interpres* sPM
Small numbers Mar-May and Aug-Sept.

Red Knot *Calidris canutus* V *
Two accepted records: 1 Kalloni Saltpans Apr 05 (S.P. Dudley: HRC 08); 1 Polichnitos Saltpans Sept-Oct 07 (T. Robinson: HRC08).
Record not submitted to HRC: 1 Polichnitos Saltpans Apr 99 (Brooks 1999); Kalloni Saltpans Apr 2000 (Brooks 2000), 2 in May 04 (Brooks 2004) & May 07.

Sanderling *Calidris alba* sPM
Small numbers seen Mar-May and Aug-Sept.

Little Stint *Calidris minuta* cPM
Can be found on almost all wetland areas Apr-May, with large concentrations at some (e.g. Kalloni Saltpans) Apr-May with smaller number Jul-Oct.

Temminck's Stint *Calidris temminckii* cPM
Can be found on almost all wetland areas Apr-May with smaller numbers Aug-Sept.

Pectoral Sandpiper *Calidris melanotos* V *
One record: juv Polichnitos Saltpans 24 Sept 08 (T. Robinson, S.P. Dudley, M. Newell: HRC08).

Curlew Sandpiper *Calidris ferruginea* cPM
Good numbers move through the island Apr-May with smaller numbers Aug-Oct.

Dunlin *Calidris alpina* sW, sPM
Surprisingly scarce Aug-May.

Broad-billed Sandpiper *Limicola falcinellus* rPM *
Recorded Apr-May but more often Aug-Sept. Flock of 20 birds Sept 02 (P. Manning) exceptional.

Ruff *Philomachus pugnax* cPM
Occurs Feb-May and Aug-Oct.

Red-necked Phalarope *Phalaropus lobatus* V *
Around 10 records inc: 2 Kalloni Saltpans May 98; a fem Kalloni Saltpans May 99 (Brooks 1999); 3 Kalloni area Aug 01 (R. Edwards: HRC07); Kalloni Saltpans May 03 & May 04 (Brooks 2003, 2004); 1 nr Kalloni Saltpans May 06 (E. Galinou); 1 Polichnitos Saltpans Aug-Sept 06 (E. Galinou).

Collared Pratincole *Glareola pratincola* cSP
Good numbers seen on passage across the island Apr-May.

Black-winged Pratincole *Glareola nordmanni* V *
Most recent records: 2 Kalloni Saltpans May 03 (N. Probonas: HRC06); 1 Kallonis Saltpans May 06 (S. Wytema: HRC06).

Slender-billed Gull *Chroicocephalus genei* sW, sPM
Occurs in small numbers Oct-Mar. Passage birds Apr-May and Aug-Sept. Few records Jun-Jul.

Black-headed Gull *Chroicocephalus ridibundus* sW
Occurs Jul-May.

Little Gull *Hydrocoloeus minutus* sW, sPM
Occurs in small numbers Aug-May. Surprisingly few seen on passage Apr-May and Aug-Sept.

Audouin's Gull *Ichthyaetus audouinii* rRB
A rare resident which breeds offshore near Petra (Brooks 2000). Recorded regularly along the north coast, especially between Molivos and Skala Sikaminias. Rare away from the north, but records occasionally from Skala Kallonis, Sigri, Vatera and the east coast areas.

Mediterranean Gull *Ichthyaetus melanocephalus* sW, sPM
Occurs in reasonable numbers Aug-May, with passage birds Mar-May and Aug-Oct.

Common Gull *Larus canus* V *
Mew Gull
Only around five records, most recent: 1 Kalloni Saltpans Aug 03 (Brooks 1998, 2003).

Yellow-legged Gull *Larus michahellis* cRB
Common resident breeding on offshore islands and seen right across the island.

Lesser Black-backed Gull *Larus fuscus* sPM
Passage birds Apr-May and Sept-Oct. Both *L. f. intermedius* and *L. f. fuscus* occur.

Gull-billed Tern *Gelochelidon nilotica* sSP
Small numbers pass through the island Apr-May.

Caspian Tern *Hydroprogne caspia* sPM
Occasionally recorded Apr-May and Aug-Sept.

Sandwich Tern *Thalasseus sandvicensis* cW, sPM
Occurs Aug-Apr.

Little Tern *Sternula albifrons* cMB
Occurs Apr-Sept.

Common Tern *Sterna hirundo* sMB, cPM
Occurs Apr-Sept.

Whiskered Tern *Chlidonias hybrida* cPM
Good numbers pass through wetlands areas Apr-May with smaller numbers Aug-Oct.

White-winged Black Tern *Chlidonias leucopterus* cPM
White-winged Tern
Good numbers pass through wetland areas Apr-May with smaller numbers Aug-Oct.

Black Tern *Chlidonias niger* sPM
Small numbers (often singles) occur Apr-May and Aug-Sept. Flocks, e.g. 18 in May 09 unusual.

Arctic Skua *Stercorarius parasiticus* V *
Parasitic Jaeger
Three records: 1 off Agios Fokas Mar 99; 2 off Kalloni Saltpans Apr 99; 2 off Kalloni Saltpans and Tsiknias River mouth Apr 03 (Brooks 1999, Brooks 2003).

Rock Dove *Columba livia* sRB
Small numbers occur around the rockier coastal areas. Feral Pigeons also occur in the towns.

Stock Dove *Columba oenas* V *
Four records, most recent: 1 Klio May 98; 2 nr Sigri May 02 (Brooks 1998, 2002).

Common Wood Pigeon *Columba palumbus* sRB, sW
Small numbers breed in pinewoods. Numbers increase with the arrival of winter migrants Oct-Mar.

Turtle Dove *Streptopelia turtur* cMB, cPM
Widespread breeder and passage migrant Apr-Sept.

Eurasian Collared Dove *Streptopelia decaocto* cRB
Widespread across the island, mainly around towns and villages.

Laughing Dove *Stigmatopelia senegalensis* V *
One record: 1 Achladeri May 94 (BoG).
Records not submitted to HRC: 1 Skala Kallonis Apr 01 (Brooks 2001).

Great Spotted Cuckoo *Clamator glandarius* sSP, rMB
Small passage Mar-May. Evidence may suggest occasional breeding (Brooks 2004). Magpie is this species' preferred host species and the lack of the host may be the reason for no confirmed breeding records. One record of Great Spotted Cuckoo on Lesvos was of a bird inspecting a Hooded Crow nest (Brooks 2004).

Common Cuckoo *Cuculus canorus* sPM
Small numbers pass through Apr-May and Aug-Oct. The rufous female form is not uncommon.

Barn Owl *Tyto alba* sRB
Small numbers breed across the island.

Scops Owl *Otus scops* sMB
Breeds across the island Apr-Jul. More often heard than seen, and birds rarely call after Jun. Some well known traditional spring roost sites inc. the Kalloni Mini Soccer pitch site (Scops Copse).

Eagle Owl *Bubo bubo* V *
Eurasian Eagle-Owl
The only confirmed records are birds been taken to the Lesvos Wildlife Hospital in winter. Reports of breeding needs to be confirmed.

Tawny Owl *Strix aluco* rRB
Known only from a handful of records of birds calling throughout the year which indicate a likely small resident breeding population.

Little Owl *Athene noctua* cRB
Occurs across the island. Breeds in rocky areas and old buildings (especially shepherd buildings).

Long-eared Owl *Asio otus* sRB
Small numbers known to breed across the island.

Short-eared Owl *Asio flammeus* rW
Odd birds Oct-Mar.

European Nightjar *Caprimulgus europaeus* sMB, sPM
Widespread but scarce Apr-Sept. Breeds in many scrub and scattered forest areas across the island inc. Potamia Valley, Mirsinia, Skala Polichnitos, nr Petra and Faneromeni.

Common Swift *Apus apus* cMB, cPM
Occurs Mar-Oct.
The Birds of Greece states that 'most birds are duller and paler than those of western Europe, tending towards *A. a. pekinensis*' and so likely confusion with Pallid Swift is increased.

Pallid Swift *Apus pallidus* sPM
Small numbers pass through Mar-Apr and Aug-Oct. Sizeable movements are recorded e.g. 110+ Meladia Valley 5 May 08. Common Swift often misidentified (usually in strong sunlight) as this species.
The Birds of Greece states that 'Pallid Swifts breeding in Greece are darker than west Mediterranean birds, intermediate between *A. p. illyricus* and *A. p. brehmorum*', coupled with the comment re. Common Swift above, likely confusion with Common Swift is greatly increased.

Alpine Swift *Apus melba* cPM, ?rMB?
Occurs on passage Mar-May and Aug-Oct. Not known to breed (but breeding suspected on offshore islands). Feeding parties seen in summer months are either the suspected breeder or from other Aegean islands or Turkey.

Little Swift *Apus affinis* V *
One record: 1 Skala Eresou Apr 04 (S.P. Dudley: HRC08).

European Roller *Coracias garrulus* sPM
Occurs more frequently in spring Apr-May than autumn Aug-Sept. Can occur in numbers, e.g. in May 03, 8 nr Sigri and 17 seen coming in off the sea Vatera.

Common Kingfisher *Alcedo atthis* sW, CB
Occurs mainly Aug-Apr with occasional breeding records, e.g. between Efthalou and Skala Sikaminias 03 (Brooks 2003).

Blue-cheeked Bee-eater *Merops persicus* V *
Only three accepted records: 1 Petra May 06 (S. Wytema: HRC06); 1 nr Tsiknias River mouth 14 Apr 08 (photo: B. Baston, K. Day: HRC08); flock of 7 Meladia River Ford 3 May 08 (S.P. Dudley: HRC08). The 2008 records were the only ones submitted from an unprecedented influx of 17 birds (10 different records) in 2008.
Records not submitted to HRC: 2 Kalloni Saltpans May 98; 1 Kalloni Saltpans Aug 98; 1 Upper Tsiknias River Apr 99 (Brooks 1998, 1999); 6 nr Gavathas Aug 2000 (Brooks 2000); influx in 2008 – 1 nr Tsiknias River mouth 19 Apr; 1 Meladia River Ford 23 Apr; 1 Skala Kallonis Pool 30 Apr; 1 nr Vourkos River mouth 30 Apr 08 (photo); 1 Sigri 1 May 08; 1 Kalloni Raptor Watchpoint 3 May 08; 1 Polichnitos Saltpans 5 May 08; 1 Meladia Valley 6 May 08.

European Bee-eater *Merops apiaster* cPM, sMB
Occurs Apr-Oct, with often large numbers passing over in spring. Breeds along dry river areas.

Eurasian Hoopoe *Upupa epops* cMB, cPM
Occurs Mar-Oct. Breeds across the island.

Eurasian Wryneck *Jynx torquilla* rPM
Occasional records Mar-Apr and Aug-Oct.

Middle Spotted Woodpecker *Dendrocopus medius* cRB
Common throughout wooded areas of the island, inc. olive groves. The Lesvos birds are thought to belong to the race *D. m. anatoliae* (BoG).

Red-backed Shrike *Lanius collurio* sMB, cPM
Scarce summer breeder (in west) and common passage migrant, often in considerable numbers, Apr-May and Aug-Oct.

Lesser Grey Shrike *Lanius minor* sMB, sPM
A scarce summer breeder and passage migrant Apr-May and Aug-Oct.

Great Grey Shrike *Lanius excubitor* V *
Probably fewer than 10 records Apr-May and Aug-Sept. no recent records. Status possibly question as the only large grey shrike record in recents years is a Steppe Grey Shrike.

Steppe Grey Shrike *Lanius pallidirostris* V *
One accepted record: nr Vatera Sept 08 (G. Sellors: HRC08). This is the only Greek record.

Records not submitted to HRC: 1 Sigri May 08.

(Steppe Grey Shrike cont.) HRC treat as subspecies of *L. meridionalis*. There are two Greek records of *L. meridionalis* (but not assigned to *pallidirostris*).

Woodchat Shrike *Lanius senator* cMB, cPM
Common summer breeder and passage migrant, often in considerable numbers, Apr-May and Aug-Oct.

Masked Shrike *Lanius nubicus* sMB
A localised summer breeder Apr-Sept. Favours olive groves and scattered deciduous woodland. Autumn migrants occur to late Sept in many habitats inc. pinewoods (e.g. Sept 07).

Golden Oriole *Oriolus oriolus* cPM
Common migrant Apr-May and Aug-Oct.

Eurasian Jay *Garrulus glandularius atricapillus* cRB
The black-crowned race *G. g. atricapillus* occurs commonly across the island.

Eurasian Magpie *Pica pica* V *
Four records: nr Kalloni Oct 95; nr Petra Jun-Sept 97; 1 Petrified Forest Oct 98 (Brooks 1998); 1 nr Mandamados May 08 (per S.P. Dudley).

Spotted Nutcracker *Nucifraga caryocatactes* V *
One record: 1 between Vafios and Agrenos May 93 (Brooks 1998).

Red-billed Chough *Pyrrhocorax pyrrhocorax* V *
Two records: 1 nr Dafia Jun 96; 1 Upper Tsiknias River Apr 03 (Brooks 1998, 2003). Recorded breeding on nearby island of Chios in 1971 but not listed as present there in 1993 (BoG).

Western Jackdaw *Coloeus monedula* sRB
Flocks are resident around Sigri, Anaxos, Skala Eresou, Gavathas, Apothika and Skala Polichnitou.

Rook *Corvus frugilegus* V *
Seven records: 2 Faneromeni Apr 86; 2 (ad and imm) wandering birds Faneromeni to Vatera Apr-May 96; 1 Ancient Andissa May 01; 1 Vatera Apr 02; 2 Achladeri Apr 02; 1 Mesa May 02 (Brooks 1998, 2001, 2002); 1 autumn 07 (Lesvos Wildlife Hospital).

Hooded Crow *Corvus cornix* cRB
Widespread and common.

Northern Raven *Corvus corax* sRB
Small numbers breed in the rockier upland areas in the west and around Mt Olympus.

Bohemian Waxwing *Bombycilla garrulus* V *
One record: unknown number of birds during a major influx of birds into Greece during the 65-66 winter (BoG).

Sombre Tit *Poecile lugubris* sRB
Widespread breeder, especially in the centre, north and west of the island. Occurs mainly around stands of deciduous trees and scattered woodland.

Coal Tit *Periparus ater* rRB
Breeds in some of the pinewoods.

Great Tit *Parus major* cRB
Common and widespread.

Eurasian Blue Tit *Cyanistes caeruleus* cRB
Common and widespread.

Eurasian Penduline Tit *Remiz pendulinus* V, CB *
Most recent records: 1 nr Mytilini Oct 97; 1 Skala Eresou Apr 98; 1 Dipi Larisos Apr 98; 2 Dipi Larisos Mar 99; 1 Haramida Oct 2000; pr bred Faneromeni River (nr lower ford) 02 (Brooks 1998, 1999, 2001, 2002); 1 nr Vatera Apr 04; 4 Faneromeni Apr 08 (D. Walbridge et al).

Bearded Tit *Panurus biarmicus* V *
Two records: 1 trapped and ringed Haramida Nov 2000 (Brooks 2001); pr Skala Kallonis Pool Apr 04 (Brooks 2004).

Calandra Lark *Melanocorypha calandra* V *
Eleven records: 2 nr Kalloni Saltpans May 96, with singles there May 97 and May 07; 1 Mesa Apr 97; 1 Skala Eresou May 97; 1 Dipi Larisos Apr 98; 1 wandering bird Skala Kallonis, Mesa and River Christou Apr-Jun 99; 1 Kalloni Saltpans Apr 2000; 1 Faneromeni River mouth Jun 2000 (Brooks 1989, 2000).

Greater Short-toed Lark *Calandrella brachydactyla* sMB, sPM
Occurs Apr-Sept. Breeds in suitable short grassland areas e.g. Alykes Wetlands.

Lesser Short-toed Lark *Calandrella rufescens* V *
One record: 1 nr Kalloni Saltpans May 04 (S. Bot, J. Poelstra, R. Gordjin, M. Bunskoek, M. Gal, C. Nengerman: HRC05).

Crested Lark *Galerida cristata* cRB
Common and widespread. The Aegean Islands population belongs to the race *G. c. caucasia* (BoG).

Woodlark *Lullula arborea* sRB, sW
Small numbers breed in suitable woodland edge and scrubby areas inc. pinewoods (e.g. Achladeri, Ipsilou). Birds found in winter in olive groves and more open areas. Birds in Greece belong to the race *L. a. pallida* but winter and passage birds also inc. *L. a. arborea* (BoG).

Eurasian Skylark *Alauda arvensis* sW
Occurs Oct-Mar. Greek birds belong to Mediterranean race *A. a. cantarella* but *A. a. arvensis* are also known in winter (BoG).

Sand Martin *Riparia riparia* sPM
Occurs on passage Mar-May and Aug-Oct.

Barn Swallow *Hirundo rustica* cMB, cPM
Common and widespread on passage Mar-May and Aug-Oct. Breeds across the island. Birds resembling *H. r. savignii* or *H. r. transitive* are reported annually in spring but with no confirmed records, these races are excluded from both the Lesvos and Greek Lists.

Eurasian Crag Martin *Ptyonoprogne rupestris* sMB, SPM, rW
Occurs Apr-Sept. Breeds in rocky gorges and cliffs of the west and north. Occasionally winters.

House Martin *Delichon urbicum* cMB, cPM
Common and widespread on passage Mar-May and Aug-Oct. Breeds across the island.

Red-rumped Swallow *Cecropis daurica* cMB, cPM
Common and widespread on passage Mar-May and Aug-Oct. Breeds across the island.

Cetti's Warbler *Cettia cetti* sRB
Found along river courses and around wetland areas.

Long-tailed Tit *Aegithalos caudatus* sRB
Localised breeder in pinewoods, e.g. Achladeri. The subspecies *A. c. tephronotus* occurs on Lesvos (BoG). This subspecies lacks all pink tones and has a black bib.

Willow Warbler *Phylloscopus trochilus* cPM
Apr-May and Aug-Oct.

Common Chiffchaff *Phylloscopus collybita* sW, sPM
Common and widespread Aug-Apr.

Eastern Bonelli's Warbler *Phylloscopus orientalis* rMB, rSP
Present Apr-Sept. Small numbers breed around Agiasos. Birds occ. breed or hold territory in central areas inc. breeding Potamia Valley 02, 03 & 04 (Brooks 2002, 2003, 2004) and single bird on territory in Lardia Valley 08 and 09 (MO). On passage noted annually in spring in the west and occ. in autumn (e.g. Aghia Ioannis (Parakila) Sept 07 (S.P. Dudley). Care should be taken in separating singing birds from Wood Warbler. Listen for the distinctive 'chip, chip' call which is also delivered before the trilling song.

Wood Warbler *Phylloscopus sibilatrix* cPM
Common on passage Apr-May, but less so Aug-Oct.

Great Reed Warbler *Acrocephalus arundinaceus* sMB, sPM
Relatively common Apr-Sept.

Moustached Warbler *Acrocephalus melanopogon* V *
Brooks (1998) states this is a localised winter visitor around Dipi Larisos (likely as good habitat) and Anaxos (unlikely due to lack of suitable habitat), but there are no recent records to support this. Apr-May records (Brooks 1998) suggest spring migrants. No autumn records.
Confusion with Sedge Warbler occurs annually. This is a real reedbed species, and whilst all birds should be studied carefully, any bird thought to be this species should be treated with caution and full details, and preferably photos, will be required by LBRC.

Sedge Warbler *Acrocephalus schoenobaenus* cPM
Common Mar-May and Aug-Oct.

Eurasian Reed Warbler *Acrocephalus scirpaceus* sMB, sPM
Small numbers Mar-Oct.

Marsh Warbler *Acrocephalus palustris* rPM
Small numbers Apr-May and, more commonly, Jul-Sept.

Eastern Olivaceous Warbler *Hippolais pallida* cMB, cPM
Common in dry scrub areas Apr-Oct.

Olive-tree Warbler *Hippolais olivetorum* sMB, rPM
This species breeds widely throughout Greece (up to 5000 pairs) (BoG), the Balkans and Turkey. In Greece it occurs south to south Mainland, Naxos and Kos; absent from both Rhodes and Crete.

On Lesvos it is widely but thinly distributed across eastern, southern and northern areas of suitable olive and oak woodland. It occurs in parkland like habitat comprising olive groves with scattered oak (occasionally just a single tree), almonds and bushes or oak parkland-like woodland with scattered olive trees and appears to show some preference for shallow undulating sites with hollows. Although thinly distributed it can occur in relatively high densities (e.g. up to six singing males singing in close proximity in Platania).

A feature of most breeding sites is the presence of Masked Shrike which regularly mimic Olive-tree Warbler. Olive-tree Warbler has a very recognisable, raucous song which is like a very loud Olivaceous Warbler. It is less guttural and rhythmic than Great Reed Warbler (migrants singing from trees occasionally confuse) and very unlike the more musical Nightingale-like Orphean Warbler song (with which it can occur alongside). Masked Shrike mimicry is usually thinner and more scratchy than the warbler's own song, but it is very passable and a shrike singing from out of sight and facing away from the observer (and so muffling the song slightly) can cause real confusion.

Better known sites on the island inc. the upper Napi Valley, Platania, Potamia Valley, around Skamnioudi, the Ambeliko Valley and Faneromeni. It does however occur in many other areas and there remain many new sites to discover!

Olive-tree Warbler arrives on the island at the very end of April and are at their most active during the first half of May. Birds depart in July with few records later than late August (later birds are probably migrants from further north).

Occasional migrant seen/heard away from known breeding areas in spring and occasionally in autumn.

Icterine Warbler *Hippolais icterina* sPM, ?rMB?
Small numbers pass through Apr-Jun and Aug-Sept. Occasionally found on territory during breeding season but no confirmed breeding records.

Common Grasshopper Warbler *Locustella naevia* rPM
Very small numbers Apr-May and Aug-Oct.

River Warbler *Locustella fluviatilis* sPM
Small numbers, usually only ever heard, Apr-May and Aug-Sept. Autumn presence confirmed by ringing (Brooks 1998).

Savi's Warbler *Locustella luscinioides* rPM
Very small numbers Apr-May and Aug-Oct.

Fan-tailed Warbler *Cisticola juncidis* fRB *
Zitting Cisticola
Former breeding species with no confirmed records since 2004 (1—2 still reported annually). Previously bred nr Kalloni Saltpans, Polichnitos Saltpans and Christou River.

Eurasian Blackcap *Sylvia atricapilla* cPM
Common, occ. in large numbers, Mar-May and Aug-Oct.

Garden Warbler *Sylvia borin* sPM
Small numbers Apr-May and Aug-Oct.

Barred Warbler *Sylvia nisoria* sPM, ?rMB?
Small numbers recorded Apr-May and Aug-Sept. Occasionally found on territory during breeding season, e.g. Meladia Valley May 05 (E. Galinou) but no confirmed breeding records.

Lesser Whitethroat *Sylvia curruca* sPM, ?rMB?
Common, occ. in large numbers, Apr-May and Aug-Oct. Suitable habitat for it to breed.

Eastern Orphean Warbler *Sylvia crassirostris* sMB, sPM
Apr-Sept. Breeds across the island. The race *S. c. crassirostris* occurs on Lesvos.

Common Whitethroat *Sylvia communis* sPM, rMB
Occurs on passage Apr-May and Aug-Oct. Several pairs breed.

Subalpine Warbler *Sylvia cantillans* cMB
Common and widespread across much of the island Apr-Sept.

Sardinian Warbler *Sylvia melanocephala* sRB, rPM, cW
Breeding birds thinly distributed along coastal areas (up to 5km inland) along the north (inland of Petra and Molivos), the east coast (between Mandamados and Mytilini) and southeast (Vatera area). Increase in winter suggests immigration from other Aegean islands and/or Turkey. Migrants can occur anywhere.

Rüppell's Warbler *Sylvia rueppelli* rMB, rPM
A localized summer breeder. The best-known area is the well-watched site at Kavaki between Petra and Molivos (Tracey Island — so named after the space-age night club structure visible as you approach the site from Petra). Males frequently found holding territory in the Kalloni-Petra corridor inc. in recent years the Kalloni Raptor Watchpoint (the 'bandstand'), the west side of Mesa (on north side of main road before the turn to Achladeri) and the east side of Mesa (along the track on the east side of the marsh just over the road bridge.

Firecrest *Regulus ignicapilla* V *
Most recent records are: 1 singing near Parakila Apr 99; up to 6 Meladia River valley nr Sigri Apr 02 (Brooks 1999, 2002); 1 Molivos Sept 07 (S.P. Dudley).

Goldcrest *Regulus regulus* sW
Localised, usually in the pinewoods, Oct–Apr.

Winter Wren *Troglodytes troglodytes* rRB, sW
Small numbers breed across the island and records indicate increase in numbers in winter.

Wood Nuthatch *Sitta europaea* rRB
Eurasian Nuthatch
Small numbers breed across the islands in oak areas inc. Napi Valley, Parivoli monastery, Skalochori, Vatousa, between Agiasos and Plomari, and along the north track between Molivos and Skala Sikaminias.

Krüper's Nuthatch *Sitta krueperi* rRB
This diminutive nuthatch is one of the main Lesvos attractions. A true Asia Minor species it is an endemic of the Western Palearctic were it is thought to be common in parts of southwest Russia, Georgia and Turkey. In Europe it occurs only on Lesvos which makes the island the accessible area for this species in the Western Palearctic. The Lesvos population is estimated at around 600 pairs (L. Kakalis *pers. comm.*).
This is a Calabrian Pine *Pinus brutia* forest species (Harrap & Quinn 1996) that occurs throughout the central and eastern pinewoods from sea level (e.g. Achladeri) up to c.800m. The species' main area lies between the Gulf of Kalloni and the Gulf of Geras and this area has formed the main research study area on the species between 2003-07 (Kakalis & Akriotis 2007), with some birds occurring in woods north of Kalloni and Parakila.
Despite extensive areas of Calabrian forest on the island, the species occurs at a low density, even for a nuthatch. This is thought to be due to the species' specialised requirement of mature forest with abundant dead trees. Current forest management on Lesvos includes the removal of much of the dead trees (Kakalis & Akriotis 2007).
Preferred nest sites are in dead standing trees (snags) with birds occasionally using dead branches of live pines (6%) with many snags having broken tops leaving a tall decaying stump. Nest holes tend to be between 3-10 meters off the ground and the taller the snag the higher the nest hole (Kakalis & Akriotis 2007). Around 250 nest boxes have been sited in the forest since 1999 but nuthatches have never been found using them (unlike in Turkey where nest box use is relatively common) (Kakalis & Akriotis 2007).
The nesting season varies depending on how cold and wet the late winter/early spring period has been. This means that in some years birds may just be going down on eggs at the end of April, but in other years they are feeding young in the first week of May. Lower altitude sites (such as Achladeri) appear to be more consistent than higher sites, with fledging being the norm around the second week in May. Incubation of the 5-6 eggs is between 14-17 days, and the young fledge after 16-19 days, with the birds keeping to the natal area for the first week or two.
Krüper's Nuthatch is resident and the Lesvos population is almost certainly isolated with no

immigration occurring from the nearest Turkish population (35km+ inc. sea crossing) (L. Kakalis *pers. comm.*). As a resident, pairs tend to be territorial throughout the year, so a pair will often be found close to their favoured breeding site throughout autumn and winter. This may indicate that birds away from these sites, especially singletons in autumn, are dispersing young birds.

Krüper's Nuthatch is often first detected by its nasal 'dwyee' or buzzy Jay-like calls.

Achladeri remains the main site for this species (1-3 pairs breeding), but it can also be seen well in the Agiasos area. It is well worth exporing other pinewood areas inc. around Kalloni and Parakila.

Western Rock Nuthatch *Sitta neumayer* cRB

Common throughout much of the rockier areas of the island, particularly the west and north. They build gourd-like nests out of mud in shaded rock crevices. Lesvos birds don't look like classic Western Rock Nuthatch *S. neumayer*, but appear to be somewhere between Western and Eastern Rock Nuthatch *S. tephronata*. They have extensive buff colouring under the tail and onto the rear flanks (pro-Eastern) as well as a medium-to-thick black eye stripe behind the eye (intermediate feature). They are however small in size and short-billed (pro-Western). *The Birds of Greece* suggests that Lesvos birds are of the race *S. n. zarudnyi*. Proving where the Lesvos birds fall in the rock nuthatch complex could prove a fascinating study.

Short-toed Treecreeper *Certhia brachydactyla* sRB

Common throughout pinewoods. Most birders see this species at Achladeri when looking for Krüper's Nuthatch and so rarely seen elsewhere. Lesvos birds may be of the Asia Minor race *C. b. harterti* (BoG).

Common Starling *Sturnus vulgaris* cW

Occurs Oct-Apr.

Rose-coloured Starling *Pastor roseus* sPM

Rosy Starling

Occurs in varying numbers annually May-Jun.

Ring Ouzel *Turdus torquatus* V *

Three recent records: a male Potamia Valley Apr 99; 1 nr Achladeri Apr 99; a male Ipsilou monastery May 99 (Brooks 1999).

Common Blackbird *Turdus merula* cRB, cW

Breeding numbers increasing and very common in winter. Shot in large numbers to reduce numbers feeding on olives.

Fieldfare *Turdus pilaris* sW

Small numbers Oct-Feb.

Redwing *Turdus iliacus* sW
Occurs Oct-Feb. Usually more numerous than Fieldfare.

Song Thrush *Turdus philomelos* cW, rB
Common and widespread in winter, with many shot (see Blackbird). Several pairs breed.

Mistle Thrush *Turdus viscivorus* sRB
Small numbers breed in pinewoods across the island.

European Robin *Erithacus rubecula* cW, rB
Occurs commonly across the island Oct-Mar. A few breeding pairs nr Mt Olympus.

Bluethroat *Luscinia svecica* V *
One accepted record: Pithariou Reservoir Sept 07 (S.P. Dudley: HRC08).
Records not submitted to HRC: most recent; Christou River spr 04 (Brooks 2004).

Thrush Nightingale *Luscinia luscinia* sPM
Occurs in small numbers Apr-May and Aug-Oct.

Common Nightingale *Luscinia megarhynchos* cMB
Apr-Oct. Breeds across the island along dry river beds and other dry, dense scrub.

White-throated Robin *Irania gutturalis* V, CB *
This species is thinly distributed throughout southern and eastern Turkey and the Middle East. It is best classed as a vagrant, sporadic breeder on Lesvos. *The Birds of Greece* lists only four records up to 1995, inc. two from Lesvos. Whilst this is a HRC description species, few observers submit their records formally so few have been officially accepted.
Three accepted records: 1 nr Molivos May 94 (Brooks 1998, BoG); 1 nr Molivos May 1995 (Brooks 1998, BoG); 1 Faneromeni May 98 (S. Gillings, S.J. Gough, P. Skerry: HRC05); 1 nr Sigri May 06 (E. Opperman, K. Mullarney: HRC06).
Unconfirmed records inc: Efthalou 95 and 96 (reportedly breeding both years); a male between Eressos and Sigri and (believed same) at Faneromeni River Ford May 97; pr on territory Ipsilou monastery May 01 were seen taking food to a nest site; 2 prs bred successfully nr Agra spr 01; 1 pr bred nr Agra 02; pr bred the old Sigri Sanatorium 06 (only a record of an adult seen on 4/5/06 submitted and accepted by HRC as above).

Rufous Bush Robin *Cercotrichas galactotes* sMB
Rufous-tailed Scrub Robin
Occurs Apr-Aug. Small numbers breed in suitable dry, scrubby areas. Signs of a decline since 2005. The eastern form *C. g. syriacus* occurs on Lesvos. It differs from the western nominate

C. g. galactotes race by lacking the rufous-toned head and mantle, with the red colouration restricted to the rump and tail with the rest of the upperparts appearing quite grey.

Lesvos holds a small population with scattered pairs across the central and western areas of the island. They seem to have a preference for coastal areas of dry stream and river beds running down to the coast.

Males sing from small trees and bushes but otherwise they spend their time skulking under and around dense low shrub cover. Better known sites inc. Kalloni Saltpans area, Meladia Valley and Madaros. Birds arrive back in Lesvos in early May (rarely late April) and depart by late August.

Black Redstart *Phoenicurus ochruros* cW
Common Oct-Mar.

Common Redstart *Phoenicurus phoenicurus* sPM
Small numbers Apr-May and Sept-Oct.

Whinchat *Saxicola rubetra* cPM
Can occur in huge numbers across the island Apr-May and Aug-Oct.

European Stonechat *Saxicola torquata* sRB, sW
Small numbers occur across the island and records indicate increase in numbers in winter.

Isabelline Wheatear *Oenanthe isabellina* sMB, rPM
Apr-Sept. Small numbers breed in the rocky west of the island. The best area to search is between the Eresos/Sigri/Kalloni road junction and Ipsilou Monastery (p. 147). Passage birds seen in other areas.

Northern Wheatear *Oenanthe oenanthe* rMB, sPM
Small numbers breed in the west inc. Apothika, Ipsilou and Sigri. Passage birds Mar-May and Aug-Oct.

Pied Wheatear *Oenanthe pleschanka* V *
Around 10 records inc: three records in May 95 — a male Skala Sikaminias, a pr near Ambeliko and a male nr Petra; a singing male nr Petra May 96; a fem/imm Mesa Aug 96; in 97, between Sigri and Eresos Aug; Potamia Valley Sept; nr Molivos Sept; a pr held territory on Mt Olympus in May 01; a possible pr on territory nr Molivos May 03 (Brooks 1998, 2001, 2003).

The Birds of Greece gives a single breeding record nr Akrasi in 88. Separating this species from the black-throated form of Black-eared Wheatear requires good views and reports frequently refer to this species.

Black-eared Wheatear *Oenanthe hispanica* cMB
Common and widespread across the island Mar-Sept. Both western (*O. h. hispanica*) and eastern (*O. h. melanoleuca*) races occur, with pale-throated and black-throated forms of both races present.

Finsch's Wheatear *Oenanthe finschii* V *
Only one accepted record: a male at Megalochori Jun 93 (BoG).
Records not submitted to HRC: a male singing at the top of Potamia Valley May 98 & Apr 99; 1 Aghia Ioannis Apr 99; pr Ipsilou monastery Apr 99; nr Molivos Irrigation Reservoir May 2000; fem between Sigri and Eresos Jun 2000; pr between Efthalou and Skala Sikaminias May 01 (Brooks 1998, 2000, 2001).
Many reports prove to be 'black and white' black-throated *melanoleuca* Black-eared Wheatear.

Rufous-tailed Rock-thrush *Monticola saxatilis* rPM
Rock Thrush
Around 16 records, most recent: 1 nr Vatousa Apr 2000, 1 Metochi Lake and 1 Napi Valley (all Apr 2000); 1 between Eresos and Ipsilou and 1 nr Vatousa (both May 2000) (Brooks 2000, 2002); 1 Efthalou Sept 05; 1 Sigri Apr 07; 1 nr Napi Apr 08.

Blue Rock-thrush *Monticola solitarius* sRB
Blue Rock Thrush
Widespread, especially in the rocky west of the island.

Spotted Flycatcher *Muscicapa striata* cPM, sMB
Widespread, and often in large numbers, Apr-May and Aug-Oct. Breeds in pinewoods across the island.

Eurasian Pied Flycatcher *Ficedula hypoleuca* cPM
Widespread Apr-May and Aug-Oct.

Semi-collared Flycatcher *Ficedula semitorquata* V *
Around 14 records, most recent: singles Faneromeni River Ford Apr 2000 & Apr 03; 1 Napi Valley Apr 2000; in Apr 04, singles at Molivos, Faneromeni River Ford and Ipsilou monastery (Brooks 2000, 2003, 2004); 1-2 Ipsilou Apr 08 (S.P. Dudley *et al*); 1 Meladia River Ford Apr 08 (per S.P. Dudley).

Collared Flycatcher *Ficedula albicollis* sSP, rAP
Occurs Apr-May. Only two autumn records: 2 Skala Eresou Oct 95 (Brooks 1998); 1 Pithariou Reservoir Sept 07 (S.P. Dudley). The west of island during good migration periods is the best chance for this species.

Red-breasted Flycatcher *Ficedula parva* rPM
Singles occasionally seen Apr-May and Aug-Sept. Four at Ipsilou Apr 08 exceptional.

Black-bellied Dipper *Cinclus cinclus aquaticus* V *
White-throated Dipper
One record: 1 Sigri Sept 07 (D. Brown) †.

House Sparrow *Passer domesticus* cRB
Widespread and common.

Spanish Sparrow *Passer hispaniolensis* sMB, sPM
Breeding groups found across the island, usually around fertile agricultural land. Distinct passage Apr-May.

Eurasian Tree Sparrow *Passer montanus* V *
Five records: 1 Skala Eresou Oct 92; between Molivos and Skala Sikaminias Apr 94; nr Anaxos Aug 96; 3 between Gavathas and Ancient Andissa May 2000 (Brooks 1998, 2000). Pr bred (amongst House Sparrows) near Agios Fokas 03 (Brooks 2003). The latter record may suggest that this species is overlooked.

Rock Sparrow *Petronia petronia* sRB
Small numbers breed in the rockier west of the island, e.g. Ipsilou, between Agra and Mesotopos.

Dunnock *Prunella modularis* sW
Occurs Oct-Mar.

Western Yellow Wagtail *Motacilla flava*
Common and widespread on passage Mar-May and Aug-Oct.
The following races are known to occur:
Black-headed Wagtail *M. f. feldegg* cPM, cMB
Blue-headed Wagtail *M. f. flava* cPM
Grey-headed Wagtail *M. f. thunbergi* cPM
Italian Yellow Wagtail *M. f. cinereocapilla* rPM
Yellow-headed Wagtail *M. f. lutea* V *
Syke's Yellow Wagtail *M. f. beema* V *
The following intergrade/variant races are also seen annually:
'Romanian' Yellow Wagtail *M. f. 'dombrowski'* sPM (*flava-feldegg* intergrade)
'Russian' Yellow Wagtail *M. f. 'superciliaris'* rPM (*thunbergi* variant)
By no means all birds can be assigned to race with many variants of each subspecies occurring. British Yellow Wagtail *M. f. flavissima* (*) is reported annually and with only a couple of Greek records, these are more likely to be variants of other races.

Citrine Wagtail *Motacilla citreola* rSM
Occurs most years in spring, often in double-figures (e.g. 15+ Apr-May 04). Most records Apr-May.
One unconfirmed autumn record: 2-5 Tsiknias River Sept 97 (Brooks 1998).
Birds all believed to be *M. c. citreola* but birds should be examined closely for *M. c. werea*.

Grey Wagtail *Motacilla cinerea* rRB, sW
Small numbers breed and numbers increase in winter Sept-Mar.

White Wagtail *Motacilla alba* sW, sPM, rB
Occurs Sept-May. A few pairs possibly breed.

Tawny Pipit *Anthus campestris* sMB, SPM
Occurs in small numbers, inc. believed breeding, Mar-Oct.

Meadow Pipit *Anthus pratensis* cW
Occurs, often in large numbers, Oct-Mar.

Tree Pipit *Anthus trivialis* sPM
Occurs Mar-May and Aug-Oct.

Red-throated Pipit *Anthus cervinus* sPM
Occurs Apr-May and Sept-Oct.

Water Pipit *Anthus spinoletta* sW
Occurs Oct-Mar.

Common Chaffinch *Fringilla coelebs* cRB
Widespread and common.

Brambling *Fringilla montifringilla* sW
Occurs in varying numbers Oct-Mar.

Red-fronted Serin *Serinus pusillus* V *
Only one accepted record: a pr nr Andissa May 94 (BoG).
Records not submitted to HRC: 2 Perivoli monastery Apr 97; a juv nr Agiasos Sept 98; 2 Skala Kallonis May 03 (Brooks 1998, 2003).

European Serin *Serinus serinus* sRB, sPM
Breeds in pinewoods across the island. Non-breeding and passage birds occur in other habitats.

European Greenfinch *Carduelis chloris* cRB
Widespread and common.

European Goldfinch *Carduelis carduelis* cRB
Widespread and common.

Pine Siskin *Carduelis spinus* sW
Occurs in varying numbers Oct-Mar.

Common Linnet *Carduelis cannabina* sRB
Scarce but widespread across the island.

Common Rosefinch *Carpodacus erythrinus* V *
Only two accepted records: a singing male Molivos May 91 (BoG); a juv (caught and ringed) Haramida Sept 96 (HBRC: HRC06).
Records not submitted to HRC: a pr Faneromeni River Ford May 97; a singing male nr Petra May 97; male Faneromeni River Ford May 2000 (Brooks 1998, 2000); 1 Ipsilou Apr 08.

Red Crossbill *Loxia curvirostra* V *
5-6 records inc: pr feeding a juv near Agiasos Apr 97; up to 8 at the Agiasos Sanatorium Aug 98; 'small group' nr Vasilika Jul 01; 2 nr Achladeri Jun 03; 1 Ipsilou monastery May 04 (Brooks 1998, 2001, 2003, 2004).

Eurasian Bullfinch *Pyrrhula pyrrhula* V *
Three records: 1 nr Kalloni Apr 84; 1 Potamia Valley Mar 86 (Brooks 1998); 2-3 nr Agiasos May 08 (T. Robinson).

Hawfinch *Coccothraustes coccothraustes* sW, rB
Scarce in winter Oct-Apr, but large flocks, e.g. 200+ nr Dipi Larisos Mar 2000 (Brooks 2000) not unexpected. Several pairs at least thought to breed.

Corn Bunting *Emberiza calandra* cRB
Widespread and common.

Yellowhammer *Emberiza citrinella* V *
Three records: 1 Mesa Mar 97; fem Faneromeni Jan 98; 3 Potamia Valley Aug 97 (Brooks 1998).

Rock Bunting *Emberiza cia* sW, ?rB? *
Most records Sept-Mar, but occasional summer records may allude to occ. breeding e.g. Mt Lepetimnos 03 (Brooks 2003).

Cinereous Bunting *Emberiza cineracea* sMB
This is another species which, at the European scale, is confined to Greece. It also occurs in neighbouring Turkey (which is thought to account for c.90% of the world population) with smaller populations in Iran and possibly in Syria and Iraq. The wintering areas are poorly known but inc. Yemen (and certainly other areas of Arabia) and Eritrea (BirdLife Species Factsheet – online at WWW.BIRDLIFE.ORG/DATAZONE).

Cinereous Bunting occurs in two forms, the nominate 'yellow-headed' western form (*cineracea* – occurs in Greece (inc. Lesvos and Turkey) and the 'yellow' eastern form (*senenowi* – from Iran). Lesvos is one of three Aegean islands along with Skyros and Chios that hold breeding populations. Elsewhere in Greece singing males have been found on Corfu and there is a single record from Kos (BoG). Lesvos remains the most important area for the species in Greece with up to 250 pairs thought to be present. The total Greek population is thought not to exceed 300 pairs.

On Lesvos, Cinereous Bunting occurs throughout the barren west of the island. Here it breeds in dry, rocky open areas with low *phrygana* (low growing, soft-leaved shrub habitat) and scattered boulders.

It is a rather inconspicuous species and is often heard long before it is seen. The yellow-headed males usually sing from the large boulders on scree slopes, but at several sites, e.g. Ipsilou, it occurs along the tree line where it uses trees and telegraph posts as song posts. Its rather drab plumage blends perfectly with lichen covered rocks and the dull greens and yellows of trees. The duller females are even less conspicuous and rarely seen away from the area they are actively feeding young. The males' song is both distinctive and far-carrying in the open country the species occurs in. The song is short and tuneful consisting of 4-6 notes (which is vaguely Reed Bunting-like in its delivery and quality), starting with a repeated short note and ending with a distinctive longer and descending double-note - zri zri zri zri zrie-zriee. It should not be confused with the more common Cretzschmar's Bunting song which is thinner, more Yellowhammer-like, (s)ji (s)ji (s)ji (s)jiuuu.

On Lesvos it is present on the breeding grounds from early April to late-July. Some may linger into August, but very few are recorded as late as September.

Like other buntings on the island it seems to have a high dependency on bush-crickets which are abundant across the island in low-shrub habitats (BoG).

Ortolan Bunting *Emberiza hortulana* sPM
Small numbers Apr-May and Aug-Sept.

Cretzschmar's Bunting *Emberiza caesia* cMB
Widespread and common across the north and west of the island Apr-Jul.

Cirl Bunting *Emberiza cirlus* cRB
Widespread and common in open country with scattered trees.

Little Bunting *Emberiza pusilla* V *
One record: 1 trapped and ringed Haramida Marsh Oct 97 (HBRC: HRC06).

Black-headed Bunting *Emberiza melanocephala* cMB
Widespread and common late Apr-Aug.

Common Reed Bunting *Emberiza schoeniclus* sW
Seven records, most recent: fem Christou River Mar 2000 (Brooks 2002); 1 Metochi Lake Dec 06; at Polichnitos Saltpans 3 winter 07/06, 2 winter 07/08 and 2 winter 08/09 (T. Robinson).

APPENDIX 1
SPECIES FORMALLY REJECTED (BY HRC) OR REPORTS OF SPECIES NEW TO LESVOS NEVER SUBMITTED AND THEREFORE CONSIDERED UNPROVEN

The species listed here remain unconfirmed (no records submitted or occurrence thought unlikely and without supporting evidence are excluded). We urge observers of these records to formally submit them to LBRC. Where records have been submitted to HRC and have been rejected, this is indicated.

Rock Partridge *Alectoris graeca* *
Records not submitted: 1 Ipsilou Apr 04 (Brooks 2004).
A very unlikely species and surely refers to Chukar.

Lesser White-fronted Goose *Anser erythropus* *
Records not submitted to HRC: several shot during the winter of 01-02 (Brooks 2002).

Barnacle Goose *Branta leucopsis* *
Records not submitted: 1 nr Kalloni Saltpans Mar 03 (Brooks 2003).

Red-crested Pochard *Netta rufina* *
Records not submitted: 1 Skala Kallonis Pool Mar 02 (Brooks 2002).

Red-throated Diver *Gavia stellata* *
Records not submitted to HRC: 1 off Skala Kallonis Apr 04 (Brooks 2004).

Storm-petrel *Hydrobates pelagicus* *
European Storm Petrel
Several records not submitted to HRC inc. 1 off Vatera Apr 01 (Brooks 1998, 2001).

Black Vulture *Aegypius monachus* *
Cinereous Vulture
Record not submitted to HRC: 1 reported May 08.

Lesser Sand Plover *Charadrius mongolus* *
Records rejected by HRC: 2 birds Christou River Sept 98 (HRC05).
Records not submitted to HRC: singles nr Kalloni Saltpans May 02 and Apr 03.
The species is not on the Greek list.

Greater Sand Plover *Charadrius leschenaultii* *
Records not submitted to HRC: singles Kalloni Saltpans Apr and May 99, 2 in May 01 and one Jun 02 (Brooks 1999, 2001, 2002).

White-tailed Plover *Vanellus leucurus* *
White-tailed Lapwing
Records not submitted to HRC: 3 Kalloni Saltpans Apr 2000 and another single there later in the month (Brooks 2000); 1 Mesa May 01 (Brooks 2001).

Baird's Sandpiper *Calidris bairdii* *
Records not submitted to HRC: one Kalloni Saltpans May 01 (Brooks 2001).

Great Black-backed Gull *Larus marinus* *
Records not submitted to HRC: 1 Mytilini Jan 98 (Brooks 1998); 1 Mytilini Apr 01 (Brooks 2001); 3 Kalloni Saltpans Oct 02 (Brooks 2003).

Lesser Crested Tern *Sterna bengalensis* *
Records not submitted to HRC: 1 Kalloni Saltpans May 01 (Brooks 2001).

Arctic Tern *Sterna paradisaea* *
Records not submitted to HRC: Tsiknias River Jun 96 (2), May 98 (1) (all Brooks 1998), Apr 99 (1) and Apr 04 (2); Kalloni Saltpans Apr 98 (1), Apr 99 (3), May 2000 (1) & Apr 04 (1); 6 Skala Kallonis Mar 02; 1 Tsiknias River mouth May 02 (Brooks 1998, 1999, 2000, 2002, 2004). Only nine accepted Greek records.

Long-tailed Skua *Stercorarius longicaudus* *
Long-tailed Jaeger
Records not submitted to HRC: 1 off Mytilini Oct 96 (Brooks 1998). Only three Greek records.

Pomarine Skua *Stercorarius pomarinus* *
Records not submitted to HRC: an adult off Vatera May 96 (Brooks 1998).

Pied Kingfisher *Ceryle rudis* *
Records not submitted to HRC: 1 off Sigri Sept 02 (Brooks 2002).

White-throated Kingfisher *Halcyon smyrensis* *
Records not submitted to HRC: a very convincing description of a single bird seen at the Christou River road bridge on the evening of 21 Sept 07.

Great Spotted Woodpecker *Dendrocopus major* *
An unlikely species but reports from Parakila, Potamia Valley, nr Gavathas, nr Petra, Papania and nr Agiasos (Brooks 1998).
This species' regional distribution is somewhat far removed (northern Greece) from the Aegean Sea area and must therefore be considered as very unlikely to occur.

Green Woodpecker *Picus viridis* *
One report: Potamia Valley May 02 (Brooks 2002).
Occurs in nearby Turkey but remains an unlikely species to occur. Golden Orioles are occasionally reported as this species.

Syrian Woodpecker *Dendrocopus syriacus* *
Reports inc. nr Arisvi May 91; Sikaminia Jun 93; Skala Eresou Aug 93; Agiasos Sept 94; nr Petra Oct 95; pr between Polichnitos and Skala Polichnitou Apr 99 (Brooks 1998, Brooks 1999).
Of all the potential vagrant woodpeckers this is the most likely species to occur.

White-backed Woodpecker *Dendrocopus leucotos* *
Unconfirmed reports: nr Skalochori Apr 87; nr Tsiknias River May 96 (both Brooks 1998); 1 Napi Valley spr 2000 (Brooks 2000).
Like Great Spotted Woodpecker, the range of this species is nowhere near the Aegean Sea area.

Black Lark *Melanocorypha yeltoniensis* *
Records not submitted to HRC: 1 after extensive snowfall during the 1986-87 winter (Brooks 1998).

Richard's Pipit *Anthus richardi* *
Records not submitted to HRC: 2 Skala Kallonis Sept 94; 1 Kalloni Saltpans Apr 98; 1 Aghia Ioannis and near Makara (believed same bird) Apr 98; Kalloni Saltpans Apr 99; 1 Ipsilou Apr 02; 1 Achladeri May 02 (Brooks 1998, 1999, 2002).

Blackstart *Cercomela melanura**
Records not submitted to HRC: 1 Meladia Valley May 2000 (Brooks 2000).
Not on the Greek list.

Desert Wheatear *Oenanthe deserti* *
Records not submitted to HRC inc. 1 nr Anaxos May 98 and a fem Mesa spr 99 (Brooks 1999).

Aquatic Warbler *Acrocephalus paludicola* *
Records not submitted to HRC: 1 Faneromeni Ford Apr 02 (Brooks 2002).

Booted Warbler *Hippolais caligata* *
Records not submitted to HRC: 1 Ipsilou May 01 (Brooks 2001).

Upcher's Warbler *Hippolais languida* *
Records not submitted to HRC: 1 nr Tavari May 96; 1 Ipsilou monastery May 99; 1 between Efthalou and Skala Sikaminias May 2000; 1 nr Efthalou May 01 (Brooks 1998, 1999, 2000, 2001).

Spectacled Warbler *Sylvia conspicillata* *
Records not submitted to HRC: 1 Faneromeni River Ford Apr 2000; 1 Ipsilou monastery Apr 2000; 1 between Efthalou and Skala Sikaminias May 01 (Brooks 2000, 2001).

Ménétries's Warbler *Sylvia mystacea* *
Records not submitted to HRC: 1 Potamia Valley May 04 (Brooks 2004).
The species is not on the Greek list.

Black-crowned Tchagra *Tchagra senegula* *
Records not submitted to HRC: 1 between Tsiknias River and Kalloni Saltpans May 98 (Brooks 1998).
The species is not on the Greek list.

Isabelline Shrike *Lanius isabellinus* *
Records not submitted to HRC inc.1 Faneromeni Apr 95; 1 near Meladia River Ford Apr 98; 1 between Petra and Vafios May 98; fem Upper Tsiknias River Apr 2000; 1 Molivos Reservoir May 01; 2 Sigri Fields May 03 (Brooks 1998, 2000, 2001, 2003).

Twite *Carduelis flavirostris* *
Records not submitted to HRC: 2 birds of the Turkish race *brevirostris* Kalloni Saltpans May 94 (Brooks 1998); 4 between Sigri and Eresos Apr 02 (Brooks 2002).
Not on Greek list.

Rustic Bunting *Emberiza rustica* *
Records not submitted to HRC: 8 Potamia Valley Mar 02 (Brooks 2002).

APPENDIX 2
ESPCAPES

The following species are thought to be of unlikely natural occurrence and therefore deemed likely escapes from captivity.

Ruddy Duck *Oxyura jamaicensis*
One reported Kalloni Saltpans Aug 02 (Brooks 2003).

Namaqua Dove *Oena capensis*
One Skala Kallonis Jun 08.

REFERENCES USED TO COMPILE THIS CHECKLIST

Brooks, R. 1998. *Birding on the Greek Island of Lesvos*. Brookside Publishing, Fakenham.

Harrap, S. & Quinn, D. 1996. *Tits, Nuthatches & Treecreepers*. Christopher Helm, London.

Hellenic Rarities Committee, 2005. *Hellenic Rarities Committee Annual Report 2005* (referred to as HRC05 in text) — see HTTP://RARITIES.ORNITHOLOGIKI.GR/EN/EAOP/ANNUAL_REPORTS.HTM

Hellenic Rarities Committee, 2006. *Hellenic Rarities Committee Annual Report 2006* (referred to as HRC06 in text) — see HTTP://RARITIES.ORNITHOLOGIKI.GR/EN/EAOP/ANNUAL_REPORTS.HTM

Hellenic Rarities Committee, 2007. *Hellenic Rarities Committee Annual Report 2007* (referred to as HRC07 in text) — see HTTP://RARITIES.ORNITHOLOGIKI.GR/EN/EAOP/ANNUAL_REPORTS.HTM

Hellenic Rarities Committee, 2008. *Hellenic Rarities Committee Annual Report 2008* (referred to as HRC08 in text) — see HTTP://RARITIES.ORNITHOLOGIKI.GR/EN/EAOP/ANNUAL_REPORTS.HTM

Brooks, R. 1999. *Lesvos update spring 1999*. Brookside Publishing, Fakenham.

Brooks, R. 2000. *Lesvos update spring-summer 2000*. Brookside Publishing, Fakenham.

Brooks, R. 2001. *Lesvos update spring-summer 2001*. Brookside Publishing, Fakenham.

Brooks, R. 2002. *Lesvos update spring-summer 2002*. Brookside Publishing, Fakenham.

Brooks, R. 2003. *Lesvos update Summer '02 — summer '03*. Brooks, R. 2003. Brookside Publishing, Fakenham.

Brooks, R. 2004. *Lesvos update autumn '03 — summer '04*. Brookside Publishing, Fakenham.

Handrinos, G & Akriotis, T. 1997. *The Birds of Greece*. A&C Black, London.

Kakalis, E. & Akriotis, T. 2007. Nest site characteristics of Krüper's Nuthatch *Sitta krueperi* on the island of Lesvos, Greece. 2nd International Congress of Eurasian Ornithology, Antalya, Turkey, 26-29 Oct 07 (poster presentation).

Website: BirdLife Species Factsheet. Cinereous Bunting — see http://www.birdlife.org/datazone/species/index.html?action=SpcHTMDetails.asp&sid=8940&m=0

Last updated 31 May 2009

WILDLIFE CHECKLISTS

BIRDS
For detailed notes on each species, taxonomy and nomenclature see pp. 188–227.

Key to status codes

c = common	RB = resident breeder	PM = passage migrant (spring and autumn)
s = scarce	MB = migrant breeder	W = winter visitor
r = rare	CB = casual/occasional breeder	V = vagrant
f = former	IB = introduced breeder	? = status uncertain
	SP = spring passage	* = description species
	AP = autumn passage	

English name	Scientific name	Status
Chukar	Alectoris chukar	sRB
Quail	Coturnix coturnix	rMB, sPM
Common Pheasant	Phasianus colchicus	rIB
Greater White-fronted Goose	Anser albifrons	sW
Red-breasted Goose	Branta ruficollis	V *
Mute Swan	Cygnus olor	rW
Whooper Swan	Cygnus cygnus	V *
Bewick's Swan	Cygnus columbianus	V *
Common Shelduck	Tadorna tadorna	sW, sPM
Ruddy Shelduck	Tadorna ferruginea	sRB, sPM
Gadwall	Anas strepera	V *
Wigeon	Anas penelope	sW
Mallard	Anas platyrhynchos	sW
Shoveler	Anas clypeata	sW
Pintail	Anas acuta	sW, sPM
Garganey	Anas querquedula	cSP, sAP
Teal	Anas crecca	sW, sPM
Pochard	Aythya ferina	V *
Ferruginous Duck	Aythya nyroca	V *
Tufted Duck	Aythya fuligula	V *
Scaup	Aythya marila	V *
Goldeneye	Bucephala clangula	V *
Smew	Mergellus albellus	V *
Red-breasted Merganser	Mergus serrator	sW
White-headed Duck	Oxyura leucocephala	V *
Black-throated Diver	Gavia arctica	sW
Little Grebe	Tachybaptus ruficollis	sRB
Great Crested Grebe	Podiceps cristatus	sW
Red-necked Grebe	Podiceps grisegena	V *
Black-necked Grebe	Podiceps nigricollis	sW
Scopoli's Shearwater	Calonectris (diomedea) diomedea	sSB
Yelkouan Shearwater	Puffinus yelkouan	cRB
Greater Flamingo	Phoenicopterus roseus	sW
Black Stork	Ciconia nigra	sMB, sPM

BIRDS

English name	Scientific name	Status
White Stork	Ciconia ciconia	sMB, sPM
Glossy Ibis	Plegadis falcinellus	cSP, sAP
Spoonbill	Platalea leucorodia	sPM
Great Bittern	Botaurus stellaris	sW, sPM
Little Bittern	Ixobrychus minutus	cSM, sAP
Night-heron	Nycticorax nycticorax	cSM, sAP
Squacco Heron	Ardeola ralloides	cSM, sAP
Cattle Egret	Bubulcus ibis	V *
Grey Heron	Ardea cinerea	sW, sPM
Purple Heron	Ardea purpurea	sPM
Great White Egret	Ardea alba	rW, sPM
Little Egret	Egretta garzetta	cSP, sAP
White Pelican	Pelecanus onocrotalus	sPM
Dalmatian Pelican	Pelecanus crispus	rPM
Pygmy Cormorant	Phalacrocorax pygmeus	rW
Cormorant	Phalacrocorax carbo sinensis	sW
Shag	Phalacrocorax aristotelis	sRB
Osprey	Pandion haliaetus	sPM
Honey-buzzard	Pernis apivorus	rMB, cPM
Red Kite	Milvus milvus	V *
Black Kite	Milvus migrans	sPM
White-tailed Eagle	Haliaeetus albicilla	V *
Egyptian Vulture	Neophron percnopterus	V *
Griffon Vulture	Gyps fulvus	V *
Short-toed Eagle	Circaetus gallicus	sMB, sPM
Marsh Harrier	Circus aeruginosus	cPM
Hen Harrier	Circus cyaneus	sW, sPM
Pallid Harrier	Circus macrourus	sPM
Montagu's Harrier	Circus pygargus	cPM
Levant Sparrowhawk	Accipiter brevipes	rMB, sPM
Eurasian Sparrowhawk	Accipiter nisus	rRB, cW, sPM
Goshawk	Accipiter gentilis	sRB, sPM
Common Buzzard	Buteo buteo	sRB, cW, sPM
Long-legged Buzzard	Buteo rufinus	sRB, sPM
Lesser Spotted Eagle	Aquila pomarina	rPM
Greater Spotted Eagle	Aquila clanga	V *
Steppe Eagle	Aquila nipalensis	V *
Imperial Eagle	Aquila heliaca	V *
Golden Eagle	Aquila chrysaetos	rPM *
Bonelli's Eagle	Hieraaetus fasciata	rPM *
Booted Eagle	Hieraaetus pennatus	rPM *
Lesser Kestrel	Falco naumanni	sMB, sPM
Common Kestrel	Falco tinnunculus	sRB
Red-footed Falcon	Falco vespertinus	cPM

BIRDS

English name	Scientific name	Status
Eleonora's Falcon	Falco eleonorae	sMB, sPM
Merlin	Falco columbarius	rW
Hobby	Falco subbuteo	sPM, ?rMB?
Lanner Falcon	Falco biarmicus	?rRB?
Saker Falcon	Falco cherrug	V *
Peregrine Falcon	Falco peregrinus	sRB, sW
Water Rail	Rallus aquaticus	rRB, rWM, rPM
Corncrake	Crex crex	V *
Little Crake	Porzana parva	cSP, rAP, rW
Baillon's Crake	Porzana pusilla	rSP
Spotted Crake	Porzana porzana	sPM
Moorhen	Gallinula chloropus	sRB, sW
Coot	Fulica atra	rMB, sW
Common Crane	Grus grus	rPM
Stone-curlew	Burhinus oedicnemus	sMB, sPM
Oystercatcher	Haematopus ostralegus	sW, sSP
Black-winged Stilt	Himantopus himantopus	sMB, cPM
Avocet	Recurvirostra avosetta	sMB, sPM
Lapwing	Vanellus vanellus	sW
Spur-winged Plover	Vanellus spinosus	sPM
Sociable Plover	Vanellus gregarius	V *
Caspian Plover	Charadruis asiaticus	V *
Dotterel	Charadrius morinellus	V *
Golden Plover	Pluvialis apricaria	sW, rPM
Grey Plover	Pluvialis squatarola	sW, sPM
Little Ringed Plover	Charadrius dubius	sMB, sPM
Ringed Plover	Charadrius hiaticula	sPM
Kentish Plover	Charadrius alexandrinus	sRB, sPM
Woodcock	Scolopax rusticola	cW
Jack Snipe	Lymnocryptes minimus	cW
Great Snipe	Gallinago media	V *
Common Snipe	Gallinago gallinago	cW, sPM
Black-tailed Godwit	Limosa limosa	sSP
Bar-tailed Godwit	Limosa lapponica	V *
Whimbrel	Numenius phaeopus	sSP
Curlew	Numenius arquata	sW, rPM
Spotted Redshank	Tringa erythropus	sPM, rW
Common Redshank	Tringa totanus	cW, sPM, ?rMB?
Marsh Sandpiper	Tringa stagnatilis	sPM
Greenshank	Tringa nebularia	sPM, sW
Green Sandpiper	Tringa ochropus	sW, sPM
Wood Sandpiper	Tringa glareola	cPM
Terek Sandpiper	Xenus cinereus	V *
Common Sandpiper	Actitis hypoleucos	sPM, rW

BIRDS

English name	Scientific name	Status
Turnstone	Arenaria interpres	sPM
Knot	Calidris canutus	V *
Sanderling	Calidris alba	sPM
Little Stint	Calidris minuta	cPM
Temminck's Stint	Calidris temminckii	cPM
Pectoral Sandpiper	Calidris melanotos	V *
Curlew Sandpiper	Calidris ferruginea	cPM
Dunlin	Calidris alpina sW,	sPM
Broad-billed Sandpiper	Limicola falcinellus	sPM
Ruff	Philomachus pugnax	cPM
Red-necked Phalarope	Phalaropus lobatus	V *
Collared Pratincole	Glareola pratincola	cSP
Black-winged Pratincole	Glareola nordmanni	rPM *
Slender-billed Gull	Chroicocephalus genei	sW, sPM
Black-headed Gull	Chroicocephalus ridibundus	sW
Little Gull	Hydrocoloeus minutus	sW, sPM
Audouin's Gull	Ichthyaetus audouinii	rRB
Mediterranean Gull	Ichthyaetus melanocephalus	sW, sPM
Common Gull	Larus canus	V *
Lesser Black-backed Gull	Larus fuscus	sPM
Yellow-legged Gull	Larus michahellis	cRB
Arctic Skua	Stercorarius parasiticus	V *
Gull-billed Tern	Gelochelidon nilotica	sSP
Caspian Tern	Hydroprogne caspia	sPM
Sandwich Tern	Thalasseus sandvicensis	cW, sPM
Little Tern	Sternula albifrons	cMB
Common Tern	Sterna hirundo	sMB, cPM
Whiskered Tern	Chlidonias hybrida	cPM
White-winged Black Tern	Chlidonias leucopterus	cPM
Black Tern	Chlidonias niger	sPM
Rock Dove	Columba livia	sRB
Stock Dove	Columba oenas	V *
Wood Pigeon	Columba palumbus	rRB, sW
Turtle Dove	Streptopelia turtur	cMB, cPM
Collared Dove	Streptopelia decaocto	cRB
Laughing Dove	Streptopelia senegalensis	V *
Great Spotted Cuckoo	Clamator glandarius	sMB, sSP
Common Cuckoo	Cuculus canorus	sPM
Barn Owl	Tyto alba	sRB
Scops Owl	Otus scops	sMB
Eagle Owl	Bubo bubo	V *
Tawny Owl	Strix aluco	rRB
Little Owl	Athene noctua	cRB
Long-eared Owl	Asio otus	sRB

BIRDS

English name	Scientific name	Status
Short-eared Owl	*Asio flammeus*	rW
Nightjar	*Caprimulgus europaeus*	sMB, sPM
Common Swift	*Apus apus*	cMB, cPM
Pallid Swift	*Apus pallidus*	sPM
Alpine Swift	*Apus melba*	cPM
Little Swift	*Apus affinis*	V *
Roller	*Coracias garrulus*	sPM
Kingfisher	*Alcedo atthis*	sW, rMB
Blue-cheeked Bee-eater	*Merops persicus*	V *
European Bee-eater	*Merops apiaster*	cPM, sMB
Hoopoe	*Upupa epops*	cMB, cPM
Wryneck	*Jynx torquilla*	sPM
Middle Spotted Woodpecker	*Dendrocopos medius*	cRB
Red-backed Shrike	*Lanius collurio*	sMB, cPM
Lesser Grey Shrike	*Lanius minor*	sMB, sPM
Great Grey Shrike	*Lanius excubitor*	V *
Steppe Grey Shrike	*Lanius pallidirostris*	V *
Woodchat Shrike	*Lanius senator*	cMB, cPM
Masked Shrike	*Lanius nubicus*	sMB
Golden Oriole	*Oriolus oriolus*	cPM
Jay	*Garrulus glandularius*	cRB
Magpie	*Pica pica*	V *
Nutcracker	*Nucifraga caryocatactes*	V *
Chough	*Pyrrhocorax pyrrhocorax*	V *
Jackdaw	*Coloeus monedula*	sRB
Rook	*Corvus frugilegus*	V *
Hooded Crow	*Corvus cornix*	cRB
Raven	*Corvus corax*	sRB
Waxwing	*Bombycilla garrulus*	V *
Sombre Tit	*Poecile lugubris*	sRB
Coal Tit	*Periparus ater*	rRB
Great Tit	*Parus major*	cRB
Blue Tit	*Cyanistes caeruleus*	cRB
Penduline Tit	*Remiz pendulinus*	V, CB *
Bearded Tit	*Panurus biarmicus*	V *
Calandra Lark	*Melanocorypha calandra*	V *
Short-toed Lark	*Calandrella brachydactyla*	sMB, sPM
Lesser Short-toed Lark	*Calandrella rufescens*	V *
Crested Lark	*Galerida cristata*	cRB
Woodlark	*Lullula arborea*	sRB
Skylark	*Alauda arvensis*	sW
Sand Martin	*Riparia riparia*	sPM
Barn Swallow	*Hirundo rustica*	cMB, cPM
Crag Martin	*Ptyonoprogne rupestris*	sMB, SPM

BIRDS

English name	Scientific name	Status
House Martin	*Delichon urbicum*	cMB, cPM
Red-rumped Swallow	*Cecropis daurica*	cMB, cPM
Cetti's Warbler	*Cettia cetti*	sRB
Long-tailed Tit	*Aegithalos caudatus*	sRB
Willow Warbler	*Phylloscopus trochilus*	cPM
Common Chiffchaff	*Phylloscopus collybita*	sW, sPM
Eastern Bonelli's Warbler	*Phylloscopus orientalis*	rMB, rSP
Wood Warbler	*Phylloscopus sibilatrix*	cPM
Great Reed Warbler	*Acrocephalus arundinaceus*	sMB, sPM
Moustached Warbler	*Acrocephalus melanopogon*	V *
Sedge Warbler	*Acrocephalus schoenobaenus*	cPM
Eurasian Reed Warbler	*Acrocephalus scirpaceus*	sMB, cPM
Marsh Warbler	*Acrocephalus palustris*	rPM
Olivaceous Warbler	*Hippolais pallida*	cMB, cPM
Olive-tree Warbler	*Hippolais olivetorum*	sMB
Icterine Warbler	*Hippolais icterina*	sPM
Grasshopper Warbler	*Locustella naevia*	rPM
River Warbler	*Locustella fluviatilis*	sPM
Savi's Warbler	*Locustella luscinioides*	rPM
Fan-tailed Warbler	*Cisticola juncidis*	fRB *
Blackcap	*Sylvia atricapilla*	cPM
Garden Warbler	*Sylvia borin*	sPM
Barred Warbler	*Sylvia nisoria*	sPM
Lesser Whitethroat	*Sylvia curruca*	sPM, ?rMB?
Eastern Orphean Warbler	*Sylvia crassirostris*	sMB, sPM
Common Whitethroat	*Sylvia communis*	sPM, rMB
Subalpine Warbler	*Sylvia cantillans*	cMB
Sardinian Warbler	*Sylvia melanocephala*	sRB, rPM
Rüppell's Warbler	*Sylvia rueppelli*	rMB, rPM
Firecrest	*Regulus ignicapilla*	V *
Goldcrest	*Regulus regulus*	sW
Wren	*Troglodytes troglodytes*	rRB, sW
Wood Nuthatch	*Sitta europaea*	rRB
Krüper's Nuthatch	*Sitta krueperi*	rRB
Rock Nuthatch	*Sitta neumayer*	cRB
Short-toed Treecreeper	*Certhia brachydactyla*	sRB
Common Starling	*Sturnus vulgaris*	cW
Rose-coloured Starling	*Pastor roseus*	sPM
Ring Ouzel	*Turdus torquatus*	V *
Blackbird	*Turdus merula*	cRB, cW
Fieldfare	*Turdus pilaris*	sW
Redwing	*Turdus iliacus*	sW
Song Thrush	*Turdus philomelos*	cW, rB
Mistle Thrush	*Turdus viscivorus*	sRB

BIRDS

English name	Scientific name	Status
Robin	*Erithacus rubecula*	cW, rB
Bluethroat	*Luscinia svecica*	V *
Thrush Nightingale	*Luscinia luscinia*	sPM
Common Nightingale	*Luscinia megarhynchos*	cMB
White-throated Robin	*Irania gutturalis*	V, CB *
Rufous Bush Robin	*Cercotrichas galactotes*	sMB
Black Redstart	*Phoenicurus ochruros*	cW
Common Redstart	*Phoenicurus phoenicurus*	sPM
Whinchat	*Saxicola rubetra*	cPM
Stonechat	*Saxicola torquatus*	sRB, sW
Isabelline Wheatear	*Oenanthe isabellina*	sMB, rPM
Northern Wheatear	*Oenanthe oenanthe*	sPM
Pied Wheatear	*Oenanthe pleschanka*	V *
Black-eared Wheatear	*Oenanthe hispanica*	cMB
Finsch's Wheatear	*Oenanthe finschii*	V *
(Rufous-tailed) Rock-thrush	*Monticola saxatilis*	rPM
Blue Rock-thrush	*Monticola solitarius*	sRB
Spotted Flycatcher	*Muscicapa striata*	cPM
Semi-collared Flycatcher	*Ficedula semitorquata*	V *
Collared Flycatcher	*Ficedula albicollis*	sSP, rAP
Pied Flycatcher	*Ficedula hypoleuca*	cPM
Red-breasted Flycatcher	*Ficedula parva*	rPM
Black-bellied Dipper	*Cinclus cinclus aquaticus*	V *
House Sparrow	*Passer domesticus*	cRB
Spanish Sparrow	*Passer hispaniolensis*	sMB, sPM
Tree Sparrow	*Passer montanus*	V *
Rock Sparrow	*Petronia petronia*	sRB
Dunnock	*Prunella modularis*	sW
Yellow Wagtail	*Motacilla flava*	
- Blue-headed Wagtail	*M. f. flava*	cPM
- Black-headed Wagtail	*M. f. feldegg*	cPM, cMB
- Grey-headed Wagtail	*M. f. thunbergi*	cPM
- Syke's Wagtail	*M. f. beema*	rPM
- Italian Wagtail	*M. f. cinereocapilla*	V *
- Yellow-headed Wagtail	*M. f. lutea*	V *
- 'Romanian' Yellow Wagtail	*M. f. 'dombrowski'*	sPM
- 'Russian' Yellow Wagtail	*M. f. 'superciliaris'*	rPM
Citrine Wagtail	*Motacilla citreola*	rPM *
Grey Wagtail	*Motacilla cinerea*	rRB, sW
White Wagtail	*Motacilla alba*	sW, sPM, rB
Tawny Pipit	*Anthus campestris*	sMB, SPM
Meadow Pipit	*Anthus pratensis*	cW
Tree Pipit	*Anthus trivialis*	sPM
Red-throated Pipit	*Anthus cervinus*	sPM

BIRDS

English name	Scientific name	Status
Water Pipit	*Anthus spinoletta*	sW
Chaffinch	*Fringilla coelebs*	cRB
Brambling	*Fringilla montifringilla*	sW
Red-fronted Serin	*Serinus pusillus*	V *
Serin	*Serinus serinus*	sRB
Greenfinch	*Carduelis chloris*	cRB
Goldfinch	*Carduelis carduelis*	cRB
Siskin	*Carduelis spinus*	sW
Linnet	*Carduelis cannabina*	sRB
Common Rosefinch	*Carpodacus erythrinus*	V *
Common Crossbill	*Loxia curvirostra*	V *
Bullfinch	*Pyrrhula pyrrhula*	V *
Hawfinch	*Coccothraustes coccothraustes*	sW, rB
Corn Bunting	*Emberiza calandra*	cR
Yellowhammer	*Emberiza citrinella*	V *
Rock Bunting	*Emberiza cia*	sW, ?rB? *
Cinereous Bunting	*Emberiza cineracea*	sMB
Ortolan Bunting	*Emberiza hortulana*	sPM
Cretzschmar's Bunting	*Emberiza caesia*	cMB
Cirl Bunting	*Emberiza cirlus*	cRB
Little Bunting	*Emberiza pusilla*	V *
Black-headed Bunting	*Emberiza melanocephala*	cMB
Reed Bunting	*Emberiza schoeniclus*	sW

BUTTERFLIES

References   *Butterflies of Britain & Europe* by Tom Tolman & Richard Lewington

English name	Scientific name					
Swallowtail	*Papilio machaon*					
Scarce Swallowtail	*Iphiclides podalirius*					
Eastern Festoon	*Zerynthia cerisyi*					
False Apollo	*Archon appollinus*					
Black-veined White	*Aporia crataegi*					
Large White	*Pieris brassicae*					
Small White	*Artogeia rapae*					
Southern Small White	*Artogeia mannii*					
Eastern Bath White	*Pontia edusa*					
Bath White	*Pontia daplidice*					
Small Bath White	*Pontia chloridice*					
Eastern Dappled White	*Euchloe ausonia*					
Orange-tip	*Anthocharis cardamines*					
Clouded Yellow	*Colias croceus*					
Cleopatra	*Gonepteryx cleopatra*					
Powdered Brimstone	*Gonepteryx farinosa*					
Eastern Wood White	*Leptidea duponcheli*					
Nettle-tree Butterfly	*Libythea celtis*					
Plain Tiger	*Danaus chrysippus*					
Southern White Admiral	*Limenitis reducta*					
Peacock	*Inachis io*					
Red Admiral	*Venessa atalanta*					
Painted Lady	*Cynthia cardui*					
Southern Comma	*Polygomum egea*					
Silver-washed Fritillary	*Argynnis paphia*					
Marbled Fritillary	*Brenthis daphne*					
Knapweed Fritillary	*Melitaea phoebe*					
Spotted Fritillary	*Melitaea didyma*					
Lesser Spotted Fritillary	*Melitaea trivia*					
Marbled White	*Melanargia galathea*					
Balkan Marbled White	*Melanargia larissa*					
Woodland Grayling	*Hipparchia fagi*					
Balkan Grayling	*Hipparchia senthes*					
Samos Grayling	*Thymelicus mersina*					
Eastern Rock Grayling	*Hipparchia syriaca*					
Turkish Meadow Brown	*Maniola megala*					
Persian Meadow Brown	*Maniola telmessia*					
Small Heath	*Coenonympha pamphilus*					
Wall Brown	*Lasiommata megera*					
Large Wall Brown	*Lasiommata maera*					
Lattice Brown	*Kirnia roxelana*					
Green Hairstreak	*Callophrys rubi*					

BUTTERFLIES

English name	Scientific name						
Ilex Hairstreak	Satyrium ilicus						
Small Copper	Lycaena phlaeas						
Scarce Copper	Lycaena virgauraea						
Grecian Copper	Lycaena ottomana						
Lesser Fiery Copper	Lycaena thersamon						
Holly Blue	Celastrina argiolus						
Brown Argus	Aricia agestis						
Green-underside Blue	Glaucopsyche alexis						
Amanda's Blue	Agrodiaetus amanda						
Common Blue	Polyommatus icarus						
Orbed Red-underwing Skipper	Spialia orbifer						
Oriental Marbled Skipper	Carcharodus orientalis						
Small Skipper	Thymelicus sylvestris						
Leventine Skipper	Thymelicus hyrax						
Mediterranean Skipper	Gegenes nostrodamus						

DRAGONFLIES

References *A Field Guide to the Dragonflies of Britain and Europe* by Klaas-Douwe Dijkstra & Richard Lewington (inc. for taxonomy and nomenclature)
The Dragonflies of Lesbos by John Bowers

English name	Scientific name
Banded Demoiselle	*Calopteryx splendens mingrelica*
Beautiful Demoiselle	*Calopteryx virgo festiva*
Odalisque	*Epallage fatime*
Robust Spreadwing	*Lestes dryas*
Migrant Spreadwing	*Lestes barbarus*
Small Spreadwing	*Lestes virens*
Dark Spreadwing	*Lestes macrostigma*
Eastern Willow Spreadwing	*Lestes parvidens*
Common Winter Damselfly	*Sympecma fusca*
Common Bluetail	*Ischnura elegans*
Small Bluetail	*Ischnura pumilio*
Common Bluet	*Enallagma cyathigerum*
Dainty Bluet	*Coenagrion scitulum*
Small Red Damsel	*Ceriagrion tenellum*
Small Redeye	*Erythromma viridulum*
Blue Redeye	*Erythromma lindenii*
Blue Featherlegs	*Platycnemis pennipes*
Migrant Hawker	*Aeshna mixta*
Blue-eyed Hawker	*Aeshna affinis*
Green-eyed Hawker	*Aeshna isosceles antehumeralis*
Blue Emperor	*Anax imperator*
Lesser Emperor	*Anax parthenope*
Vagrant Emperor	*Anax ephippiger*
Hairy Hawker	*Brachytron pratense*
Eastern Spectre	*Caliaeschna microstigma*
Turkish Clubtail	*Gomphus schneiderii*
Small Pincertail	*Onychogomphus forcipatus albistibalis*
Turkish Goldenring	*Cordulegaster picta*
Blue-eyed Goldenring	*Cordulegaster insignis*
Yellow-spotted Emerald	*Somotochlora flavomaculata*
Broad-bodied Chaser	*Libellula depressa*
Blue Chaser	*Libellula fulva*
Black-tailed Skimmer	*Orthetrum cancellatum*
Southern Skimmer	*Orthetrum brunneum*
Epaulet Skimmer	*Orthetrum chrysostigma*
Keeled Skimmer	*Orthetrum coerulescens anceps / O. ramburii*
Small Skimmer	*Orthetrum taeniolatum*
Red-veined Darter	*Sympetrum fonscolombii*
Ruddy Darter	*Sympetrum sanguineum*
Common Darter	*Sympetrum striolatum*

DRAGONFLIES

English name	Scientific name
Southern Darter	Sympetrum meridionale
Broad Scarlet	Crocothemis erythraea
Violet Dropwing	Trithemis annulata
Black Pennant	Selysiothemis nigra

OTHER SELECTED INSECTS

English name	Scientific name
Mole Cricket	Gryllotalpa gryllotalpa
'Ephippiger' Bush-cricket	Ephippiger ephippiger
Egyptian Grasshopper	Anacridium aegyptiacum
'Red-winged' Grasshopper	Oedipoda germanica
'Blue-winged' Grasshopper	Oedipoda caerulans
'Stick' grasshopper sp.	Acrida ungarica
Praying Mantis	Iris oratoria
Mantid sp.	Ameles spallanziana
Mantid sp.	Empusa fasciata
Lesvos Cicada	Cicada orni lesbosiensis (Lesvos endemic)
Giant Peacock Moth	Saturnia pyri
Oleander Hawkmoth	Daphnis nerii
Hummingbird Hawkmoth	Macroglossum stellatarum
Cream-spotted Tiger	Arctia villica
Violet Carpenter Bee	Xylocarpus violacea
Great Potter Wasp	Delta unguiculata
Antlion sp.	Palpares libelluloides
Thread Lacewing	Nemoptera sinuata

ORCHIDS

References
Field Guide to Orchids of Britain and Europe by Karl Peter Buttler
Orchids of Lesvos by Y.A. Karatzas & A. Karatza
Orchids of Lesvos by Brian & Eileen Anderson

Notes
1. var = variant
2. species with same English names are species some authorities consider as separate species whilst other authorities treat them as subspecies

Scientific name	English name	Flowering period
Epipactis helleborine	Broad-leaved Helleborine	mid-May to end Jun
Epipactis microphylla	Small-leaved Helleborine	mid-May to end Jun
Cephalanthera damasonium	Large White Helleborine	mid-May to end Jun
Cephalanthera rubra	Red Helleborine	Jun-Jul
Cephalanthera longifolia	Sword-leaved Helleborine	end Apr to end May
Cephalanthera epipactoides	Spurred Helleborine	end Apr to mid-Jun
Limodorum abortivum	Violet Limodore	mid-Apr to end May
L. abortivum var. *rubrum*		mid-Apr to end May
L. abortivum var. *albiflorum*		mid-Apr to end May
Listera ovata	Twayblade	mid-May to mid-Jun
Spiranthes spiralis	Autumn Lady's Tresses	Sep-Oct
Platanthera holmboei	Holmboë's Butterfly	May to mid-Jun
Dactylorhiza romana	Roman Orchid	mid-Apr to end May
D. romana var. *albifora*		mid-Apr to end May
Comperia comperiana	Komper's Orchid	end Apr to end Jun
Neotinea maculata	Dense-flowered Orchid	mid-Mar to end Apr
Aceras anthropophorum	Man Orchid	Apr-May
Orchis coriophora	Bug Orchid	May-Jun
Orchis sancta	Holy Orchid	end Apr to end May
Orchis sancta var. *alba*		end Apr to end May
Orchis laxiflora	Loose-flowered Orchid	mid-Apr to mid-Jun
Orchis palustris	Bog Orchid	May to mid-Jun
Orchis pinetorum	Pinewood Orchid	end Apr to mid-Jun
Orchis provincialis	Provence Orchid	end Apr to end May
Orchis anatolica	Anatolian Orchid	mid-Mar to mid-Apr
Orchis collina	Fan-lipped Orchid	mid-Mar to end Apr
Orchis collina var. *albiflora*		mid-Mar to mid-Apr
O. papilionacea heroica	Pink Butterfly Orchid	mid-Feb to mid-Apr
O. p. heroica var. *alba*		mid-Mar to mid-Apr
O. p. heroica var. *rubra*		mid-Mar to end Apr
Orchis quadripunctata	Four-spotted Orchid	mid-Mar to end Apr
Orchis morio morio	Green-winged Orchid	mid-Mar to mid-Jun
O. m. morio var. *albiflora*		mid-Mar to mid-Jun
Orchis morio picta		mid-Mar to mid-Jun
Orchis tridentata	Toothed Orchid	mid-Apr to mid-Jul
Orchis lactea	Milky Orchid	mid-Mar to mid-Apr
Orchis purpurea	Lady Orchid	mid-Apr to late May

ORCHIDS

Scientific name	English name	Flowering period
Orchis italica	Naked Man Orchid	mid-Mar to end Apr
Orchis italica var. *albiflora*		mid-Mar to mid-Apr
Orchis simia	Monkey Orchid	mid-Apr to early May
Anacamptis pyramidalis	Pyramidal Orchid	end Apr to mid-Jun
A. pyramidalis var. *albiflora*		end Apr to mid-Jun
Barlia robertiana	Giant Orchid	Apr-May
Himantoglossum caprinum	Balkan Lizard Orchid	Jun-Jul
Himantoglossum affine	Eastern Lizard Orchid	May-Jun
Himantoglossum montis-tauri		May-Jun
Serapias cordigera	Heart-flowered Orchid	mid-Apr to early May
Serapias vomeracea	Plough-share Orchid	mid-Mar to mid-May
Serapias orientalis carica	Eastern Orchid	mid-Mar to mid-Apr
Serapias parviflora	Small-flowered Orchid	Apr
Ophrys fusca	Dull Orchid	Feb-Apr
Ophrys attaviria		mid-Mar to early May
Ophrys iricolor	Rainbow Orchid	mid-Feb to end Apr
Ophrys sitiaca	Omega Orchid	mid-Mar to mid-Apr
Ophrys sicula	Yellow Orchid	mid-Feb to end Apr
Ophrys phryganae	Yellow Orchid	mid-Mar-Apr
Ophrys tenthredinifera	Sawfly Orchid	mid-Mar-Apr
Ophrys apifera	Bee Orchid	mid-Apr to mid-May
Ophrys speculum or	Mirror Orchid	
O. vernixia orientalis	Mirror Orchid	mid-Mar-Apr
Ophrys bombyliflora	Bumble Bee Orchid	mid-Mar to mid-Apr
Ophrys reinholdii	Reinhold's Orchid	mid-Mar to early May
Ophrys umbilicata	Carmel Orchid	mid-Mar-Apr
Ophrys attica	Carmel Orchid	mid-Mar-Apr
Ophrys bucephala	Carmel Orchid	mid-Mar-Apr
Ophrys cornutula	Woodcock Orchid	mid-Mar to early May
Ophrys minutula	Woodcock Orchid	end Mar to early May
Ophrys oestrifera	Woodcock Orchid	mid-Mar to early May
Ophrys lesbis	Lesbos Orchid (endemic)	mid-Mar to early May
Ophrys ferrum-equinum	Horse-shoe Orchid	mid-Mar to early May
Ophrys labiosa	Horse-shoe Orchid	mid-Mar-Apr
Ophrys holoserica	Late Spider Orchid	mid-Mar-Apr
Ophrys homeri	Homer's Orchid	mid-Apr to mid-May
Ophrys candica	Kandia's Orchid	end Apr to late May
Ophrys spruneri	Spruner's Orchid	mid-Mar to mid-Apr
Ophrys aesculapii	Aesculapius Orchid	mid-Mar to mid-Apr
Ophrys mammosa	Mammosa Orchid	mid-Mar-Apr

MAMMALS (selected)
Reference *Mammals of Britain & Europe* by David Macdonald & Pricilla Barrett

English name	Scientific name
Fallow Deer	*Dama dama*
Persian Squirrel	*Sciurus anomalus*
Beech Marten	*Martes foina*
Weasel	*Mustela nivalis*
Lesser Mole-rat	*Nanospalax leucodon*
Brown Hare	*Lepus capensis*
Rabbit	*Oryctolagus cuniculus*
Eastern Hedgehog	*Erinaceus concolor*
Red Fox	*Vulpes vulpes*
Otter	*Lutra lutra*
Mediterranean Monk Seal	*Monachus monachus* (very rare Med endemic)
Bottled-nosed Dolphin	*Tursiops truncatus*
Common Dolphin	*Delphinus delphis*
Striped Dolphin	*Stenella coeruleoalba*

AMPHIBIANS, REPTILES & ALLIES (selected)
Reference *Amphibians and Reptiles of Europe* (website — www.herp.it)
by Paolo Mazzei & Ilaria Pimpinelli

English name	Scientific name
Green Toad	*Bufo viridis*
Bedriaga's / Levant Marsh Frog	*Pelophylax bedriagae*
Tree Frog	*Hyla arborea*
Turkish Gecko	*Hemidactylus turcicus*
Starred Agama	*Laudakia stellio*
Snake-eyed Lizard	*Ophisops elegans ehrenbergi*
Balkan Green Lizard	*Lacerta trilineata*
Snake-eyed Skink	*Ablepharus kitaibelii*
Glass Lizard	*Pseudopus apodus*
Ottoman Viper	*Montivipera xanthina*
Eastern Montpellier Snake	*Malpolon insignitus*
Grass Snake	*Natrix natrix*
Dice Snake	*Natrix tessellata*
European Cat Snake	*Telescopus fallax*
Four-lined Snake	*Elaphe quatuorlineata*
Leopard Snake	*Zamenis situla*
Sand Boa	*Eryx jaculus*
Spur-thighed Tortoise	*Testudo graeca*
Sripe-necked Terrapin	*Mauremys rivulata*
European Pond Terrapin	*Emys orbicularis*

DUTCH AND GREEK BIRD NAMES

Nomenclature and taxonomy follow Gill & Wright (2009) – see p. 188. For English names – see also pp. 188–227 or 228–35.
Duth names follow *Dutch Birding* (www.dutchbirding.nl).
Greek names follow Hellenic Rarities Committee (http://rarities.ornithologiki.gr).

Scientific name	Dutch name	Greek name
Alectoris chukar	Aziatische Steenpatrijs	Νησιώτικη Πέρδικα
Coturnix coturnix	Kwartel	(Κοινό) Ορτύκι
Phasianus colchicus	Fazant	(Κοινός) Φασιανός
Anser albifrons	Kolgans	Ασπρομέτωπη Χήνα
Branta ruficollis	Roodhalsgans	Κοκκινόχηνα
Cygnus olor	Knobbelzwaan	(Βουβός) Κύκνος
Cygnus cygnus	Wilde Zwaan	Αγριόκυκνος
Cygnus columbianus	Kleine Zwaan	Νανόκυκνος
Tadorna tadorna	Bergeend	Βαρβάρα
Tadorna ferruginea	Casarca	Καστανόπαπια
Anas strepera	Krakeend	Καπακλής
Anas penelope	Smient	(Ευρωπαϊκό) Σφυριχτάρι
Anas platyrhynchos	Wilde Eend	Πρασινοκέφαλη Πάπια
Anas clypeata	Slobeend	(Ευρασιατική) Χουλιαρόπαπια
Anas acuta	Pijlstaart	Ψαλίδα (του Βορά)
Anas querquedula	Zomertaling	(Ευρωπαϊκή) Σαρσέλα
Anas crecca	Wintertaling	(Ευρωπαϊκό) Κιρκίρι
Aythya ferina	Tafeleend	Γκισάρι
Aythya nyroca	Witoogeend	(Ευρωπαϊκή) Βαλτόπαπια
Aythya fuligula	Kuifeend	Μαυροκέφαλη Πάπια
Aythya marila	Topper	Σταχτόπαπια
Bucephala clangula	Brilduiker	(Ευρωπαϊκή) Βουκεφάλα
Mergellus albellus	Nonnetje	Νανοπρίστης
Mergus serrator	Middelste Zaagbek	Θαλασσοπρίστης
Oxyura leucocephala	Witkopeend	(Ευρωπαϊκό) Κεφαλούδι
Gavia arctica	Parelduiker	Λαμπροβούτι
Tachybaptus ruficollis	Dodaars	(Κοκκινόλαιμο) Νανοβουτηχτάρι
Podiceps cristatus	Fuut	Σκουφοβουτηχτάρι
Podiceps grisegena	Roodhalsfuut	Κοκκινοβουτηχτάρι
Podiceps nigricollis	Geoorde Fuut	Μαυροβουτηχτάρι
Calonectris (diomedea) diomedea	Scopoli's Pijlstormvogel	Αρτέμης
Puffinus yelkouan	Yelkouanpijlstormvogel	Μύχος (της Μεσογείου)
Phoenicopterus roseus	Flamingo	(Ευρωπαϊκό) Φοινικόπτερο

Scientific name	Dutch name	Greek name
Ciconia nigra	Zwarte Ooievaar	Μαύρος Πελαργός
Ciconia ciconia	Ooievaar	Λευκός Πελαργός
Plegadis falcinellus	Zwarte Ibis	(Ευρασιατική) Χαλκόκοτα
Platalea leucorodia	Lepelaar	(Ευρασιατική) Χουλιαρομύτα
Botaurus stellaris	Roerdomp	(Ευρασιατικός) Ήταυρος
Ixobrychus minutus	Woudaap	(Ευρωπαϊκός) Μικροτσικνιάς
Nycticorax nycticorax	Kwak	(Κοινός) Νυχτοκόρακας
Ardeola ralloides	Ralreiger	(Ξανθός) Κρυπτοτσικνιάς
Bubulcus ibis	Koereiger	Γελαδάρης
Ardea cinerea	Blauwe Reiger	Σταχτοτσικνιάς
Ardea purpurea	Purperreiger	Πορφυροτσικνιάς
Ardea alba	Grote Zilverreiger	Αργυροτσικνιάς
Egretta garzetta	Kleine Zilverreiger	(Κοινός) Λευκοτσικνιάς
Pelecanus onocrotalus	Roze Pelikaan	Ροδοπελεκάνος
Pelecanus crispus	Kroeskoppelikaan	Αργυροπελεκάνος
Phalacrocorax pygmeus	Dwergaalscholver	Λαγγόνα
Phalacrocorax carbo	Aalscholver	(Ευρωπαϊκός) Κορμοράνος
Phalacrocorax aristotelis	Kuifaalscholver	(Ευρωπαϊκός) Θαλασσοκόρακας
Pandion haliaetus	Visarend	Ψαραετός
Pernis apivorus	Wespendief	(Ευρωπαϊκός) Σφηκιάρης
Milvus milvus	Rode Wouw	Ψαλιδιάρης
Milvus migrans	Zwarte Wouw	Τσίφτης
Haliaeetus albicilla	Zeearend	(Ευρωπαϊκός) Θαλασσαετός
Neophron percnopterus	Aasgier	Ασπροπάρης
Gyps fulvus	Vale Gier	Όρνιο
Circaetus gallicus	Slangenarend	Φιδαετός
Circus aeruginosus	Bruine Kiekendief	Καλαμόκιρκος
Circus cyaneus	Blauwe Kiekendief	Χειμωνόκιρκος
Circus macrourus	Steppekiekendief	Στεπόκιρκος
Circus pygargus	Grauwe Kiekendief	Λιβαδόκιρκος
Accipiter brevipes	Balkansperwer	(Κοινό) Σαΐνι
Accipiter nisus	Sperwer	(Κοινό) Ξεφτέρι
Accipiter gentilis	Havik	Διπλοσάϊνο
Buteo buteo	Buizerd	(Κοινή) Γερακίνα
Buteo rufinus	Arendbuizerd	Αετογερακίνα
Aquila pomarina	Schreeuwarend	Κραυγαετός
Aquila clanga	Bastaardarend	Στικταετός
Aquila nipalensis	Steppearend	Στεπαετός
Aquila heliaca	Keizerarend	(Ανατολικός) Βασιλαετός
Aquila chrysaetos	Steenarend	Χρυσαετός

Scientific name	Dutch name	Greek name
Aquila fasciata	Havikarend	Σπιζαετός
Hieraaetus pennatus	Dwergarend	Γερακαετός
Falco naumanni	Kleine Torenvalk	(Ευρωπαϊκό) Κιρκινέζι
Falco tinnunculus	Torenvalk	Βραχοκιρκίνεζο
Falco vespertinus	Roodpootvalk	(Ευρωπαϊκό) Μαυροκιρκίνεζο
Falco eleonorae	Eleonora's Valk	Μαυροπετρίτης
Falco columbarius	Smelleken	Νανογέρακο
Falco subbuteo	Boomvalk	Δεντρογέρακο
Falco biarmicus	Lannervalk	Χρυσογέρακο
Falco cherrug	Sakervalk	Στεπογέρακο
Falco peregrinus	Slechtvalk	Πετρίτης
Rallus aquaticus	Waterral	(Ευρωπαϊκή) Νεροκοτσέλα
Crex crex	Kwartelkoning	Ορτυκομάνα
Porzana parva	Klein Waterhoen	Μικροπουλάδα
Porzana pusilla	Kleinst Waterhoen	Νανοπουλάδα
Porzana porzana	Porseleinhoen	Στικτοπουλάδα
Gallinula chloropus	Waterhoen	(Κοινή) Νερόκοτα
Fulica atra	Meerkoet	(Κοινή) Φαλαρίδα
Grus grus	Kraanvogel	(Ευρωπαϊκός) Γερανός
Burhinus oedicnemus	Griel	(Ευρωπαϊκή) Πετροτουρλίδα
Haematopus ostralegus	Scholekster	(Ευρωπαϊκός) Στρειδοφάγος
Himantopus himantopus	Steltkluut	Καλαμοκανάς
Recurvirostra avosetta	Kluut	(Ευρωπαϊκή) Αβοκέτα
Vanellus vanellus	Kievit	(Ευρωπαϊκή) Καλημάνα
Vanellus spinosus	Sporenkievit	Αγκαθοκαλημάνα
Vanellus gregarius	Steppekievit	Αγελοκαλημάνα
Charadrius morinellus	Morinelplevier	Βουνοσφυριχτής
Pluvialis apricaria	Goudplevier	(Ευρωπαϊκό) Βροχοπούλι
Pluvialis squatarola	Zilverplevier	Αργυροπούλι
Charadrius dubius	Kleine Plevier	Ποταμοσφυριχτής
Charadrius hiaticula	Bontbekplevier	Αμμοσφυριχτής
Charadrius alexandrinus	Strandplevier	Θαλασσοσφυριχτής
Scolopax rusticola	Houtsnip	(Ευρασιατική) Μπεκάτσα
Lymnocryptes minimus	Bokje	Κουφομπεκάτσινο
Gallinago media	Poelsnip	Διπλομπεκάτσινο
Gallinago gallinago	Watersnip	(Κοινό) Μπεκατσίνι
Limosa limosa	Grutto	(Ευρωπαϊκή) Λιμόζα
Limosa lapponica	Rosse Grutto	Θαλασσολιμόζα
Numenius phaeopus	Regenwulp	Σιγλίγουρος
Numenius arquata	Wulp	(Ευρασιατική) Τουρλίδα

Scientific name	Dutch name	Greek name
Tringa erythropus	Zwarte Ruiter	Μαυρότρυγγας
Tringa totanus	Tureluur	Κοκκινοσκέλης
Tringa stagnatilis	Poelruiter	Βαλτότρυγγας
Tringa nebularia	Groenpootruiter	Πρασινοσκέλης
Tringa ochropus	Witgat	Δασότρυγγας
Tringa glareola	Bosruiter	Λασπότρυγγας
Xenus cinereus	Terekruiter	Ρωσότρυγγας
Actitis hypoleucos	Oeverloper	Ακτίτης
Arenaria interpres	Steenloper	Χαλικοκυλιστής
Calidris canutus	Kanoet	Κοκκινοσκαλίδρα
Calidris alba	Drieteenstrandloper	Λευκοσκαλίδρα
Calidris minuta	Kleine Strandloper	(Κοινή) Νανοσκαλίδρα
Calidris temminckii	Temmincks Strandloper	Σταχτιά Νανοσκαλίδρα
Calidris melanotos	Gestreepte Strandloper	Θωρακωτή Σκαλίδρα
Calidris ferruginea	Krombekstrandloper	Δρεπανοσκαλίδρα
Calidris alpina	Bonte Strandloper	Λασποσκαλίδρα
Limicola falcinellus	Breedbekstrandloper	Ραβδοσκαλίδρα
Philomachus pugnax	Kemphaan	Μαχητής
Phalaropus lobatus	Grauwe Franjepoot	Ερυθρόλαιμος Φαλαρόποδας
Glareola pratincola	Vorkstaartplevier	(Κοινό) Νεροχελίδονο
Glareola nordmanni	Steppevorkstaartplevier	Μαυρόφτερο Νεροχελίδονο
Chroicocephalus genei	Dunbekmeeuw	Λεπτόραμφος Γλάρος
Chroicocephalus ridibundus	Kokmeeuw	Καστανοκέφαλος Γλάρος
Hydrocoloeus minutus	Dwergmeeuw	Νανόγλαρος
Ichthyaetus audouinii	Audouins Meeuw	Αιγαιόγλαρος
Ichthyaetus melanocephalus	Zwartkopmeeuw	Μαυροκέφαλος Γλάρος
Larus canus	Stormmeeuw	Θυελλόγλαρος
Larus fuscus	Kleine Mantelmeeuw	Μελανόγλαρος
Larus michahellis	Geelpootmeeuw	Ασημόγλαρος της Μεσογείου
Stercorarius parasiticus	Kleine Jager	Γερακοληστόγλαρος
Gelochelidon nilotica	Lachstern	Γελογλάρονο
Hydroprogne caspia	Reuzenstern	Καρατζάς
Thalasseus sandvicensis	Grote Stern	Χειμωνογλάρονο
Sternula albifrons	Dwergstern	(Ευρωπαϊκό) Νανογλάρονο
Sterna hirundo	Visdief	Ποταμογλάρονο
Chlidonias hybrida	Witwangstern	Μουστακογλάρονο
Chlidonias leucopterus	Witvleugelstern	Αργυρογλάρονο
Chlidonias niger	Zwarte Stern	Μαυρογλάρονο
Columba livia	Rotsduif	Αγριοπερίστερο
Columba oenas	Holenduif	Φασσοπερίστερο

Scientific name	Dutch name	Greek name
Columba palumbus	Houtduif	(Κοινή) Φάσσα
Streptopelia turtur	Zomertortel	(Ευρωπαϊκό) Τρυγόνι
Streptopelia decaocto	Turkse Tortel	(Ευρασιατική) Δεκαοχτούρα
Streptopelia senegalensis	Palmtortel	Φοινικοτρύγονο
Clamator glandarius	Kuifkoekoek	Κισσόκουκος
Cuculus canorus	Koekoek	(Ευρωπαϊκός) Κούκος
Tyto alba	Kerkuil	Τυτώ
Otus scops	Dwergooruil	(Ευρωπαϊκός) Γκιώνης
Bubo bubo	Oehoe	(Κοινός) Μπούφος
Strix aluco	Bosuil	(Κοινός) Χουχουριστής
Athene noctua	Steenuil	(Ευρωπαϊκή) Κουκουβάγια
Asio otus	Ransuil	Νανόμπουφος
Asio flammeus	Velduil	Βαλτόμπουφος
Caprimulgus europaeus	Nachtzwaluw	(Ευρωπαϊκό) Γιδοβύζι
Apus apus	Gierzwaluw	(Κοινή) Σταχτάρα
Apus pallidus	Vale Gierzwaluw	Ωχροσταχτάρα
Apus melba	Alpengierzwaluw	Βουνοσταχτάρα
Apus affinis	Huisgierzwaluw	Μικροσταχτάρα
Coracias garrulus	Scharrelaar	(Ευρωπαϊκή) Χαλκοκουρούνα
Alcedo atthis	IJsvogel	(Ευρωπαϊκή) Αλκυόνη
Merops persicus	Groene Bijeneter	Πράσινος Μελισσοφάγος
Merops apiaster	Bijeneter	(Ευρωπαϊκός) Μελισσοφάγος
Upupa epops	Hop	Τσαλαπετεινός
Jynx torquilla	Draaihals	Στραβολαίμης
Dendrocopos medius	Middelste Bonte Specht	Μεσαίος Δρυοκολάπτης
Lanius collurio	Grauwe Klauwier	Αετομάχος
Lanius minor	Kleine Klapekste0	Σταχτοκεφαλάς
Lanius excubitor	Klapekster	Διπλοκεφαλάς
Lanius pallidirostris	Steppeklapekster	
Lanius senator	Roodkopklauwier	Κοκκινοκεφαλάς
Lanius nubicus	Maskerklauwier	Παρδαλοκεφαλάς
Oriolus oriolus	Wielewaal	(Ευρωπαϊκός) Συκοφάγος
Garrulus glandarius	Gaai	(Ευρωπαϊκή) Κίσσα
Pica pica	Ekster	(Κοινή) Καρακάξα
Nucifraga caryocatactes	Notenkraker	Καρυοθραύστης
Pyrrhocorax pyrrhocorax	Alpenkraai	Κοκκινοκαλιακούδα
Coloeus monedula	Kauw	(Ευρωπαϊκή) Κάργια
Corvus frugilegus	Roek	Χαβαρόνι
Corvus cornix	Bonte Kraai	(Σταχτιά) Κουρούνα
Corvus corax	Raaf	(Κοινός) Κόρακας

Scientific name	Dutch name	Greek name
Bombycilla garrulus	Pestvogel	(Ευρωπαϊκή) Βομβυκίλα
Poecile lugubris	Rouwmees	Κλειδωνάς
Periparus ater	Zwarte Mees	Ελατοπαπαδίτσα
Parus major	Koolmees	Καλόγερος
Cyanistes caeruleus	Pimpelmees	Γαλαζοπαπαδίτσα
Remiz pendulinus	Buidelmees	Υφάντρα
Panurus biarmicus	Baardman	Μουστακαλής
Melanocorypha calandra	Kalanderleeuwerik	(Κοινή) Γαλιάντρα
Calandrella brachydactyla	Kortteenleeuwerik	(Ευρωπαϊκή) Μικρογαλιάντρα
Calandrella rufescens	Kleine Kortteenleeuwerik	Μικρογαλιάντρα της Ερήμου
Galerida cristata	Kuifleeuwerik	Κατσουλιέρης
Lullula arborea	Boomleeuwerik	Δεντροσταρήθρα
Alauda arvensis	Veldleeuwerik	(Κοινή) Σιταρήθρα
Riparia riparia	Oeverzwaluw	Οχθοχελίδονο
Hirundo rustica	Boerenzwaluw	Σταυλοχελίδονο
Ptyonoprogne rupestris	Rotszwaluw	(Ευρωπαϊκό) Βραχοχελίδονο
Delichon urbicum	Huiszwaluw	Λευκοχελίδονο
Cecropis daurica	Roodstuitzwaluw	Μιλτοχελίδονο
Cettia cetti	Cetti's Zanger	(Ευρωπαϊκό) Ψευταηδόνι
Aegithalos caudatus	Staartmees	Αιγίθαλος
Phylloscopus trochilus	Fitis	Θαμνοφυλλοσκόπος
Phylloscopus collybita	Tjiftjaf	Δεντροφυλλοσκόπος
Phylloscopus orientalis	Balkanbergfluiter	Βουνοφυλλοσκόπος
Phylloscopus sibilatrix	Fluiter	Δασοφυλλοσκόπος
Acrocephalus arundinaceus	Grote Karekiet	Τσιχλοποταμίδα
Acrocephalus melanopogon	Zwartkoprietzanger	Ψαθοποταμίδα
Acrocephalus schoenobaenus	Rietzanger	Σχοινοποταμίδα
Acrocephalus scirpaceus	Kleine Karekiet	Καλαμοποταμίδα
Acrocephalus palustris	Bosrietzanger	Βαλτοποταμίδα
Hippolais pallida	Oostelijke Vale Spotvogel	Ωχροστριτσίδα
Hippolais olivetorum	Griekse Spotvogel	Λιοστριτσίδα
Hippolais icterina	Spotvogel	Κιτρινοστριτσίδα
Locustella naevia	Sprinkhaanzanger	Θαμνοτριλιστής
Locustella fluviatilis	Krekelzanger	Ποταμοτριλιστής
Locustella luscinioides	Snor	Καλαμοτριλιστής
Cisticola juncidis	Graszanger	(Ευρωπαϊκή) Κιστικόλη
Sylvia atricapilla	Zwartkop	Μαυροσκούφης
Sylvia borin	Tuinfluiter	Κηποτσιροβάκος
Sylvia nisoria	Sperwergrasmus	Γερακοτσιροβάκος
Sylvia curruca	Braamsluiper	Βουνοτσιροβάκος

Scientific name	Dutch name	Greek name
Sylvia crassirostris	Oostelijke Orpheusgrasmus	Μελωδοτσιροβάκος
Sylvia communis	Grasmus	Θαμνοτσιροβάκος
Sylvia cantillans	Baardgrasmus	Κοκκινοτσιροβάκος
Sylvia melanocephala	Kleine Zwartkop	Μαυροτσιροβάκος
Sylvia rueppelli	Rüppells Grasmus	Αιγαιοτσιροβάκος
Regulus ignicapilla	Vuurgoudhaan	Πυροβασιλίσκος
Regulus regulus	Goudhaan	Χρυσοβασιλίσκος
Troglodytes troglodytes	Winterkoning	(Ευρωπαϊκός) Τρυποφράχτης
Sitta europaea	Boomklever	Δεντροτσοπανάκος
Sitta krueperi	Turkse Boomklever	Τουρκοτσοπανάκος
Sitta neumayer	Rotsklever	(Δυτικός) Βραχοτσοπανάκος
Certhia brachydactyla	Boomkruiper	Καμποδεντροβάτης
Sturnus vulgaris	Spreeuw	(Ευρωπαϊκό) Ψαρόνι
Pastor roseus	Roze Spreeuw	Αγιοπούλι
Turdus torquatus	Beflijster	Χιονοκότσυφας
Turdus merula	Merel	(Κοινός) Κότσυφας
Turdus pilaris	Kramsvogel	Κεδρότσιχλα
Turdus iliacus	Koperwiek	Κοκκινότσιχλα
Turdus philomelos	Zanglijster	(Κοινή) Τσίχλα
Turdus viscivorus	Grote Lijster	Γερακότσιχλα
Erithacus rubecula	Roodborst	Κοκκινολαίμης
Luscinia svecica	Blauwborst	Γαλαζολαίμης
Luscinia luscinia	Noordse Nachtegaal	Τσιχλαηδόνι
Luscinia megarhynchos	Nachtegaal	(Κοινό) Αηδόνι
Irania gutturalis	Perzische Roodborst	Λευκόλαιμο Αηδόνι
Cercotrichas galactotes	Rosse Waaierstaart	Κουφαηδόνι
Phoenicurus ochruros	Zwarte Roodstaart	Καρβουνιάρης
Phoenicurus phoenicurus	Gekraagde Roodstaart	(Κοινός) Φοινίκουρος
Saxicola rubetra	Paapje	Καστανολαίμης
Saxicola torquatus	Roodborsttapuit	(Ευρωπαϊκός) Μαυρολαίμης
Oenanthe isabellina	Izabeltapuit	Αμμοπετρόκλης
Oenanthe oenanthe	Tapuit	Σταχτοπετρόκλης
Oenanthe pleschanka	Bonte Tapuit	Παρδαλοπετρόκλης
Oenanthe hispanica	Westelijke Blonde Tapuit	Ασπροκωλίνα
Oenanthe finschii	Finsch' Tapuit	Βουνοπετρόκλης
Monticola saxatilis	Rode Rotslijster	Πυροκότσυφας
Monticola solitarius	Blauwe Rotslijster	Γαλαζοκότσυφας
Muscicapa striata	Grauwe Vliegenvanger	Σταχτομυγοχάφτης
Ficedula semitorquata	Balkanvliegenvanger	Δρυομυγοχάφτης
Ficedula albicollis	Withalsvliegenvanger	Κρικομυγοχάφτης

Scientific name	Dutch name	Greek name
Ficedula hypoleuca	Bonte Vliegenvanger	Μαυρομυγοχάφτης
Ficedula parva	Kleine Vliegenvanger	Νανομυγοχάφτης
Cinclus cinclus	Waterspreeuw	(Ευρωπαϊκός) Νεροκότσυφας
Passer domesticus	Huismus	Σπιτοσπουργίτης
Passer hispaniolensis	Spaanse Mus	Χωραφοσπουργίτης
Passer montanus	Ringmus	Δεντροσπουργίτης
Petronia petronia	Rotsmus	Πετροσπουργίτης
Prunella modularis	Heggenmus	(Κοινός) Θαμνοψάλτης
Motacilla flava	Gele Kwikstaart	Κιτρινοσουσουράδα
Motacilla citreola	Citroenkwikstaart	Κιτροσουσουράδα
Motacilla cinerea	Grote Gele Kwikstaart	Σταχτοσουσουράδα
Motacilla alba	Witte Kwikstaart	Λευκοσουσουράδα
Anthus campestris	Duinpieper	Ωχροκελάδα
Anthus pratensis	Graspieper	Λιβαδοκελάδα
Anthus trivialis	Boompieper	Δεντροκελάδα
Anthus cervinus	Roodkeelpieper	Κοκκινοκελάδα
Anthus spinoletta	Waterpieper	(Ευρωπαϊκή) Νεροκελάδα
Fringilla coelebs	Vink	(Κοινός) Σπίνος
Fringilla montifringilla	Keep	Χειμωνόσπινος
Serinus pusillus	Roodvoorhoofdkanarie	Μαύρο Καναρίνι
Serinus serinus	Europese Kanarie	Σκαρθάκι
Carduelis chloris	Groenling	(Ευρωπαϊκός) Φλώρος
Carduelis carduelis	Putter	(Κοινή) Καρδερίνα
Carduelis spinus	Sijs	(Κοινό) Λούγαρο
Carduelis cannabina	Kneu	(Κοινό) Φανέτο
Carpodacus erythrinus	Roodmus	(Κοινή) Ροδόπιζα
Loxia curvirostra	Kruisbek	(Κοινός) Σταυρομύτης
Pyrrhula pyrrhula	Goudvink	(Κοινός) Πύρρουλας
Coccothraustes coccothraustes	Appelvink	(Ευρωπαϊκός) Κοκκοθραύστης
Emberiza calandra	Grauwe Gors	Τσιφτάς
Emberiza citrinella	Geelgors	Χρυσοτσίχλονο
Emberiza cia	Grijze Gors	Βουνοτσίχλονο
Emberiza cineracea	Smyrnagors	Σμυρνοτσίχλονο
Emberiza hortulana	Ortolaan	Βλαχοτσίχλονο
Emberiza caesia	Bruinkeelortolaan	Φρυγανοτσίχλονο
Emberiza cirlus	Cirlgors	Σιρλοτσίχλονο
Emberiza pusilla	Dwerggors	Νανοτσίχλονο
Emberiza melanocephala	Zwartkopgors	Αμπελουργός
Emberiza schoeniclus	Rietgors	(Μεγάλο) Καλαμοτσίχλονο

LESVOS PLACES NAMES

Achladeri	Αχλαδερή	ΑΧΛΑΔΕΡΗ	Ach-la-derry
Aghios Ioannis	Άγιος Ιωάννης	ΑΓΙΟΣ ΙΩΑΝΝΗΣ	Ageos E-owa-niss
Agiasos	Αγιάσος	ΑΓΙΆΣΟΣ	Eye-ass-oss
Agiasos Sanatorium	Σανατόριο Αγιάσου	ΣΑΝΑΤΟΡΙΟ ΑΓΙΆΣΟΥ	Sana-torio Ay-ass-u
Agia Paraskevi	Αγία Παρασκενή	ΑΓΙΑ ΠΑΡΑΣΚΕΥΉ	Ag-ee-a Parra-ske-vee
Agios Fokas	Άγιος Φωκάς	ΆΓΙΟΣ ΦΩΚΆΣ	Eye-ee-oss Fok-as
Agra	Άγρα	ΆΓΡΑ	Agg-ra
Agreilia	Αγριελιά	ΑΓΡΙΕΛΙΆ	Agree-lia
Alikoudi Pool	Αλικούδι λίμνη	ΑΛΙΚΟΥΔΙ ΛΙΜΝΗ	Ally-koo-dee
Almiropotamos River	Αλμυροπόταμος Ποτάμι	ΑΛΜΥΡΟΠΟΤΑΜΟΣ ΠΟΤΆΜΙ	Al-miro-pot-amos
Alykes Wetlands	Αλυκές έλος	ΑΛΥΚΈΣ ΈΛΟΣ	Ally-kess
Ambeliko	Αμπελικό	ΑΜΠΕΛΙΚΌ	Am-vell-ee-ko
Anemotia	Ανεμώτια	ΑΝΕΜΌΤΙΑ	Anne-mot-ea
Anaxos	Άναξος	ΑΝΑΞΟΣ	An-axe-soss
Andissa	Άντισσα	ΆΝΤΙΣΣΑ	An-dissa
Apothika	Αποθήκα	ΑΠΟΘΉΚΑ	Apoth-ika
Chrousos	Χρούσος	ΧΡΟΎΣΟΣ	Chroo-sos
Christou River	Ποταμός Χριστού	ΧΡΙΣΤΟΥ ΠΟΤΆΜΙ	Pot-am-oss Chris-tu
Dafia	Δάφια	ΔΆΦΙΑ	Daf-ea
Dipi Larisos	Ντίπι Λάφισος	ΝΤΊΠΙ ΛΆΦΙΣΟΣ	Dippi La-fiss-os
Efthalou	Ευθαλού	ΕΥΘΑΛΟΎ	Eff-ta-loo
Evergetoulas (River)	Ευεργέτουλας	ΕΥΕΡΓΈΤΟΥΛΑΣ	Ever-get-oo-lass
Eresos	Ερεσσός	ΕΡΕΣΣΟΣ	Er-ess-oss
Faneromeni	Φανερωμένη	ΦΑΝΕΡΩΜΈΝΗ	Fan-err-o-many
Filia	Φίλια	ΦΊΛΙΑ	Fil-ia
Gavathas	Γαββαθάς	ΓΑΒΒΑΘΆΣ	Gavva-thass
Gera (Gulf of)	Κόλπος Γέρας	ΚΌΛΠΟΣ ΓΕΡΑΣ	Gerra
Haramida	Χαραμίδα	ΧΑΡΑΜΙΔΑ	Harra-meeda
Ipsilou Monastery	Μονή Υψηλού	ΜΟΝΉ ΥΨΗΛΟΎ	Ip-sil-oo
Kalami River	Καλάμι Ποτάμι	ΚΑΛΆΜΙ ΠΟΤΆΜΙ	Kal-ammi
Kalloni	Καλλονή	ΚΑΛΛΟΝΉ	Kall-o-ni
Kato Stavros	Κάτω Σταυρός	ΚΆΤΩ ΣΤΑΥΡΌΣ	Cat-o Stav-ros
Katsinia Bay	Παραλία Κατσίνια	ΠΑΡΑΛΊΑ ΚΑΤΣΊΝΙΑ	Cat-sin-ia
Kavacki	Καβάκι	ΚΑΒΑΚΙ	Ka-vacki
Keramia	Κεραμεία	ΚΕΡΑΜΕΊΑ	Kerr-amia
Klio	Κλειώ	ΚΛΕΙΩ	Cleo

Korakas headland	Ακρωτήριο Κόρακας	ΑΚΡΩΤΉΡΙΟ ΚΌΡΑΚΑΣ	Akrot-ee-rio Kore-ack-as
Koriani	Κοριανή	ΚΟΡΙΑΝΉ	Kor-ia-ni
Lardia Valley	Κοιλάδα Λαρδιά	ΛΑΡΔΙΆ ΚΟΙΛΆΣ	Ke-lad-dah Lar-dia
Limonos monastery	Μονή Λειμώνος	ΛΕΙΜΏΝΟΣ ΜΟΝΑΣΤΉΡΙ	Lim-o-noss
Loutra	Λουτρά	ΛΟΥΤΡΆ	Loo-tra
Loutropoli Thermis	Λουτρόπολη Θερμής	ΛΟΥΤΡΌΠΟΛΗ ΘΕΡΜΉΣ	Loo-tro-polly
Madaros	Μαδαρός	ΜΑΔΑΡΌΣ	Mad-a-ross
Makara	Μάκαρα	ΜΆΚΑΡΑ	Mack-ar-ah
Mandamados	Μανταμάδος	ΜΑΝΤΑΜΆΔΟΣ	Mant-a-mad-oss
Megalochori	Μεγαλοχώρι	ΜΕΓΑΛΟΧΏΡΙ	Mega-low-chori
Meladia Valley	Κοιλάδα Μελάδια	ΜΕΛΆΔΙΑ ΚΟΙΛΆΣ	Kee-la-dah Mel-add-ear
Mesa	Μέσα	ΜΕΣΑ	Messa
Mesotopos	Μεσότοπος	ΜΕΣΌΤΟΠΟΣ	Messo-top-poss
Metochi Lake	Λίμνη Μετόχι	ΜΕΤΟΧΙ ΛΊΜΝΗ	Lim-nee Met-och-ee
Milopotamos River	Ποταμός Μυλοπόταμος	ΜΥΛΟΠΟΤΑΜΟΣ ΠΟΤΆΜΙ	Pot-am-oss Mill-o-pot-am-oss
Molivos (Mithimna)	Μόλυβος (Μήθυμνα)	ΜΌΛΥΒΟΣ (ΜΉΘΥΜΝΑ)	Molly-voss (Myth-im-na)
Mt Lepetimnos	Ορ Λεπέτυμνος	ΟΡ ΛΕΠΕΤΥΜΝΟΣ	Lep-et-im-nos
Mt Olympus	Ορ Όλυμπος	ΟΡ ΟΛΥΜΠΟΣ	Ol-lym-pus
Mytilini	Μυτιλήνη	ΜΥΤΙΛΗΝΗ	Mitt-ee-lee-knee
Mytilini airport	Μυτιλήνη αεροδρόμιο	ΜΥΤΙΛΗΝΗ ΑΕΡΟΔΡΌΜΙΟ	Mitt-ee-lee-knee Aero-drom-io
Napi (Valley)	(Κοιλάδα) Νάπη	ΝΆΠΗ (ΚΟΙΛΆΣ)	(Koy-lad-dah) Nappy
Palia Vigla chapel	Παλιά Βίγλα παρεκκλήσι	ΠΑΛΙΆ ΒΊΓΛΑ ΠΑΡΕΚΚΛΉΣΙ	Pal-ia Vig-la
Palios	Παλιός	ΠΑΛΙΌΣ	Pal-eos
Panaghia chapel	Παναγία παρεκκλήσι	ΠΑΝΑΓΊΑ ΠΑΡΕΚΚΛΉΣΙ	Pan-a-gee-a
Parakila (Marsh)	Παράκοιλα (βάλτος)	ΠΑΡΆΚΟΙΛΑ (ΒΆΛΤΟΣ)	Parra-keela
Perama	Πέραμα	ΠΕΡΑΜΑ	Per-am-ah
Perasma	Πέρασμα	ΠΕΡΑΣΜΑ	Pe-rass-ma
Perevolis Monastery	Μονή Περιβολής	ΜΟΝΉ ΠΕΡΙΒΟΛΉΣ	Perry-vollis
Petra	Πέτρα	ΠΕΤΡΑ	Pet-ra
Petrified Forest	Απολιθωμένο Δάσος	ΑΠΟΛΙΘΩΜΈΝΟ ΔΆΣΟΣ	Apoli-tho-meno Da-soss
Pirgi	Πύργοι	ΠΎΡΓΟΙ	Peer-gee
Pithariou reservoir	Πιθαρίου δεξαμενή	ΠΙΘΑΡΊΟΥ ΔΕΞΑΜΕΝΉ	Pith-are-ee-oo
Platania	Πλατάνια	ΠΛΑΤΆΝΙΑ	Plat-anya
Plomari	Πλωμάρι	ΠΛΩΜΆΡΙ	Plom-are-ee
Polichnitos Saltpans	Πολιχνίτος Αλυκές	ΠΟΛΙΧΝΊΤΟΣ ΑΛΥΚΈΣ	Polly-chn-ee-toss
Polichnitos	Πολιχνίτος	ΠΟΛΙΧΝΊΤΟΣ	Polly-chn-ee-toss
Potamia	Ποταμιά	ΠΟΤΑΜΙΆ	Pot-am-ear
Sideras (Agra)	Σιδεράς (Άγρα)	ΣΙΔΕΡΆΣ (ΆΓΡΑ)	Sid-err-ass

Sigri	Σίγρι	ΣΙΓΡΙ	Sig-ri
Sikaminia	Συκαμνιά	ΣΥΚΑΜΝΙΆ	Sick-a-min-ea
Skala Eresou	Σκαλα Ερεσού	ΣΚΑΛΑ ΕΡΕΣΟΎ	Skar-la Eress-oo
Skala Kallonis	Σκάλα Καλλονής	ΣΚΆΛΑ ΚΑΛΛΟΝΉΣ	Ska-la Kallo-knees
Skala Polichnitou	Σκάλα ΠολιΧνίτου	ΣΚΆΛΑ ΠΟΛΙΧΝΊΤΟΥ	Skar-la Polly-chn-ee-too
Skala Sikaminias	Σκάλα Συκαμνιάς	ΣΚΆΛΑ ΣΥΚΑΜΝΙΆΣ	Skar-la Sick-a-min-ee-ass
Skala Vasilikon	Σκάλα Βασιλικών	ΣΚΆΛΑ ΒΑΣΙΛΙΚΏΝ	Skala Vas-illy-kon
Skalochori	Σκαλοχωρι	ΣΚΑΛΟΧΩΡΙ	Skall-o-chory
Skamnioudi	Σκαμνιούδι	ΣΚΑΜΝΙΟΎΔΙ	Skam-nee-oo-di
Skoutaros	Σκουτάρος	ΣΚΟΥΤΑΡΟΣ	Scoot-ah-ross
Stavros	Σταυρός	ΣΤΑΥΡΌΣ	Stav-ross
Tavari	Ταβάρι	ΤΑΒΆΡΙ	Tav-ar-ee
Tsiknias River	Ποταμός Τσικνιάς	ΤΣΙΚΝΙΆΣ ΠΟΤΆΜΙ	Pot-am-oss T-sick-knee-ass
Tsonia	Τσόνια	ΤΣΟΝΙΑ	T-sonya
Vafios	Βαφειός	ΒΑΦΕΙΌΣ	Va-feos
Vasilika	Βασιλικά	ΒΑΣΙΛΙΚΆ	Vass-ee-li-ka
Vatera	Βατερά	ΒΑΤΕΡΆ	Vat-err-ra
Vatousa	Βατούσσα	ΒΑΤΟΎΣΣΑ	Vat-oo-sa
Voulgaris River	Βούλγαρης Ποτάμι	ΒΟΎΛΓΑΡΗΣ ΠΟΤΆΜΙ	Pot-am-oss Voul-garis
Vourkou River	Βούρκού Ποτάμι	ΒΟΎΡΚΟΎ ΠΟΤΆΜΙ	Pot-am-oss Vour-kou
Vouvaris River	Βούβάρης Ποτάμι	ΒΟΎΒΆΡΗΣ ΠΟΤΆΜΙ	Pot-am-oss Vou-varis
Vrisa	Βρίσα	ΒΡΊΣΑ	Vree-ssa

REFERENCES & BIBLIOGRAPHY

Amphibians and Reptiles of Europe (website). 2009. — WWW.HERP.IT

Anderson, B. & E. 2007. *Lesvos Landscapes* (car tours and walks). Sunflower Books, London.

Anderson, B. & A. *Orchids of Lesvos*. 2001. Privately published.

BirdLife Species Factsheet: Cinereous Bunting (website). 2009.
  — see WWW.BIRDLIFE.ORG/DATAZONE/SPECIES/INDEX.HTML

Bowers, J. 2008. *The Dragonflies of Lesbos*. Friends of Green Lesbos, Lesvos.

Brooks, R. 1998. *Birding on the Greek Island of Lesvos*. Brookside Publishing, Fakenham.

Brooks, R. 1999. *Lesvos update spring 1999*. Brookside Publishing, Fakenham.

Brooks, R. 2000. *Lesvos update spring-summer 2000*. Brookside Publishing, Fakenham.

Brooks, R. 2001. *Lesvos update spring-summer 2001*. Brookside Publishing, Fakenham.

Brooks, R. 2002. *Lesvos update spring-summer 2002*. Brookside Publishing, Fakenham.

Brooks, R. 2003. *Lesvos update Summer '02 — summer '03*. Brooks, R. 2003. Brookside Publishing, Fakenham.

Brooks, R. 2004. *Lesvos update autumn '03 — summer '04*. Brookside Publishing, Fakenham.

Buttler, K.P. *Field Guide to Orchids of Britain and Europe*. 1991. The Crowood Press Ltd, Marlborough.

Chinery, M. 1997. *Insects of Britain & Western Europe*. HarperCollins, London.

Dijkstra, K-D. & Lewington, R. 2006. *A Field Guide to the Dragonflies of Britain and Europe*. British Wildlife Publishing, Dorset.

Handrinos, G. & Akriotis, T. 1997. *The Birds of Greece*. A&C Black, London.

Harrap, S. & Quinn, D. 1996. *Tits, Nuthatches & Treecreepers*. Christopher Helm, London.

Harrap, S. 1993. *Corsican and Krüper's Nuthatches*, two Western Palearctic endemics. Birding World 6: 111-114.

Harris, A., Shirihai, H. & Christie, D. 1996. *The Macmillan Birder's Guide to European and Middle Eastern Birds*. Macmillan, London.

Hellenic Rarities Committee, 2005. *Hellenic Rarities Committee Annual Report 2005* (referred to as HRC05 in text) — see HTTP://RARITIES.ORNITHOLOGIKI.GR/EN/EAOP/ANNUAL_REPORTS.HTM

Hellenic Rarities Committee, 2006. *Hellenic Rarities Committee Annual Report 2006* (referred to as HRC06 in text) — see HTTP://RARITIES.ORNITHOLOGIKI.GR/EN/EAOP/ANNUAL_REPORTS.HTM

Hellenic Rarities Committee, 2007. *Hellenic Rarities Committee Annual Report 2007* (referred to as HRC07 in text) — see HTTP://RARITIES.ORNITHOLOGIKI.GR/EN/EAOP/ANNUAL_REPORTS.HTM

Hellenic Rarities Committee, 2008. *Hellenic Rarities Committee Annual Report 2008* (referred to as HRC08 in text) — see HTTP://RARITIES.ORNITHOLOGIKI.GR/EN/EAOP/ANNUAL_REPORTS.HTM

Kakalis, E. & Akriotis, T. 2007. Nest site characteristics of Krüper's Nuthatch *Sitta krueperi* on the island of Lesvos, Greece. 2nd International Congress of Eurasian Ornithology, Antalya, Turkey, 26-29 Oct 07 (poster presentation).

Karatzas, Y.A. & Karatza, A. *Wild Orchids of Lesvos*. Εκδοσεισ Εντελεχεια. Mytilini.

Lesvos Birding (website). 2009. — see WWW.LESVOSBIRDING.COM

Macdonald, D. & Barrett, P. *Mammals of Britain & Europe*. HarperCollins, London.

Maunder, M. 2003. *On Foot in North Lesvos*. The Olive Press, Brighton.

Tolman, T. & Lewington, R. 1997. *Butterflies of Britain & Europe*. HarperCollins, London.

SCIENTIFIC NAME INDEX

Normal type   introductory sections and main birdchecklist.

Note, the 'tick lists' have not been indexed!

Bold type   species and place names from the individual site sections (place names are main places and those names detailed on maps — not all mentions of all places from within the text)

Italic type   illustrated in the colour plate section

Accipiter brevipes 30, 32, 45, 48, 51, **117, 119, 121, 133, 149, 154, 172, 178**, 196

Accipiter gentilis 29, 30, 34, 35, 48, 53, 73, 75, 102, **116, 117, 119, 120, 121, 122, 130, 135, 172, 178, 181, 182**, 196

Accipiter nisus 29, 48, 52, 53, **117, 120, 122, 181, 182**, 196

Acrocephalus arundinaceus 30, 51, 68, **98, 99, 101, 103, 104, 139, 140, 158, 162, 163, 177, 184**, 211

Acrocephalus melanopogon **184**, 211

Acrocephalus paludicola 226

Acrocephalus palustris 50, 211

Acrocephalus schoenobaenus 50, 211

Acrocephalus scirpaceus 50, 51, **184**, 211

Actitis hypoleucos 30, 48, **104, 112, 114, 160, 162, 173**, 202

Aegithalos caudatus 55, **167, 168, 181, 182, 183**, 210

Aegypius monachus 48, 56, 224

Alauda arvensis 29, 49, 53, 60, **173**, 210

Alcedo atthis 28, 35, 48, 85, **98, 103, 104, 106, 112, 128, 152, 166, 167, 173, 184, 186, 187**, 207

Alectoris chukar 46, 53, 67, 76, 79, 83, 84, **114, 128, 130, 132, 133, 140, 141, 142, 143, 145, 147, 149, 150, 154, 155, 156, 157, 159**, 190

Alectoris graeca 223

Anas acuta 52, 60, **165, 172, 173**, 191

Anas clypeata 191

Anas crecca 52, **172, 173**, 191

Anas penelope 52, 191

Anas platyrhynchos 52, 60, 191

Anas querquedula 29, 60, 70, **98, 99, 110, 111, 112, 113, 165, 172, 173, 184**, 191

Anas strepera 56, 191

Anser albifrons 56, 190

Anser erythropus 56, 223

Anthus campestris **111, 112, 113, 114, 152, 166, 170, 171, 173**, 220

Anthus cervinus 31, 49, **110, 111, 112, 113, 114, 117, 152**, 220

Anthus pratensis 53, 220

Anthus richardi 56, 225

Anthus spinoletta 29, 220

Anthus trivialis 51, 125, 127, 220

Apus affinis 56, 206

Apus apus 31, 49, 51, 99, 206

Apus melba 31, 34, 49, **99, 142**, 206

Apus pallidus 29, 31, 49, **99**, 206

Aquila chrysaetos 35, 48, 197

Aquila clanga 197

Aquila fasciata 35, 48, **117**, 197

Aquila heliaca 48, 56, **117**, 197

Aquila nipalensis 48, 56, 197

Aquila pomarina 48, 196

Ardea alba 47, 84, **111, 166, 173, 184**, 194

Ardea cinerea **111**, 194

Ardea purpurea 31, 47, *90*, *91*, **99, 104, 111, 142, 166, 174, 175**, 194

Ardeola ralloides 47, 81, *91*, **98, 99, 111, 162, 163, 178**, 193

Arenaria interpres 48, **112**, 202

Asio flammeus 53, **112, 114**, 206

Asio otus 46, 54, 86, **99, 116, 167, 168, 178 182**, 206

Athene noctua 54, 84, **112, 119, 120, 121, 122, 130, 147, 149, 150, 154, 155, 156, 157, 159, 165, 166, 170**, 206

Aythya ferina 36, 56, 191

Aythya fuligula 56, 60, 191

Aythya marila 191

Aythya nyroca 56, 191

Bombycilla garrulus 209
Botaurus stellaris **139, 184**, 193
Branta leucopsis 56, 223
Branta ruficollis 56, 190
Bubo bubo 54, 205
Bubulcus ibis 47, 193
Bucephala clangula 56, 192
Burhinus oedicnemus 29, 48, 51, 54, 65, **98, 100, 105, 108, 109, 110, 111, 112, 113, 114, 141, 162, 166, 169, 189**, 199
Buteo buteo 30, 48, 52, 53, **111, 115, 117, 120, 122, 130, 137, 149, 177, 182**, 196
Buteo rufinus 30, 48, 53, 54, 56, 66, 67, 73, 75, 92, **98, 100, 101, 102, 103, 104, 105, 106, 107, 111, 115, 116, 117, 119, 120, 121, 122, 123, 127, 130, 135, 136, 137, 140, 143, 144, 145, 149, 150, 153, 158, 159, 160, 161, 163, 167, 168, 173, 177, 178, 184**, 196
Calandrella brachydactyla 31, 49, 51, 56, **110, 111, 112, 113, 114, 132, 166, 170, 173**, 209
Calandrella rufescens 56, 209
Calidris alba 48, 111, 114, 202
Calidris alpina 48, 111, 114, 203
Calidris bairdii 224
Calidris canutus 202
Calidris ferruginea 30, **111, 114, 172, 173**, 202
Calidris melanotos 56, **171**, 202
Calidris minuta 30, 48, 11, **114, 172, 173**, 202
Calidris temminckii 30, 48, 68, 69, **111, 114, 160, 162, 171, 172, 173**, 202
Calonectris diomedea diomedea 30, 46, 47, **128, 129, 162, 176**, 192
Caprimulgus europaeus 33, 51, 85, **101, 102, 165, 166**, 206
Carduelis cannabina 55, **166**, 221
Carduelis carduelis 55, 221
Carduelis chloris 55, 221
Carduelis flammea 56, 226
Carduelis spinus 24, 29, 221
Carpodacus erythrinus 56, 221
Cecropis daurica 30, 49, 51, **99, 101, 137, 149**, 210
Cercomela melanura 225
Cercotrichas galactotes 31, 33, 51, 67, 79, 80, **109, 110, 112, 113, 114, 115, 125, 143, 144, 145, 153, 155, 157, 158, 159, 165, 166**, 216
Certhia brachydactyla 55,85, 86, **167, 168, 181, 182**, 215

Ceryle rudis 56, 225
Cettia cetti 29, 55, **98, 99, 103, 162, 163, 184**, 210
Charadrius alexandrinus 48, **98, 100, 104, 111, 113, 114, 172, 173**, 200
Charadrius asiaticus 30, 113, 200
Charadrius dubius 48, 51, 69, **100, 104, 111, 114**, 200
Charadrius hiaticula 48, **104, 111, 114, 173**, 200
Charadrius leschenaultii 56, 224
Charadrius mongolus 56, 224
Charadrius morinellus 56, 200
Chlidonias hybrida 32, 48, **99, 112**, 204
Chlidonias leucopterus 32, 48, **99, 112**, 204
Chlidonias niger 48, **112**, 204
Chroicocephalus genei 30, 48, **99, 110, 112, 184, 187**, 203
Chroicocephalus ridibundus **112**, 203
Ciconia ciconia 47, 50, **91, 99, 111, 117, 119, 120, 121, 122, 123, 132, 173**, 193
Ciconia nigra 47, 50, **101, 111, 117, 119, 120, 121, 122, 137, 149, 173**, 193
Cinclus cinclus 56, 219
Circaetus gallicus 30, 46, 48, 61, 66, 67, 73, 74, 75, **101, 102, 103, 104, 105, 109, 111, 115, 116, 117, 119, 120, 121, 122, 130, 135, 136, 137, 140, 143, 144, 145, 149, 150, 153, 155, 158, 159, 161, 163, 165, 167, 168, 172, 177, 178, 181, 182, 184, 186, 187**, 195
Circus aeruginosus 29, 30, 36, 48, **99, 100, 106, 111, 114,139, 152, 173, 184**, 196
Circus cyaneus 30, 36, 48, **99, 100, 106, 111, 114, 152, 173**, 196
Circus macrourus 30, 48, **106, 111, 114, 152**, 196
Circus pygargus 30, 48, **99, 100, 106, 111, 114, 173**, 196
Cisticola juncidis 55, **111, 112, 184**, 212
Clamator glandarius 49, 51, **122, 125, 127, 149, 154**, 205
Coccothraustes coccothraustes 29, 45, 55, **128**, 221
Coloeus monedula 55, 60, **140, 141, 152**, 208
Columba livia 54, 60, 83, **140, 141**, 204
Columba oenas 56, 205
Columba palumbus 205
Coracias garrulus 30, 49, 79, 85, **105, 121, 122, 143, 148, 153, 167, 168, 173**, 206
Corvus corax 55, **107, 115, 149, 181, 182**, 209
Corvus cornix 55, 60, 205, 208

Corvus frugilegus 208
Coturnix coturnix 29, 51, 60, **108, 109, 110, 113, 141, 162, 173,** 190
Crex crex 47, 60, 198-9
Cuculus canorus 49, **125, 127, 140,** 149, **153, 154, 168, 173, 181, 182,** 205
Cyanistes caeruleus 55, 209
Cygnus columbianus 56, 190
Cygnus cygnus 56, 190
Cygnus olor 190
Delichon urbicum 49, 210
Dendrocopos leucotos 56, 225
Dendrocopos major 56, 225
Dendrocopos medius 33, 45, 54, 73, 75, 87, **101, 102, 104, 105, 106, 114, 120, 121, 122, 123, 130, 131, 136, 137, 144,** 149, **154, 165, 168, 169, 170, 175, 176, 177, 178, 180, 181, 182, 183, 187,** 207
Dendrocopos syriacus 56, 225
Egretta garzetta 47, **111, 166, 173,** 194
Emberiza caesia 30, 34, 46, 52, 72, 74, 76, 79, 95, **114, 116, 117, 121, 123, 124, 125, 128, 130, 133, 139, 140, 141, 142, 143, 144, 145, 147, 148,** 149, **150,** 154, **155, 156, 157, 159,** 222
Emberiza calandra 29, 34, 55, **166,** 221
Emberiza cia 221
Emberiza cineracea 30-31, 34, 46, 52, 76, 77, 84, 95, **139, 140,** 142, **143, 147, 148,** 149, **150,** 154, **156, 157, 159,** 222
Emberiza cirlus 55, 66, **119, 120, 121, 122, 123, 124, 125, 126, 127, 128, 137, 140, 142, 145, 148,** 149, **160, 161, 165, 168, 181, 182,** 222
Emberiza citrinella 56, 221
Emberiza hortulana 30, 80, **105, 112, 117, 122, 128, 159, 173,** 222
Emberiza melanocephala 31, 34, 52, 79, 80, **101, 105, 107, 112, 123, 124, 125, 126, 127, 130, 133, 145, 155, 157, 159, 173,** 223
Emberiza pusilla 56, 223
Emberiza schoeniclus **173, 184, 186, 187,** 223
Erithacus rubecula 29, 53, 54, **89, 180, 181, 182,** 216
Falco biarmicus 49, **166,** 198
Falco cherrug 56, 198
Falco columbarius 29, 56, 198
Falco eleonorae 30, 32, 34, 49, 51, 78, **111, 117, 125, 127, 137, 139, 143, 145,** 149, **150, 152, 153, 154, 155, 158, 159, 161, 163, 166, 172,** 198

Falco naumanni 30, 49, 51, 78, 83, **109, 110, 117, 137, 139, 140, 141, 142, 143, 145,** 149, **150, 151, 152, 153, 154, 155, 157, 158, 159, 166,** 197
Falco peregrinus 49, 52, 53, 67, **101, 103, 104, 105, 107, 111, 116, 117, 119, 120, 125, 130, 133, 136, 137, 145,** 149, **150, 154, 159, 160, 161, 163, 166,** 198
Falco subbuteo 30, 49, **99, 117, 150, 166,** 198
Falco tinnunculus 49, 53, **99, 117, 159, 160,** 197
Falco vespertinus 30, 32, 49, 84, 92, **99, 109, 110, 111, 117, 139, 149, 150, 151, 153, 154, 159, 166, 173,** 198
Ficedula albicollis 30, 35, 36, 50, 56, 78, 94, **153, 155, 158,** 218
Ficedula hypoleuca 50, 218
Ficedula parva 31, 50, **128,** 219
Ficedula semitorquata 30, 50, 218
Fringilla coelebs 55, 220
Fringilla montifringilla 220
Fulica atra 28, 54, 199
Galerida cristata 159, 210
Gallinago gallinago 48, 52, 60, **112, 114,** 201
Gallinago media 32, 48, **106, 112,** 113, **114,** 153, 201
Gallinula chloropus 54, 199
Garrulus glandarius 55, **103**, **105, 114, 131,** 149, 208
Gavia arctica 29, 46, 52, 54, 56, **99, 173, 186,** 192
Gavia stellata 56, 223
Gelochelidon nilotica 30, 48, **99, 112,** 204
Glareola nordmanni 203
Glareola pratincola 30, 48, **99, 109, 110, 111, 112, 114,** 203
Grus grus 199
Gyps fulvus 48, 56, 195
Haematopus ostralegus **111,** 199
Haliaeetus albicilla 56, 195
Halycon smyrensis 56, 225
Hieraaetus pennatus 35, 48, **117,** 197
Himantopus himantopus 48, 51, **99, 100, 108, 111, 139, 173,** 199
Hippolais caligata 56, 226
Hippolais icterina 30, 50, 51, **137, 149, 158, 159,** 212
Hippolais languida 226
Hippolais olivetorum 31, 45, 51, 67, 73, 87, **101, 102, 120, 121, 122, 135, 140, 144, 153, 158, 159, 169, 170,** 211

Hippolais pallida 31, 68, 69, **99, 101, 115, 139, 184**, 211
Hirundo rustica 49, 51, 210
Hirundo rustica 49, 51, 210
Hydrocoloeus minutus 48, **112**, 203
Hydroprogne caspia 184, **187**, 204
Ichthyaetus audouinii 30, 46, 54, **128, 129, 130, 152**, 203
Ichthyaetus melanocephalus 29, 30, 48, **99, 112, 169, 170, 173, 184, 186, 187**, 203
Iphiclides podalirius 96
Irania gutturalis 32, 51, 56, **129, 130, 155**, 216
Ixobrychus minutus 31, 32, 43, 47, 66, 68, 78, 80, 81, *90*, **98, 99**, 103, **104, 105**, 140, **151, 152, 153, 158, 162, 163, 175, 178, 184**, 193
Jynx torquilla 31, 49, 207
Lanius collurio 31, 50, 52, 80, 81, **99, 101, 112, 115, 154, 155, 159, 166, 173**, 207
Lanius excubitor 56, 207
Lanius isabellinus 226
Lanius minor 31, 50, 52, 80, **112, 157, 159, 166, 173**, 207
Lanius nubicus 31, 46, 50, 52, 67, 73, 86, **101, 102, 112, 120, 121, 122, 129, 130, 135, 136, 137, 153, 154, 167, 168**, 208
Lanius pallidirostris 56, 207
Lanius senator 31, 50, 52, 80, **99, 101, 112, 114, 115, 119, 120, 121, 122, 125, 130, 137, 148, 149, 154, 155, 159, 166, 168, 170, 173, 184**, 208
Larus canus 56, 203
Larus fuscus 29, 48, 53, **112, 166, 167, 170**, 204
Larus marinus 56, 224
Larus michahellis 46, 54, **99, 107, 129, 140, 160, 186**, 204
lepidoptera 236
Limicola falcinellus **112, 114, 172, 173**, 203
Limosa lapponica 56, **112**, 201
Limosa limosa **112**, 201
Locustella fluviatilis 31, 50, 67, **114, 115, 125**, 212
Locustella luscinioides 212
Locustella naevia 212
Loxia curvirostra 29, 56, 221
Lullula arborea 29, 46, 76, 85, 86, **119, 120, 121, 122, 149, 157, 159, 165, 166, 167, 168**, 210
Luscinia luscinia 30, 32, 50, **128, 137, 149, 154, 155, 158, 159**, 216

Luscinia megarhynchos 13, 31, 51, 69, *93*, **101, 120, 122, 137, 139, 181, 182**, 216
Luscinia svecica 36, 56, **161**, 216
Lymnocryptes minimus 52, 201
Martes foina 57
Melanocorypha calandra 49, **112, 113, 114**, 209
Melanocorypha yeltoniensis 56, 225
Mergellus albellus 56, 192
Mergus serrator 36, 52, **99**, 192
Merops apiaster 31, 35, 49, 51, 68, 82, 99, **104, 105, 106, 111, 112, 114, 115, 120, 121, 122, 125, 127, 128, 133, 135, 139, 140, 141, 142, 143, 145, 151, 153, 155, 157, 158, 159, 161, 163, 166, 167, 178**, 207
Merops persicus 56, **158**, 207
Milvus migrans 30, 48, **173**, 195
Milvus milvus 56, 195
Monachus monachus **128, 141**
Monticola saxatilis 50, 218
Monticola solitarius 54, 74, 75, 84, **101, 102, 103, 116, 117, 120, 124, 125, 133, 136, 137, 140, 145, 147, 148, 149** 154, **156, 159, 160, 165, 166, 167, 177, 178, 181, 186**, 218
Motacilla alba 29, 36, **112, 114, 152, 160, 173, 178**, 220
Motacilla cinerea 29, 53, **160, 166, 167, 173, 181, 182**, 220
Motacilla citreola 30, 50, 68, **112, 113, 114, 152, 170, 188**, 220
Motacilla flava 30 ,49, **98, 100**, 107, 110, 113, **140, 142, 152, 160, 173, 184, 186, 187**, 219
Motacilla flava beema 219
Motacilla flava cinereocapilla 219
Motacilla flava drombrowski 219
Motacilla flava feldegg 51, **99, 112, 114**, 219
Motacilla flava flava 99, **112, 114**, 219
Motacilla flava flavissima 219
Motacilla flava lutea 219
Motacilla flava superciliaris 219
Motacilla flava thunbergi **112, 114**, 219
Muscicapa striata 35, 50, 218
Nemoptera bipennis 96
Neophron percnopterus 48, 56, 195
Netta rufina 223
Nucifraga caryocatactes 208
Numenius arquata 48, **114**, 201
Numenius phaeopus 48, 112, *114*, 201

Nycticorax nycticorax 31, 33, 43, 47, 78, *90*, **99**, 103, 104, 110, 111, 149, 152, 167, 168, 184, 189, 193

odonata 238

Oena capensis 227

Oenanthe deserti 226

Oenanthe finschii 56, **129**, 218

Oenanthe hispanica 29, 46, 50, 51, 56, 66, 72, 74, 76, 79, 83, 84, 85, **101**, **102**, **103**, **104**, **105**, **107**, **114**, **115**, **116**, **117**, **124**, **125**, **126**, **127**, 130, 133, 136, 137, 139, 140, 141, 142, 143, 145, **147**, 148, 149, 150, 154, 155, 156, 157, 159, 161, 165, 167, 168, 176, 181, 186, 218

Oenanthe isabellina 30, 46, 50, 51, 76, **147**, **148**, 149, 150, 156, 217

Oenanthe oenanthe 29, 50, 51, 112,114, 140, 141, 148, 149, 154, 155, 156, 173, 217

Oenanthe pleschanka 56, 217

Oriolus oriolus 30, 50, 75, 77, **120**, **121**, **122**, **128**, 130, 131, 135, 136, 137, 139, 140, 141, 142, 143, 144, 145, 149, 152, 153, 154, 159, 178, 208

Onychogomphus forcipatus 96

Ophrys lesbis 96

Otus scops 51, 72, *93*, **99**, **114**, **115**, **116**, **136**, **137**, **186**, 205

Oxyura jamaicensis 227

Oxyura leucocephala 56, 192

Pandion haliaetus 30, 48, 111, 186, 187, 195

Panurus biarmicus 56, 209

Parus major 55, 209

Passer domesticus 50, 55, 219

Passer hispaniolensis 50, 81, 98, 99, **105**, **112**, **125**, **127**, **154**, **162**, 219

Passer montanus 219

Pastor roseus 33, 50, **99**, **112**, **113**, 215

Pelecanus crispus 31, 47, 111, 194

Pelecanus onocrotalus 31, 35, 47, *90*, **98**, **100**, 111, 173, 194

Periparus ater 55, **168**, **181**, **182**, **183**, 209

Pernis apivorus 32, 34, 35, 48, 51, **116**, **117**, **120**, **122**, **133**, **149**, **159**, **177**, **178**, **181**, **182**, 195

Petronia petronia 55, 75, 76, 84, *94*, **106**, **136**, **137**, **142**, **143**, **144**, **145**, **147**, **148**, **149**, 150, 219

Phalacrocorax aristotelis 29, 53, **129**, **140**, **169**, **172**, 194

Phalacrocorax carbo 29, 36, 46, 52, **99**, **105**, **169**, **171**, **172**, 194

Phalacrocorax pygmeus 29, 36, 43, 46, 52, 85, **166**, **167**, **184**, 194

Phalaropus lobatus 56, 203

Phasianus colchicus 190

Philomachus pugnax 48, 112, 114, 203

Phoenicopterus roseus 28, 30, 35, 36, 47, 50, 71, 108, **111**, **160**, **161**, **165**, **166**, **173**, 192

Phoenicurus ochruros 29, 36, 53, **99**, **112**, **114**, 148, 149, 170, 173, 217

Phoenicurus phoenicurus 30, **99**, **131**, **154**, **181**, **182**, **183**, 217

Phylloscopus collybita 29, 35, 50, **99**, **149**, 211

Phylloscopus orientalis 30, 35, 36, 52, 89, **137**, **140**, **149**, **158**, **180**, **181**, **182**, 211

Phylloscopus sibilatrix 35, 50, **158**, **159**, **181**, **182**, 211

Phylloscopus trochilus 35, 50, **149**, 210

Pica pica 60, 208

Picus viridis 56, 225

Platalea leucorodia 47, **172**, **173**, 193

Plegadis falcinellus 47, 70, *91*, **99**, **110**, **111**, **112**, **113**, **114**, 193

Pluvialis apricaria **111**, **114**, 200

Pluvialis squatarola 48, **111**, **114**, 200

Podiceps cristatus 29, 30, 35, 36, 46, 52, **99**, **111**, **113**, **160**, **167**, **169**, **172**, **173**, **184**, **186**, **187**, 192

Podarcis tauricus 95

Podiceps grisegena 192

Podiceps nigricollis 29, 30, 36, 46, 52, **99**, **101**, **102**, **111**, **113**, **160**, **167**, **169**, **172**, **173**, **184**, **186**, **187**, 192

Poecile lugubris 31, 34, 45, 55, 73, 77, 81, 84, 87, **101**, **102**, **104**, **119**, **120**, **121**, **122**, **123**, **124**, **125**, **126**, **127**, **128**, **129**, **130**, **139**, **140**, **142**, **144**, **145**, **147**, **148**, **149**, **155**, **157**, **158**, **159**, **161**, **176**, 209

Porzana parva 31, 47, 66, **99**, **103**, **104**, **162**, **163**, **175**, 199

Porzana porzana 31, 47, **99**, **104**, 199

Porzana pusilla 33, 47, *92*, **104**, **158**, 199

Prunella modularis 53, 54, 219

Ptyonoprogne rupestris 30, 49, 51, 75, **101**, **136**, **137**, **149**, **160**, **161**, 210

Puffinus yelkouan 30, 46, 47, **128**, **129**, **176**, 192

Pyrrhocorax pyrrhocorax 208

Pyrrhula pyrrhula 221

Rallus aquaticus 28, **99**, **138**, **139**, **170**, **184**, **187**, 198

Recurvirostra avosetta 48, 51, **99**, **108**, **111**, **173**, 199

Regulus ignicapilla 213
Regulus regulus 53, 214
Remiz pendulinus 50, 56, **153**, 209
Riparia riparia 49, 210
Rustic 56, 226
Saxicola rubetra 30, 35, 50, **98, 99** 103, **105, 112, 114, 115, 154, 173**, 217
Saxicola torquatus **166, 167**, 217
Scolopax rusticola 52, 200
Serinus pusillus 56, 220
Serinus serinus 29, 55, **178, 180, 181, 182**, 220
Sitta europaea 55, **102, 119, 120, 121, 122, 123, 131**, 214
Sitta krueperi 10, 31, 33, 40, 41, 46, 55, 85, 86, 94, **165, 166, 167, 168, 180, 181, 182, 183**, 214
Sitta neumayer 31, 34, 46, 55, 72, 73, 76, 79, 83, 84, *94*, **101, 102, 103, 104, 105, 107, 114, 115, 116, 117, 120, 121, 122, 123, 125, 127, 128, 130, 133, 137, 139, 140, 141, 142, 145, 147, 148, 149, 150, 154, 155, 156, 159, 161, 165, 166, 167**, 215
Stercorarius longicaudus 56, 224
Stercorarius parasiticus 56, 204
Stercorarius pomarinus 56, 224
Sterna benegalensis 56, 224
Sterna hirundo 51, 204
Sterna paradisea 56, 224
Sternula albifrons 51, **108, 112**, 204
Streptopelia decaocto 205
Streptopelia senegalensis 56, 205
Streptopelia turtur 35, 45, 51, 60, **125, 127, 130, 137, 140, 149, 153, 154, 172, 173, 181, 182**, 205
Strix aluco 54, 206
Sturnus vulgaris 29, 53, 60, **184**, 215
Sylvia atricapilla 29, 50, **137, 149**, 213
Sylvia borin 50, 137, 149, 213
Sylvia cantillans 51, 66, 72, **101, 102, 115, 116, 117, 119, 120, 121, 122, 123, 124, 125, 127, 128, 130, 131, 135, 136, 137, 149, 158, 165, 166, 177, 178, 181, 182**, 213
Sylvia communis 50, 213
Sylvia conspicillata 56, 226
Sylvia crassirostris 30, **101, 114, 115, 121, 122, 124, 125, 128, 130, 135, 136, 149, 166, 168, 177, 178**, 213

Sylvia curruca 50, 213
Sylvia melanocephala 29, 32, 51, 89, **125, 132, 158, 175, 176, 177, 178, 186**, 187
Sylvia mystacea 226
Sylvia nisoria 31, 50, 51, **115, 123, 124, 125**, 128
Sylvia rueppelli 30, 52, 74, *93*, **107, 124, 125, 158, 165**, 213
Tachybaptus ruficollis 53, **99, 101, 104, 161, 184**, 192
Tadorna ferruginea 43, 44, 53, 70, 82, 84, 85, *90*, **105, 107, 109, 110, 111, 113, 114, 115, 123, 131, 132, 135, 136, 165, 166, 167, 172**, 190
Tadorna tadorna 52, 107, 173, 190
Tchagra senegula 226
Testudo graeca 57, 76, *95*, **141, 142**, 149
Thalasseus sandvicensis 53, **99, 112,** 173, **184, 186, 187**, 204
Tringa erythropus 30, 48, **112, 114, 172**, 201
Tringa glareola 30, 48, **99, 104, 112, 114, 173, 186**, 202
Tringa nebularia 30, 48, **112, 114**, 201
Tringa ochropus 48, 52, **104, 112, 114, 173, 184**, 202
Tringa stagnatilis 30, 47, 48, **99, 112, 114, 172, 173**, 201
Tringa totanus 48, 112, 114, 201
Troglodytes troglodytes 53, 54, **104, 137, 181, 182**, 214
Turdus iliacus 29, 53, 60, 216
Turdus merula 36, 53, 54, 215
Turdus philomelos 29, 36, 53, 54, 89, **181, 182**, 216
Turdus pilaris 29, 53, 215
Turdus torquatus 56, 215
Turdus viscivorus 54, **180, 181, 182**, 216
Tyto alba 54, 99, 186, 205
Upupa epops 30, 31, 49, 51, 57, **103, 104, 105, 115, 119, 121, 120, 122, 128, 130, 137, 140, 141, 149, 154, 155, 159, 161, 163, 172, 181, 182**, 207
Vanellus gregarius 56, 200
Vanellus leucrus 56, 224
Vanellus spinosus 30, 48, *93*, **111, 114**, 200
Vanellus vanellus 29, 60, 200
Xenus cinereus 56, **173**, 202

ENGLISH INDEX

This index covers English species names, place names and main subjects referred to throughout this guide.

Normal type — introductory sections and main birdchecklist.
Note, the 'tick lists' have not been indexed!

Bold type — species and place names from the individual site sections (place names are main places and those names detailed on maps — not all mentions of all places from within the text)

Coloured bold type — main site pages

Italic type — illustrated in the colour plate section

A

Achladeri Forest 40, 46, *86*, **164**, 167–8, **169**
Aghios Ioannis 31, *84*, 138–9
Agia Paraskevi 64, 97, **118**, **119**
Aghias Taxiarchis **134**, 135
Agiasos 44, 64, **179**, 180–1
Agiasos area 44, 179–184
Agiasos Sanatorium **179**, 180–1
Agios Fokas 22, 32, 40, **174**, 175–6
Agra 64, *84*, **138**, **141**
Alikoudi Pool 43, *86*, 169–70
Akrasi **174**
Almiropotamos River (Vatera) 43, 63, 174–5
Almyropotamos River (Lisvorio) *87*, **171**, **172**
Alykes Wetlands 42, 48, 49, 62, **97**, 112–13
Ambeliko Valley 63, 64, *89*, **174**, 177–8
Anaxos 44, **134**
Andissa 22, 64, **134**
Anemotia **101**, **134**
Apothika *83*, **138**, **140**, **141**
Argenos **123**, **128**, **133**
Asomatos **179**
Avocet 48, 51, **99**, **108**, **111**, **173**, 199

B

Bee-eater
   Blue-cheeked 56, **158**, 207
   European 31, 35, 49, 51, 68, 82, 99, **104**, **105**, **106**, **111**, **112**, **114**, **115**, **120**, **121**, **122**, **125**, **127**, **128**, **133**, **135**, **139**, **140**, **141**, **142**, **143**, **145**, **151**, **153**, **155**, **157**, **158**, **159**, **161**, **163**, **166**, **167**, **178**, 207

Bicycles (for hire) 25
birdwatchers code of conduct 37
Bittern
   Great **139**, **184**, 193
   Little 31, 33, 43, 47, 66, 68, 78, 80, 81, *90*, **98**, **99**, **103**, **104**, **105**, **106**, **140**, **151**, **152**, **153**, **158**, **162**, **163**, **175**, **178**, **184**, 193
Blackbird 36, 53, 54, 215
Blackcap 29, 50, **137**, **149**, 213
Blackstart 225
Bluethroat 36, 56, **161**, 216
Brambling 220
Bullfinch 221
Bunting
   Black-headed 31, 34, 52, 79, 80, **101**, **105**, **107**, **112**, **123**, **124**, **125**, **126**, **127**, **130**, **133**, **142**, **145**, **155**, **157**, **159**, **173**, 223
   Cinereous 30-31, 34, 46, 52, 76, 77, 84, *95*, **139**, **140**, **142**, **143**, **147**, **148**, **149**, **150**, **154**, **156**, **157**, **159**, 222
   Cirl 55, 66, **119**, **120**, **121**, **122**, **123**, **124**, **125**, **126**, **127**, **128**, **137**, **140**, **142**, **145**, **148**, **149**, **160**, **161**, **165**, **168**, **181**, **182**, 222
   Corn 29, 34, 55, **166**, 221
   Cretzschmar's 30, 34, 46, 52, 72, 74, 76, 79, *95*, **114**, **116**, **117**, **121**, **123**, **124**, **125**, **128**, **130**, **133**, **139**, **140**, **141**, **142**, **143**, **144**, **145**, **147**, **148**, **149**, **150**, **154**, **155**, **156**, **157**, **159**, 222
   Little 56, 223
   Ortolan 30, 80, **105**, **112**, **117**, **122**, **128**, **159**, **173**, 222
   Reed **173**, **184**, **186**, **187**, 223
   Rock 221

Rustic 56, 226

buntings 45, 52, 34, 68, 69, 71, 76, 80, 88, **98**, **102**, **103**, **104**, **106**, **107**, **109**, **111**, **113**, **114**, **117**, **123**, **124**, **125**, **126**, **127**, **128**, **130**, **140**, **142**, **149**, **152**, **155**, **157**, **158**, **159**, **160**, **161**, **171**, **172**, **173**, **175**

buses 24

butterflies 8, 9, 58, **125**, **127**, **128**, **130**, **149**, **167**, **168**, 182, 186, 236—7

    Scarce Swallowtail 96

Buzzard

    Common 30, 48, 52, 53, **111**, **115**, **117**, **120**, **122**, **130**, **137**, **149**, **177**, **182**, 196

    Long-legged 30, 48, 53, 54, 56, 66, 67, 73, 75, 92, **98**, **100**, **101**, **102**, **103**, **104**, **105**, **106**, **107**, **111**, **115**, **116**, **117**, **119**, **120**, **121**, **122**, **123**, **127**, **130**, **135**, **136**, **137**, **140**, **143**, **144**, **145**, **149**, **150**, **153**, **158**, **159**, **160**, **161**, **163**, **167**, **168**, **173**, **177**, **178**, **184**, 196

C

Cape Lena **185—6**

car hire 24

chats 45, 78, 88, **101**, **104**, **106**, **109**, **111**, **125**, **127**, **130**, **131**, **132**, **135** 139, **140**, **141**, **142**, **145**, **151**, **152**, **153**, **155**, **157**, **158**, **159**, **160**, **161**, **162**, **163**, **167**, **169**, **170**, **171**, **172**, **173**, **175**, **176**, **178**, **184**, **186**, **187**

Chaffinch 55, 220

Chough 208

Chiffchaff (Common) 29, 36, 50, **99**, **149**, 211

Christou River 20, 22, 42, 48, 55, 62, 65, **97**, **98**, **100**, **101**, **102**, **103**

Chrousos **138**, **144—5**

Chukar 46, 53, 60, 67, 76, 79, 83, 84, **114**, **128**, **130**, **132**, **133**, **140**, **141**, **142**, **143**, **145**, **147**, **149**, **150**, **154**, **155**, **156**, **157**, **159**, 190

Cisticola, Zitting (see Fan-tailed Warbler)

Coot 28, 54, 199

Cormorant

    (Great) 29, 36, 46, 52, **99**, **105**, **169**, **171**, **172**, 194

    Pygmy 29, 36, 43, 46, 52, 85, **166**, **167**, **184**, 194

Corncrake 47, 60, 198—9

Crake

    Baillon's 33, 47, 92, **104**, **158**, 199

    Little 31, 47, 66, **99**, **103**, **104**, **162**, **163**, **175**, 199

    Spotted 31, 47, **99**, **104**, 199

crakes 29, 33, 43, 47, 80, 81, **98**, **102**, **103**, **104**, **105**, **106**, **114**, **139**, **157**, **158**, **159**, **162**, **163**, **171**, **175**, **178**, **184**, **187**

Crane (Common) 199

Crossbill (Common) 29, 56, 221

Crow, Hooded 55, 60, 205, 208

Cuckoo

    Common 49, **125**, **127**, **140**, **149**, **153**, **154**, **168**, **170**, **173**, **181**, **182**, 205

    Great Spotted 49, 51, **122**, **125**, **127**, **149**, **154**, 205

Curlew (Eurasian) 47, 48, **114**, 201

D

Dafia 97, **105**, **116**

Dimitrios 63, **179**, 182

Dipi Larisos 29, 43, 46, 52, **179**, 184

Dipper, Black-bellied 56, 219

Diver

    Black-throated 29, 46, 54, 56, **99**, **173**, **186**, 192

    Red-throated 56, 223

dolphins **128**

Dotterel 56, 200

Dove

    Collared 205

    Laughing 56, 205

    Namaqua 227

    Rock 54, 60, 83, **140**, **141**, 204

    Stock 56, 205

    Turtle 35, 45, 51, 60, **125**, **127**, **130**, **137**, **140**, **149**, **153**, **154**, **173**, **181**, **182**, 205

dragonflies 9, 43, 57, 58, **101**, **102**, **103**, **128**, **130**, **132**, **142**, **167**, **168**, **170**, 238—9

    Small Pincertail 96

driving 26

Duck

    Ferruginous 56, 191

    Ruddy 227

    Tufted 56, 60, 191

    White-headed 56, 192

Dunlin 48, **111**, **114**, 203

Dunnock 53, 54, 219

Dutch bird names 243—250

E

Eagle
- Bonelli's 35, 48, **117**, 197
- Booted 35, 48, **117**, 197
- Golden 35, **48**, 197
- Greater Spotted 197
- Imperial (Eastern) 48, 56, **117**, 197
- Lesser Spotted 48, 196
- Short-toed 30, 46, 48, 61, 66, 67, 73, 74, 75, **101**, **102**, **103**, **104**, **105**, **109**, **111**, **115**, **116**, **117**, **119**, **120**, **121**, **130**, **135**, **136**, **137**, **140**, **143**, **144**, **145**, **149**, **150**, **153**, **155**, **158**, **159**, **161**, **163**, **165**, **167**, **168**, **172**, **177**, **178**, **181**, **182**, **184**, **186**, **187**, 195
- Steppe 48, 56, 197
- White-tailed 56, 195

eagles 32, 48, 119, **120**, **121**, **122**, **172**

economy 14—15
- olives 15
- ouzo 15
- tourism 15

Efthalou 32, 41, 62, 74, **123**, 128—30

Egret
- Cattle 47, 193
- Great White 47, 84, **111**, **166**, **173**, **184**, 194
- Little 47, **111**, **166**, **173**, 194

egrets 28, 29, 33, 34, 36, 43, 47, 67, 70, 71, 84, 88, **98**, **100**, **101**, **104**, **105**, **106**, **107**, **109**, **110**, **112**, **113**, **153**, **157**, **158**, **159**, **160**, **161**, **163**, **165**, **166**, **167**, **170**, **172**, **175**, **176**, **177**, **184**

Eresos 14, 22, 27, 34, 44, 46, 62, 64, 82, **146**, **160**, **162**

F

Falcon
- Eleonora's Falcon 30, 32, 34, 49, 51, 78, **111**, **117**, **125**, **127**, **137**, **139**, **143**, **145**, **149**, **150**, **152**, **153**, **154**, **155**, **158**, **159**, **161**, **163**, **166**, **172**, 198
- Lanner 49, **166**, 198
- Peregrine 49, 52, 53, 67, **101**, **103**, **104**, **105**, **107**, **111**, **116**, **117**, **119**, **120**, **125**, **130**, **133**, **136**, **137**, **145**, **149**, **150**, **154**, **159**, **160**, **161**, **163**, 198
- Red-footed 30, 32, 49, 84, 92, **99**, **109**, **110**, **111**, **117**, **139**, **149**, **150**, **151**, **153**, **154**, **159**, **166**, **173**, 198
- Saker 56, 198

falcons 30, 32, 34, 45, 46, 48, 49, 69, 71, 88, **102**, **105**, **106**, **110**, **111**, **119**, **120**, **121**, **122**, **139**, **140**, **141**, **142**, **145**, **148**, **149**, **150**, **152**, **153**, **157**, **166**, **169**, **170**, **171**, **172**, **177**, **178**

Faneromeni (inc. fields, fords) 7, 41, 44, *78*, *79*, **94**, **146**, 151—4

Fieldfare 29, 53, 60, 215

Filia **134**

finches 29, 34

Firecrest 213

Flamingo, Greater 28, 30, 36, 47, 50, 71, **108**, **111**, **160**, **161**, **165**, **166**, **173**, 192—3

Flycatcher
- Collared 30, 35, 36, 50, 78, *94*, **153**, **155**, **156**, **158**, 218
- Pied 50, 218
- Red-breasted 31, 50, **128**, 219
- Semi-collared 30, 50, 218
- Spotted 35, 50, 218

flycatchers 30, 50, 77, 78, 80, 83, **104**, **127**, **130**, **135**, **136**, **137**, **140**, **141**, **142**, **144**, **145**, **148**, **149**, **151**, **152**, **153**, **154**, **155**, **156**, **158**, **159**, **160**, **161**, **163**, **167**, **168**, **169**, **175**, **176**, **178**, **181**, **182**, **183**, **184**, **186**, **187**

flowers 13, 22, 37, 45, 57, 76, **98**, **99**, **147**, **149**, **167**, **180**, **181**

Fox, Red 57

G

Gadwall 56, 60, 191

Garbias Island **140**, **141**

Garganey 29, **110**, **111**, **112**, **113**, **165**, **172**, **173**, **184**, 191

getting to Lesvos 18

Godwit
- Bar-tailed Godwit 56, **112**, 201
- Black-tailed 48, **112**, 201

Goldcrest 53, 214

Goldeneye (Common) 56, 192

Goldfinch 55, 221

Goose
- Barnacle 56, 223
- Greater White-fronted 56, 60, 190
- Lesser White-fronted 56, 223
- Red-breasted 56, 190

Goshawk 29, 30, 34, 35, 48, 53, 73, 75, **102**, **116**, **117**, **119**, **120**, **121**, **122**, **130**, **135**, **172**, **178**, **181**, **182**, 196

Grebe
- Black-necked 29, 30, 36, 46, 52, **99, 101, 102, 111, 113, 160,** 167, **169,** 172, 173, **184, 186, 187,** 192
- Great Crested 29, 30, 35, 36, 46, 52, **99, 111, 113, 160,** 167, **169,** 172, 173, **184, 186, 187,** 192
- Little 53, **99, 101,** 104, **161, 184,** 192
- Red-necked 192

grebes 98, **105, 124, 161, 166, 184, 186, 187**

Greenfinch 55, 221

Greenshank 30, 48, **112,** 114, 201

Greek bird names 243—250

Gulf of Kalloni 83, 164—73

Gull
- Audouin's 30, 46, 54, **128, 129, 130, 152,** 203
- Black-headed **112,** 203
- Common 56, 203
- Great Black-backed 56, 224
- Lesser Black-backed 29, 48, 53, **112, 166, 167, 170,** 204
- Little 48, **112,** 203
- Mediterranean 29, 30, 48, 99, **112, 169, 170, 173, 184, 186, 187,** 203
- Slender-billed 30, 48, **99,** 110, **112, 184, 187,** 203
- Yellow-legged 46, 54, **99,** 107, **129, 131, 140, 160, 186,** 204

gulls 29, 68, 88, **98, 99, 101, 102, 105, 106, 107, 110, 112, 113, 124, 132, 155, 167, 169, 170, 172, 173, 184, 186, 187**

H

Haramida Marsh 32, 44, 63, 186—7

Harrier
- Hen 30, 36, 48, **99, 100, 106, 111, 114, 173,** 196
- Marsh 29, 30, 36, 48, **99, 100, 106, 111, 114,** 139, **152,** 173, **184,** 196
- Montagu's 30, 48, **99, 100, 106, 111, 114, 152, 173,** 196
- Pallid 30, 48, **106, 111,** 114, **152,** 196

harriers 48, 71, 78, 86, 88, 98, **105,** 109, **110, 111, 113, 117, 119, 120, 121, 122, 148, 150, 151, 153, 157, 158, 159, 169, 171,** 172

Hawfinch 29, 45, 55, **128,** 221

health 18

Heron
- Grey **111,** 194
- Purple 31, 47, 90, 91, **99, 104, 111, 166, 175,** 194

Squacco 47, 81, 91, **98, 99, 111, 142, 162, 163, 178,** 193

herons 28, 29, 31, 36, 43, 65, 66, 70, 71, 78, 84, 87, 88, 91, **98, 100, 101, 102, 103, 104, 105, 106, 107, 109, 110, 112, 113, 114, 138, 139, 140, 141, 151, 152, 153, 157, 158, 159, 160, 161, 163, 165, 166, 167, 170, 171, 172, 175, 176, 177, 178, 184, 187**

Hellenic Rarities Committee (HRC) 56

hirundines 29, 31, 34, 35, 49, 66, 68, 98, **99, 101, 102, 103, 104, 105, 106, 112, 114, 115, 120, 122, 128, 131, 133, 137, 139, 140, 141, 142, 145, 149, 153, 154, 155, 157, 158, 159, 160, 161, 163, 173, 181, 182, 187**

Hobby 30, 49, **99, 117, 150, 166,** 198

Honey-buzzard, (European) 32, 34, 35, 48, 51, **116, 117, 120, 122, 133, 149, 159, 177, 178, 181, 182,** 195

Hoopoe 30, 31, 49, 51, 57, **103, 104, 105, 115, 119, 120, 121, 122, 128, 130, 137, 140, 141, 149, 154, 155, 159, 161, 163, 172, 181, 182,** 207

hot springs **128**

hunting 60

I

insects 239

Ibis, Glossy 47, 70, 91, **99, 110, 111, 112, 113, 114,** 193

Ipsilometopo **118, 123, 133**

Ipsilou (Monastery) 16, 20, 31, 32, 39, 46, 55, 76, 77, **146,** 147—9

J

Jackdaw 55, 60, **140, 141, 152,** 208

Jay 55, **103, 105, 114, 131, 149,** 208

K

Kalami 43, 165—6

Kalloni (area) 42, 51, 53, 54, 64, 97—117, **105, 113, 114**

Kalloni Mini Soccer Pitch 72, **97,** 115—16

Kalloni Raptor Watch Point 32, 62, 72, **97,** 116—7

Kalloni Saltpans / Saltworks 20, 30, 32, 34, 41, 42, 43, 47, 48, 49, 70, 71, **97,** 108—12, **113, 118**

Kapi **123,** 132—3

Katepetros Valley **134,** 135—6

Kato Stavros 89, **174,** 177—8

Kato Tritos **179**

Kavaki 41, 64, 74, **123,** 124—5

Kestrel
- Common 49, 53, **99**, **117**, **159**, **160**, 197
- Lesser 30, 49, 51, 78, 83, **109**, **110**, **117**, **137**, **139**, **140**, **141**, **142**, **143**, **145**, **149**, **150**, **151**, **152**, **153**, **154**, **155**, **157**, **158**, **159**, **166**, 197

Kingfisher
- (Common) 28, 35, 48, 85, **98**, **103**, **104**, **106**, **112**, **128**, **152**, **166**, **167**, **173**, **184**, **186**, **187**, 207
- Pied 56, 225
- White-throated 56, 225

Kite
- Black 30, 48, **173**, 195
- Red 56, 195

Klio 44, 75, **123**, **131**, 132–3
Knot 56, 202
Konditsia Valley **138**, 141–2
Korakas **123**, 131
Koriani **118**, 120–1
Kremestes **118**

L

Lapwing (Northern) 29, 60, 200
Lardia Valley 41, *75*, **134**, 136–7
Lark
- Black 56, 225
- Calandra 49, **112**, **113**, **114**, 209
- Crested **159**, 210
- Lesser Short-toed 56, 209
- Short-toed (Greater) 31, 49, 51, 56, **110**, **111**, **112**, **113**, **114**, **132**, **166**, **170**, **173**, 209
- Sky (see Skylark)
- Wood (see Woodlark)

larks 34, 45, 49, **98**, **99**, **101**, **106**, **109**, **111**, **166**, **169**, **173**
Lepetimnos **123**, **128**, **133**
Lepetimnos, Mt (see Mt Lepetimnos)
Lesvos Bird Records Committee (LBRC) 56
Linnet 55, **166**, 221
Lisvorio 87, **164**
lizards 57, **149**, 242
- Wall Lizard 95

local people 38
Loutra **185**

M

Madaros 53, 56, *67*, **97**, **104**, **105**, 114–15
Magpie 60, 208
Makara (inc. River) 7, 44, 72, *83*, **138**, 140–2
Mallard 52, 60, 191
mammals 57, 242
Mandamados 19, 26, 27, 32, 44, 50, 64, **118**, **119**, **123**, 130–2
marsh terns 32, 66, 71, 98, **103**, **104**, **106**, **108**, **110**
Marten, Beech 57
Martin
- Crag 30, 49, 51, 75, **101**, **102**, **136**, **137**, **149**, **160**, **161**, 210
- House 49, 210
- Sand 49, 210

Mavria **121**
Mediterranean Monk Seal **128**, **141**
Megali Limni, **183**
Megalochori Valley **179**
Meladia Valley (inc. River and Ford) 31, 41, 44, 46, 47, *79*, *80*, *81*, **146**, **151**, **154**, **155**, 156–9
Merganser, Red-breasted 36, 52, **99**, 192
Merlin 29, 56, 198
Mesa 33, 40, 43, 64, *84*, **164**, 165–6, **167**, **168**
Mesotopos 62, 64, **138**, **141**, **142**, **144**, **143**, **145**
Metochi Lake 31, 36, 42, 43, 45, 47, 53, 57, *66*, **97**, **100**, **101**, 102–4
Mikri Limni 63, **164**, **170**
military areas 39, 40, **116**, **132**, **147**, **166**, **167**, **168**, **169**, **175**, **176**
Milopotamos River 42, **108**, **112**
Mirsinia *85*, 165–6
Molivos (Mythimna) 6, 13, 19, 20, 22, 27, 32, 35, 40, 44, 54, 61, 64, **123**, **125**, 126–127, **128**, **132**
money 18
Moorhen 54, 199
Mt, Lepetimnos 13, 16, 32, 45, 54, **123**, 132–3
Olympus 16, 32, 43, 44, 45, 54, 70, 89, **179**
Mythimna (see Molivos)
mythology 13
Mytilini 12, 13, 14, 18, 19, 20, 21, 23, 24, 25, 26, 27, 44, 54, 64, 185–6
Mytilini airport 23, 185–6

N

Napi **118,** 119—20

Napi Valley 26, 32, 41, 64, 73, **97,** 118—22

natural history 16

Neapoli 23, 185

Neochori **174, 179**

Night-heron, (Black-crowned) 31, 33, 43, 47, 78, *90,* **99, 103, 104, 110, 111, 152, 167, 168, 184 189,** 193

Nightingale
  Common 13, 31, 51, 69, *93,* **101, 120, 122, 137, 139, 181, 182,** 216
  Thrush 30, 32, 50, **128, 137, 149, 154, 155, 158, 159,** 216

Nightjar, (European) 33, 51, 85, **101, 102, 165, 166,** 206

no go areas 38

North coast 21, 23, 32, 35, 41, 46, 54, 64, *74, 75,* 123—33

Nutcracker 208

Nuthatch
  Krüper's 10, 40, 41, 46, 55, 85, 86, *94,* **165, 166, 167, 168, 180, 181, 182, 183,** 214
  Rock 31, 34, 46, 55, 72, 73, 76, 79, 83, 84, *94,* **101, 102, 103, 104, 105, 107, 114, 115, 116, 117, 120, 121, 122, 123, 125, 127, 128, 130, 133, 137, 139, 140, 141, 142, 145, 147, 148, 149, 150, 154, 155, 156, 159, 161, 165, 166, 167,** 215
  Wood 55, **102, 119, 120, 121, 122, 123, 131,** 214

O

Olympus, Mt (see Mt Olympus)

orchids 8, 58, 89, *96,* **180, 181,** 240—1
  Lesbos Orchid *96*

Oriole, Golden 30, 50, 75, 77, **120, 121, 122, 128, 130, 131, 135, 136, 137, 139, 140, 141, 142, 143, 144, 145, 149, 152, 153, 154, 159, 178,** 208

Osprey 30, 48, **111, 184, 186, 187,** 195

Ouzel, Ring 56, 215

Owl
  Barn 54, 99, **186,** 205
  Eagle 54, 205
  Little 54, 84, **112, 119, 120, 121, 122, 130, 147, 149, 150, 154, 155, 156, 157, 159, 165, 166, 170,** 206
  Long-eared 46, 54, 86, **99, 116, 167, 168, 178 182,** 206
  Scops 51, 72, *93,* 99, **114, 115, 116, 136, 137, 186,** 205
  Short-eared 53, **112, 114,** 206
  Tawny 54, 206

Oystercatcher **111,** 199

P

Palia Vigla Chapel (nr Vatera) 174—6

Palios 44, 53, **132**

Panaghia Chapel (nr Agiasos) 63, **179,** 183

Parakila 27, 31, 64, **138, 139**

Parakila Marsh 44, 62, 138—9

Partridge, Rock 223

passerines 31, 34, 35, 36, 43, 52, 72, 74, 78, 79, 81, 88, 89, **98, 110,** 111, **114, 116, 123, 124, 126, 142, 147, 150, 151, 152, 153, 155, 157, 158, 159, 160, 175, 178**

Pelican
  Dalmatian 31, 46, 47, **111,** 194
  White 31, 35, 47, *90,* **98, 100, 111, 173,** 194

pelicans 32, **110, 175**

Pelopi **123, 133**

Perasma (inc. reservoir) 34, 44, **123,** 124—5, **126, 127, 177**

Perivolis Monastery **134,** 136—7

Petra 6, 21, 25, 32, 44, 52, 54, 61, 64, **123, 124, 126, 127**

Petra reservoir (see Perasma)

Petrified Forest 12, 16, 59, 62, **146,** 150, **152, 154, 155, 158**

petrol 27

Phalarope, Red-necked 56, 203

Pheasant (Common) 190

photographers 41

Pigeon, Wood 205

Pintail (Northern) 52, 60, **165, 172, 173,** 191

Pipit
  Meadow 53, 220
  Red-throated 31, 49, **110, 111, 112, 113, 114, 117, 152,** 220
  Richard's 56, 225
  Tawny **111, 112, 113, 114, 152, 166, 170, 171, 173,** 220
  Tree 51, **125, 127,** 220
  Water 20, 220

pipits 45, 88, **98, 99, 100,** 104, **105, 106, 109, 110, 111, 113, 123, 124, 151, 157, 158, 161, 163, 169, 171, 173**

Pithariou Reservoir 34, 35, 36, 44, 53, 81, *82,* 87, **146,** 160—1, **162**

place names 61, 251—3

Platania 73, **118,** 120—2

Plomari 64
Plover
    Caspian 30, **113**, 200
    Golden **111**, **114**, 200
    Greater Sand 56, 224
    Grey 48, **111**, **114**, 200
    Kentish 48, **98**, **100**, **104**, **111**, **113**, **114**, **172**, **173**, 200
    Lesser Sand 56, 224
    Little Ringed 48, 51, 69, **100**, **104**, **111**, **114**, 200
    Ringed 48, **104**, **111**, **114**, **173**, 200
    Sociable 56, 200
    Spur-winged 30, 48, *93*, **111**, **114**, 200
    White-tailed 56, 224
Pochard
    (Common) 36, 56, 191
    Red-crested 223
Polichnitos 7, 27, 32, 35, 47, 50, 64, **164**
Polichnitos Saltpans 7, 34, 43, 47, 55, 86, 87, *88*, **164**, 171–3
political history 13—14
Potamia Reservoir 34, **97**, 100–2
Potamia Valley 33, *66*, *67*, **97**, 100–2, **134**
Pratincole
    Black-winged 203
    Collared 30, 48, **99**, **109**, **110**, **111**, **112**, **114**, 203
Pterounda **134**,

Q

Quail 29, 51, 60, **108**, **109**, **110**, **113**, **141**, **162**, **173**, 190

R

Rail, Water 28, **99**, **138**, **139**, **170**, **184**, **187**, 198
raptors 20, 28, 29, 30, 32, 34, 35, 43, 46, 48, 51, 53, 55, 66, 67, 72, 73, 74, 76, 78, 79, 81, 82, 83, 88, 89, **98**, **99**, **101**, **102**, **103**, **104**, **105**, **107**, **110**, **111**, **114**, **115**, **116**, **117**, **119**, **120**, **121**, **122**, **123**, **124**, **125**, **126**, **127**, **128**, **130**, **131**, **132**, **133**, **135**, **136**, **137**, **139**, **140**, **142**, **143**, **144**, **145**, **147**, **148**, **149**, **150**, **151**, **152**, **153**, **154**, **155**, **157**, **158**, **159**, **160**, **161**, **163**, **165**, **167**, **168**, **169**, **170**, **171**, **172**, **173**, **175**, **176**, **177**, **178**, **180**, **181**, **182**, **184**, **186**, **187**
Raven 55, **107**, **115**, **149**, **181**, **182**, 209
Redshank
    (Common) 48, **112**, **114**, 201
    Spotted 30, 48, **112**, **114**, **172**, 201

Redstart
    Black 29, 36, 53, **99**, **112**, **114**, **148**, **149**, **170**, **173**, 217
    Common 30, 50, **99**, **131**, **154**, **181**, **182**, **183**, 217
Redwing 29, 53, 60, 216
Revna **134**
River
    Almiropotamos (Vatera) 32, 43, 174–5, **176**
    Almyropotamos (Lisvorio) 87, **171**, **172**
    Christou 20, 22, 42, 48, 55, *65*, **97**, 98–100, **101**, **102**, **103**
    Kalami 43
    Makara 44
    Meladia (see Meladia Valley)
    Potamia (see Potamia Valley)
    Tsihliotas (see Meladia Valley)
    Tsiknias 20, 41, 42, 43, 47, *68*, *69*, **97**, **98**, **108**, **109**, **111**, **114**, 104–7
    Vergias 44, *81*, **146**, **160**, **161**, 162–3
    Voulgaris 44, 53, 62, *82*, **134**, 135–6, **137**
    Vourkos 43,, **174**, 176–8
    Vouvaris 40, *85*, **164**, 166–7, **168**
Robin
    (European) 29, 53, 54, 89, **180**, **181**, **182**, 216
    Rufous Bush 31, 33, 51, 67, 79, 80, **109**, **110**, **112**, **113**, **114**, **115**, **125**, **143**, **144**, **145**, **153**, **155**, **157**, **158**, **159**, **165**, **166**, 216
    White-throated 32, 51, 56, **129**, **130**, **155**, 216
Rock-thrush
    (Rufous-tailed) 50, 218
    Blue 54, 74, 75, 84, **101**, **102**, **103**, **116**, **117**, **120**, **124**, **125**, **133**, **136**, **137**, **140**, **145**, **147**, **148**, **149**, 154, **156**, **159**, **160**, **165**, **166**, **167**, **177**, **178**, **181**, **186**, 218
Roller 30, 49, 79, 85, **105**, **121**, **122**, **143**, **148**, **153**, **167**, **168**, 73, 206
Rook 208
Rosefinch, Common (Scarlet) 56, 221
Ruff 48, **112**, **114**, 203

S

Saltpans
    Kalloni 20, 30, 32, 34, 41, 42, 43, 47, 48, 49, *70*, *71*, **97**, 108–12, **113**, 118
    Polichnitos 7, 34, 43, 47, 55, 86, 87, *88*, **164**, 171–3
Sanderling 48, **111**, **114**, 202
Sandpiper
    Baird's 224

Broad-billed 112, 114, 172, 173, 203
Common 30, 48, **104**, **112**, **114**, **160**, **162**, **173**, 202
Curlew 30, **111**, **114**, **172**, **173**, 202
Green 48, 52, **104**, **112**, **114**, **173**, **184**, 202
Marsh 30, 47, 48, **99**, **112**, **114**, **172**, **173**, 201
Pectoral 56, **171**, 202
Terek 56, **173**, 202
Wood 30, 48, **99**, **104**, **112**, **114**, **173**, **186**, 202

Scaup, (Greater) 191

scooters (for hire) 25

Serin
(European) 29, 55, **178**, **180**, **181**, **182**, 220
Red-fronted 56, 220

Shag, (European) 29, 53, **129**, **140**, **169**, **172**, 194

Shearwater
Scopoli's (Cory's) 30, 46, 47, **128**, **129**, **162**, **176**, 192
Yelkouan 30, 46, 47, **128**, **129**, **176**, 192

shearwaters **123**, **130**, **141**, **162**, **174**, **176**, **186**, **187**

Shelduck
Common 52, **173**, 190
Ruddy 43, 44, 53, 70, 82, 84, 85, *90*, **105**, **107**, **109**, **110**, **111**, **113**, **114**, **115**, **123**, **131**, **132**, **135**, **136**, **165**, **166**, **167**, **172**, 190—1

Shoveler (Northern) 191

Shrike
Great Grey 56, 207
Isabelline 226
Lesser Grey 31, 50, 52, 80, **112**, **157**, **159**, **166**, **173**, 207
Masked 31, 46, 50, 52, 67, 73, 86, **101**, **102**, **112**, **120**, **121**, **122**, **129**, **130**, **135**, **136**, **137**, **153**, **154**, **167**, **168**, 208
Red-backed 31, 50, 52, 80, 81, **99**, **101**, **112**, **115**, **154**, **155**, **159**, **166**, **173**, 207
Steppe Grey 56, 207—8
Woodchat 31, 50, 52, 80, **99**, **101**, **112**, **114**, **115**, **119**, **120**, **121**, **122**, **125**, **130**, **137**, **148**, **149**, **154**, **155**, **159**, **166**, **168**, **170**, **173**, **184**, 208

shrikes 34, 35, 45, 50, 68, 69, 78, 80, 83, 85, 87, 88, **98**, **102**, **103**, **104**, **105**, **106**, **109**, **111**, **114**, **122**, **123**, **124**, **125**, **126**, **127**, **128**, **129**, **130**, **131**, **132**, **135**, **136**, **137**, **139**, **140**, **141**, **142**, **144**, **145**, **148**, **149**, **151**, **152**, **153**, **154**, **155**, **157**, **158**, **159**, **161**, **162**, **163**, **167**, **168**, **169**, **170**, **171**, **172**, **173**, **175**, **176**, **178**, **181**, **182**, **184**, **186**, **187**

Sideras**138**, 142—3
Sigri (inc. fields) 21, 22, 32, 44, 46, 64, 78, *78*, 151—5
Sigri Old Sanatorium 79, **146**, 154—5
Sikaminia 35, 64, 75, **123**, **133**, **128**
Siskin 29, 221
Skala Eresou 10, 12, 21, 23, 44, 64, 81, **146**, **160**, **162**—3
Skala Kallonis 6, 10, 20, 21, 22, 31, 41, 50, 54, 55, 62, 64, 97, **98**—9
Skala Kallonis Pool 20, 55, 58, 64, *65*, **97**, 98—9
Skala Sikaminias 20, 23, 32, 41, 54, 74, **123**, 128—30
Skala Polichnitou 11, 34, 43, **164**, **172**
Skala Vasilikon **164**, 169—70
Skalochori (area) 64, 134—7
Skamnioudi 43, *87*, **164**, 169—70, **171**, **172**
Skoutaros **134**

Skua
Arctic 56, 204
Long-tailed 56, 224
Pomarine 56, 224

Skylark 29, 49, 53, 60, **173**, 210
Smew 56, **192**
snakes 57

Snipe
Common 48, 52, 60, **112**, **114**, 201
Great 32, 48, **106**, **112**, **113**, **114**, **153**, 201
Jack 52, 201

Sparrow
House 50, 55, 219
Rock 55, 75, 76, 84, *94*, **106**, **136**, **137**, **142**, **143**, **144**, **145**, **147**, **148**, **149**, **150**, 219
Spanish 50, 81, **98**, **99**, **105**, **112**, **125**, **127**, **154**, **162**, 219
Tree 219

sparrows 50, **102**, **106**, **107**

Sparrowhawk
Eurasian 29, 48, 52, 53, **117**, **120**, **122**, **181**, **182**, 196
Levant 30, 32, 45, 48, 51, **117**, **119**, **121**, **133**, **149**, **154**, **172**, **177**, **178**, 196

Spoonbill (Eurasian) 47, **172**, **173**, 193

Starling
(Common) 29, 53, 60, **184**, 215
Rose-coloured 33, 50, **99**, **112**, **113**, 215

Stilt, Black-winged 48, 51, **99**, **100**, **108**, **111**, **139**, **173**, 199

Stint
Little 30, 11, 48, **114**, **172**, **173**, 202

Temminck's 30, 48, 68, 69, **111**, **114**, **160**, **162**, **171**, **173**, 202
Stipsi **123**, 132—3
Stonechat, (European/Common) **166**, **167**, 217
Stone-curlew 29, 48, 51, 54, 65, **98**, **100**, **105**, **108**, **109**, **110**, **111**, **112**, **113**, **114**, **141**, **162**, **166**, **169**, **189**, 199
Stork
    Black 47, 50, **101**, **111**, **117**, **119**, **120**, **121**, **122**, **137**, **149**, **173**, 193
    White 47, 50, *91*, **99**, **111**, **117**, **119**, **120**, **121**, **122**, **123**, **132**, **173**, 193
    storks 29, 32, 34, 35, 43, 65, 70, 71, 81, 84, 87, 88, **98**, **100**, **104**, **105**, **106**, **108**, **109**, **110**, **112**, **113**, **114**, **116**, **117**, **119**, **128**, **132**, **136**, **151**, **152**, **153**, **157**, **158**, **159**, **160**, **161**, **165**, **167**, **168**, **170**, **172**, **173**, **175**, **176**, **177**
Storm-petrel 56, 223
Swallow
    (Barn) 49, 51, 210
    Red-rumped 30, 49, 51, **99**, **101**, **137**, **149**, 210
Swan
    Bewick's 56, 190
    Mute 190
    Whooper 56, 190
Swift
    Alpine 31, 34, 49, **99**, **142**, 206
    Common 31, 49, 51, **99**, 206
    Little 56, 206
    Pallid 29, 31, 49, **99**, 206
    swifts 24, 49, 76, **98**, **99**, **101**, **102**, **103**, **104**, **112**, **114**, **115**, **120**, **122**, **128**, **131**, **133**, **137**, **139**, **140**, **141**, **142**, **143**, **145**, **147**, **149**, **153**, **154**, **157**, **158**, **159**, **161**, **163**, **168**, **173**, **181**, **182**, **186**, **187**

T
taxis 24
Tavari **138**, **144**, **145**
Tchagra, Black-crowned 226
Teal (Eurasian) 52, 172, **173**, 191
Terrapins 57, **103**
    European Pond **103**
    Stripe-necked 57, 80, 101, 103
Tern
    Arctic 56, 224
    Black 48, **112**, 204
    Caspian **184**, **187**, 204
    Common 51, 204

    Gull-billed 30, 48, **99**, **112**, 204
    Lesser Crested 56, 224
    Little 51, **108**, **112**, 204
    Sandwich 53, **99**, **112**, **173**, **184**, **186**, **187**, 204
    Whiskered 32, 48, **99**, **112**, 204
    White-winged Black 32, 48, **99**, **112**, 204
terns 68, 88, **98**, **99**, **102**, **105**, **106**, **109**, **110**, **112**, **113**, **170**, **173**, **184**, **186**, **187**
Thrush
    Blue Rock (see Rock-thrush, Blue)
    Mistle 54, **99**, **102**, **173**, **181**, **182**, 216
    (Rufous-tailed) (see Rock-thrush, Rufous-tailed)
    Song 29, 36, 53, 54, 89, **181**, **182**, 216
Thread Lacewing 57, *96*
Tit
    Bearded 56, 209
    Blue 55, 209
    Coal 55, **168**, **181**, **182**, **183**, 209
    Great 55, 209
    Long-tailed 55, **167**, **168**, **181**, **182**, **183**, 210
    Penduline 50, 56, **153**, 209
    Sombre 31, 34, 45, 55, 73, 77, 81, 84, 87, **101**, **102**, **104**, **119**, **120**, **121**, **122**, **123**, **124**, **125**, **126**, **127**, **128**, **129**, **130**, **139**, **140**, **142**, **144**, **145**, **148**, **149**, **155**, **157**, **158**, **159**, **161**, **176**, 209
Tortoise, Spur-thighed 57, 76, *95*, **141**, **142**, 149
Treecreeper, Short-toed 55, 85, 86, **167**, **168**, **181**, **182**, 215
Tsiknias River 41, 42, 43, 47, *68*, *69*, *97*, 104—7
Turnstone 48, **112**, 202
Twite 56, 226

V
Vafios 23, **123**, 132—3
Vasilika **164**
Vatera 21, 22, 32, 35, 43, 49, 64, **174**
Vatousa 64, **134**
Vergias River 44, *81*, **146**, **160**, **161**, 162—3
Vigla (nr Ipsilou) 147—8
Voulgaris River 44, 53, *82*, **134**, 135—6
Vourkos River 43, **174**, 176—8
Vouvaris River *85*, **164**, 166—7
Vrisa **174**
Vulture
    Black 48, 56, 224
    Egyptian 48, 56, 195
    Griffon 48, 56, 195

W

waders 28, 29, 30, 32, 34, 36, 43, 47, 48, 65, 68, 69, 70, 71, 78, 81, 84, 86, 88, 92, **98**, **100**, **101**, **102**, **103**, **104**, **105**, **106**, **107**, **108**, **109**, **110**, **111**, **112**, **113**, 124, **131**, **132**, **138**, **139**, **140**, 142, **151**, **152**, **153**, **155**, **157**, **158**, **159**, **160**, **161**, **162**, **163**, **165**, **166**, **167**, **169**, **170**, **171**, **172**, **173**, **175**, **177**, 184, **186**, **187**

Wagtail
  Black-headed (Yellow) 51, 99, **112**, **114**, 219
  Blue-headed (Yellow) **99**, **112**, **114**, 219
  British Yellow 219
  Citrine 78, **112**, **113**, **114**, 152, 170, 220
  Grey 29, 53, **160**, **166**, **167**, **173**, **181**, **182**, 220
  Grey-headed (Yellow) **112**, **114**, 219
  Italian (Yellow) 219
  Romanian (Yellow) 219
  Russian (Yellow) 219
  Syke's (Yellow) 219
  White 29, 36, **112**, **114**, 152, **160**, **173**, **178**, 220
  Yellow-headed (Yellow) 219
  'yellow' 30, 49, **98**, **99**, **100**, **107**, **110**, **111**, **113**, **140**, **142**, 145, **152**, **160**, **173**, 184, **186**, **187**, 219
wagtails 45, 49, 68, 81, 83, 87, **98**, **99**, **101**, **104**, **105**, **106**, **109**, **110**, **113**, **124**, **135**, **141**, 145, **151**, **152**, **157**, **158**, **160**, **161**, **162**, **163**, **169**, **170**, **171**, **172**, **173**, **175**, **177**, 184

walking 25

Warbler
  Aquatic 226
  Barred 31, 50, 51, **115**, **123**, **124**, **125**, **128**, 213
  Booted 56, 226
  Cetti's 29, 55, **98**, **99**, **103**, **162**, **163**, **184**, 210
  Eastern Bonelli's 30, 36, 52, 89, **137**, **140**, **149**, **158**, **180**, **181**, **182**, 211
  Eastern Orphean (see Orphean)
  Eurasian Reed (see Reed)
  Fan-tailed (Zitting Cisticola) 55, **111**, **112**, 212
  Garden 50, **137**, **149**, 213
  Grasshopper (Common) 212
  Great Reed 30, 51, 68, **98**, **99**, **101**, **103**, **104**, **139**, **140**, **158**, **162**, **163**,, 184, 211
  Icterine 30, 50, 51, 91, **137**, **149**, **158**, **159**, 212
  Marsh 50, 211
  Ménétries 226
  Moustached 184, 211
  Olivaceous (Eastern) 31, 45, 51, 67, 68, 69, 73, 87, **99**, **101**, **115**, **139**, **184**, 211
  Olive-tree 31, 45, 51, 67, 73, 87, **101**, **102**, **120**, **121**, **122**,**135**, **136**, **140**, **144**, **153**, **158**, **159**, **169**, **170**, 211
  Orphean 30, **101**, **114**, **115**, **121**, **122**, **123**, **124**, **125**, **128**, **130**, **135**, **136**, **149**, **166**, **168**, **177**, **178**, 213
  Reed 50, 51, **184**, 211
  River 31, 50, 67, **114**, **115**, **125**, 212
  Rüppell's 30, 52, 61, 74, *93*, **107**, **123**, **124**, **125**, **130**, **158**, **165**, 213
  Sardinian 29, 32, 51, 89, **125**, **132**, **158**, **175**, **176**, **177**, **178**, **186**, **187**, 213
  Savi's 212
  Sedge 50, 211
  Spectacled 56, 226
  Subalpine 51, 66, 72, **101**, **102**, **115**, **116**, **117**, **119**, **120**, **121**, **122**, **123**, **124**, **125**, **127**, **128**, **130**, **131**, **136**, **137**, **149**, **158**, **165**, **166**, **177**, **178**, **181**, **182**, 213
  Upcher's 226
  Willow 35, 50, **149**, 210
  Wood 35, 50, **158**, **159**, **181**, **182**, 211

warblers 29, 30, 35, 43, 45, 50, 51, 66, 68, 77, 78, 80, 81, 83, **98**, **101**, **102**, **103**, **104**, **105**, **106**, **107**, **109**, **110**, **111**, **114**, **122**, **124**, **125**, **126**, **127**, **128**, **130**, **131**, **132**, **135**, **136**, **137**, **138**, **139**, **140**, **141**, **142**, **144**, **145**, **148**, **149**, **151**, **152**, **153**, **154**, **155**, **158**, **159**, **160**, **161**, **162**, **163**, **165**, **166**, **167**, **168**, **169**, **172**, **175**, **176**, **177**, **178**, **181**, **182**, **183**, **184**, **186**, **187**

Waxwing 209

weather 17, 28, 29, 30, 32, 33, 35, 36

websites 59

what to take 19–20

Wheatear
  Black-eared 29, 46, 50, 51, 56, 66, 72, 74, 76, 79, 83, 84, 85, **101**, **102**, **103**, **104**, **105**, **107**, **114**, **115**, **116**, **117**, **124**, **125**, **126**, **127**, **130**, **133**, **136**, **137**, **139**, **140**, **141**, **142**, **143**, **145**, **147**, **148**, **149**, **150**, **154**, **155**, **156**, **157**, **159**, **161**, **165**, **167**, **168**, **176**, **181**, **186**, 218
  Desert 226
  Finsch's 56, **129**, 218
  Isabelline 30, 46, 50, 51, 76, **147**, **148**, **149**, **150**, **156**, 217
  Northern 29, 50, 51, **112**,**114**, **140**, **141**, **148**, **149**, **154**, **155**, **156**, **173**, 217
  Pied 56, 217

wheatears 34, 35, **101, 104, 105, 106, 132, 140, 142, 145,** 149, **152, 154,** 158, 159, 160, 161, 163, 166, 170, 173, **176, 186**

Whimbrel 48, **112, 114,** 201

Whinchat 30, 35, 50, **98, 99** 103, 105, **112,** 114, **115, 154, 173,** 217

Whitethroat

    Common 50, 213

    Lesser 50, 213

Wigeon 52, 191

wildfowl 28, 29, 30, 36, 43, 50, 52, **99, 124, 138, 139, 160, 161, 165, 166,** 170, 173, 184

Woodcock 52, 200

Woodlark 29, 46, 76, 85, 86, **119, 120, 121, 122,** 149, **157, 159,** 165, 166, 167, **168,** 210

Woodpecker

    Great Spotted 56, 225

    Green 56, 225

Middle Spotted 33, 45, 54, 60, 73, 75, 87, 98, 101, 102, 104, 105, 106, 114, 120, 121, 122, 123, 130, 131, 136, 137, 144, 149, 154, 165, 168, 169, 170, 175, 176, 177, 178, 180, 181, 182, 183, 187, 207

Syrian 56, 225

White-backed 56, 225

Wren, (Winter) 53, 54, **104, 137, 181, 182,** 214

Wryneck 31, 49, 207

Y

Yellowhammer 56, 221

Z

Zitting Cisticola (see Fan-tailed Warbler)

SITE INDEX

Kalloni area
- Skala Kallonis Pool — 97
- Christou River — 98
- Potamia Valley — 99
- Potamia Reservoir — 100
- Metochi Lake — 100
- Tsiknias River (Lower) — 102
- Tsiknias River (Upper) — 107
- Kalloni Saltpans — 108
- Alykes Wetlands — 112
- Madaros — 115
- Kalloni Mini Soccer Pitch — 115
- Kalloni Raptor Watch Point — 117

Napi Valley
- Napi — 120
- Koriani — 120
- Platania — 120

North Coast
- Kavaki — 124
- Perasma — 125
- Molivos — 126
- Efthalou to Skala Sikaminias — 128
- Korakas — 131
- Molivos to Klio road — 132
- Petra to Kapi road — 132

Skalochori area
- Aghias Taxiarchis — 135
- Katapetros Valley — 135
- Voulgaris River — 136
- Lardia Valley — 137
- Perivolis Monastery — 137

South West
- Parakila Marsh — 138
- Aghia Ioannis — 139
- Makara — 140
- Konditsia Valley — 142
- Sideras — 142
- Mesotopos — 144
- Chrousos — 145

Far West
- Ipsilou — 147
- Petrified Forest — 150
- Sigri & Faneromeni area — 151
- Sigri Old Sanatorium — 154
- Meladia Valley — 156
- Pithariou Reservoir — 160
- Vergias River, Skala Eresou — 162

Eastern Gulf of Kalloni
- Mesa — 164
- Vouvaris River Mouth — 166
- Achladeri Forest — 168
- Achladeri to Skala Vasilikon — 169
- Skala Vasilikon to Skamnioudi — 170
- Alikoudi Pool — 170
- Mikri Limni — 170
- Polichnitos Saltpans — 171

Vatera area
- Almiropotamos River — 174
- Agios Fokas — 176
- Palia Vigla Chapel — 176
- Vourkos River Mouth — 176
- Ambeliko Valley — 178

Agiasos area
- Agiasos — 180
- Agiasos Sanatorium — 180
- Megalochori Valley — 182
- Dimitrios — 182
- Panaghia Chapel — 183
- Dipi Larisos Reedbed — 184

Mytilini area
- Mytilini — 186
- Airport area — 186
- Cape Lena — 186
- Haramida Marsh — 187

ESSENTIAL GREEK

Hello	ya-sass
Goodbye	ad-io
Please	para-kallo
Thank you	ef-harri-sto
Yes	neh
No	ocky
Sorry	sigh-no-me
Excuse me	me sing-ho-rite
Help!	vo-ith-ia
OK	en-taxi
Toilet	tua-le-tah
Bill please	ton logha-reaz-moz para-kallo

1	ena	6	eksi
2	theo	7	efta
3	tria	8	okh-to
4	tess-erra	9	en-ia
5	ped-deh	10	thek-ka